D1442802

THE BOOK OF

MARTYRDOM

AND

ARTIFICE

ALSO BY ALLEN GINSBERG

POETRY BOOKS

Collected Poems 1947–1997

Death & Fame: Last Poems, 1993–1997

Selected Poems 1947–1995

Illuminated Poems

Cosmopolitan Greetings Poems 1986–1993

White Shroud Poems 1980–1985

Howl Annotated

Plutonian Ode and Other Poems 1977–1980

Mind Breaths: Poems 1972–1977

The Fall of America: Poems of These States, 1965–1971

Planet News: 1961–1971

Reality Sandwiches

Kaddish and Other Poems: 1958–1960

Howl and Other Poems

PROSE AND PHOTOGRAPH BOOKS

Family Business: Selected Letters Between a Father & Son

Deliberate Prose: Selected Essays 1959–1995

Spontaneous Mind: Selected Interviews

Indian Journals

Journals Mid-Fifties

Allen Ginsberg Photographs

Journals: Early Fifties Early Sixties

RECORDINGS

Kaddish

First Blues

New York Blues: Rags Ballads, Harminium Songs

First Thought Best Thought

Allen Ginsberg Audio Collection

The Voice of the Poet: Allen Ginsberg

Wichita Vortex Sutra

For further bibliographic information visit
www.allenginsberg.org

. . .

ALSO BY BILL MORGAN

I Celebrate Myself: The Somewhat Private Life of Allen Ginsberg

The Beat Generation in San Francisco

Literary Landmarks of New York

The Beat Generation in New York: A Walking Tour of Jack Kerouac's City

The Works of Allen Ginsberg 1941–1994: A Descriptive Bibliography

The Response to Allen Ginsberg, 1926–1994: A Bibliography of Secondary Sources

Lawrence Ferlinghetti: A Comprehensive Bibliography

Howl on Trial: The Struggle for Free Expression (editor)

An Accidental Autobiography: The Selected Letters of Gregory Corso (editor)

Deliberate Prose: Selected Essays, 1952–1995 (editor, by Allen Ginsberg)

Death & Fame: Last Poems, 1993–1997 (editor with Bob Rosenthal and Peter Hale, by Allen Ginsberg)

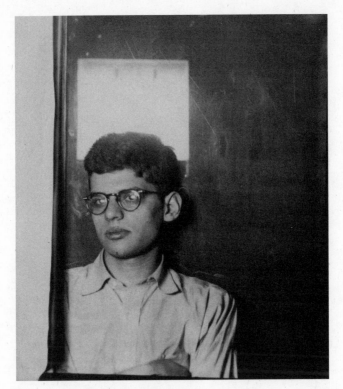

Allen Ginsberg looking in a mirror, 1940s

ALLEN GINSBERG

THE BOOK OF

MARTYRDOM

AND

ARTIFICE

[*First Journals and Poems, 1937–1952*]

EDITED BY

Juanita Liebermann-Plimpton
and Bill Morgan

DA CAPO PRESS

A MEMBER OF THE PERSEUS BOOKS GROUP

FIRST DA CAPO PRESS EDITION 2006

Library of Congress Cataloging-in-Publication Data
Ginsberg, Allen, 1926-1997.
   The book of martyrdom and artifice : first journals and poems, 1937-1952 / / [Allen Ginsberg] ; edited by Juanita Lieberman-Plimpton and Bill Morgan. — 1st Da Capo Press ed.
      p. cm.
   Includes journals from Ginsberg's formative years that document his relationships with Carl Solomon, Lucien Carr, and Herbert Huncke, Ginsberg's conversations with Jack Kerouac, Neal Cassady, and others, an appendix of more than 100 of Ginsberg's earliest poems.
   Includes index.
   ISBN-13: 978-0-306-81462-4 (hardcover : alk. paper)
   ISBN-10: 0-306-81462-5 (hardcover : alk. paper) 1. Ginsberg, Allen, 1926-1997. 2. Poets, American—20th century—Biography. 3. Ginsberg, Allen, 1926-1997—Friends and associates. 4. Beat generation—Biography. I. Lieberman-Plimpton, Juanita. II. Morgan, Bill, 1949- III. Title.
   PS3513.I74Z46 2006
   811'.54—dc22

                                                                     2006026893

Published by Da Capo Press
A Member of the Perseus Books Group
http://www.dacapopress.com

Da Capo Press books are available at special discounts for bulk purchases in the U.S. by corporations, institutions, and other organizations. For more information, please contact the Special Markets Department at the Perseus Books Group, 11 Cambridge Center, Cambridge, MA 02142, or call (800) 255-1514 or (617) 252-5298, or e-mail special.markets@perseusbooks.com.

Book design and composition by Mark McGarry, Texas Type & Book Works
Set in Monotype Dante with Gotham display

10 9 8 7 6 5 4 3 2 1

For Peter Orlovsky

and the memory of Allen Ginsberg

CONTENTS

ACKNOWLEDGMENTS

The very fact that it took twenty-three years to publish this volume should make it clear that it could not have been put together without the help of a host of people. Although we began working on the book with Allen Ginsberg, we had to complete it after his death without his friendly encouragement. First, and foremost, we would like to thank Allen for the honor of entrusting us with his earliest words. We thank him for the support, assistance, and insight he shared with us during our time together. His presence is missed more than ever, and we acknowledge that if this volume is successful it is through his efforts. Where there are errors, we trust that he would forgive us those mistakes.

Several people have displayed such generosity of spirit that we feel they deserve special gratitude. Bob Rosenthal and Peter Hale at the Allen Ginsberg Trust have both been enthusiastic in their support of the presentation of this book.

The editors would also like to acknowledge the help of the following people in the creation of this book. For their memories, their guidance, and their cooperation: George Anderson, Gordon Ball, Paul Bertram, Justin Brierly, Eugene Brooks, William Burroughs, Lucien Carr, Carolyn Cassady, Joel Gaidemak, Bill Gargan, Edith Ginsberg, Herb Gold, James Grauerholz, Janet Hadda, Jack W. C. Hagstrom, John Hollander, Bill Keogan, Norman Krinick, William Lancaster, Elbert Lenrow, Paula Litzky, Bruce Mazlish, Tim Moran, Edie Kerouac Parker, Helen Parker, Paul Roth, John Snow, Carl Solomon, and Ed White.

This book would not have been possible without the resources and help of several libraries. In particular, we'd like to thank Bernard Crystal, Rudolph Ellenbogen, Henry Rowen, Ken Lohf, and the staff of the Special Collections

Department at Columbia University; and Polly Armstrong, Margaret Kimball, William McPheron, and the staff of the Special Collections Department at Stanford University.

In addition, Juanita Plimpton would like to thank Peter Orlovsky for confidence, creative encouragement, and support. Thanks also to Vicki Stanbury, Althea Crawford, Kate Mailer, Kathy Wiess, and especially to Dede Wilson and Rachel Schwartz for laughter and friendship. Thanks to my parents, Ted and Dorita Lieberman, and my brother, Richard Lieberman, for always being there. And finally to Tom Plimpton for teaching me and showing me love and to Daniel Plimpton, the light of my life.

Special thanks are due to Ben Schafer, our editor at Da Capo Press, for recognizing the importance of these journals and helping to shepherd this book through the publication process. Mention should also be made of Allen's literary agent, Andrew Wylie, and his assistant, Jeffrey Posternak, for all their efforts.

Loving thanks to Judy Matz for her patience and support during this and all other projects.

INTRODUCTION

Dear Diary is a salutation that nearly every child has written at least once in their lives. Frequently, a diary is begun and continues for a week, a month, or maybe a few years, but rarely does anyone stick to it for an entire lifetime. Very few writers are remembered for their diaries—Samuel Pepys in London and George Templeton Strong in New York come to mind. But generally, diaries are of interest because they illuminate the lives of their famous creators. Such is the case with Allen Ginsberg, a poet who kept his own journal for sixty years. Of the more than three hundred journals he filled, perhaps his earliest diaries are the most interesting. They were written during the years when he was forming lasting friendships with the likes of Jack Kerouac, Neal Cassady, and William S. Burroughs, long before he came to prominence with the publication of his poem, "Howl," in 1956. Ginsberg's circle of friends was the nucleus of a group that became widely known as the Beat Generation. During the 1940s and 1950s, Ginsberg and his friends developed individual writing styles that would change the course of American literature forever. The stories of their first meeting and early relationships make Ginsberg's journal entries extremely interesting. These journals also illustrate how Ginsberg had the gift for spotting genius among his friends and encouraged them to become writers.

During the early 1980s, I began working on a two-volume bibliography of Ginsberg's poetry for Greenwood Press, and during the course of that research I cataloged Ginsberg's enormous archive as well. Through that organizational work, I uncovered earlier diaries stretching back to 1937, the year Ginsberg turned eleven. In 1977, Ginsberg had published what he considered his early journals for Grove Press under the title, *Journals: Early Fifties*

Early Sixties. Those chronicled his life beginning in 1952 and continued some-
what intermittently through the early 1960s. At the time, his earlier diaries
had been lost and somewhat forgotten within the hundreds of cardboard
boxes in which his papers were stored. Although he knew that he had kept a
journal during the 1940s, he felt that the period of his life that would be of
greatest interest to his readers came after he had discovered his mature po-
etic voice, met Peter Orlovsky, his lifelong companion, and accepted his own
homosexual nature. Who could possibly be interested in his early impres-
sions upon meeting Jack Kerouac, William S. Burroughs, and Neal Cassady,
he must have thought? Or who could be interested in his inner conflict as he
struggled to fit into a heterosexual world? Or who would want his opinion
on the murder that gave birth to the Beats, or the burglary ring he was
involved with that led to his admittance into a psychiatric hospital where he
met Carl Solomon (to whom "Howl" was addressed), or his own battles with
depression that led to suicidal daydreaming? There were many tragedies,
deaths, and broken hearts along the way, all of which Ginsberg had carefully
noted and recorded.

In 1984, after I had incessantly extolled the virtues of these revealing diaries,
Ginsberg's literary agent, Andrew Wylie, asked Juanita Lieberman and me to
undertake the editing of his journals for publication. At the time, Lieberman
was dating Peter Orlovsky and worked for Ginsberg in his office, as his secre-
tary's right hand. Her discerning faculty for winnowing all but the most salient
entries has led to the pleasant readability of this volume. Our method was sim-
ple. We collected all the journal material available for the period we planned
to cover. Then, we found contemporary manuscripts and letters to supple-
ment it. We even searched for other documents from the period, such as Gins-
berg's report cards, photographs, and papers written as class assignments.
After transcribing all the materials from their original handwritten pages onto
neatly typed sheets, we were able to collate them chronologically, since Gins-
berg often wrote in more than one notebook at a time and jumped from one
to another to register entries. Then, we made a list of suggested deletions,
striking out classroom notes and superfluous, redundant, and unnecessary
lists. We spent the better part of two years on the foregoing and the addition
of notes for further explication where needed. We went to great pains to pre-
serve Ginsberg's original syntax, but occasionally we corrected his spelling. In
some cases, like when he wrote about the Italian dictator, *Mooselini,* we kept
his charming and creative spelling. Additions and notes are always inserted

within square brackets, [ ], and were not original parts of the journals. In keeping with the organization of Ginsberg's original notebooks, all his poetry is placed at the end of the narrative, also in chronological order. It was his habit to record his daily entries in the front of a diary, and then write his poetry on the last pages of the book, working back to front.

The most interesting part of the project came next, when we sat down with Ginsberg to review the edited manuscript. Once or twice a week we spent a few hours with Ginsberg while he carefully read through the manuscript. Each entry seemed to bring a long-forgotten memory that remained vivid in his brain. He remembered (and sang for us) each of the ditties that he and his classmates had learned as Columbia freshmen. He described all his childhood homes in Paterson and various events that had taken place while he was living in each one. And he took a special interest in each of the dreams that he had recorded in his earliest years. Footnotes written by him at that time are identified as such. Unattributed footnotes were created by the editors. In the end, it proved to be great fun to be a part of this autobiographical process, a labor of love for Ginsberg, Lieberman, and me.

At the time, Ginsberg's oldest and closest friend, Lucien Carr, was still very much alive, and as Ginsberg came across his frequent, albeit veiled, references to the homosexual crush that he had on the decidedly heterosexual Carr, Ginsberg became convinced that if he published his comments, it might embarrass Carr and focus unwanted attention on the very private man. For fear of embarrassing Carr and some of his other friends, as well as the press of other engagements at the time, Ginsberg decided to put this journal project on hold, after finishing about a third of the complete manuscript.

As time passed, Lieberman moved away to pursue her own career in publishing and raise a family, and Allen's hectic reading schedule took up more of his time throughout the world. In the end, his health deteriorated, and he died in 1997 of liver cancer before he ever returned to the manuscript. Carr attended his old friend's funeral but continued to shy away from any publicity that would identify him with the Beat Generation. Surprisingly, he was always willing to answer questions cordially for my many other Ginsberg-related projects. It was because of his openness that I took several trips to Washington to visit Carr in his retirement, and we discussed many unanswered questions about people and events mentioned in the *First Journals*. He was always generous with his time and candid in his answers about everything, and also said that he didn't mind if the journals were published. When I asked him to write a preface for the volume, he silently declined. He preferred to remain anonymously in the background, as he had for more than fifty years. Carr passed away in 2005, six months after I saw him for the last time. He was the last of that group of friends who first met around the Columbia campus to form the nascent Beat Generation. With his passing, it seemed that the time had finally come to publish Ginsberg's *First Journals*.

Bill Morgan
New York City, 2006

SECTION I

CHILDHOOD IN NEW JERSEY

Louis, Eugene, Naomi, and Allen Ginsberg, 1930s

[When the young Allen Ginsberg received a small pocket diary for his eleventh birthday in 1937, no one had any way of knowing that it would be only the first of hundreds of journals he would fill over the course of the next sixty years of his life. His parents were intelligent, creative people, who considered literature and writing to be among the most important things in life, but no one knew that this boy would develop into one of the greatest poets of the century. His first entries were brief, autobiographical notes, and were entered sporadically. It would take him several years to develop the daily habit of writing in his journal, but the earliest entries from his preteen life help paint a picture of a young, sensitive boy who was doing his best to cope with the events that surrounded his mother's long decline into schizophrenia and madness. His time is spent reading and watching every movie he could see, and early on, he exhibited an interest in politics that would last throughout his life.]

1937

Name—Allen Erwin [sic] Ginsberg
Age—11
Grade—6A
School—No. 12
Brother—Eugene Brooks Ginsberg
Father—Louis Ginsberg
Mother—Naomi Ginsberg
Chief Cousins—Arthur Ginsberg
　　　　　　　Claire Gaidemak
　　　　　　　Joel Gaidemak
　　　　　　　Johanna Meltzer
　　　　　　　Morton (A., S., G.) Ginsberg
Aunts and Uncles—Hannah Litzky [—] Leo Litzky
　　　　　　　　Rose Gaidemak—Sam Gaidemak
　　　　　　　　Clara Meltzer—Harry Meltzer
　　　　　　　　Abe Ginsberg—Anna Ginsberg

Grandmother and Grandfather—Rebecca Ginsberg—Pinya Ginsberg
[Judith] Levy—Max Levy

Don't mind my spelling, writing, or language.

June 1937. Diary, ever since about January a change has come over my brother, he assumes an air of lordly importance, in other words he thinks he's big, but I think he's exasperating. My mother [had] a nervous breakdown but she is better now. She thinks she will not get well, but is making good progress toward health. She has a chance of 1 in 1,000,000 to die.[1]

Friday. June 11, 1937. Diary, had planned to go to Newark where my cousin lives, but my brother wanted to stay, [I] liked the idea, but my father made me go. While I am writing I am in Newark. There was some trouble about the key of this diary.[2]

Saturday. [June 12], 1937. [I] forgot to write on June 12 and it is June 13 when I am writing. I came back to Paterson about 2 o'clock in the afternoon, and went directly to the movies. I saw the pictures *They Gave Him a Gun* and *50 Roads to Town*. After that I read the book *Doctor Dolittle's Garden* after three years of waiting to read it.

Sunday. June 13, 1937. Got a dime in the morning and went to the movies. Was going to go to the U.S.[3] but I forgot that they charged more on Sunday. So I went to the Regent and saw *Good Old Soak* and *Café Metropole*. Had seen *Café Metropole* before.

Thursday. June 17, 1937. Had some of my exams and have had some good marks including 100, 100, 93, 92. I also went to the movies and saw *I Met Him in Paris* and *Michael O'Halloran*. The reason I didn't write on the three preceding days is because I had nothing to write about.

---

1   Naomi Ginsberg (1894–1956). Ginsberg's note about his mother's condition at this time: "In and out of Greystone State Hospital, Morristown, NJ. Had attack of hyperaesthesia. Had to be in dark room curtain closed soundless half year. Sound, touch, light hurt. Grand crisis of her nervous break downs. Maybe a suicide attempt?"

2   Ginsberg's diary had a leather cover and an attached lock. Here, he complains about someone reading his diary since he could not lock it.

3   U.S. A movie theater on Main Street in Paterson, New Jersey, where the admission was 15¢ on Sundays.

Friday. June 18, 1937. Well, we have five more days of school. I found out that we [will] have to sit around doing nothing [for] the five days—we were forbidden to bring any books! It is a rainy day. As yet I haven't gotten your key, diary. [There] was nothing else interesting today.

Saturday. June 19, 1937. Went to the movies and saw *Parnell* and *Hotel Haywire*. My mother thinks she is going to die and is not so good. Haven't received the key yet. Expect to go to the movies tomorrow. My brother is to graduate from high school soon, and will go to Montclair State Teachers College.

Sunday. June 20, 1937. Diary, went to the movies again and saw *This Is My Affair* and *Oh, Doctor*.[4] The later would set a good example for my mother as she is pretty bad today. Her sickness is only mental, however, and she has no chance of dying. My brother still has the idea that he is big.[5]

Monday. June 21, 1937. I heard the story of *Monsieur Beaucaire* by Booth Tarkington over the radio, it was about time. I haven't received the key yet, and my mother is worse today. I found the book *Speaking of Operations* by Cobb[6] and I expect to read it soon.

Tuesday. June 22, 1937. Haven't received the key and I stayed home from school to mind my mother. I got a haircut and two pairs of shoes and heard the Louis-Braddock fight over the radio. [Joe] Louis won and is now champion of the world.

Wednesday. June 23, 1937. My brother graduated from high school today and we had a party. The party broke up about 12 o'clock at night. We had an excellent time and my brother (for once) kissed my aunts good-by. I stayed home from school to take care of my mother.

Thursday. June 24, 1937. I stayed home from school again, only today I went to high school and saw my father teach.[7] My mother locked herself in the

4 *Oh Doctor*. A comedy film starring Edward Everett Horton as a lovable hypochondriac.

5 Ginsberg's note about his brother: "Eugene thought he was a 'big shot,' because he was older than me."

6 *Speaking of Operations* (Garden City, NY: Doran, 1915) by Irvin S. Cobb. A best-selling, humorous account of visiting the doctor and hospital. After undergoing his own operation, Cobb came to understand why people like to talk about them so much.

7 Louis Ginsberg (1896–1975). Ginsberg's father was an English teacher at Eastside High School and an accomplished poet.

bathroom early in the morning and my father had to break the glass to get in.[8] She also went back to the sanitarium.

Friday. June 25, 1937. I saw a newsreel of the Louis-Braddock fight. [I] also [saw] *Dangerous Number* and another picture in the movies. I developed a sty below my eye.

Wednesday. September 7, 1937. Dear Diary, I went to the shore beginning of summer and did not write anything as you were not along. Worst summer ever had—poison ivy—impetigo—bad weather—cold. Saw many pictures there including *The Life of Emile Zola* [starring Paul Muni], *Firefly* [with Jeanette MacDonald] and *Saratoga* with Jean Harlow.

Thursday. September 8, 1937. Started school again, my teacher is Mrs. Biscut— she isn't good or bad. The day was uneventful. [Allen's father wrote the following in his son's diary] "P.S.—She was bad. Dear dairy [sic]—. Miss Biscut wood [sic] give anyone indigestion."

Thursday. December 23, 1937. Coming home from movies (allegedly) shouting 'Four blows'.

Friday. December 31, 1937. Celebrated New Year by seeing two movies in succession. [Four years later, on May 22, 1941 Allen annotated his diary and criticized himself by noting: "Should have put down which."]

1938

Saturday. January 22, 1938. "Life is but an empty dream." I had a couple of vocabulary tests and I rated [as high as] high school graduates. My brother still has his 'bigness' complex.

Sunday. January 23, 1938. Came back from Newark today. My mother is still in Greystone.[9] I saw *Hollywood Hotel* and *Sgt. Murphy* [with Ronald Reagan]. I just had another quarrel with my brother.

---

8 One of Naomi's occasional suicide attempts.
9 Greystone Park Psychiatric Hospital, Morris Plains, New Jersey.

Allen Ginsberg reading, 1937   © ALLEN GINSBERG TRUST.

Wednesday. February 2, 1938. [Ground Hog Day]. Saw *Rosalie* with Nelson Eddy and Eleanor Powell. Am listening to Ben Bernie[10], who said the ground hog came out, took a look at [Walter] Winchell[11] and ducked in again. When Winchell opened his mouth Sam Goldwin[12] got the idea for *Hurricane.*

Friday. February 25, 1938. Came to Newark.[13]

Saturday. February 26, 1938. I saw *Hurricane* with Jon Hall and *All American Sweetheart.* The actor in the leading man's role [Scott Colton] was exceedingly good.

Sunday. February 27, 1938. Had a puppet show: "A Quiet Evening with the Jones Family." Am in Newark.

Monday. February 28, 1938. Went to school. Miss Biscuit still "cracked or crackered..." P.S. (this my better half's writing). [Allen's father, Louis, who was a famous punster, wrote the phrase within the quotation marks.] In case you don't know, I moved.[14] So did my brother. "And father and the rest of the furniture." [Again Louis wrote the phrase within the quotation marks]. Got some new furniture. [My brother's] bigness still going strong.

Tuesday. March 1, 1938. Nothing new today. Naomi is still in the sanitarium but will be out in about one month.

Saturday. March 5, 1938. Saw [Walt Disney's] *Snow White and the Seven Dwarfs*[15] —exceedingly good. I sat through the picture three times.

---

10 Ben Bernie (1891–1943). Popular radio personality on WABC, New York, whose jazz program aired nightly at 9:30 P.M.

11 Walter Winchell (1897–1972). Powerful newspaper columnist and radio commentator whose opinions helped make and break many celebrities.

12 Sam Goldwyn (1882–1974). Motion picture producer whose movie about a tropical hurricane was one of the very first "disaster" genre films.

13 While his mother was ill and in mental hospitals, Ginsberg frequently spent weekends with his father's family in Newark, New Jersey. Rose Gaidemak was his father's oldest sister, Clara Meltzer was the next oldest, and Honey Litzky was his youngest sister. From time to time he stayed with them as a respite from the family problems in Paterson.

14 The Ginsberg family moved from 155 Haledon Avenue to an apartment at 72 Haledon Avenue in Paterson.

15 Ginsberg remembered going to Radio City Music Hall in Manhattan to see *Snow White.*

Thursday. March 10, 1938. Nothing so new today, but I tried my hand at making puppets. It was unsuccessful. My brother also smeared paint on a Humpty.

Monday. March 14, 1938. What fools these Nazis be. In later years I expect to use this book for history. The world is now in a turmoil. A party headed by Hitler (Germany) and Mooselini [sic] (Italian) and some daffy emperor of China are killing all the Jews in their countries (a little exaggeration there). It really is a tough situation (I haven't mentioned this subject before in my diary).

[*As a young boy, Ginsberg saved newspaper clippings and reported the headlines of the stories in his diary, a practice he would follow as an adult when he used newspaper headlines in his poetry.*]

September 9, 1937—Italy, Reich reject bid to parley [with Russians about piracy].

September 10, 1937—[English and French] draft plan to annihilate [submarine] pirates.

September 11, 1937—Soviet balks, British plans its war on pirates—piracy conference reaches agreement—patrol of Mediterranean [to keep neutral shipping safe].

September 17, 1937—Britain and France defy Italy [over piracy patrol].

February 3, 1938—Reich war rift with Nazis widens.

February 5, 1938—Hitler takes Army control ousts 15 generals shifts 25 puts Goering in command.

February 16, 1938—Austria capitulates to Germany. Pro-Nazis get key posts in cabinet. Berlin outlines policy for Austria, gloom pervades Vienna.

February 21, 1938—England speeds [peace] pact with Italy [Germany and France]. Many Jews predicting what will happen in Austria flee in panic. [Anthony] Eden resigns in crisis over Hitler's speech. Hitler defies world, next move is Czechoslovakia. Hitler wants [African] colonies back [which are now British colonies]. War invited by Eden policy says [Neville] Chamberlain.

February 22, 1938—House of Commons backs Chamberlain policy [to restore friendship with Mussolini].

March 11, 1938—Was Hitler's first important move. [Kurt] Schuschnigg [Austria's chancellor] is going to have plebiscite, either free Austria or German lands.

March 12, 1938—[Schuschnigg resigns] Hitler takes army into Austria and conquers it so that it will not have a plebiscite because he knows that the majority is against him.

March 14, 1938—Austria absorbed into German Reich. Hitler commander of united armies, plebiscite on April 10 Chamberlain shocked—and there you have it. Seeing Schuschnigg was going to have a plebiscite Hitler marches his troops into Austria because he knows that he will lose. All the countries see his open hand Schuschnigg made him show his real self.

March 15, 1938—Nazi Deputy warns Czech chamber.

March 17–20, 1938—Lithuania-Poland have a [border] controversy. It nearly led to war. Poland won without bloodshed.

March 24, 1938—Britain will go to <u>war</u> to defend its World War treaties. But denies help to Czechs. There sure is a hot time in the old world today.

March 28, 1938—A civil war in Spain, with bombing on a grand high in one day (last week) 1,200 were killed in Barcelona [Loyalist stronghold city]. It's bad the war is about over and those damn Rebel fascists are winning. Mussolini is sending soldiers by the thousand (and that is a confirmed fact admitted by certain Italian sources) and is ready to go to war if France (or any other country) helps the loyalists. A nice kettle of fish. But there is also war in China (Chinese against the invaders which is Japan) the war has been going on, people killed and it still is an undeclared war. Thank heavens the Chinese are winning. It was even at first, then the Japanese gained so many victories that Japan thought (and other countries) that it would be a cinch for her to win. Then or rather now the Chinese have cornered the Japanese in a triangle in the midst of Chinese territory (not so fast or wonderfully though). Something is likely to break soon in Europe the tension is not so great but the dictators' next move may start another European (or most likely world) war.

April 10, 1938—Germany Austria approve of Hitler's grab of Austria (99%). Mussolini and England signed a treaty that may avert war for the present. The Sudeten Germans in Czechoslovakia (Nazis) are demanding a separate tract of land for themselves.

May 22, 1938. The world is all agog, nothing much happened since I spoke to you last. Today, oh, am I having fun. Oh boy, my brother thinks I saw *Girl of the Golden West* (he-he). I am leading him around the bush by telling [him] the stories and happenings of that and another picture. I really didn't see either of them. I got [the] information from a friend.

Briefly there's a war in China; Brazil had a fascist uprising (the government won, thank heavens); Mexico is on the verge of a civil war; there's a war in Spain; but most important of all [is] Czechoslovakia. There is a party in Czechoslovakia called the 'Sudeten Germans' headed by a man called Konrad Henlein. The Sudeten Germans are Nazis consisting of [only] 3 million out of 14 3/4 million people in Czechoslovakia. They are demanding autonomy for themselves and a lot of other outrageous demands [even though] they are a small minority. The Sudetens are backed by Hitler. If [he] grabs [Czechoslovakia] it will be by an excuse of saving her from internal troubles. He hesitates to take her because she is armed and will fight back and France is on her side. If France fights [Germany], Great Britain will too and also Russia; if Hitler fights he will be backed up with Italy.

I haven't told you much about myself. I am [the] smallest boy in class. Hobbies—stamps, coins, minerals, chemistry and most of all (at present) movies. They afford me great pleasure and they are about the only relief from boredom which seems to hang around me like a shadow. So don't be surprised at the movies I've seen in succession. On March 14, 1938, Clarence Darrow[16] died at 80.

[*Ginsberg continued to list selected headlines in his diary.*]

August 4–8, 1938—Held a little border dispute with Russia and Japan.

August 8, 1938—Japan army concedes Soviet victory at border.

---

16 Clarence Darrow (1857–1938). American criminal lawyer and social reformer, most famous for his work on the Scopes trial. At the time, the young Ginsberg hoped to follow in his footsteps and become a lawyer.

August 29, 1938—British envoy to Berlin called home for talks in move to keep peace.

September 4, 1938—Hitler army of 50,000 on Rhine.

September 6, 1938—Hitler defies blockade. (War is coming, I'm pretty sure). France pours reserves into frontier defenses. Blames German arming.

September 9, 1938—War crisis at explosion point.

September 10, 1938—Britain will fight, Nazis told, Romania agrees to let Russians trespass through it to defend Czechoslovakia.

September 11, 1938—Nazis demand annexation of Sudeten.

[*At this point, Ginsberg stopped keeping a journal, not to resume again for nearly three years, just before his fifteenth birthday. During those three years, the family moved to 288 Graham Avenue in Paterson, Ginsberg entered Central High School, and spent his summers with his father's family at the beach in Belmar, New Jersey.*]

1939–1940

[*No entries for the years 1939 and 1940 have been found. During those years, Ginsberg graduated from the sixth grade at P.S. 6 in Paterson and moved on to Central High School, where Allen excelled in English, algebra, and civics. The family moved to 288 Graham Avenue, and his mother Naomi continued to be in and out of mental hospitals for treatment. In 1940, the family spent what was to be their last summer together as a group and rented a bungalow in Arverne, a seaside resort in Queens. While there, they visited the World's Fair, then being held in Flushing Meadow Park, where some of the last photographs of Allen with his mother were snapped. Just as they returned to Paterson, Allen's favorite aunt, Rose Gaidemak, died at the age of forty. By the end of the year, Naomi was seized by a fit of "frenzied insistent accusation" and condemned Allen as a spy for his father and grandmother. That year she demanded that Allen help her escape and forced him to take her on a horrible bus trip to Lakewood, New Jersey. There, he left her in paranoiac fear surrounded by police in a drugstore. Later much of that event was recalled in his greatest poem, "Kaddish."*]

Elanor Frohman (Naomi's sister), Naomi, Allen, and Louis Ginsberg
at the New York World's Fair, 1940

1941

May [22], 1941. Began writing to (I suppose) satisfy my egotism. My writing has improved (slightly). A lot happened since I first entered notes in [this] book and stopped. Biggest things were graduation from public school, classical course and extracurricular activities in high [school]: L. D. S. (Literary and Debating Society), Dramatic Club, S.G.A. (Student Government Association) Board of Publications. I was a good writer so I got a $2 a week position beginning September 1941 as Central [High School] columnist for *Paterson Evening News.* Will be layout editor of the *Tatler*[17] (school paper) next term. I'm running for Treasurership of S.G.A. against Robert Hanson and Saul Liss. Haven't <u>too</u> good a chance. Am counting on my father's name and a lot of people who know me but not vice versa. Don't mind my succession of different thoughts. I have a lot to say. As I said, I am writing to satisfy my egotism. If some future historian or biographer wants to know what the genius thought and did in his tender years, here it is. I'll be a genius of some kind or other, probably in literature. I really believe it. (Not naively, as whoever reads this is thinking). I have a fair degree of confidence in myself. Either I'm a genius, I'm egocentric, or I'm slightly schizophrenic. Probably the first two.

I'm president of LDS [the Literary and Debating Society]. As for international affairs, I have a collection of newspaper headlines. I made a collection with my brother, who by the way is a senior at college and has recovered from his attack of '17'.[18] The [headline] collection dates from somewhere in 1937 or '38 to '40. I became lazy. By the way, I'm an atheist and a combination of Jeffersonian Democrat [and] Socialist Communist. I don't agree with communist foreign policy and dictatorship. Also to satisfy my egotism (and for the benefit of future historians) I'm outlining and giving my opinion on every book I read, hereafter. I'm a lover of classical music and like some swing [such as:] *Playmates, Alexander the Swoose* [recorded by Johnny Messner], and *Three Little Fishes.*

Started to compose my own piano concerto. Succeeded in getting introduction and main theme, about 25 bars, and didn't have patience to finish. What I have is excellent. I like Tchaikovsky, Beethoven, Chopin, Schubert—

---

17 *Tatler.* Ginsberg became layout editor in September 1941.

18 Ginsberg's note: "My brother was merely boasting at being all of seventeen years old." This is in reference to earlier "big shot" comments.

long list. I prefer rhapsodies, overtures, piano concertos and a few suites and dances, [just] about everything. My latest fad is Tchaikovsky especially Piano Concerto #1 and [his] 4th, 5th and 6th symphonies. Wagner too.

Mommy came home about a year ago. Is still a little ---- [the dashes are Ginsberg's, used to camouflage her mental state that he couldn't bring himself to put in writing]. She came home to find Lou $3,000 in debt. Is very fat, lost her girlish laughter and figure. I don't blame her for her condition. For about four months, there were violent quarrels. Lou should have known better. As for the $3,000—*Je ne sais pas.*

Heywood Broun[19] died and a columnist by the name of Samuel Grafton[20] has almost taken his place. Grafton's style is humorous, witty, satirical, cynical, not [as] sentimental as Broun. Grafton is more cold, political, full of facts. I admire him very much. Typical of his humor and fine phraseology is, "I get my knowledge thru osmosis." His columns are both entertaining and educational. Roosevelt elected for third term, awhile ago.

I saw a great deal of movies including: *Make Way for Tomorrow, Pygmalion, Grapes of Wrath, Of Mice and Men, Great Dictator,* and other Charlie Chaplin films, *Fantasia, Dark Victory, The Letter, The Old Maid* (Bette Davis), *Wuthering Heights, Mr. Deeds Goes to Town, You Can't Take It with You,* Laurel and Hardy pix, Ed Cantor's pix, Jack Benny's pix, Bob Hope and Bing Crosby's pix, *Snow White and the Seven Dwarfs,* Sabu's pix (*Aladdin?*), *Three Comrades* (with Robert Taylor, Margaret Sullavan), *It Happened One Night, All Quiet on the Western Front,* lives of Emile Zola, Louis Pasteur, *Goodbye, Mr. Chips, Lost Horizon, The Hurricane, Count of Monte Cristo, The Prisoner of Zenda* [with Ronald Colman], *My Time, Naughty Marietta* [Jeanette MacDonald and Nelson Eddy], *Last Train from Madrid* and *Firefly.* My capitalization has not improved with age [*Note:* the editors have corrected Ginsberg's capitalization errors for the sake of clarity.]

I weigh 95 lb., by the way, and am comparatively fragile. I'm coming thru a stage of puberty and new horizons are opening up, though I can remember the baser emotions since I was about seven. In a modified way, of course. I'm capable of almost anything. Well, if I'm equipped to do things why not? I suppose I'm a coward, because I haven't exercised my beautiful theories. By the way, the lock on this [diary] is broken because I lost the key a few years ago.

I am no longer bored by life in general (as mentioned in a previous year) because of my extra-curricular activities. I haven't the time to be bored.

---

19 Heywood Broun (1888–1939). Popular commentator and newspaper columnist of the day.
20 Samuel Grafton. Local radio commentator and *New York Post* columnist.

[*At a very early age, Ginsberg became interested in politics and world affairs. Three weeks after Pearl Harbor, he wrote a letter to the* New York Times *expressing his views.*]

December 28, 1941.

I have long believed, in principle, the ideals of Woodrow Wilson and regretted that we did not choose to live with the world when the time came to 'resolve that our dead shall not have died in vain' by joining the League of Nations.

I am normally a more or less passive individual. However, I think I am growing cynical. I chuckle and feel a bit of grim humor when I read of our growing regret for the world's biggest blunder, our refusal to join the League. One can almost see a pained and astonished expression growing on the faces of America as the people now realize what they did to the world and themselves in 1920.

So now, finally we have a reflowering of Wilson's vision: witness Winston Churchill's speech before congress; a fine speech on the 28th by Senator Guffey; and a passionate appeal for a new league by Edwin L. James in last Sunday's Times. However, it seems that our futile regret is too little and too late. Our stupidity has reaped its harvest and we have a bumper crop. The death toll in this war has been at least four million (including Spanish, Chinese, and Abyssinian wars). There is no preventable catastrophe in recorded history paralleling this.

That is a grim joke on ourselves, four million dead as the result of mental impotence and political infirmity on the part of a handful of U.S. Congressmen. But in the midst of all this tribulation one can gather infinite consolation by speculation as to what will happen to those Congressmen when they get to hell. We will know better this time, but in any case, the devil has prepared a nice, hot bath ready for many more Senators.

[*In the spring of 1941, Ginsberg published his first articles in the* Central High School Spectator, *and before long he was writing a column about high school events for the* Paterson Evening News, *for $2 a week. At one point, he even ran for class treasurer, relying on his father's popularity to be elected, instead of campaigning, but he lost. In September of 1941, Ginsberg had to transfer to East Side High School in Paterson for his junior and senior years, as he had been incorrectly assigned to Central High School. Once again, he proved to be a good student and earned respectable grades, especially in English where his teacher, Mrs. Durbin, encouraged him to write poetry. During the summer of 1942, he* *returned to his father's family in Belmar, New Jersey, a noticeably sadder place after the death of his Aunt Rose. He continued to spend much of his time at the movies and reading. With World War II in full swing, his brother Eugene enlisted in the Army Air Corps.*]

1942

Saturday. September 24, 1942. The weather today was coolish, with choppy clouds. I did not sleep well during the night because I had a cold and coughed every once in a while. I woke up and drowsily asked the time. It was a quarter to nine. I jumped up and began swearing. My mother told me it was Saturday today; I dozed back to sleep for a half hour.

When I finally awoke, I ate, dressed, listened to the radio, and read the papers till lunch. I heard [Eric] Coates' *London Again Suite* over WQXR and was humming its tunes for the rest of the day. Listening to it, I started comparing his version of London to Gershwin's version of New York. I almost began feeling nostalgic for dear old London and Piccadilly Circus, wherever that is.

I had planned to start writing a letter to the editor today. I thought, with elections so near, I would write my last one. I had decided to try to show, from the isolationist's viewpoint, how this war is different. The war which the united nations are fighting is to free humanity, etc. Also, I thought I would quote from the *Daily News* to show what the isolationist idea of peace would be.

So, after lunch, I carried a bundle of clothes downtown to Russian War Relief for my mother and then dropped into the Abramson[21] Headquarters to write. There was too much noise and bustle there, so I picked up my mother and bought a *Life* magazine, and sat in Barbour's Park[22] to read for the balance of the afternoon.

I had supper at 6:30, after working on my journal for a half hour. Then I took a nap till 8:15 and left for work: minding a baby. When I got to my place of business, being still a little tired, I lay down for another hour. At 10 o'clock I got up and read three acts of *Hamlet*. I am almost finished with it. The parents of the baby (it had been quiet all night) came home at 12:30. When I got home I skimmed thru a copy of the *American Mercury* I found lying on my father's desk. I went to bed at 1:30.

---

21 Irving Abramson. Democratic candidate for the 8th Congressional District of New Jersey, against incumbent Gordon Canfield, the Republican isolationist and colleague of Hamilton Fish.

22 Barbour's Park. Park near Ginsberg's home in Paterson.

Friday. October 23, 1942. The weather today is mediocre; a little on the overcast side, slightly muggy. I woke up today with a slight feeling of dread: my school-work [has] not been good the past month and today is marking day. I finished the last portion of a box of Shredded Wheat my mother makes me eat and heaved a sigh of relief.

I was nervous and did little studying during my first period study class. My math teacher, Mr. Dougherty, gave (literally) me an 80 on my report (I had failed my algebra monthly). I am beginning to think that he isn't half bad, maybe. I felt cheated of five points when Miss Green gave me a 90 in European History. I wanted to complain, but didn't have the nerve, so I merely asked her what I would have to do to get a 95. I was annoyed when she explained that perhaps I was a 95 student, but on the first marking period she felt that she should be conservative. I began to feel like a martyr. Of course, you realize that I am purely objective in this matter of marks; I am merely searching for the truth. I was a little ashamed to get a 90 in English after I saw others, such as Robert Brotman, who knew much more about the English texts, get an 80. This put me in a good mood, so didn't give a damn when I got an 80 in French. P.A.D. [public address and debate] gave me an E.

I came home at three, read the papers till five thirty. I was incensed when I read of that hypocrite Canfield's charge that Abramson was smearing him, and that Abramson was a "Red." I sat down immediately and wrote 500 words in reply. My idea was to ghost write a statement for Abramson, counter-charging that Canfield was obscuring the issues and smearing Abramson. Fire fights fire.

I had supper and went down to the movies with my parents to see *Pride of the Yankees*. I liked the picture very much because it refrained from over-sentimentality, stressed the human angle, and had Theresa Wright. The scene in Yankee Stadium at the end impressed me very much; enough to make me cry a little.

After the movies we went back to Bickford's[23] and had pancakes and coffee. Then I went to the Abramson Headquarters and talked to Hi Zimel,[24] his publicity manager. My idea was a good one, but they already had adopted it and had sent statements to the papers. One such statement by Loftus[25] appeared in the papers Saturday. It seemed effective. I came home and still being in the

---

23 Bickford's. Chain of inexpensive cafeterias.

24 Hyman Zimel. Friend of Ginsberg's father and publisher of the *Passaic Valley Examiner*. Years later, Ginsberg would interview the poet, William Carlos Williams, for the *Examiner*.

25 Martin Loftus. Democratic lawyer.

mood to write, I wrote a two page letter to Canfield himself. I said that I was interested in the campaign because I'd have to live in the world the next Congress would help make; that I thought that there were great issues involved in the election; and that I was disappointed in his refusal to meet those issues.

[*The following is the text of that letter.*]

As you probably know, I have been very much interested in the current Congressional campaign and have sent several letters to the *Morning Call* opposing your re-election and arguing for the election of Mr. Abramson. I am interested in this campaign because I have a personal stake in the matter: I am a high school student and may fight in this war or not, but in any case I will have to live in the world which the next Congress will help make, if it helps win the war. I am sure that you will understand why I have raised my voice.

However, I am sure that I am quite fallible and may be mistaken in either the facts or logic of the matter. For that reason, I have eagerly awaited your return from Washington, at which time I knew that you would present your side of the case. May I say that I was deeply disappointed in this respect by your first statement since you returned as reported in the *News* and *Call* of today. You assailed your opponent for 'smearing' you; you charged that he was using unfair and generally un-American tactics; and most dismaying of all you intimated in no uncertain terms that he is a communist (though I am sure that you are aware that he is not) and dares not repudiate communist support. And while you did mention your voting record, saying that "when I was voting for measures of defense in the Congress, the communists...etc.," you neglected to offer specific, unequivocal proof of this from your record which was what I was looking for.

In my humble opinion, this is the most important Congressional election in our history and the issues involved are of such great significance that it would be a tragedy for those issues to be denied or obscured by smearing, Red-baiting, political tomfoolery or name calling, conscious or unconscious. I am sure that you will be one of the first to admit that state C.I.O. leader Abramson is a sincere liberal, working tirelessly for what <u>he</u> believes to be the good of the country. And I have read newspaper reports in which he credits you with being patriotic and sincere. I do not believe that at any time he has "smeared" you. He <u>has</u> at all times attacked your record or convictions.

Therefore, I think it is unjust of you to attack and insult him personally, as you did in your speech, though perhaps you really did not mean to do so. I am sure that you will admit that it is legitimate and just for your opponent to attack your record and point of view. Therefore the debate resolves itself into an open and sincere discussion of principles which is as it should be.

And so I am sincerely waiting to hear your side of the picture, for I am sure that you have not acted in the past without some reason. I am waiting and the public is waiting for that frank and honest discussion of principles involved: your conservatism versus his liberalism or your documented, recorded denial of conservatism; your Isolationism versus his International-ism, or your specific, documented denial and repudiation of Isolation. These are the issues involved and these are the issues which you must face frankly, if this election is not to be a farcical demonstration of the degradation of the democratic philosophy of representative government.

Sunday. October 25, 1942. The weather today was clear and there was some cold sunshine. Today I slept late. Me and Reilly.[26] I got up at 11:30, yawned till twelve, and read the papers till two thirty. I was disgusted to read that Con-gress put the training amendment on the draft bill.[27] Somewhere in the papers I saw a comment that the President has denounced this Congress as inefficient and generally lousy because it disagrees with him. I commented mentally that, to that observer, a "rubber stamp" Congress is one which the observer doesn't agree with. I think that there is a scandal shaping up on the prosecution of the war in the South Pacific. I hope that it won't react too unfavorably on the Pres-ident.

There was a lot of good music on the radio today. I heard Siegfried's *Rhine Journey* at least twice on two different stations. Schubert's *Unfinished Symphony* sounded as good, if not better, as ever. I don't think I've heard it since the beginning of summer. WQXR played *Scheherazade* [by Rimsky-Korsakov]. I've heard it often lately, but it still has that same oriental appeal to me. Irving Deakin's commentary and records on the ballet over WQXR was very good. I liked the snatch of Aaron Copland's new score *Rodeo* that they played as over-ture. Copland himself gave a very interesting talk. I like Deakin's program because he conducts it with rare intelligence and good humor.

---

26 Probably a reference to the radio program, *The Life of Reilly*, whose main character was a great loafer.

27 The draft bill lowered the draft age to eighteen but provided that no inductee under twenty would be placed in combat without a full year of training. Ginsberg was sixteen at the time.

I was running around the eastside section [of Paterson] looking for 21st St. the last half of the afternoon. I was running on an errand for Abramson. As a politician he has to buy tickets to every clambake and coffee klatch that's put on by the local clubs. This one was for some Polish society, and he had to send them $2 for the tickets; [that's] where I came in.

After supper I was posted for patrol duty for Civilian Defense. I walked the rounds of my sector with two other wardens—two young ladies. I was supposed to go with them to protect them in case anything happened on a dark street, etc. Fortunately, I didn't have to put my commando tactics into use. When I came home, I did my homework till 11:00 o'clock, and then got in bed and finished *Hamlet*. I liked it, but I'd like to see it played before I pass judgment.

[Ginsberg's candidate of choice, Abramson, lost the election, and Ginsberg wrote the following congratulatory letter to Canfield.]

November 4, 1942.
May I take this occasion to congratulate you on your re-election and the decisive majority by which it was accomplished. The campaign has been at times bitter and hard fought, nevertheless I am sure that it was a healthy sign in respect to the vigor of the democratic system even in wartime. In any case, it was no doubt beneficial to have the issues thoroughly thrashed out and disposed of.

Eastside High School (Paterson, New Jersey) Yearbook, 1943

SECTION II

COLUMBIA COLLEGE

Allen Ginsberg with Columbia College friends, ca. 1944   © ALLEN GINSBERG TRUST.

[On May 14, 1943, Allen Ginsberg was accepted at Columbia College in New York. He applied to Columbia for several reasons. A friend of his from Paterson, Paul Roth, who Ginsberg had a secret crush on, had gone to Columbia a year earlier. That, coupled with the fact that his own father had gone to Columbia for his Master's degree, was enough to make that Ginsberg's first choice for college. It was also one of the best schools in the country and close enough to Paterson for frequent trips home. As soon as he graduated from East Side High School in late June, Ginsberg began classes at Columbia during the summer term. At first, he roomed with Jerry Rauch and Arthur Lazarus in an apartment on Morningside Drive, but before long, Columbia found a dorm room available for him at the Union Theological Seminary at 122nd Street and Broadway. Much of his writing of the time takes the form of class notes, reports, and lists of all sorts. By the time his journal entries resumed, he was becoming acclimated to college life in the city.]

1943

[Ginsberg made no actual journal entries in his notebooks during his first term at Columbia. He did record the words to several bawdy songs popular among students at the time. He told the editors that these were sung to the tunes of familiar standard songs, which he still remembered clearly enough forty years later to sing. He noted that he did not write these songs but was merely recording them. The following are a few examples of those songs.]

August 23, 1943

[Title unknown]

We are from Barnard[28]
Barnard are we
We haven't lost
Our virginity

---

28 Barnard. An undergraduate college for women just across Broadway from the Columbia campus.

We have no scandals
We all use candles
We are from Barnard,
Balls, balls, balls, balls (repeat)

Every night at just nine o'clock
We watch the watchman piss on the rock.
We like the way he handles his cock,
We are from Barnard, balls, etc.
Every year at our Christmas dance
We never ever wear any pants
We like to give the boys all a chance
We are from Barnard, balls, etc.

Carr's Melody[29]

Violate me
In violent times
The vilest way that you know.
Ruin me
Ravage me
Utterly savage me
On me no mercy bestow.

Saga of Redwing (Alan Schanes[30])

There once was an Indian maid
Who always was afraid
That some buckaroo would shove it up her goo
as she lay in the shade

That maid had an idea grand:
She filled her crack with sand,

---

29 Lucien Carr (1925–2005). One of Ginsberg's first and best friends at Columbia College. Ginsberg learned this and other 1920's mock vaudeville songs from him.
30 Alan Schanes. Columbia student who taught Ginsberg this well-known bawdy song.

So no buckaroo would shove it up her goo
and reach the promised land

Refrain:
Oh, the moon shines tonite on pretty Redwing,
As she lay sleeping
A warrior's creeping,
The lovelight in his eyes agleaming
As he lay dreaming of promised joy.

Now, this buckaroo was wise:
He crept between her thighs
With a condom cute on the end of his toot
And a love that never dies.

But Redwing came to life
and seized her Bowie knife—
With one mighty pass cut the balls from his ass
And ended that warrior's life.

Refrain:
Oh, the moon shines tonite on pretty Redwing,
As she lays snoring, there hangs a warning,
That two warrior's balls adorning
From nite to morning,
Her wigwam door.

[Title unknown][31]

I ain't got no use for the women,
A true one can seldom be foun'
They'll stick with a man when he's winning
And laugh in his face when he's down.

They're all alike at the bottom
Selfish and grasping for all

---

31 Ginsberg's note: "A lugubrious song, long winded, sung as a parody or comedy act."

They'll use a purse for his money
And laugh in his face at his fall.

My pal was an honest cow puncher
Honest and upright and true
But he turned to a hard shootin' gunman
On account of a gal named Lou

He fell in with evil companions
The kind that are better off dead
When a gambler insulted her picture,
He filled him full of lead.

All thru the long nite they trailed him
Through mesquite and thick chaparral
And I couldn't help think of that woman
With her I saw him pitch and fall.

If she'd been the pal that she should have
He might have been raising a son
Instead of out there on the prairie
To die by a ranger's gun.

He raised his head on his elbow
The blood from his wounds flowed red.
As he gazed at the pals grouped around him
He whispered to them and said

"Bury me out on the prairie
Where the coyotes can howl o'er my grave
Bury me out on the prairie—
But from them my bones please save.

Wrap me up in my blankets
And bury me deep in the ground
Cover me over with boulders
Of granite grey and round."

They buried him there on the prairie
With boulders protectin' his corpse
They said a prayer on the prairie,
And led away his horse

And many another young rancher
As he rides past that pile of stones
Recalls some similar woman
And thinks of his moldering bones.

[Song]³²

There was blood on the saddle
And blood on the ground
A great big puddle of blood all around
A cowboy lay in it all gory and red
His bronco had fallen and smashed in his head.
Oh, pity the cowboy all gory and red
He ain't gonna ride his horse no more now
Because the poor guy's dead.

[*In December 1943, Ginsberg's new friend, Lucien Carr took Ginsberg to Greenwich Village to meet William Burroughs³³ and David Kammerer. On December 17, 1943, Ginsberg wrote a letter to his brother Eugene, which reads like a journal entry. Since the meeting of these characters was to play such an important role in his life, part of that letter is reproduced here.*]

This was my last day of school before Christmas vacation, which begins tomorrow and lasts until the 27th. I don't know what I'll be doing Christmas—nothing much I suppose, out of the ordinary. Saturday I plan to go down to Greenwich Village with friend of mine who claims he's an "intellectual" (that has a musty flavor, hasn't it?) and know queer and interesting people there. I plan to get drunk Saturday evening, if I can. I'll tell you the result. Sunday I'll be around Hastings Hall, probably reading *Anna Karenina*, which I've been reading on and off for a week. Sunday night I'm going to a Japanese

---

32 Ginsberg believed that Carr may have taught him this song as well.

33 William Seward Burroughs (1914–1997). Author of *Naked Lunch* and one of Ginsberg's closest friends.

restaurant with the Jap in the dorm here. I think I told you about him. I want to see how it compares with the Chinese delicacies. Sunday evening I'll probably go to the movies. Monday I'll be either in Paterson, or at the Metropolitan Opera with Naomi. Tuesday I'll be in Paterson, reading *Tom Jones*. Wednesday evening Lou and I have tickets for the Met to see Lilly Pons in *Lucia Di Lammermoor*. God knows, the opera isn't too wonderful, but we want to see Cesare Sodero conduct. He's invited us to visit him backstage if we go. Thursday, Friday, and Saturday are open, except that I have to finish *Tom Jones*, and also finish the whole of Milton's *Paradise Lost*. I don't look forward to reading it.

The Book of Martifice[34]

Being the

NOTE BOOK

of

Allen Ginsberg

"Now, from the cracked and bleeding heart,
   Triumphantly, I fashion—Art!"[35] —Allen Renard

   (salvage?)

Absorber tout, et en faire de l'ideal![36]

"No more in Hell than when in Heaven" —Milton

"Prove all things: Hold fast to that which is true" —Thessalonians

"Everything that is profound loves a mask" —Nietzsche

The symbol of Martifice. As Stephen Dedalus in Joyce's *Portrait of an Artist [As A Young Man]* states, the suicide of the artist enables him to transcend the particular of time and place. He passes beyond death. If he once existed, now he lives. He experiences a transmigration of spirit, that he spreads about him

---

34 Ginsberg titled his notebook, "The Book of Martifice" explaining that the word *martifice* came from Kerouac who combined *martyrdom* with *artifice*. Ginsberg said that he was thinking of people like Van Gogh who were martyrs to art.

35 Ginsberg's note: "These epigrams probably refer to closet frustrations. I was gay and hadn't come out yet, these represent an inner neurotic condition."

36 Loosely translated from the French: "Absorb all and in so doing, attain the ideal!"

wherever he passes. When he touches an object, it too dies, and becomes a living soul, a symbol. He is beyond life, beyond good and evil; rather he is good; he is the high priest of God. He must therefore be worshipped.

[*Ginsberg made the following notes for an unrealized novel. Ginsberg's fictional name for himself was to be Gillette.*]

Gillette reached over his well-ordered desk and plucked a small blue notebook from under a pile of history tests. On the cover he had printed: "Out of the cracked and bleeding heart / Triumphantly I fashion—Art!"

In a weaker moment, one of acute self-consciousness, he had titled the couplet "Whee." The title had no literal significance but indicated generally that the author was aware of the sentimentality of the lines. Gillette took out his pen, and smiling, crossed out the "Whee!"

Sexual Vocabulary

infibulation—act of clasping or fastening genitals in such a way as to prevent copulation

clitoridectomy

ovariotomy

erethism, sexual—condition of excessive redness

coitus—copulation

onine (animal)

Satanism—Diabolism

catharides

polymorph—perverse general infantile sexuality (Freud)

epilated—hair removed?

Sapphism—Lesbianism

uranism

cunnulinctus—muff diving

analinctus—ass diving

pederasty—child sodomy

post coitus triste

hyperasthesia—over sexuality, early discharge

onanism—uncompleted coitus?

bucal onanism—mouth (oral?)

perineal-coitus—with thighs

perineum—region between thighs (genitalia and anus)

fellatio—mouth sodomy

tribadism—mutual friction in Sapphistic contact

coprophilia—licking excrement

coprophagous—feeding on dung

micturition—excessive urination

suborn—to perjure, procure for corruption

pander (from pandarus)—a pimp, go between also, verb to minister to evil
    passions of others

panderism

penunda

necrophilia—sexual love of dead bodies

pedophilia—love of little boys

erogenous—sexually excitable

moral hyperasthesia

eructation—volcano-belch forth

ructation

urolagniac

urogenous—producing urine

flatus—puff or wind, stomach gas, fart gas

smegma

cryptorchiditic—adj. undescended testicle?

aperient—gentle laxative

aperitive

abstergent—purger, wipe clean, n. (to absterge)

abstersive—adj. of above

clyster—a lust

restringents

cacoethes—a lust

oliguresis (ah lig u ree sis)—deficiency in urine

cloacae—sewer, privy, wc, toilet

incunabular cacoethes

He was conceived in a cloacae

eonism (after diplomat Chevalier d'Eon, who posed as woman)
　　psych: the tendency to adopt the mental habits, costumes, characteristics
　　of other sex

transvestition—adoption of customs of other sex

cacoethes—lust

hetaerism—state of primitive concubhage

hetaera—high class whore

polychesia—excessive defecation

bromidrosis—body odor

otiose

Galfanati—Romans, pederastic prostitutes, wore green gaudy robes

uranism

androgyny

algolagnia—pleasure in inflicting or suffering pain, Sadism and
　　masochism

mons veneris—mount around cunt

godmiche—candle (artificial phallus) (Sade)

enculer—anal sodomy (Sade)

encylade

brundus—rump (Sade)

spunk—sperm (Sade)

priapus—penis ("bursting priapus" - Sade)

pego—penis ("bursting priapus" - Sade)

gamahucke

sphincter—rectal muscles

tribade—Lesbian sexual satisfaction by rubbing erogenous zones mutually

Havelock Ellis. *Philosophy of Conflict*: Infantile sexuality: "You will not be wrong in attributing to the child a fragment of homosexual aptitude." This aptitude is a "wish." The wish is suppressed by mores, "disappears into the unconscious to be replaced in the conscious by some other manifestation." Censors: shame and disgust. "Fragments on infantile state of desire remain as fixed perversions or are transmitted as neuroses."

"He's promiscuous, obviously...he even has a baby with his wife."—J. Kingsland[37] (on Charlie Chaplin at table, supper, in International House, with Bruce Maezlich [sic: Mazlish],[38] moi, Carr, Lancaster.[39])

"After all, a deficiency in manners is a deficiency in perception." —H. R. Steeves[40]

"Just like a glass of beer!" Lucien Carr on Brahms' *Academic Festival Overture*.

1944

[*Ginsberg had a lifelong fascination with dreams. The following are the very first of the thousands of dreams he would record in his journals. From this point on, Ginsberg is much more consistent entering items in his diary.*]

I sleep with my desires. The poisoned dreams of fantasy and lust. Dreams—my poisoned dreams. Dream of sexplay on the fence with the degrading Italian slut.

---

37 John Kingsland. College classmate, who Ginsberg described as, "an overdeveloped and world-ly-wise sybarite."

38 Bruce Mazlish (b. 1923). College classmate who became a professor of history, focusing on Western intellectual and cultural history.

39 William Wort Lancaster. Another of Ginsberg's college roommates and later a professor of law at the University of Arkansas at Fayetteville. Ginsberg described him as "a socialist of sorts, a neurotic."

40 Harrison Ross Steeves (1881–1981). Until 1948, the chairman of the Columbia College English Department and an authority on the work of Jane Austen.

Dreams of Childhood:

1. Running up the concrete pavement at 155 Haledon Avenue[41] to porch, on which mother or father mopped. Water on porch. Creature chasing me. Slow, sticky, impossible, frustrating running.

2. Dream of flying—of running inside houses and flying down hallways and in and out of rooms. Buoyant exhilarating feelings. Piano, white walls. At Aunt Rose's house.

3. Dream of creatures staring at me, clasping fire escape and glaring in window from side. I screamed in dream (but not in life) for father to come rescue me. Relief and rescue in father (with long stick?).

4. Dream of father dead. In school. Walked up silent, almost stoical, the aisle, through the teacher's desk—determined and triumphant and violently aggressive—and then tears and crying while I walked.

June 2, 1944.

Dream: I am conversing with Arthur Lazarus[42] in a sun parlor of a home, probably 288 Graham Avenue.[43] It also is on the long road in Belmar (Aunt Clara association). We are talking, and are somehow hinting back and forth, drawing closer; for he is essentially a lover of my type. We concord to embrace. But there is another man around, a Spaniard (Maurice Levett?[44] Don Alvirez?[45]). The man is in our way and does not leave. He stays in a sun parlor like the kitchen. Arthur doesn't know what to do. I go into the other room and indicate to the man that we have private sexual business. The man is not at all adamant but he wavers around and as he finally exits he wants to give us advice about such marriages not lasting. I am not considering the affair as a marriage. As I go back to Arthur, he is seated on chaise lounge or chair. I sit him on me and take him in my arms, kiss him. He is warm and pliable, almost feminine to my touch. It appears to be a permanent marriage. We are under 60th Street dancehall embracing. Arthur has a cunt it seems, so that I am delighted that he promises varied, important experience. Loving him (normalcy) I will have sexual contact with a woman's cunt.

41 155 Haledon Avenue. One of Ginsberg's childhood homes in Paterson, New Jersey.
42 Arthur Lazarus. One of Ginsberg's roommates while he was living at the Union Theological Seminary dormitories on Broadway at West 122nd Street. Lazarus studied pre-law at the time. Carr described Ginsberg's roommates as a "nest of intellectuals."
43 288 Graham Avenue. Another of Ginsberg's Paterson homes.
44 Maurice Levett. French friend of Ginsberg's father.
45 Don Alvirez. Ginsberg was unable to remember who this was.

Allen Ginsberg, Lucien Carr (center), and William Burroughs

We are a family, a wandering one. There are six of us of varying sizes. What relationship there is I know not. We stand on the corner of Bridge and Fair Streets and will meet my family. I wish to keep my father incognizant of my new married life. My brother, or a brother of mine, about six, comes, recognizes me and the children of my marriage. My father, aged, white-haired, doddering with cane, and blind, comes to the corner. He is told that I am here and my brother does not tell my father that the people my father recognizes as his own likeness in the crowd are part of me.

June 2, 1944.

Dream: I am visiting [William] Lancaster. His house is like Aunt Honey's or Dr. Chester's. Going to visit Lancaster, I go through a small village searching, like the time I searched for Kerouac[46] in Ozone Park. I take three trips from Lancaster's house.

The first is with a group of boys at some school or organization. I am at the school—a barn, like on Fair Street or a frame cottage like at the YMHA camp. I have a candle as it is night. I go around the back and place the candle on an eave. I come back with Hal Chase[47] to find the candle has set fire to the eave. I rip out a wet board or two or else a cardboard wall to get to the glimmering flame. I stamp it out with my hands. It reappears on the side of the eave. Hal, taking sympathy, says that if there's trouble in regard to the fire he'll take responsibility since I'm already scandalized with college. He is very good and generous. The fire goes out. Back at Mrs. Lancaster's I fear her disapproval at my escapades.

The second trip I am alone, I am searching for marijuana. I go into negro bar or grocery on corner like grocery at Ozone Park. I ask dark owner who says no, but tells me that the doctor nearby can supply me.

I go to doctor. He is a negro, small, like elevator fag at Warren Hall.[48] He indicates no but leads me back to private room. He opens a drawer, takes out bottles of pills, which are tea,[49] and I ask how much? He gives me two, at a dollar apiece; I return one, saying I will be back for more. I wonder how to take

---

46 Jack Kerouac (1922–1969). Novelist, author of *On the Road* and a lifelong friend. Kerouac lived with his mother in Ozone Park, Queens, at the time.

47 Hal Chase (b. 1923). One of the key figures in the early circle of friends around Columbia. Chase came from Denver and introduced the group to Neal Cassady in 1946.

48 Warren Hall. Rooming house at 404 W. 115th Street, near the Columbia campus, where Ginsberg, Carr, and other friends stayed from time to time.

49 Tea. Slang for marijuana.

the tea; I don't know the strength of each pill. I leave, taking the keys to his house with me, gloating on the possibility of stealing more.

I return to Lancaster's at six or seven in the morning and upstairs I meet Kerouac. He and I leave to do something about the M [marijuana]. When last seen, he and I are sitting on telephone wires or flyboard outside. He begins to piss down to street; I do so myself. My fly is closed, but piss bubbles out of my pants without wetting them. [End of dream]

The old fellow mumbled in a broken voice about the orators in Columbus Circle, "Fools, they are. The Jews damn the Protestants and the Protestants damn the Catholics, and the Catholics damn them all. All fools! Lis'n, let me tell you. I been to Italy and Greece. I lived there a long time. In Greece the peasants live in mud huts with a bed and a picture. A picture on the wall—you know who?"

"The Virgin?"

"Saint Mary, that's right and underneath the picture a candle burns all night. And underneath the candle the man and wife are in bed making monkey business. Fools! They no understand Christianity!"

I think that I shall lie in my coffin with a look of pain in my face. It will be a very touching gesture.

If there is a God he is too obviously a failure or a fool who cannot demand my thanks and reverence. This is a world that God forgot, and until I am satisfied with it, I must continue to demand my money back from God.[50]

Creation and Waste

Art = conscious selective creative self expression, which is therefore potentially communicative.

It is wasteful for an artist to create uncommunicative art. It is creative for him to communicate, creative because of the physical fact that more people are enriched by communicative than uncommunicative art. The uncommunicative artist's value is lost to all but himself.[51]

---

50 Ginsberg's note: "I was imitating someone's smart aleck style, can't recall exactly whose."
51 Ginsberg's note: "During an argument, William Burroughs said that art is just a three letter word—that's all. It means whatever you want it to mean."

June 22, [1944].

Dialogue: <u>Aesthetics and Morality</u>. (7:45 am, after a session with [Lucien] Carr.)

Allen: Well, art should communicate.

Lucien Carr: Come now, Ginsberg, do you really think that art is communication?

Allen (hesitatingly): No.

Carr: But you just said that art is communication. Really Ginsberg, you ought to straighten these things out in your mind before you presume to argue with me.

Allen: Abide with me. I'll get it out.

Carr: Really Ginsberg, you bore me.

Allen: Perhaps that shows a limitation on your part?

Carr (insultingly): Now, Ginsberg, don't take refuge in insult.

Allen: You're hypersensitive to insult.

Carr: Ah, first you say I'm hypersensitive, then you tell me I'm limited. Really Ginsberg, you bore me.

Allen (smiling shyly): I have a right to change my mind.

Carr: Which just about shows how light your mind is.

Allen (pensively, absently, as if he'd been thinking about it all along): But has art no communicative faculty at all?

Carr (with assurance): If Michelangelo went over to the moon, would he be appreciated? But it still would be art.

Allen: Well, what is <u>art</u>, then?

Carr: Creative self-expression.

Allen: With no thought of satisfying others?

Carr: No. Self-expression, self-satisfaction. Though the true artist could never be satisfied.

Allen (beginning to see gleams of light): Well, maybe we're not talking about the same things, then.

Carr: <u>I'm</u> talking about art!

Allen: I am too, in a sense.

Carr: Oh, no, you're beginning to qualify.

Allen: Perhaps. Don't <u>argue</u> with me.

Carr: Well, what the hell do you think you're doing, Mr. Ginsberg, setting an absolute? "Don't <u>argue</u> with me." Hah!

Allen: I didn't mean <u>that</u>.

Carr: You said it.

Allen: No, I meant I didn't like your attitude. Let's get back to art.

Carr: That's what I'm talking about.

Allen (shyly): You mean I'm not?

Carr (smirking, precious, raising and lowering eyebrows): Well, in a way.

Allen (seriously, but trying to suppress a smile): Look, our trouble is about definition.

Carr: I've defined it already, as creation.

Allen: Perhaps that's our trouble. You've defined it and are arguing on your terms with me while I try to work communication into the definition, as an imperative.

Carr: Art has no imperatives!

Allen: Oh?

Carr: Except self-expression.

Allen: Come now, Mr. Carr, will you talk seriously?

Carr: I am talking seriously. What's the matter with you tonight, Ginsberg?

Allen (retreating): I'm sorry. But about art (slowly, a bit uneasily, trying, as Carr is not, to get something settled besides his mind). We're not talking about the same things. Art is, perhaps, creative self-expression, but only in a sense. If art is purely self-expression, then the two terms need not be used. Why not use the same words, say self-expression rather that art? Both a slap of paint and a Renoir represent the realization of the artistic desire, the consummation of the self-expressive impulse. If art is pure expression, we cannot define good and bad art, nor censure bad art. It fulfills the creative need.

Carr: Well, I'm not defining good and bad art, except, that art that appeals to me or repels me is good. Art that bores me is bad.

June 23, 1944.

Dialogue on Morality [continued]

Carr[52]: I tell you that I repudiate your little loves, your little derivative morality, your hypocritical altruism, your foolish humanity obsessions, all the cares and tenets of your expedient little modern bourgeois culture.

Ginsberg: And I reply that I repudiate your priggish cynicism, your own equally coerced amorality, your escapist egotism, your foolish obsessions with your narrow personal devices, all the petty appurtenances of your neurotic escapist mechanism.

---

52 Ginsberg fictionalized names in his notebook. For example, here he used the name Claude de Maubri as a pseudonym for Lucien Carr. Ginsberg was not consistent in the use of pseudonyms, and the editors have changed the names back to the true names for the sake of clarity.

Carr: That's no argument; don't take refuge in insult.

Ginsberg: Well, then, we shall repudiate personal attack, and consider our respective cases on their merits—that is, if we can disembody them from their proponents.

Carr: I am willing because you are too mediocre a person for me to devote my time to. So I prefer the issue.

Ginsberg: I prefer to do so because I think that you are perhaps mislead—that you may be too good to consider as an argument for your confusions.

Carr: We are both terribly confused.

Ginsberg: Thus we reach for unobtainable absolutes.

Carr: What is an absolute?

Ginsberg: A womb! Confusion! We have no absolutes in morality, as in art—they are interchangeable.

Carr: I have an absolute—*moi...j'existe!*

Ginsberg: Prove it, point by point with reason, with logic. You can prove it with love alone.

Carr: Love. Ha! *Moi, j'existe.*

Ginsberg: But you can find no intellectual justification for that. We are not intellectually conscious of our existence. We intuit it, we do not know it.

Carr: *Moi! J'existe.*

Ginsberg: And on those terms we agree. There is no justification, no reason, no love, and no morality.

Carr: *J'accord.* But why do you insist on bringing your dirty old morality into this? Modern bourgeois culture, Ginsberg, has you stuck on its fat sticky paws.

Ginsberg: It has. It has you, too. You react to it.

Carr: I react against it.

Ginsberg: You are a product of it.

Carr: You are it.

Ginsberg: I have taken from it what I wish.

Carr: It has given you what you wish. You have submitted to the mores. You are influenced by your environment. You are weak!

Ginsberg: I am human. It has influenced me—that is inescapable. It has equally inescapably influenced your *Weltanschauung*[53] and your private environment has determined your thought. You are equally weak.

Carr: But I have succeeded in escaping M.B.C. [modern bourgeois culture]

Ginsberg: You have escaped nothing. We are equally weak. I am firmly

53 *Weltanschauung:* Philosophy of life.

convinced that I am as right as you—or that we are equally wrong. You have also submitted to intellectual nihilism.

Carr: *Moi?*

Ginsberg: *J'existe?* What are you? Not heaven nor hell nor the intellect can show you! *J'existe.* You are not cut away completely from M.B.C.

Carr: Well, what do you expect me to do? The nihilism…

Ginsberg: Would lead to suicide?

Carr: I've tried that.

Ginsberg: But even that cannot satisfy the demands of nihilism. If you are truly—emotionally and intellectually convinced of nihilism, you could not attempt suicide, for that would be a positive action. If you were convinced—the result would be paralysis, slow vegetative starvation, final, dull, barren death.

Carr: I find no compunction or desire to allow others to enter my universe.

Ginsberg: I find compunction and desire to fraternize with others in this universe. Perhaps I am happier in my universe than you in yours!

Carr: The happiness of insensitivity! Stupid altruism. Bourgeois convenience.

Ginsberg: The happiness of bourgeois convenience, at times, but the happiness of selection. Finally, I avow, the happiness of acute sensitivity—a sensitivity which it has been determined, shall not exclude others. Stupid altruism? All is stupid in our nihilistic universe! Both of us. But my heart's desire leads me to the hearts of others. Yours leads you to your own heart. Ideals are the extension of the ego. We both seek our hearts—I in others, you in yourself.

Carr: The lyric cry!

Ginsberg: *Moi! J'existe!* I exist; I and my desire. I follow my heart's desire. I espouse, we espouse, creation as good, waste as bad—temporarily. We do this because we desire to create. We are artists, shall we say?

Carr: Yes, I am an artist.

Ginsberg: I am unhappy in a world of Philistines. I respect the quality of my creativeness. Since I prize creativeness as a quality, I also tend to love it in quantity. The more the merrier! Sweet reasonableness! I seek my pleasure, therefore, by following this morality: that I shall undertake to add to the quality of art as an artist, and add to the quantity of artistry as a politician. In this nihilistic world, I see no less reason for making a world of artists, than for making myself an artist. Following my heart's desire, I see reason in fashioning, with politics, a future art. At the same time I pursue to the limits of my capacity, my own artistic—conscious selective creative self-expressive desires. *C'est* my morality. You have the sensitivity of the extreme, I have the sensitivity of balance and in the long run, more creative. For surely, through me, others shall create—I shall enable them to.

Carr: Then art as communication?

Ginsberg: All art is communicative, consciously or no. The artist heightens the sensitivity of the recipients, enriches them—how small the number!—and this enriches the society of which it is part, and enriches the future society of which it is the patrimony.

Carr: Then art need not be consciously didactic, consciously communicative?

Ginsberg: Perhaps not. It may be more creative for the artist to attempt to communicate, if in doing so he does not compromise his art.

Carr: Will this not destroy his art?

Ginsberg: Perhaps so. Perhaps not, if he is an artist. But he will be more creative than the self-expressive obscurantist because of the physical fact that his creation enriches other artists and spurs them to communicate. Thus, accepting the morality of creation and waste, it is wasteful for the artist to chant his poems to the wandering winds or live his art, and not record it. The uncommunicative artist's value is lost to all but himself.

Carr: Again, communication self-consciously attempted, will destroy art! Joyce in the *Ladies Home Journal.*

Ginsberg: Not so, because his art would be what we would consider inferior and not heightening the sensitivity or enriching the patrimony of the race. The *Ladies Home Journal's* communicativeness does not enrich people, it bemuses them. Our moral systems are intertwined and inextricably part of one another. The artist may be a free spirit; artistry may be moral. Everybody's satisfied. (and he wept a big tear...)

August 3, 1944.
Carr on Nancy Nash:[54]

Nancy filled a fulsome bodice*
of bacchantes she the goddess**
Freely of her body giving
Denying neither dead nor living
Not a thing her lips had tasted***
But was shriveled and well wasted.

* And for that matter many a large mouth.
** And for that matter many a maypole.
*** Lips in foursomes if you get me.

---

54 Nancy Nash. One of Carr's St. Louis girlfriends.

—God! the drunken robber in the heavens. "God is an Indian giver who gives only occasionally." Jack Kerouac

—Most people spend half their lives creating memories, the other half, remembering them. In doing so, they create new ones.

—A paraphrase of Proust: "He became a dishwasher in a cafe. The job was first easy, but he soon resented the fact that his brothers had made more illustrious careers in a grocery store."

—Business genius: The infinite capacity for taking gains.

—Artistic genius: The infinite capacity for giving pains.

—All work and no play makes Jack.

July 28, 1944.
Pre-Induction Physical:[55]
"I remember you," said a boy named Sidney. "You were in Mrs. Pierpont's English class with me." A man walked up, flicked his cigarette away, and said roughly, "I'm going in, for good, today."

"We aren't, yet—they gave us a couple weeks."

"No," said he, "Hell, they're so hard up for men, they're taking them now right away. They'll send you right off."

After a while, Sidney accepted one of my cigarettes, and asked, half seriously as if very interested, "Are you scared?"

"No."

The bus started singing, release of cramped and worried spirits. "No 4-F's[56] allowed on this bus!" When we got there, the officer in charge gave us instructions. He made a speech. He listed the diseases we might have, ending with "no balls, one ball, clap, diabetes, gonorrhea, syph, dandruff—whatever you want."

"Make sure you don't go to table 17 or you'll find your ass in Ft. Dix tonight."

"Oh, yes, better be careful of the doctor when he makes you spread your cheeks. There've been rumors going around lately."

On the examining line, the prick doctor looked us over, "Squeeze," said he, bored. Then he leaned over to another doctor. "Do you know anything about these damned Civil Service lists? I've been trying to fill one out for two weeks.

55 When Ginsberg turned eighteen, he was required to sign up for the wartime draft and take a physical examination prior to induction into the military.
56 4-F. Classification number given to those people who are medically unfit for military service.

They ask you everything you forgot about—what you do, how you do it, who you do it to, how long you been at it, where your mother lives, where your great uncle lives, where are your deceased relatives living?—"

"If you run an abortion ring do you have to put that down too?" laughed a clean young doctor in the corner, as he tested a urine bottle.

The army doctor asked me about my feet. "Did ya know you we're going to be examined today?"

"Yes," said I worried.

"Well, why didn't you wash your feet?"

When I got to the psychiatrist I was able to answer all his questions truthfully, for my battle for LS [light service] had already been won with the eye doctor. "Ever have a nervous breakdown?"

"Nope."

"Do you make friends easily?"

"Nope!" He looked up a little worried. "You have difficulty in making friends?"

"Well, of course," I answered philosophically—for he did look the philosophical hoary-headed type—"Assuming that one can really have true friends, one must admit that some selection is necessary. I don't want to be friends with everybody! I pick mine. Don't you?"

He looked somewhat relieved. "Do you like the girls?" I smiled shyly and nodded "Yes,"—was I blushing?—and he was so touched by my innocence that he pursued this no further, but he patted me paternally on the head and gave me his OK. [This is a somewhat fictional account. Later Ginsberg, following his own doctor's advice, was actually classified as 4F and determined to be unable to serve based on his admitted homosexual tendencies.]

On Art

As life wounds us, so art must wound us. We are tormented by the delicate, indefinite pain in art; the heart cry of the lover, the failure of realization of the desire, the finite mind stretching to comprehend infinity—these are our sorrows. We pleasure in the perfection of our self torture; we love to mock and sneer at ourselves; we flagellate ourselves with our own failures. Masochists all, we love to be hurt and we love to have our unhealing wounds opened and reopened again; we sit staring in the mirror of art, fascinated by our own deformities.

Why is the perfect lover always jealous? He must be if he is the perfect lover. He sees his own love in everybody's eyes. [David Kammerer[57]]

July 28, 1944. Afternoon.

Dream: Brother comes back in officer's uniform. Looms ruddy and broad. When Gene [Eugene Ginsberg] spoke, he spoke in Louis's [Louis Ginsberg] voice and accents with characteristics peculiar to Lou in tone and attitude. Lou hovered about, but I don't remember seeing him. I confessed to them that their voices were alike and seemed at the time to say or think that the Army experience had matured him. (While walking in the street today, the idea of alignment against me, they having same characteristics proved interesting.)

[Dream]: Dream of needing a few dollars for known use (forgotten since dream) and of finding it. Usually in this dream, I find pennies, then nickels, dimes, quarters, half dollars, and no bills. I pick them up—usually from grass, gutter. Once from under and between boards that cover floor behind soda fountain.

August 3, 1944. Afternoon.

Dream: We were at a convention? It was held in a large house perhaps Aunt Clara's house[58] with some territory added. I, full of ebullience and strength flipped a somersault on the wet grass. A woman pointed out to me that I shouldn't do that, for I had a clean brown two-tone suit on. I wondered if there were any brown color left on the grass from my suit (suit stain) and then asked if there were any grass stains on the coat. We walked on around the back of the house, where there was a pavilion looking like a made over outhouse—its side cut to make room for a counter. There, in a barrel, were standing some flowers, which Jack Turvey[59] wanted to buy. I loathed to spend my money on them and made believe that I'd never seen these flowers (so that if he wanted them he would spend his money) and didn't know what they were good for, for, it seems, they did have some special use at the convention. Perhaps one dried, crinkled, and burned them. Turvey may have bought some.

---

57 David Kammerer (1911–1944). St. Louis friend of Carr and Burroughs who followed Carr to New York City hoping for a sexual liaison with him. Kerouac depicts him as Waldo Meister in *The Town and the City*.

58 Aunt Clara. *loc. cit.*, Louis Ginsberg's sister.

59 Jack Turvey (b. 1927). Another of Ginsberg's Columbia classmates who lived on the same floor as Ginsberg in the Union Theological Seminary dormitory.

At any rate, the dream ended somehow, with me, in my sleep, reciting a poem: "Magellan Discovers The Big World"—The court of Spain? Magellan first sees the earth. Magellan is fêted and feasted, and has Queen Elizabeth, and "Magellan Discovers The Little World," and it is, I intend, the little round cunt of Queen Elizabeth. But in my dreams, formulating the poem clearly, I have some reservations. It'll be another long, dull poem like MacLeish or Hart Crane or Benét, that no one will read. It will be [only] interesting to me, and thus it won't be a work of art. Maybe I could make it a short poem—2 $^1/_2$ pages like my dream poem of yesterday ("Corybantic Lycanthropy"). I wake up on the poem.

August 3, 1944.
Essay in Character Analysis: Lucien Carr
Carr is strangely limited by subliminal repressions, which he rationalizes, unconsciously enough, and makes capital of. He declares that he is 'bored' with me, with places, with things. A truly hypersensitive artist would not be so. Besides, <u>can</u> one be so bored? He declares that he cannot write, that he is a perfectionist and until he squeezes perfection from himself he will not write or show what he writes, or publish what he writes. He makes much of this perfectionism. His bohemianism—a result of what?

It all seems to be a result of inquietude from the usual reasons—no parents, no standard, no security, intellectual or moral; most important, an inquietude coming from a comparison not with the world around him, myself, Adams,[60] etc., but with his higher imagined self or his few mundane heroes—Trilling,[61] Daiches,[62] etc.

He confesses that he fears sterility at the bottom of everything. This is much the same fear as that of not realizing his dreams, of not reaching his standards. He feels sterile? That is impersonalising his failure. He really fears that he is not creative. That is still less invidious than it really is. He feels that he lacks artistry. Thus, he is a perfectionist, he would have it. Thus, if he turns out a poor story—that is excusable, for he turned out a poor story and has not had time to revise it to perfection. What he says is that it's excusable because it's imperfect and therefore not truly representative of his potential. Secretly he

---

60 Walter Adams. Friend and classmate whom Ginsberg described as a "literary anarchist." Adams also lived in the Union Theological Seminary dorm at the time.

61 Lionel Trilling (1905–1975). Noted author, critic, and Ginsberg's English literature professor at Columbia.

62 David Daiches (b. 1912). Scottish author and literary critic.

knows that he has never achieved this potential and fears that he never shall. Thus he is a perfectionist. Thus he rationalizes, in part, his social failures, his intellectual failures, desiring social-recognition in place of intellectual achievement that is, the social recognition as the intellectual, the bohemian, the libertine. He would hate to be known as a mere boor, an eccentric, crankish fool, or a worthless bull-like, stupid, oafish exhibitionist. His ego demands intellectual recognition. Thus he adopts the postures and attitudes of the intellectual with which he is familiar—the bohemian. All the appurtenances of the bohemian become his and this pathogenic dread of non-self-recognition and non-social recognition drives him to red shirts, wild songs, drink, women, queer shoes, loud talk, arrogance, infantilism on a high intellectual level. It is thus vicarious intellectual recognition. It is a palliative to his scarred ego. Either he is a genius or he...but he can recognize no other alternative. He must prove that he is a genius. He cannot do so in creative labor—for he has not the patience, says he, nor the time, says he, nor the occasion, says he. None of these reasons is correct. He seems not to have the talent. Since creativeness can't satisfy, he turns to his defense mechanism, his outlet. His bohemianism. And he can temporarily satisfy himself with his social versatility, his eccentricity, his victories over little Allen, his conquests of women, his love affairs.

Unfortunately he has enough talent in him to encourage his hopes. Unfortunately he has too little talent for him to realize himself in some artistic creation.

Thus Allen, in the Dialogue on Morality, is his Lucifer, or at any rate, his second devil. They are the successful artists, practicing and flourishing, creative and fertile. To him, their success is unworthy, their creation is uninspired, their fertility is never energy and volume. Sensitivity thus becomes the key word. Carr is sensitive, Ginsberg is complacent. Yet he (Carr) has enough respect for the complacent, therefore happy and creative artist, to accord him some modicum of praise. He is a technician. He has energy. In the dialogue, Ginsberg, the successful, is the technician, the complacent, the somewhat stupid, the insensitive. In life, Ginsberg seems to occupy the same position in the Carr microcosm.

So Ginsberg is not the real devil, as much as is modern bourgeois culture. In the dialogue, modern bourgeois culture is what stifles the artist. In the south seas the artist can paint. Not in the middle of M.B.C. [modern bourgeois culture]. The artist, Carr, is disgusted with the bourgeois fancies in poetry and art, all the cute tricks. He rejects them and does not create his own, but vegetates. "To hell with those pismires," said Lucien bitterly. "That was rubbish, disgusting banal rubbish. I am satisfied by no forms of poetry any more. There must be some new way, some new visionary method to deal with art and beauty. I must find this unknown method, otherwise I'll give up art altogether and try life."

Now, this is crucial. He must find the new way. Otherwise, he says prophetically, he'll give up art for life. His plea is that art can't satisfy him. His plea may be true. He does not finish by saying that the reason he is not satisfied is that he has no artistic fire, that he cannot make new forms of art. He takes refuge in life, in exhibitionism. Then he continues significantly, "I'll never find it around here. Everything about the people here drives me away from them. The whole character of this God-damn mire forces me to find a new vision of life. I'm leaving tomorrow to be alone somewhere. Anywhere to get out of this muck." This is his plea, that he is being oppressed by M.B.C. The true artist could find enough in him to defy M.B.C. and remain an artist in it. Carr cannot unfortunately develop enough artistry—or perhaps he has that and lacks the self confidence to *"absorber tout et en faire de l'ideal,"* to use the M.B.C. for his purposes and thereby escape from it. He flees it. He also flees art. He flies to liberty. He flies to life. Perhaps he does not comprehend the true liberation of the artist—the self-liberation, the liberation of the soul, the inner freedom, the wild high flying jubilation of creativeness. So he, of course, resents M.B.C. Is his resentment a foolish, an unphilosophic and an inartistic passion? Is it grounded in his delicate sensitivity or has it a deeper base? Does he fear that he is modern bourgeois culture, or if he is <u>not</u>, does he fear that he is not enough of an artist to rise above it? To rise above it in other's eyes? To do so, as well, in his own eyes? Does he resent it because he fears it? Fears, not that it will physically destroy him, but that he is intellectually at one with its unanimous and insincere mediocrity? Does he resent artistic "success" because it is invidious, and the mob because he sees his face in the mob's face? That perhaps is overdramatic. He knows that in his eyes he is superior. But, after all, how much superiority is he sure of? Especially with his <u>sterility</u>, which is at once cause and effect of his inquietude.

He declares that he must satisfy himself; that he must express himself. Perhaps he believes this and clings to it emotionally, because he is afraid of his mediocrity and desires therefore to satisfy only himself? But he next finds, or will find, that he cannot satisfy himself except in terms of others. "As for denying future generations of poets, it's my own soul I want to look into and my own soul I want to satisfy. Other poets be damned!" But this is really unconvincing, for it is partly insincere, partly front. He is intellectually unconvinced of its righteousness. It is amusing to note that, in his own terms, to find his soul, he must flee an outside environment. He does not realize that his soul follows him around. "It's bad enough being torn apart like this without everyday looking into the bourgeois faces, dulled with misery. No wonder I've been living in all engrossing sloth and carnality. But it won't work anymore, I have to leave. Do you see what I'm talking about, Allen?"

Then his conscience bothers him. "Allen's hand clasped Lucien's which was holding his arm more and more tightly as he spoke." This, however, sounds as if Lucien were in the position of the laboring mother, the creative earth spirit, the sensitive sufferer, while Ginsberg is the dull, complacent, and somewhat bewildered husband, holding his wife's hands while she gives birth.

Know these words and you will speak the Carr language: fruit, phallus, clitoris, cacoethes, feces, fetus, womb, Rimbaud.

August 3, 1944.
Suicide note. Written in melancholy mood, consciously, to be used in a novel:

Good creatures, I am no more. Compose yourselves to the fact of my inexistence. No doubt you will either smile or pity me. That you do neither, I must explain my death. That you do neither, I must justify myself. If it be that I am merely satisfying my ego in justifying myself, in inviting your attention to my misfortunes, then I must accept and espouse my egotism. I am determined that you shall know my predicament.

I am a lost child, a wandering child, in search of the womb of love. I have been intellectually perverted by insanity and adultery in my home. I have dreamed obscenities that would shock you as they once shocked me. I have thought thoughts of wildly imaginative insanity, of perversion, of humor, of loveliness and beauty. I have desired many things—the important ones, I have been denied. They are stability (economic and familial) and love (emotional). I could be very happy with love *sans argent*; we all could. Love mints its own currency. I can not be happy living with neither.

I have loved twice. Helen of Paterson was calm, merry, complacent, intelligent. Her beauty roused my desire, her intelligence roused my love. I was jealous of her. When I loved her I was insane with rapture. I was childish in my courtship. But she is no longer primary in my affections. I still love her...but I shall pass to Jean—infinitely more intelligent, more beautiful, more versatile, more sensitive. I am now prepared for suicide, for she reformed me, and leaves me. She will not know me...and I can see you, my lovers and friends, pitying me! Mocking me! No, I would have none of your self-satisfied pity, your patronizing and righteous condescension. In my evil and in my love I was higher than all of you! You, you mean and priggish creatures, who walked your narrow ways through narrow lives, were incapable of feeling the bitterness of it. If you did not sink into what you called evil, it was because you accepted the rut you were in, and stayed in it by force of habit. It is because you were not shocked and grieved, and because you never transvalued into maturity all the provincial beliefs of childhood. Yours was the comforting and stable life. Yours was the easy complacence of self. Satisfaction and satisfaction with others. Mine was the life without childhood, the adolescence without love, the loneliness of the perverted genius. I defy your pity! and in my weakness, I feel humiliation. Have you truly triumphed over me, my lovers and friends, my enemies all? Has life been your high card, and death my futile hand? Do you rise above me in existence? No! I will not have it. I have been more than all of you. I have seen and suffered more than all of you—that I am dead, proves this. I was touched with a fire that you in your cold existence cannot feel. I felt the nervous singing flame of unrealized longing burn on inside of me while I was alive. I wept to the wandering winds and sang to the moon at night and wrote verse and spoke charmingly. You merely speak charmingly! Did _you_ ever love? Did _you_ ever deny yourself love? Did _you_ ever torture yourself with the sight, the voice, even the touch of the beloved, and yet ever restrain yourself from rushing blindly, wildly into her arms, kissing her violently, clasping her body, tasting her breasts, declaring your love madly, sinking into the graceful curves of her back with your face? Have you ever denied yourself this—so near to love and yet sacrifice for some higher more ennobling love? Have you ever consciously transformed a powerful personal desire into a general attitude? Have you found it necessary to sublimate the passion for an individual to a passionate love for all humanity? Have you felt your weakness, your inability, your final failure, your utter hopelessness? Have you drawn back in revulsion from your higher, ennobling love? Have you heeded duty and love together? or have you sacrificed? or have you felt neither? _Can_ you have felt them, and felt them as agonizingly as I have? I defy you! I defy your wills! I defy your law, your Gods, your idols, your principles, yourselves! And I defy myself! I kill my conscience! I kill myself! Whee!

I want friends! I want to unburden my soul to a loved one! and yet, if people knew me, I should have to commit suicide!

Several times in my life I have come to the conclusion that life is profoundly painful for me. Rather than end it, which would have painful effect on others, I dedicate myself in these sorrowful days to making other people happy. In hours when I am happy—when I forget, and forgive, which hours are not rare—I am unconscious of my consecrated task. I am still able to forget myself in righteous indignation for other people's wrongs. This is the only true altruism. It is a sublimation of personal desire, a result of repression, an extension of my ego, but it is nonetheless quite sincere.

August 3, 1944. Thursday Evening, Written 3:05–3:15.
The street, 115th between Amsterdam Ave. and Morningside....and as I walked along the street, the dark, quiet evening seemed to make the buildings shrink to miniature size and I felt myself lifted above the sidewalk and looking down on it. How singular was the feeling—and how often I have felt it. Looking down on the street, I was struck by the fact that it was a stage—really, truly, a stage. I played my part on it. I walked the street, lonely, in love, recovering from love. I had a tragic role. Yet I was conscious of my role, so conscious, in fact, that I almost treasured it for its nobility. Now I am acting this tragedy. In years to come I shall walk down this street, this stage, and look at it in retrospect. It shall not then be a part of the present, but a reminder of the past to me. I shall value it and love it for what it once meant. And so walking the stage, peering at the backdrop, I was taken with awe by it! So real and so unreal did it seem. So unreal was my sorrow, viewed from above and in the future, yet how real to me in this present!

Thus musing I stopped suddenly and stared intensely at it, as if to memorize its every detail, to be fully conscious, completely sensitive to the present while it was the present, the living, the portentous, the sorrowful, the memorable present. I was actually in it! It was mine—but only now. It would not be in a day, in a month, a year! Grasp it, clutch it tightly, claim it, it is your own for this short time. This is your single moment of life, Allen!

August 10, 1944, around 6:30 A.M.
Dream: Arthur Lazarus and I were hitchhiking on our way to France (association with Carr's trip)[63] though it was really England we were going to (association with Eugene's army station). We ride with all sorts of people on a road that reminds me of upper Main Street Paterson: stores, trolley tracks, churches, red house. With one eye I see a car coming along, it has a sleek continental front, cream and clean colored, straight cut with a curious hood. Its sides are

---

63 Carr was planning to ship out as a merchant seaman on a freighter to France in order to escape David Kammerer's homosexual advances.

open and strangely enough, it is driverless. It turns a corner from a bridge and we get out of its way. Then Arthur seizes his opportunity and jumps on, for he wants a hitch of any kind. The two front seats of the car are unoccupied. Art gets in and rolls along. The car travels ahead of me. Suddenly, I see that the back of the car has sled runners immediately behind the rear wheels. Even more surprising, there is a third seat in the back, hidden from front view, on which is seated an old woman, Queen Victoria perhaps, her head sticking just above seat level. I try to warn Arthur of her presence, but he doesn't hear me and I'm afraid to shout to him openly for fear of arousing the lady, who seems to be half-conscious of his presence, but she sees me warn him. I attempt an indirect communication, "Look behind you," I whisper. Finally, desperate, I shout in euphoria, "Discretion is the better part of valor."[64] Lazarus finally turned and jumped off the car and the car went ahead. We continue hitching for a moment, when suddenly I remind Arthur that he left his glasses on the car. He runs off to find them saying that he'll be back. The car rides ahead at a little faster than walking speed and is lost in the traffic. I suddenly resolve not to waste time but to follow them. I prepare to run ahead—I take off my glasses and coat and put them on a grey ledge jutting out from the rough grey building. I make my way thru the garbage piled against the buildings but am unable to sight them ahead. I run forward, but, as in dreams, my speed is agonizingly slow—my running is repressed. I seem to blame my slow progress on my lack of glasses, and so with some difficulty I make my way through the garbage back to the ledge and pick up the eyeglasses. I go on ahead now, faster, and finally come to an intersection where there is much traffic (Clinton and Bergen Streets in Newark?). There seems to be a long square—I am about to enter England, looking sadly for Arthur. I enter what resembles the entrance to the stage door canteen—a somewhat high tin door leading into a sort of waiting room—like that at the Susquehanna bus terminal. There is a crowd milling about. At the end of the room is a man taking tickets by a turnstile which leads to England. I look for Arthur. I am first inclined to enter. But since I would not enter England without him, I check myself. I see Bill Lindmen with a little brother that resembles him, and I ask, "Did you see Arthur Lazarus?" He suddenly seems to really be someone else, of a smaller build, as does his little brother who, in the change, still looks like the older. They resemble Lindmen a little still, but are obviously different people. I observe they are

---

64   This inversion of Shakespeare's "The better part of valor is discretion" is interesting because Ginsberg later remembered that these were the first words he ever spoke to Jack Kerouac.

Englishmen, they turn away. The crowd stumbles about with people entering by the tin door. I see people coming up and down a clean modern buff-colored stairway and I wonder if I should too. I convince myself that if he comes along I'll be able to find him because no matter how many people enter England, they all must pass through this little space. Still, I ought to communicate with him—perhaps by hanging Carr's picture of the violin player on the narrow stairway wall so that Arthur will know I'm around and be able to locate me when he comes. I wake.

August 13, 1944.
<u>Ginsberg in Love</u>

I decided that I was in love with her about two months after I met her. <u>She</u> was quite different, Helen. I was in the season of the death of beautiful adolescent love, when the trance was wearing off, but had not yet left me completely. Love, at best, in Paterson was a 'doleful joy' as Hardy puts it. Because I did not know this Helen, because she was more of a mystical goddess than a personal friend, because in high school terms, she was popular and I was Allen Ginsberg. I spent my spare hours and my study hours idealizing her. She was intelligent, yes, and rather good-looking. She had black hair, short, but thick. When I did not see her I imagined her to be plump; when she was in my eyes I discovered that she was beautifully slender. Her breasts were overlarge; her throat was tanned and shortened. Well, so much for the bitch. I asked her to the movies. She did not hear me for she was walking in the corridor with Louise. I asked her again, almost running after her, undignified. She turned and said casually, "Yes." I stifled my jubilant ecstasy. I slowed my walk. I banged my book on my knee. Mine! Done! Once! Alone! At last! Tonight? Mine! Mine! Helen! I walked home in a dream. I was enervated and beaten. My body no longer existed. Oh, it was a famous victory!

I said hello to my father—the fool! He didn't know the horrible joy that was mine that day—he was that much the fool for not knowing. He was that much beneath me. I sank listless into the easy chair. I stared in apathy and bliss. I ruminated and raptured. I near wept, I near bit my leg off. My cock shriveled to the size of a peanut—this was too pleasurable to be disrupted by the nasty necessities of sex. Thus the day dragged on; I counted my hours and found that platitudes were, oh, so true! Supper was not for me. And all the while, the world whirled as usual! My brother studied law, my mother cooked, my father wrote at his desk. The sun went down and I prepared myself. Oh, how I handsomed myself! I smiled brightly and told the family I was going to the movies. Goodnight, have a nice time, hideous creatures!

I came to the theater, where we were to meet, early, and waited. Then, to add to my impression, I bought a copy of the [New York] Times and stood there, my eyes fixed unmoved on the page. I lost myself in delightful fancies. Suddenly she tapped the paper; I looked up; she smiled at me—she smiled at me—the world stopped; my heart beat no more; my mind was out of order; my watch forgot to tick—she smiled at me—her breasts were in front of her—her little round cunt was behind it all—she smiled at me. "Oh, hello," I cried gaily. "Just in case I got bored tonight I brought along a paper..."

That was the first time we went together. We went, again and often—but she never loved me, never reciprocated. I left for college. I wrote her each week—it would not be discreet to write more. I did not tell her of my love—I continued to love her for a year—I saw her once every month—once every two months. Soon my love became habit; in college I became sharpened; I saw how limited and dull she was; I saw how much lower than myself she was; I was tied to her in human bondage still, but no longer did my lonely mutterings ring true. When I saw her, I could smile and jest—and no longer feel hurt as I hurt her—I could mock her and view her hideousness—and love her, perhaps. But she is over—Helen has lost.

August 13, 1944.
West End[65] Sunday: A Romanticized Version of a Tragedy

The Cast:[66]

> [Lucien] Carr
> [David] Kammerer
> [Allen] Ginsberg
> [John] Kingsland
> [Walter] Adams

Kammerer walked into the room as Adams and I were sitting there talking about the *Jester Review*.[67] "Hello," I greeted him. "You're out of luck tonight. Carr was here about ten minutes ago to see me and left. I wasn't home. But what brings you here?"

---

65 West End. A popular bar across Broadway from Columbia University between 113th and 114th streets, in business until 2006.

66 Ginsberg sometimes used fictional names in his journal: Carr was Claude, Kammerer was Klavier, and Ginsberg was the narrator. Kingsland and Adams were identified by their actual names, but occasionally Ginsberg became mixed up and used the real names of other characters as well.

67 *Jester Review.* The *Columbia Jester* was Columbia's literary and humor magazine, and Ginsberg was on its staff in various capacities.

"Oh, Lucien out? Well, I came to see <u>you</u>, Ginsberg. I wanted to read that wonderful new story of yours."

"Well, I'm delighted that the news leaked out so quickly and forcefully. But where did you hear about it?"

"Oh, it's in the air."

"Now, tell me—what <u>did</u> you come for?" I asked, smiling.

"Well, if you insist, Ginsberg," he declared with a tone intended to convey an attitude of boredom discreetly disguised as interest. "I thought I'd pay you a visit to borrow some money."

"Aha!" I smiled, rocking my chair, "truth will out!"

"And I hope money will, too. I'm broke and Edie[68] and Jack [Kerouac] said you've got a pile, if you want to help an old friend like me, or do you?" He threw his head to one side and laughed in conscious and delicate delight.

"Well," I said "you know how loyal I am to my friends; I'd like to think up something charming to say other than 'I haven't the money.' Anyway, I haven't the money." I leaned forward quickly. "Now Adams, here...." I hurried on and smiled sardonically.

"Adams has no money either," said Adams quietly, with a weepy look on his face.

"Well," said Kammerer, imitating a look of umbrage. "This is a fine way to treat a friend."

"It's the only way under the circumstances. Where are you headed, by the way?" I asked.

"Oh, out," he said casually. "By the way, did you know I'm shipping off soon."

"Oh, you too? Where?"

"Who knows?"

"Well, the *Wanderjahr* riot has caught you now. First Carr, now Kammerer."

"Well, we traveling souls, you know. Ginsberg why don't you ship out?"

"Who, me? Don't be silly, that would be indiscreet."

"Indiscreet? Foolish, maybe."

"Well foolishly valorous, and therefore indiscreet; at least, in my position."

"That's right, you want to save the world, don't you. I don't suppose you could ship out then. Oh, Ginsberg, heed the call of the artist. Reverend Sybarite, forsake thy calling!"

"Art waits on humanity for the moment," said Ginsberg.

"That's right, Burroughs called you the bourgeois Rimbaud last night."

---

68   Edie Parker (1923–1992). Kerouac's girlfriend at the time and soon to be his first wife.

"Well, anyway, when are you leaving?"

"Who knows? Soon enough, I suppose, soon enough."

"And where?"

"I said I didn't know...you never know where you're shipped to."

"Oh, come, be more specific."

"Insistent little pismire, isn't he?" said Kammerer, turning to Adams. "By the way, Adams, why don't you ship out?"

"I've no working papers," replied Adams complacently.

"Well, they're not hard to buy. You just have to know the right people...like me."

"Oh," asked Adams, interested. "Can you get the Merchant Seaman's papers for me?"

"Sure, of course, for a price."

"Well, that's taken for granted. About how much would that be, though?"

"Depends on the salesman. I'll sell you mine for $50."

"Sounds like a good idea, but I've already arranged for a motorcycle trip," Adams said.

Kammerer had risen to leave. "I'll go with you. Are Edie and Jack outside?" I asked.

"Yes, but I wouldn't go, if I were you," he replied darkly. "It would not be discreet."

"Is this a hint?" I replied.

"Oh, no, when I want to tell you something I'll say it outright. But you'd better not come—do so if you want to—I'd advise not."

"This all sounds quite mysterious. Well, I won't go with you, but Walt [Adams] and I are going over the West End for a drink now. Come downstairs with us."

We walked downstairs, chatting. Adams told of his proposed trip to Vermont.

"Well, then, I suppose we won't be seeing each other again," said Kammerer, "for I'll be leaving soon!"

"Then this is goodbye," said Walt, "maybe I'll see you again."

"Probably not," laughed Kammerer. "We don't travel in the same circles."

He and Adams shook hands. I wanted to shake his hand and say goodbye, for I was not sure that I'd see him again after he left. I thought that would be too sentimental however; for I knew that, once shipped out, he'd never run across me again. So I trusted that I'd see him later in the evening and walked with Adams to the West End. As we crossed Broadway, Carr met us.

"Why, hello, Ginsberg. Did you get my message?"

"What message? Oh, I see, I haven't been up to my room since this morning. What'd it say?"

"Oh, I'm sorry you missed it. Nothing much, except that I'd looked through your notebook."

"You what?"

"Don't be angry now; it won't do you any good."

"Well, that was…indelicate of you. And to admit it, too! Anyway, what did you see?"

"Oh, a lot. I skipped most of that self-conscious sentimental stuff about yourself."

"Oh, what a shame! You missed the most charming part!"

"Well, I'm glad you picked up the word recidivous," said Carr.

"You have a special place in your heart for it?"

"Oh, yes. Someone was chanting that in the village! 'Recidivous and solipsistic, recidivous and solipsistic.' Anyway, I left tears all over your book, when I read that long sketch of me."[69]

"How touching! But it wasn't a sketch, it was a clinical report."

"Well, it wasn't tears that it drew. I was sweating like a bitch."

"The truth hurts, eh?"

"Well, it was competent, I suppose. You know Jack said the same thing about sterility. Anything strike home?"

"How much of you was in my report?" I asked.

"Well, the best part was that about my identifying myself with the bourgeois and desiring to be something different." "Oh," he started up, "did I tell you about the fight I had with my mother?"

"You mentioned it before."

"I had a time with the old girl tonight. She's good in an argument. An old Phi Beta baby!"

"What was it about?" I asked.

"My insanity record. She finally got me to burn it."

"No! Oh, what a misfortune. You've lost the only family heirloom that you had."

"Yes, I felt kinda sentimentally moved, burning it."

"Well, how did she get you to?"

"She just asked me. So I argued. I told her to put a $20 bill in it and I'd do

69 See "Essay in Character Analysis: Lucien Carr," pp. 47–50.

it. She said OK, but with my money. I offered to put $10 in if she put in ten, so she smiled and said no, either all your money or none at all. Then I offered to burn it free, only on the carpet. She said no, so I gave in and we put a big ashtray on the table, lit the paper and giggled while it burned. We even turned all the lights out," said Carr.

"Well, now your mother must feel relieved."

"Yup, it's symbolic of something, I suppose," he mused.

"Of her dear little Lucien's normalcy," I said.

"Well, then, maybe I shouldn't have burned it."

There was a lull in the conversation as we ordered a few beers and lit cigarettes. "Where's Celine?"[70] I asked.

"Oh, up in Pelham. She asked me up tonight. I don't know why I didn't go. I should have. There's nothing doing here."

"By the way, is she still madly, desperately in love?" I asked.

"Yes, but why ask that?"

"Oh, Kingsland was telling me a long, long story last night. He was very bewildered about it all. Friday night when you and Celine slept at Edie's, you got up and went to the bathroom or to get a drink. While you were out, Kingsland said that Celine came over, half dressed, to the couch where he was laying, sat down on his lap and began to neck with him. He told me that at the time he thought they were both drunk for he had been gulping pernod with Edie all evening, so he let himself go. He didn't get far, however, because you came back and Celine left him. When he woke up in the morning, he remembered it, smiled weakly, and then—BY GOD! Celine wasn't drunk! He had been, but not she! He felt as if he had strangled someone in a dream and awakened to find some of the dead man's flesh under his fingernails."

"As a matter of fact, Celine told me about it."

"He said that showed that she had fallen out of love with you, she seemed to him to be cooling towards you. I said that she was still deeply in love and had done it as a gesture of defiance, for she didn't feel that you were the right one to fall in love with."

"No, she's still in love. As a matter of fact, that night, we copulated for the first time," said Carr.

My face lit up. "Mon Dieu! At last!" I extended my hand, "Congratulations." Carr did not offer his, as I withdrew mine, a little embarrassed.

---

70   Celine Young. Barnard student who was dating Carr at the time. Her family lived in Pelham, just north of New York City.

"Anyway," I added, "it takes a load off my mind."

"Incidentally, I didn't know about Celine and Kingsland," Lucien added with a smile.

"And I knew you didn't know," I glared up.

"Well, well, fighting as usual!" Kammerer's voice came to us as he leered down upon us from the side of the table. Kingsland and Frank Grosz walked up to the table as well.

We all got up from the table and went to the bar. Carr approached Kingsland and began to ask him about Celine.

I pulled Carr's sleeve, raised an eyebrow, and murmured *"restez."*[71] He did not seem to understand, and so I continued *"Ne demandez pas des questions embarassantes de cet homme."*[72]

Carr's face lit up! He had me in a most painful position and he exploited his opportunity.

"Come now, don't embarrass me further."

"What's it worth to you?"

"Oh, come, Carr, I gave you my last half buck for the beers."

"Give me what you have left," he said.

I put my foot down, *"Pas une centime, Crapuade."*[73]

He asked seriously, "Would it really embarrass you?" He smiled sardonically at this.

I said yes and turned to Kingsland who had walked to the bar. I went over to him to draw him away and he asked, "What the hell is this all about anyway?"

In desperation I began to confess. "OK, I'll tell you."

"Was it about something I told you last night?" meaning Celine's conduct.

"Damn him," I thought, "Why doesn't he give me a chance to talk?"

"Yes, I told Carr and he was going to tell you; I stopped him, but now I don't give a damn!" Suddenly, someone kicked my foot. I turned to see Carr retire. "God!" I thought, "I've given myself away, he wouldn't have talked." Someone kicked my foot and I turned resentfully to Carr, who looked at the heavens and pointed to Kammerer. Kammerer smiled queerly at me, leaned his head to one side and said with surprising bitterness, "damn fool." I turned around, Kammerer kicked me again with violence. I became annoyed and pulled my foot back into his groin, missing him by inches. He raised an eyebrow, smiled sardonically and sidled away.

---

71 French: "Stay."
72 French: "Don't ask this man embarrassing questions."
73 French: "Not a penny."

"I'm so embarrassed," said Kingsland.

"So am I," I replied, "but why are you?"

"I feel quite guilty."

"Guilty?"

"I feel as if I had seduced Celine."

"Then rest assured," I assured him, "that Carr doesn't want it."

"But Celine will resent my telling it. How will she feel?"

"Well, I'll speak to Carr and tell him not to ask her about it."

Carr and Kammerer, meanwhile, sat at the bar. Carr was entirely absorbed in conversation while Kammerer stared down at him seriously, they seemed to be arguing heatedly. I could not hear what they were arguing about....

I noticed that Carr and Kammerer had left, it was one thirty. We rose from the table, walked to the soda fountain and ordered sandwiches. I walked to the door and looked outside to see if I could spy Kammerer and Carr. They had completely disappeared. I returned, disappointed, to the bar. We left immediately afterwards. Kingsland and I walked to Kerouac's. He was in bed with Edie, writing a poem.

"See Carr or Kammerer?"

"No, they haven't been here. But we're going to bed now."

We stayed a moment more and left. I assured Kingsland that he didn't need to feel guilty about Celine.

Returning home, I looked in my notebook. There was a note of Carr's. "Really, Allen, the call was only condescension and by request. Notice the tears in your most definitive work. Glad to see you've picked up recidivous, by the way, lovely word."

I read Marx for an hour and retired, it was 3 o'clock.

August 13, 1944.
Dream: Helen stroking cock under cover. Unfortunately, only one stroke: the shock was so great that I woke up. I imagined that four strokes would bring orgasm. Too bad.

August 14, 1944.
Dream: I was in Newark, seemingly with Louis Ginsberg. I had come in with several bags and valises (association of going to farm with Naomi[74]). I was

---

74 Ginsberg's mother Naomi had spent many years in and out of various sanatoriums and mental institutions, commonly called "farms" at the time, as in "funny farm."

leaving for a visit to N.Y. and there was some trouble. I wouldn't need all the valises myself and Lou could take some back to Paterson. I went to get the train at its station on the top of an embankment; a long sloping grassy land led up to the embankment, much like Naomi's farm. I arrived latish and put down my bags next to a ditch. There were too many people there for me to be able to walk directly over to the train, so I crossed over to the other side of the tracks somehow, and found myself, as before, with many people waiting. I wanted to find what time the train was to leave. What if it would leave before I could get my bags? Trains to N.Y. run often—every 20 minutes probably.

I was on a train with Arthur Lazarus and W. Scott, perhaps Stuart Scheuer and some others, to Far Rockaway, to Coney Island. I made the trip twice with them and had a nice time the first trip. The second time they filed out of the train, a whorish looking slack legged woman entered my car in the train as I tried to go with them. I left late to find them. I went on to the boardwalk where there seemed to be two parallel walks, one going to the sea, one coming back inland with a few amusements. I wandered out looking in vain for Scotti and Lazarus.

I am on the beach, on the path. The scene is pallid, almost anemically white, with the sand broken by two long thin delicate paths. Lifeguards are going empty handed down to the sea; dozens of lifeguards are walking up from the ocean—on their back are curled people they've rescued. There seems to have been a major accident (association with Coney Island fire[75]). A guard comes down the path from the sea, carrying a man on his back. At orders of the man, stops near me on the beach and dumps him from his back onto the sand. He has recovered and is being brought back.

August 15, 1944.
I had a horrible headache.

Kammerer Dead! Another lover hits the universe![76]
Life—it moves! —?

Like all sad people,
I am a poet.

75 Coney Island fire. On August 12, 1944, a spectacular fire gutted nearly half of the Luna Park amusement attractions at Coney Island.

76 In the early morning hours of August 14, 1944, Lucien Carr killed David Kammerer with his pocket knife.

August 19, 1944.[77]

And now, this curtain has been rung down! Everything I have loved of the past year has fled into the past. My world is no longer the same—Lancaster has left—he was the first to escape the stage; his flight presaged the finale! Then all of Hastings Hall[78] was dissolved—Rauch[79] went into the army, Smith[80] graduated, Hoffman[81] left, Mazlish[82] left. But these were the least dear, except for Lancaster. Arthur [Lazarus] and I no longer were roommates—this was a sharp parting and sad, although neither he nor I realized it. When we meet now, we carry the vestigial remains of our former proximity into our attitudes. Kingsland moved. I was reconciled to the dissolution by a new friendship with Carr, which was quite rewarding. There was a quick inter-crystalization of principles. Both of us were stimulated. But the frenzied acceleration of life was the passing climax of a longer pleasure; it was the prelude to the decay of this life. Now the omened deed is done. The shadow has closed down on us and engulfed us all. Carr is in prison, Kammerer is dead—wonderful, perverse Kammerer—Burroughs has fled, Edie has come to like me and Kerouac will end the tantalizing marriage prolegomenon. The libertine circle is destroyed with the death of Kammerer. If Carr is released, it can never be the same. We will certainly leave, Celine may not return and Kingsland lives at home. Burroughs will probably leave town. Edie will return to Detroit (Grosse Point!) and Jack to the sea—only I will remain faithful to the past. I walked into the West End tonight. That place into which I could once step and be greeted by a half dozen carousers, was peopled by a mob of strange faces—old swaybacked women, midshipmen, pock-faced Italians, alien voices all. No more, "It's love, love, love." The strains of "You Always Hurt the One You Love," that mawkish, accurate, melancholy air that haunted last Sunday evening, is dying. It is only a reminiscence of a past now. I walked to the bar, ordered a beer with the little money I had left and sipped it, lonely and wandering, eagerly seeking some familiar face to greet me. I finished it in silence, smiled, and walked out...

---

77 The Carr-Kammerer tragedy of a week before had dramatically upset the circle of friends that Ginsberg had made around the Columbia campus.

78 Hastings Hall. The building at the Union Theological Seminary where they all lived.

79 Jerry Rauch. Another of Ginsberg's classmates at Columbia.

80 Grover Smith. Friend who Ginsberg described in a letter to his brother as "a Miniver Cheevy medievalist who is translating Sir Thomas More's *Utopia* from the Latin." Later he called him an "antiquarian, lean and lantern jawed [with a] voice from the whirlwind."

81 Ted Hoffman. Friend who Ginsberg described as "a hunch-backed poet, a good one too."

82 Bruce Mazlish. *loc. cit.*

August 19, 1944.

Reminiscences of Kammerer, whom it would be best not to forget:

1. First meeting—in John Jay[83]—white uniform and red of hair.

2. Stories told about him before introduction by Carr—esp. bloody gums. Meeting in street. Unctuous smile.

3. Walking into room with cakes, which they devoured and quick retirement.

4. Evening in Village—*Anna Karenina*—Carr's blister—shower—Allen in Wonderland—Downtown—K's room for the first time—"I'm thirsty," with innuendo. Hints. My sphinx-like smile to cover embarrassment and ignorance. Bars—humankindness—Minetta's, others (argument or what?)—Subway home—talk about Carr while C. slumbers. Off at 123rd St. Sleeping over. Awakening early, coitus, going through Lazarus' bookcase. Kammerer awakens, comes in, talks. Great B's [Burroughs'] long talk, me seated shyly rocking Jerry's chair, questioning Kammerer about ambitions, past a bit.

5. Long evening talks with Kammerer about his troubles—on Mann and German mind, beloved's return.

6. Long evening talk. "I need a wise man." "I've read a lot of books." Treated me in Chock-Full-Of-Nuts. Sitting on bench above subway, 116th St. Sterility. Compact—you write, I'll encourage Carr. Escape from influence, grasping for steady principle, emotional rock of Carr's. Walking to Hastings [Hall], sharing pack of cigs. Amiability. "I'll come up and read your paper on Pascal."

7. Evening of wrenched ankle. Fight with Carr. Fight with both. M. [marijuana] downtown—throw away Chemistry homework, take book downtown as gesture of conformity to necessity of passion make-up. Discourse on finger in taxi. Drink—orange juice, then across the street, milk. Trouble with Danish pastry—hard. Louise, puffing-circle—me on bed—Carr and Kammerer puffing away. Kammerer stamping making faces in the mirror. Then at Burroughs, Burroughs as sphinx. Typewriter. Giddiness of Carr and Kammerer. Little result. Refusal of Burroughs to give more—whisky, I intend… "If you're not drunk then no more will help." First time at this brand. Taxi home, me limping. I get off at 115th St., to go to Edie's. They to Warren [Hall].

---

83 John Jay Hall. Building on the Columbia campus where the grill room called the Lion's Den was located. It was a popular hangout with many of the students, and Kammerer waited tables there occasionally.

8. Evening with Donna[84] at George's. Humankindness argument by bar.[85] Breaking of glasses. I take mine out, Carr fails, Kammerer succeeds. Lying in doorway, talk about bank cashier and husband with fake checks. Passerby staring.

Edie Parker—Jack Kerouac—*Recherché*.[86]

1. First meeting Edie—West End—Talk and questions about C.I.O.
2. Tales all about Edie—by Kingsland, Grover Smith,[87] Bill Lown[88] and Celine. Rathenberg, Celine, Carr, Lown, Helen Stevens at ballet—"Fair at Sorochinsk" [opera by Mussorgsky]. Carr and I compare notes. They were drunk. Wordsworth's "Intimations." My reactions.
3. First time at Edie's—Strange front. Walk up.
4. Woof It[89]—curious behavior toward anyone walking in. Barking and jumping. L. Carr petting and rolling around with Woof It. Celine's story: My affairs with Woof It. Repression.
5. Kit Kat—on my chest at night. Pugnacity.

August 19, 1944.
[Dream]: Woke up in night dreaming of picking up money. Pennies and dimes. Believe I dreamed that consciously, out of sheer perversity, for I knew it was a dream while it still clung to my brain, yet it didn't flee for a few moments.

August 20, 1944.
1.) Write of old drunken painter in bar who starts talking to young guy. Theories of art, ennobling creative expression, selective expression, communication. Use bartender's conversation, guy gets drunker and drunker. I ask then if only sin is wasted as opposed to creation gets very vehement while he repudiates himself by wasting himself. The subconscious knowledge of which may make him drink.

---

84 Donna Leonard. Another nubile girlfriend of Carr's, who remembered her as a pretty young girl from Chicago, often on the scene.
85 Humankindness. A reference to Shakespeare's distinction between human-kindness and humankind-ness.
86 French: "Refind."
87 Grover Smith. *loc. cit.*
88 Bill Lown. One of Ginsberg's intellectual classmates at Columbia.
89 Woof It. The name of Edie's dog, given to her by Kerouac.

2.) In bed an unpublished author and an unknown sculptress. Dialogue opens with his remark that they have been carefree all day according to her dictates and now he wants to hear of the departure she is threatening him with. Mentions she has been packed since previous day and is she going back to work in Saint Louis? *"Comme les autres fois."*[90] She reproves him saying perhaps he doesn't believe her because the two other times she has left him one or the other of them has been able to effect a reunion.

August 22, 1944.
Dream: That I received this praise from the Big Jesus. He recommended me to someone as the most versatile, erudite, strongly intelligent person around here. I was respected then for the solidity and variety of my politico-artistic accomplishments.

August 25, 1944.
Dream: I walked along seaside with someone, possibly Grover Smith, and explored the coral reefs. I picked up large snail shells and many colored conch shells, which I broke open for the poems hidden within.

August 26, 1944.
I went through the old preliminaries, opening the history book, reading, noting, musing; finally I put it aside and tried to write poetry. No—my soul was overflowing with lyric wailings—my pen was full of—ink! Black, borrowed ink, without a flash of gold flowing from the nib of the pen! Disgusted, sad, I got up and read Emily [Dickinson]! Old sweet Emily. All she knew! I picked up my book and walked out to the West End—no one but the bartender was familiar. Again, again, all alone. I bought my cigarettes—opened the pack as I walked out, and puffed passionately. Suddenly I wheeled about, and walked rapidly to the Gold Rail.[91] I was intoxicated with the cigarette! I was vital and full! To demonstrate this to the passing people I walked lightly and unsteadily. My sleeves were rolled up; I felt the cold wind flow on my bare arms and stimulate me to wild, energetic despair! I stumbled across Broadway and strode in the Gold Rail—no one I knew was there; it was full of faces. Out, again, up to the benches by the subway. I seated myself in the same bench I had once occupied with Kammerer. Self consciously I stared at his seat. A trolley rolled by

---

90   French: "Like the other times."
91   Gold Rail. Chain of inexpensive bars.

STUDENT IS INDICTED IN 2D-DEGREE MURDER

Lucien Carr, 19-year-old Columbia University sophomore, was indicted yesterday for second-degree murder in the stabbing of David Kammerer, 33, on Aug. 14. At the same time the police revealed that they had uncovered a second material witness, William Seward Borroughs, 30, of 69 Bedford Street. He is free in bail of $2,500, set by General Sessions Judge John J. Sullivan, before whom young Carr will plead to the indictment Tuesday.

Borroughs, the police said, admitted that after Carr had stabbed Kammerer, former college instructor, and then weighted his body with rocks and tossed it into the Hudson River, he had heard the story from the youth and had done nothing because Carr said he was on his way to surrender. It was almost twenty-four hours later before Carr gave himself up.

After Carr had told Borroughs he repeated the story to John Kerouac, former Columbia student, who has been held as a materail witness in default of $5,000 bail. The police escorted Kerouac to the Municipal Building on Tuesday to witness his marriage to Miss Edith Parker of Detroit and then took him back to Bronx prison.

August 25, 1944, page 15   © NEW YORK TIMES.

noisily; I shouted above the roar "Kammerer, Kammerer, where are you? No more Kammerer?" I laughed and then cried! .... "Dead? So soon? Dead? Kammerer? Where are you?" Then gently I repeated, "Don't you think that's a rationalization of your passionate nature?" Mockingly I said this, attempting to recapture my tone. It was hollow. I could not force mockery. "Kammerer?" I looked down at his seat, half expecting to see him. Another trolley came— "Kammerer!!" I shouted, my voice lost in the noise. The quick and the dead! I am quick, he is dead! I first realized, then, that he was dead.

August 27, 1944.

There is something seductive about decadence. Perhaps it is because it is accompanied by bohemianism, in its turn, an outgrowth of libertinism. Charming libertinism! Who can resist its appeal? Who can deny the whirl and the sway of the soul, fettered by convention, yet trembling in anticipation of life. Why not, fear you the siren call, why not, renounce responsibility? If you are the artist, it chides flatteringly, you are the creator. Will you bind yourself to the inartistic; will you bury yourself among the million sands of faceless mediocrities? Can you deny your creative desire? Come, then, come, and throw away the bonds that restrain you, your inhibitions and dependencies, become free and jubilantly high flying! Soar above the rabble and the wrong. You are buffeted by evil and by vice? Then forget, deny all social vice. If you must be beaten, take it at the hands of God and nature, not at the hands of your inferiors. If you must suffer, suffer nobly. Love, laugh through your tears, or cry, create and perhaps, perish. Oh, which is best? Buffeted by the hush winds is the artist! Is he to swing with the brute tempest, or stand up against it?

September 1, 1944.

After visiting Grant's Tomb[92]—Grant's Tomb is merely pretty; it is not moving. The man buried there was no prophet, no inspirer. Lincoln's Memorial is beautiful and moving; the spirit that pervades the place makes all the difference. One brings no memories but distaste to Grant's Tomb. The spirit of Lincoln lives in his memorial and summons up visions of humanity marching to the millennium.

---

92 Grant's Tomb. Well-known New York City landmark a short walk from the Columbia campus on Riverside Drive at West 122nd Street.

September 1, 1944.

Suicide Note

Chaqu'un a son gout[93]—My apologies, however, to anyone my death will inconvenience. I am sure they will be consoled by my contrition.

To my father I leave my books and my desires,

To my mother, my contempt and forgiveness,

To my brother, my affection,

To the world at large, my love,

To certain individuals I distribute variously my hatred,

To all my friends I present my rue and disgust.

September 1–17, 18, 1944.

Suicide Note: Revised

I have no other possessions of value but my soul. I do not owe it to earth; I will it to oblivion. I have attempted little and been satisfied by nothing. I desired much and rejected equally. All love is foul because it is a compromise with hatred; all friends are fools and all fools are friends. All desire is hopeless; all dreams, dream; all faith, false; and all gods faithless.

Remember to write about Nay [Naomi Ginsberg] on Dr. Luria's[94] couch, stricken with the desire to become the Messiah, vainly trying to grasp the inspiration that floated in his head. She sat on the couch self-consciously, closed her eyes, refused to be interrupted, and began to speak words of beauty, wishing she were really in a trance of genius. She spoke on for several minutes, pronouncing fierce truisms about educating the world from street corners, and ended lamely, unable to think of anything more to say other than we should build a new world as our hearts tell us. Then she sank back, as I launched uncharitably into her economic theory, knowing that she was a failure, and a fat, middle aged, neurotic housewife.

As an artist I design to extract from the welter of contradictions, a set of values. I would see beauty in what has no care for beauty, and truth in a universe too complex to be simplified to apothegms. I desire to shape meaning out of confusion, standardize my desires, understand my passions, and direct them rather than be directed. I search for values. I am a moralist. I could not eat breakfast unless I were a moralist.

---

93 French: "To each his own (taste)."

94 Leon Luria. For a while Ginsberg's mother had a job in Manhattan as a receptionist for Dr. Leon Luria, a medical examiner for the Maritime Union. After her split with Louis Ginsberg, Naomi dated Dr. Luria and often slept overnight on a couch in his office.

September 2, 1944.

Half dream—1:30 at nite: I consider the printing advertisements in the bookstore. I talked with Lucien and Eugene about it. I do not like it but they find something good in it. I confess that I do not understand it—cannot comprehend its technique. Is this my fault? How will they look on me if I say this? The wisdom of the humble or the confession of the fool? Should I say like Turvey that I'm not as good as this stuff? I can't...I'm pre med....Oh, how much better to be shrewd and wise, to be the Socrates and completely understand it, to see it through and through, and then damn it.

September 3, 1944.

[Dream]: I dreamed that on the 6th floor landing of Hastings Hall, I embraced a beautiful girl. She was nude and white skinned, fair, virginal, shy, coy, eloquently beautiful, eminently desirable. She was frightened and nervous. She was a marble fawn, caught momentarily in my arms before bounding nervously away. (The creature was Isabella, the association being to Dickens' *Great Expectations* which I'd been reading.) We tore petals of roses and dropped them down from the window—until we were interrupted by the shrewish Miss Havisham who broke up our idyll.

September 4, 1944.

I went to the movies with Claire[95] and put my arms around her tenderly.

[Dream]: I was at Dumbarton Oaks Residence House located in the midst of the forest on 122nd St. and Riverside Drive, or near the Cloisters overlooking the river. There Claire and I met young Nazis in brown two-tone uniforms. They were adolescents—college age. They saluted, heiling furtively as they paraded in twos around the corners of the mansion's patio. They were arrogant. I sat down next to one of them on a couch to talk to him and convert him. As soon as I spoke, he rose in disdain and threw his paper away on the couch. I looked at it in resignation; it was the *Paterson Evening News*.

September 7, 1944.

[Dream]: A wild night fantasy in which the demon was caught in a castle, having committed some crime. He fled his pursuers over turret and battlement, in and out of gaunt corridors; he hid behind idols and draperies, hid himself in masks and costumes, secreted himself in closets and mystic passageways. The

---

95   Claire. Probably Claire Gaidemak, Ginsberg's cousin.

king, queen, and court were assembled. (Was the king, Kerouac? And the queen, Celine? Perhaps at first, not later.) The mob roared after the demon. He succeeded in escaping and hid himself in the labyrinth of the upper part of the castle. He was daring and miserable, haunted, hunted, fear ridden, persecuted. Was he suddenly apprehended? He slipped away, his face taut with excitement, his yellow uncombed hair flowing wildly. He threw himself into the closet with the queen's dresses. The demon was followed by a fat subordinate guard. Stealthily he untied a small, sharp, silver clasp from one of the robes and then pounced on the guard. He attempted to stifle his screams with his left hand. The guard's moans attracted the attention of the pursuers. A face poked into the closet, a hand ran along the dresses, the demon was seen and the door was closed. When the door was reopened the demon rushed out but the king and queen were there and took part in the chase themselves. I remember the king clasping the queen to comfort and restrain her. She was frightened and eager. The king grappled with the demon. The door to the rooms of sleeping courtiers were burst open revealing the enthusiastic, questioning, and morally outraged gentlemen. It was 12 o'clock. The hour had struck. Retribution was no more! Vengeance had to be foregone—all was changed. And so the demon was judged and released, for it was the beginning of the New Evil Years. The dream ended and continued. I found myself down and out of the castle, across the street from it, immediately afterwards, with Edie and Celine. I put my arms around them brotherly, and coyly told Celine: "No! You aren't leaving me too! Both of you can't go." It seems she was going somewhere too. (Edie was going with Jack to Detroit.)

Associations:

1. The demon chased and criminal—Carr's crime and punishment. My sympathy for his sense of persecution.
2. Castle—associated with Jane Eyre movie I saw with Edie?
3. Silver Clasp—associated with boy scout knife? [Carr used a boy scout knife to stab Kammerer.]
4. The changing times—the clock and New Year.
   a. With Louis and Scott's Ghost of Christopher Welles?
   b. Perhaps new term (I remember the day to have been October 1 in the dream).
5. The frightened courtiers at their doors—Jack Levine's[96] picture.
6. The easy punishment—plea for self defense.

96 Jack Levine (b. 1915). American social realist painter.

September 7, 1944.

Dream: I was walking down Fair Street or Hamilton Street in Paterson and New York at the same time. I had a Susquehanna Railroad ticket in my hand. I was going to the bus stop, located by the big sign before the railroad bridge on Straight St. (perhaps the laundry with new windows). I met two girls, one in red, one in green. The youngest was desirable. They told me they were not virgins. We stopped in a sandwich shop to have a bite. I asked for her address. It seemed so convenient and easy to get a lay from her! I had to leave the restaurant to get something somewhere up the street (perhaps in another restaurant). I left my bags. I came back; they were still there. I asked for the address which she had been writing and picked up my bag, for I had to go. My train was leaving 20 after and it was 12:15. She had lost the address! She looked quickly and found it in her handbag (a little white edge of paper). I grabbed it and ran...

September 9, 1944.

Dream: Eugene came back on furlough, bemoaning his former life, its waste. He sneered at me: "I'll end up in bed with you." "Well, what do you want me to do?..." He was angered that I was merely a male and a brother. I offered to pander for him—to call up Celine, and arrange a date. He was delighted. I fumbled at the phone and inserted dimes and nickels in the slots, at the wrong places, jamming them in. I shook the phone to release the money I'd inserted. Into the long, wide mouthed tray (like a cigarette vending machine) fluttered tickets; and brushing them aside I found a tidy pile of dimes. The objecting crowd that gathered around the bakery wagon into which our phone booth had metamorphosed, would not let us free. They shouted like cattle, and jumped on the running board to stop us. I shouted with an air of authority that they must retreat. Most backed away, except for one tenacious busybody and a man in a public service dress uniform whom I confused momentarily for a policeman. He suggested we drive to the police station to verify our claim to the dimes and we assented. Eugene drove. He went straight ahead, and then drove right and curved around past pastures like out the Newark airport beyond the city. "To the police station," I cautioned from his side. Soon we arrived at a baroque pile of buildings, very clean and modern, which I first took to be the police court buildings. Yes, this was our real goal...the baking company.

An aristocrat had expropriated all the peon land around the beautiful country. He had amassed his wealth by trucking oppressed paisanos into his service at low wages. The peons were gathered downstairs. "How many of you owned land here before he bought you out?" "Many!" We walked up the long rough-rail stairway to a high porch to interview the Señor. He was a cruel, brown, hard, and cynically self-interested exploiter. He had a wicked glance and a black mustache. He defied, quite coolly, all our questions. Our leader, who had driven me in the trucks, asked shrewd questions of him. He replied curtly. I was incensed. I shouted, "You cannot talk this way! The man to whom you speak is a professor at the university! He is a man of learning." There was a murmur of defiance in the crowd as the professor gently rebuked me with his glare, for betraying his identity. I was adamant; the owner could not talk to him in that manner. Then the capitalist-traitor put his foot down on our demands, "No!" He comfortably seated himself on the railing and ordered his men to give the peasants their white trays of pastry. I could stand it no longer; I resolved to push him off the porch to his death. I hesitated, and he began to slip off the rail. I grasped his white trousered foot and attempted to force him over the rail. He grappled with me, but I succeeded in pushing him off. We fell together, for he clung to me. I persisted in striking him violently on the shoulders with my feet, thus he dropped. Presumably, he died. (There is no indication that I was at all affected.)

The trays meanwhile had been given to the peasants who went pell-mell into the square trapdoor in the middle of the porch and fell down in wild disarray to their wagons. The white trays fell gracefully, mixed with bodies, settling safely down to earth. I even glimpsed the surprised complacency of John Kingsland's face, descending between two trays.

September 13, 1944.
Dream: I walked up the riverlakeside. It was on the street on the other side of the lake in Asbury Park. It was 5th Avenue and 66th St. It was Riverside Drive. There was Lucien Carr, stalking up the drive stiffly erect, his heals clicking the ground. People watched him as he postured in imitation of himself. He wore a white topcoat, with a yellow wig. He crossed over the street and into a two story modest looking house. In the living room, on the couch, he made love to Kerouac's sister. Kerouac stayed in the living room. After a while Lucien sickened of the face staring at him and disappeared. I felt it my duty to help him. I went in, took his place, put on his white coat, and walked out of the house, through a crowd. I walked past the staring policemen to the bus....up to 122nd St. and Riverside Drive....into the cathedral. Then down 122nd St. to Broadway...on the corner was a clean saloon with mirrors and curved bar. I

met an author, with whom I sensed I was a kindred spirit. He leaned over milk. I ordered a yellow drink (ginger ale?)....I showed him a poem of Whitman—mine, going, in part:

"We are brothers, man—with —mania / We are brothers, you with pen—and—statistics. / We are not animal eaters."

There were other verses which I cannot remember. (The tone and portent was a justification of the politician as an artist and an anti-Philistine. The last line is distinctly of Kerouac's style!) In the dream I was perhaps occupied with my new job. (This was dreamed under the jaundice illness, with the strain of joblessness hanging over.) My job was at Hastings location. There was a restaurant...My job had extremely short hours. The job was my residence and it was located on some street in Greenwich Village. There were young girls working with me that lived across the street. The food was creamy wonderful, sweet pastry and cherry fantasies. The boss, when I arrived for work, was at his wits end berating negroes for their inefficiency. He had them climb in a washing machine to illustrate.

September 21, 1944, Thursday P.M.

[*The following is a letter from Carr, which Ginsberg copied into his notebook.*]

Cher Breton—

First my future. I think I can expect a future one half as gloomy, temporarily speaking, as Sebastian Pere's.[97] A more sanguine outlook would countenance freedom. I express myself obscurely for the benefit of others besides yourself who will read this epistle.

Do you know a song called "Night Time Is The Right Time To Be With The One You Love?" I am being bombarded with a rendition of it for the hundredth time today by the colored guy in the next cell. I have learned a lot about jazz and the blues, purely their vocal aspects of course, since my incarceration. Wilson, the guy in the next cell, has a deep and vibrant voice which reduces the whole row of cells to silence when he starts moaning out a blues tune.

The population here is varied, from men who have spent most of their lives in jail and are so full of larceny it comes out of their ears, to men of character and intelligence far above that of most of the free population of New York. The one thing common to us all is that we are all under duress.

97 Sebastian Pere. Probably a reference to the martyr, St. Sebastian.

The way men react to the Tombs[98] gives us one pretty lucid insight into their character in general. There are men here facing inevitable death who take it as resignedly and philosophically as the best of Tolstoy's characters. And there are men with misdemeanor raps over their heads who squawk and snarl and worry incessantly. Most veterans claim two months in the Tombs far less endurable than two years "upstate." They say this is where men's wills are broken, where they cop pleas rather than try to beat their raps, which might entail months here. The discipline is purely negative; there are many things one cannot do but nothing one must do. Nevertheless the Tombs does its work. Last year there was a 97% conviction rate because of plea copping.

One thinks in jail. But it takes power to direct your mind so that its activity may be dignified with the time of thought rather than garbled day-dreaming. In the exegeses of the two *Weltanschauung* that you sent me I think you draw too distinct a demarcation line. The "Romantic Eclectic" and the "Introspective Visionary" are not at antipodes with one another. Into which class would you allocate Joyce, the Dublin Eclecticist and the Dedalusian Visionary? He must be in both. I would hesitate to put Breton or de Maubri [Carr] into either class. Can you place Breton with his talk of artistic completion of spiritual circles in the former class or de Maubri (whose guise I assume with distinct misgivings) with his hatred of generalities and anthropological preoccupations in the latter?

Eh bien, mon frère. This all preambles a novel I am planning. The novel of Claude de Maubri, if you will. But Lucien has changed somewhat since you last saw him due to various vicissitudes which he has undergone. Still the introspective, he will never cease to see, like Thoreau, all of life in a drop of water. He is still convinced that the secret of morality lies within and not without the self, though he has learned that the self is a far fuller (pardon the solecism) entity than he ever thought it before. He is not disillusioned with the intellect and its power but he has relegated it to the position of less importance. He has begun to wonder about the meaning of the "spirit." But *nôtre garçon* still worships fervently at the shrine of parturience. And he has begun to see a little more clearly along the ascendant paths of self-consummation!

Once when de Maubri read *The Symposium* he said, "Ah, Aristophanes, how true was thy half-jest!" and then he wondered what that rhetorical outburst meant. Now he has begun to find out. My greatest reason for desiring

98 The Tombs. Familiar name for the New York City prison.

to be spared a jail sentence concerns Bebe [Celine Young]. Because she had more faith and confidence in me than anyone else, I feel that my arch betrayal has been to her. This may seem strange to you, when you consider others that have been betrayed—Breton and Bleistein. Nonetheless I will consider that I have betrayed her even more basely if I get sent upstate, although I have little control over that now. The communication of love is paradoxical and perhaps impossible. It is ultimately bound up with the loss, and at the same time, the gain of spiritual freedom. It is perhaps the one way to escape the prison of blindness and find the greater self, yet it is also a blind alley impeding the fulfillment of what it seems to permit. It sterilizes as it impregnates the possibility of a new vision. Love is both a resignation and a never ending struggle. Be that as it may, I am in love.

I, too, dream of the Rive Gauche. P.S. Write Bebe. I know she wants you to. 542 2nd Ave. Pelham, NY. Also write me quickly for if I am sent upstate I will be able to communicate with you only by subterfuge through *ma mère* or *peut-être* Bebe.

I miss music more than anything else. Oh to have my Brahms sextet to teach me the meaning of tortured introspection. [end of letter]

October 1, 1944.
Wrote three poems: "Elegy on Cemetery Rosebush," "Monologue on Deathbed" and "Jupiter Symphony."

Against Masturbation: *Fait accompli!*

1. It limits heterosexual drive, social versatility.
2. It becomes boring; you become jaded. Its excitement is in inverse proportion to frequency.
3. It is not satisfying: you take from yourself, whereas in copulation you take from another. You are repressed—your hand substitutes for a woman's cunt and is a poor substitute unless you have a good imagination.
4. Which I haven't.

What you demand, my love, is far beyond my power to grant either to you or to me. Love!…I am too much the poet to be a lover! I am too much the artist to be satisfied upon your bed. Desire's echo is for me the sole reality—the virgin dream can be my only life of lust. And if, my love, you are not sated by a dream, and if you cannot salvage reality out of desire, then let my poems be your lovers; let my rhymes kiss your round mouth, let my phrases fondle your ears, let my music swell your breasts, and my meanings stab your heart as a lover would—let my loneliness be your lover!

Jean walked over to the edge of the roof and leaned over the rough stone railing, staring at the street below. The shadowed darkness was punctuated only by lonely lights that glimmered through the mist from the apartment house across the street. Suddenly, passionately, Jean stared up at the quick stars that ruined the heavy sky. He looked at them singly, and then intently swept his glance over the whole canopy of the heavens. Then he closed his eyes....the stars continued to shine for the rest of the night. [Later in his journals, Ginsberg rewrote this paragraph using the name of Lucien as the character.]

[*The following entries are in Kerouac's handwriting.*]

Society bleeds geniuses.
*

He was conscience-stricken because he was to betray his kind; I had no kind to betray, really.
*

If such be the rules of the game, I can eat cake while the other man starves. Who would invent such a game? God.
*

The conscience is a rusty grating pendulum.
*

There is an old woman who goes by this house down there every morning at six with her bag of wood. Who is that old witch? Perhaps a ballet-dancer long exiled by the Bolsheviks.
*

About the streets at night...now let's examine the contents of this garbage pail. Who sleeps in the alley?
*

J'ai la maladresse au travaux. Je veux ecrire; c'est tout, c'est tout, ça. Quel travail— quel espêce de misère. Je suis en amour pour ne rien. Naturaliste! J'ai toujours mal au coeur—ont dirai que je veut me quitter du coeur. Je ne peux pas, j'ai peur du froid.
*

The Hollywood-*New Yorker-Esquire* axis corrupts the style of American prose— it does so unerringly, pervasively, silently like evil.

*

A style, a prose: weigh each sentence with gold (like Mann). Exercise selectivity over detail. Ignore the cosmopolitan gesturism of the Hollywood-*New Yorker-Esquire* style. Wasted years!

*

Corinthians, Chapter 3:15: "If any man's work shall be burned, he shall suffer loss; but he shall be saved; yet so as by fire."

*

Nietzsche: "Art—the complement and consummation of existence." The Apollonian interposition between life and death. "—art seducing one to a continuation of life."(!)

*

Life's meaning is not sanctioned for us on conditions of truth or reason; we persist on emotional grounds, and love it.

*

In my love's smile is the approval of the cosmos. When she blights me, the cosmos has cruelly rejected me off somewhere alone, where I shiver at the cold of life's outer perimeter.

She does not want to love him, but he can seduce her to love him by his kisses; life does not want to love him, but he can seduce life to love him by his art.

A persuasion, then, of one's self, and of the object <u>out of necessity</u> (an emotional necessity) to be seduced. There is no rational, philosophical ground to art's purpose?

*

A child bewildered me today. A charming child who can bewilder with his wit. He is nine, I am twenty-two.

*

Tonight is Halloween night! So let us all remove our masks.

*

The ultimate issue of "SDTK"—the psyche and society.

*

[*This was the last entry in Kerouac's handwriting.*]

"I read each book for a special purpose—one, to see what a drink cure is like, etc."
Burroughs reading—yoga, *The Castle* [by] Franz Kafka, Blake, *Opium* [by] Jean Cocteau, Shakespeare, Rimbaud, Baudelaire, *The Ox-Bow Incident*—Egyptian Grammar [by] O'Hara, Spengler, Pareto, *The Folded Leaf* [by] William Maxwell, Gogol, *Moby Dick, The Lost Weekend* [by] Charles Jackson, *Maiden Voyage* [by] Den-

ton Welch, *Crime and the Human Mind* [by] David Abrahamsen, *The Brick Foxhole* [by Richard Brooks], hypnotism analysis, *Nightwood* [by] Djuna Barnes.

[Ginsberg recorded several arguments between his father and mother in his journal.]

I.

November 10, 1944.

Argument, money [as] usual.

Naomi: Sorry I ever married you, could've married richer smarter handsomer. I don't want to stay in same house any more, starts for door.

Louis: Where are you going? Don't go, stay.

Naomi: You're rotten to the core. Get out of my life.

Louis: Don't go.

Naomi: Go to hell! (slams door)

II.

Few days later—

Louis: Where have you been?

Naomi: Won't tell. (goes to closet packs) (one hour)

Louis: Why are you doing this to me?

Naomi: I've had enough talk. Don't want more, I'm going. (leaves). "Allen, I don't want you to come with me because if you do you'll tell him where I'm living." Allen offers to carry bags, she lets him unwillingly. [They] walk to Hamilton Avenue boarding house to room.

Naomi: This is where I live. I have a cute room here. I'm happy where I am now but not at home. Glad I'm here. Never going back again.

Allen: Returns home—tells of Naomi's attitude. When father asks for her address advises him to let her cool off a few days. Father does. When they go over to boarding house she's gone.

III.

Naomi: (surprised) What are you doing here? I don't want anything to do with you.

Louis: I want to get you to come back with me again.

Naomi: I don't ever want anything to do with you. I told you that before. Why do you bother me? (rising) Either you go or I go! (raises her voice)

Louis: Don't speak so loud. People will hear.

Naomi: (in louder tones) I don't care. Either you go or I go.

IV.

At boarding house.

   Naomi: Get out of my life!

November 17, 1944, Sunday Evening.

"Do you remember me?" I asked.

   "Yes," replied Bodenheim.[99]

   "I don't believe you," I said charmingly.

   "Why do you come here?"

   "I like to look around."

   "Does it interest you?"

   "Yes…in a morbid sort of way."

He displays Roosevelt button. "See you are on the right side."

   "Yes, I'm Communist. I'm one of those lousy Communists."

   "You have been admirably deloused."

   "I've got to go. (puts up hand.) My name is Maxwell Bodenheim."

   "Mine is Allen Ginsberg."

   (squints) "We're both of the same Irish blood." (leaves)

Souvenir of Bodenheim: Pipe tobacco.

   [John] Kingsland: "Oh it's so dull here, always the same women looking seductive in a corner. We met Mr. Syrinx. He designed the Museum—everyone thinks it's a horrible monstrosity; it's not even functional. So we just sat and scowled at him." Should Kingsland marry Jerri Lust?[100] Imagine what would happen if she copulated with other men. How would he look, wandering around shouting, "I've been betrayed by my wife!"?

   Grover Smith: "Women just won't have anything to do with me, after they find out my intentions…all right, Celine. I'll be magnanimous! I won't be petty! I'll offer it again in 20 years."

   Jack in West End: "Ginsberg why don't you actively help me seduce Celine?" [Kerouac wrote the following word in Ginsberg's notebook] "Inaccurate."

   Celine, the "simpering school girl—she would vomit to drink the blood of a poet."

   The most individual, uninfluenced, unrepressed, uninhibited expression of self is the true expression and the true art. And since the artist is convulsed in

   99 Maxwell Bodenheim (1893–1954). Eccentric New York poet and novelist, author of *My Life and Loves in Greenwich Village*.
   100 Jerri Lust: Geraldine Lust.

violent reaction to the extension of the outside social more and repression into his free expression, he tends toward anarchism and solipsism. He rejects the subliminal influence, if he can, of the superego, preventing him from exposing and expressing the lower depths of himself. He resents being perverted in creation by the intrusion of the demands of society.

But wherein does the artist desire the pleasure of creation? The pleasure of artistry? Is it the release of the pent up soul in self expression? Is it truly merely in exposition of his thoughts. Then why must he commit them to paper? Why not think to himself, or aloud. Why not take out his energy in mere impermanent life? Why make his passing fancies immutable and permanent? Ah, because his ego basks in the reflected glory of his finished art— The ego, the eagle, feeding on the carrion of our desires! The ego, which is the philoprogenitive organ of the soul, is the true cause of permanent art, and not the drive to self expression in permanent form. The artist's pleasure is, greatly, societal. He loves recognition. He communicates—his ego is the dynamo that moves the transmission belt of his art. Self expression is in actuality—brutal reality—the communication, not the mere expression, of self. Creation is reducible to communication. Art is by nature communicative. Ego the producer, experience and soul the raw material, art the commodity, the intellectual, the consumer.

Gauguin? He defeated his own end—indifference—by taking the positive step of setting fire to his pictures. If he really had been freed from his ego, he would have seen no need, have felt no desire, to destroy his art. His method of communication—was destruction. His ego-pleasure was in the *beau geste*, the vicarious pleasure of destruction, the big defiance, the completely self-conscious—and self-defeating attitude of indifference. His greatest work of art was his attitude—and that he reasonlessly carried to an extreme and corruption by burning his pictures. He thought he freed himself from the ego and superego. He merely expressed it in a different form.

Where Was The World?
...Lucien walked to the edge of the roof and stood silently, leaning over the rough stone edging. He stared down calmly at the shadowy sidewalk. A light illuminated the window across the street. Suddenly, passionately, he looked up at the stars, beaconing from the heavy sky. The stars continued to shine for the rest of the night.[101]

---

101 Ginsberg reworked this paragraph originally written on October 1, 1944, several times.

Les etoiles qui blessent leur ciel.[102]

Killing of porcupine: Lucien naked, strides out of lonely cabin in woods, and strikes down a baby porcupine which had grunted irritatingly for a time. Then, conscience stricken, he fled inside, cowering behind the door to hear the mother porcupine squealing and wailing over her cub's body.

Dip birds in kerosene, touch them with fire and watch them fly up, burning, in the night!

"It is because they deny the ground beneath them that they are insecure."
—Celine Young

"It's more important to me that you get satisfaction from it than I."
—Lucien Carr to Celine Young

"A man will seduce all the women he can and marry the one he can't."
—Lucien Carr

    Ginsberg: "I heard you wrote a novel."
    Burroughs: "It is not a novel, it's only twenty pages long. I finished that and decided that I had said everything I have to say. I haven't written a word since."
    Burroughs to Elayne Fritzl: "I like disreputable characters. They amuse me."

Burroughs approves of my poetry. Immediately my estimation of him went down.

Bum in Village as related by Kerouac: "Life is a bowl of cherries my son, but try and get one."

Burroughs is the <u>authentic</u> devil.—Jack Kerouac

"When you put cutlets in cans they copulate."—Jack Kerouac

"When you put cattle in cars they copulate."—Lucien Carr

I am writing a naturalistic-symbolistic novel. If detail is merely disgusting and dirty, it has no place in the novel. If the dirtiness of actions or motives represents something important other than itself, if it is necessary background. In short,

---

102 French: "The stars that bless their sky."

if it is a symbol, I use it. I am resting natural facts for universal significance.

Kingsland Visits the Department Store

Do you know where I went shopping today? Di Penna's—it was simply a tragic experience. I went over to the tie counter and started fingering their beautiful silk ties—I turned my head and saw the salesman staring at me! Oh, what a sight. He had flaxen hair and a very light moustache. But his eyebrows were so dark! The crowning touch was mascara on his eyelashes and a gentle rouging all over his face. It even embarrassed me.

But the most horrible part was when this old matron walked in with her chauffeur at her heels like a kept man and said she wanted to exchange a pocketbook that "a very dear friend" had given her—return! This was too simple for her—just a useful simple black satin thing. What she probably wanted was something about four feet long with dangling braids and bows and rhinestones dripping from it. The manager looked at the purse and told her that that type had been out of stock for over a year.

She was so embarrassed that her very dear friend have given her this old trashy sow's ear that had been laying around an attic for so long, that she became indignant and raised her finger in the air and told him "Well! I like this! I'm never coming back into this store and I'll use my influence to see that not one of my friends ever steps in here again." Then she looked at him haughtily and flung, "and I have very great influence you know." Then she motioned contemptuously to her chauffeur to go.

The manager came over in a huff and said, "Madame...I have come from Saks Fifth Avenue and the policy is just as it is here!"

She didn't even reply and stormed out.

> In N.Y.C. did Kubla Klein[103]
> A stately department store decree
> Where 5th the sacred avenue ran
> Thru caverns measureless to man
> Down to lightlit Broadwee.

Ivresse[104]

We were in the little room on 60th St.[105] Next door the mother told the kid to sleep. Burroughs paced the floor and extemporized the plot of his mostly

---

103 Klein's. Popular discount department store on Union Square.
104 French: "Drunkenness."
105 60th St. Burroughs rented a room over Riordan's Bar at 42 W. 60th Street.

symbolic novel concerned with the decline of the west. Kerouac sat forward intently and made suggestions. Ginsberg lay on the couch absorbed in a morphine stupor.

Morphine—*Mort et Phoebus—L'homme est mort. Phoebus brule la chair avec son grand flamme de la vie.*[106] The sun rises behind the head of the dead man stretched languidly out on the earth.

Thus one learns the equality of his little loves and great despairs.

Moral weight in the back of the head.

From the great bow of naturalism I, the symbol, fly like an arrow directly toward the absolute.

Die and enter the world of reality, where symbols and dreams collect the whole of the world's truth. Reality clusters in the shadow of the icon. The air sings, the wind breathes, the world waylays god.

Try: [107]

Morphine (M)*

Opium poppy—codeine cough medicine*

   paregoric

Laudanum

Marijuana (Tea)*

Cocaine

Heroin

No Doz—Caffeine*

Phenobarbital*

Codeine*

Pantopon*[108]

Delauded*

Benzedrine*

Nembutal*

Effects:

<u>Morphine</u>: Flesh falls from bones; relaxation; quietness. Mental awakening; brilliance and straight thoughts. —$^1/_2$ grain. Effect 6 hours.

---

106 French: "The man is dead. Phoebus burns the flesh with his great flame of life."

107 Ginsberg compiled this list of drugs that he wanted to experiment with. As he sampled each one, he checked it off the list with an *.

108 Pantopon. Ginsberg frequently referred to pantopon as pentaphon. It is a mixture of the alkaloids of opium and has a beautiful pink color.

No Doz: 2 tablets—at night—semiconscious energy; good for writing, brings out subliminal thoughts, bad for absorbing idea.

Phenobarbital: Relaxation. Same effect on me as morphine, but quicker. 3 grains. Relax, awake in bed.

Codeine: Relaxation; sexual stimulation if it comes. Wakeness. Few images. 4 oz. licorice or orange tasting = 4 or 5 hours.

Opiates: Pantopon dreams.

Benny:—Benny integration and amiability. And Benny depression.

I love women as I love food when I am full. I am surfeited but despairing—I would take the forbidden fruit. How I envy the man who has appetite!

Now I have discovered, impelled by my own neuroses, the pleasures of decadence. I have been introduced to the problem of good and evil, and may have solved it for both practical and metaphysical purposes.

Out of the great mysterious cultural unconscious will emerge the elemental poetry, metaphors and symbols. Out of the great subconscious well of the mind I will find the great motives. I will stare back into the womb, place the penis in my mouth, gasp in the vagina, eat feces, swim in semen, murder the father, copulate with the mother, injure the brother, unravel the silver cord of consciousness and trace it back to its elemental Godhead. Here is the birth of poetry—a recognition and an intellectual exploitation of the subconscious.

Knowing all of psychology, history, literature, art (plastic), music, anthropology, religion, platitudes, one will synthesize decadence and creation, surrealism and sanity and comprehensibility both emotional and intellectual. Surrealism seems to be the rise of unconscious symbols. It is the key to future art. Dadaism will help; psychic research; yogism; oriental philosophy will be essential.

Lord, what a task!

Try at the Acropolis Restaurant: Dolmades / Chicken broth: with lemon, egg, rice. A soup / Stuffed peppers / Moussaka

[In October, Ginsberg began making notes for a novel based on the Carr-Kammerer affair of August 1944. On November 4, 1944, he began writing the book using fictional names, occasionally slipping and using the real names. The editors have used the character's actual names wherever possible.]

Scenes for Novel: the plot

[*October 1, 1944.*]

1.) Fight in West End Bar

2.) Consolation of Celine

3.) Jack's circular return—

    1. Self Ultimacy in Minettas; Wonder of Lucien's death; Mills Hotel[109] and Rimbaud

    2. Love for Celine

       a. Her unresponsiveness and neurotic nature.

    3. Recollections of Sebastian [Sampas];[110] beginning of *Galloway*.[111]

    4. Picture of Warren Hall—Grossman's[112] refusal to let three stay in room.

4.) Evening in Village—

    Donna Leonard; in Pastors;[113] her story

       a. Mother; Baltimore; Friends' car trip

       b. Louise McMahon

       c. Recollection of Lucien

       d. Her reading list in the West End.

       e. Her job at the 5 and 10¢ Store

       f. Sleeping with everybody; Valeska Gert,[114] Jack's job.

       g. Brings us to Burroughs

5.) Bill Burroughs

       a. Recollection of Lucien in Persian Palace

       b. Gangster friends; *Daily News* and *Journal* clippings

       c. Taxes: His cosmology misinterpreted

       d. Imperialism in Persia; Decline of West.

       e. Satire on policemen and bureaucrats; essay on constipation; perspective of frog.

       f. Donna's loan and decamping, "She can borrow my gun."

---

109 Minetta's. An Italian bar and restaurant at 113 MacDougal in the Greenwich Village. The Mills Hotel at 160 Bleecker Street, was a cheap hotel where both Kerouac and Ginsberg stayed from time to time.

110 Sebastian Sampas. Kerouac's boyhood friend from Lowell, Massachusetts, who had been killed in World War II.

111 *Galloway*. Original title of Kerouac's first novel, *The Town and the City*.

112 Grossman. Probably the manager of the residence hall.

113 Tony Pastor's. Well-known bar in the Village.

114 Valeska Gert. Another popular Village bar in the 1940s.

g. Attempted seduction of Celine, "What are you doing?" His comments on Celine as the typical American female.

h. Morphine; Burroughs moving to Columbus Circle over bar.

i. Kerouac and Burroughs write novel: Sequence in notebook. Morphine dreams.

    1.) Jesus Christ

    2.) Cow

j. Jack drunk after rejection of novel; wakes with bugs on elbow

k. Burroughs' sermon to Jack on neurosis and drink; Circle of neuroses.

l. Jack goes to Lowell

m. I settle philosophy with Burroughs

n. Kingsland steals jewels

6.) Closing chapter

    a. Me writing "Last Voyage" in dorm

    b. Jack returns; talks about neurotic circle, goes off in it—goes to sea; I give lecture on the New Vision

7.) Epilogue

    a. I get kicked out of school

    b. Jack goes to sea; Sermon of Johnny Bartender,[115] Burroughs

    c. John Buys opening in museum

    d. Burroughs goes to Persia

    e. Celine gets married

Philosophic Structure

1. Creation and Waste—Artistic Morality

2. Self Expression

3. Self Ultimacy

4. Dionysian orphic/Decline of West (merged) Theories of archetypal and cultural emotion forces

5. Supreme Reality—Rejection of Immortality
Art as Ego: Various expressions of Ego: Gauguin
Jean White: Burroughs

6. New Vision—acceptance. Prospero?

---

115 Johnny. Bartender of the West End Bar.

Problems of Novel:

1. Personal: Struggle of Lucien from decadence
2. Moral: Decadence—Nihilism and cross causality
3. Cultural: Mechanism and determinism
4. Aesthetic: Moral art vs. creative
   Communicative vs. expressive
5. Political: Split between aesthetic and social
   [Split between] artistic and political
   Politician as artist.

Incident: Kammerer getting money for Lucien by prostituting self.
Food—fighting over it; meat—wildness.
Ripping Burroughs' coat off to festoon room.

The Bloodsong

We were spread out, the three of us, in a dim red booth in the Radical Café.[116] We liked the bar mostly because it served pernod and it had always attracted the campus bohemian, the whores, the fags, the sterile drunkard, and all the intellectual maniacs that clustered around the college. Jack Kerouac had just come back from a visit to his wife in Cleveland [sic: Detroit]—Edie Parker, a rich, bird-brained intelligent female who had been his mistress for two years before he married her. Tonight was his last night and we were all a bit melancholy.

As usual, we were talking about art, and Jack was becoming more and more lonely as he drank. He really didn't want to go to sea again. He'd been in the Merchant Marine for three years and was sick of it.

"That bitch Edie…" He banged his beer glass unsteadily on the table and ran his fingers through his black hair. Celine smiled and began putting lipstick on with her brush. "If it weren't for money I wouldn't ship out."

"Well, why did you marry her in the first place?" I asked.

"I don't know. She's an animal and I'm used to laying her. Sometimes I run away and never want to see her again and then I write halfway through a novel in some lonely hole in the city and I begin to feel guilty and father-like and I run back to her."

Celine began to defend Edie's intelligence and I patted her on the head. She resented it.

---

116 Radical Café. Fictional name Ginsberg gave to the West End Bar. Later in the story, he reverts to its actual name.

"While I'm away I'm going to write the big novel." The big novel was called *Galloway*,[117] it was a variant of *Portrait of an Artist as a Young Man*. Jack had been writing it on and off for five years, never finishing it. "The trouble with you is that you don't write about your own environment. In *Galloway* I'm going to throw away all this damned decadence. All you can write about is Rimbaud and Lautréamont. Look at you—a Jew from Jersey City and you don't have a feeling for your country."

I snickered. He glared at me.

"You know what I mean, don't smile ironically. You have no sense of the present, of land. I've been to New Orleans in whoring time and I've laid women in Washington and I grew up in Lowell, Massachusetts. I want to put all of that in *Galloway*. I want Ian MacKenzie in it and his Beethoven Quartets and his mansion in Lowell. Here is a type—he's closeted up and writing away and burning what he writes. When he's 40 he's going to write and publish and be another Tolstoi. I want to put Sebastian [Sampas] in it."

Sebastian had been a poet in Lowell, a Greek, and he was killed in Italy. Jack had all Sebastian's beautiful old letters and all his poetry in a trunk in Long Island, where Jack's parents lived.

"I want to write something of growth that springs from energy. I want to get Wolfe and the College and the football team in it. I want to get the South in it, and the Puritans and Jazz and Hollywood, and even the bourgeois of Jersey City.

I replied, "I'm looking for a novel too, but one that has cultural roots in the whole west, and has a sane moral philosophy."

"Well, you swallowed Rimbaud, which is all right," Jack replied, "but you're just plodding along—what is it, Lautréamont now? The trouble with you is that you're not a spawner, a poet. You're an academician. You can't understand creation as your only good. There's your morality; throw everything else aside;—the damned bourgeois, even your decadence. Be Orpheus, be Dostoyevsky, and write and multiply."

Celine had been flirting with a sailor that had been standing listening to us talk. He was drunk and aggressive. He smiled nastily to us and called across the barroom to another sailor. "Hey Joe, come 'ere and listen to these two talk over here. Looks like the real stuff." Celine smiled. The sailor looked to me. "Hey kid, what's your name."

"Ginsberg, Allen." I turned to Jack to talk.

---

117 *loc. cit. Galloway* was published in 1950 under the title, *The Town and the City*.

"I'll bet you go to the college here, huh, kid?" The other sailor had come over and decided to make Celine.

"Yes."

"See, Joe? Real brains. Just like I said, intellectuals." He put his foot up on the bench and leaned over me. "No kidding, tell me. What are you doing here? You won't learn nothing from this place. The only people that come here are stumblebums and dumb sailors like us."

I looked up modestly and sensed trouble.

"I mean, Jesus,—what do you think of people like us? No kidding? Where do we fit in?"

"I don't pass judgments," I laughed.

Jack looked up annoyed. Celine kept flirting with the other sailor.

"No kidding, have you ever been laid?" both laughed hugely. "Shit," he scowled, "when the army and navy comes home all you yellow shits are going to get a knife up your ribs."

Jack muttered, "We can do some knife slinging too."

"Keep quiet," I told Jack. "He's drunk and sadistic already."

"I know your type. I've seen hundreds of little pipsqueaks like you before," returned the sailor.

"Never one like me," I smiled. The sailor sneered and turned to Jack. "Why aren't you in the army? You look old enough."

"I was in the navy for half a year before I went into the merchant marine," said Jack, a little angered.

"Let's see your discharge papers." The other sailor began pulling him away and stopped when Jack said, "Like hell. I was discharged because I was a Communist."

"And I suppose you are, too," the sailor looked at me. "Where were you born? No kidding," he asked Jack.

Jack looked up to him innocently and said "Moscow."

"I won't take more of your shit." The sailor stood up, "We'll have knives for you."

"And blackjacks too?" Jack was being edged into a fight.

"And fists too. Come on outside and I'll show you what we'll have for you."

"Don't," I said to Jack, "you're drunk and it's unphilosophic."

"Shit," said the sailor. "Keep out of this you little asshole."

I told Jack to come back, but when he went out, I followed.

Outside the bar a crowd had gathered to watch. Both of the sailors were together and both jumped on Jack. He was ready for them; the first he just sidestepped. The argumentative one fell down in his haste onto the pavement and skinned his jaw. Jack began beating away at the second and knocked him down but both jumped up again. There wasn't much I could do but grab the sleeve of one while Jack fought with the other.

"Get away you little bastard before you get hurt." I was pushed and sprawled on the sidewalk. When I got up Jack was sitting on top of one, telling him to stop fighting. The sailor that had pushed me down pulled Jack on to his back while the other rolled over and sat on Jack's chest. Johnny the bartender wouldn't do anything to stop the fight so I had to rush over and pull at one of the sailors again. They were trying to beat Jack's head against the pavement. I distracted them and they backed me up against the bar's plate glass window and began slapping me, telling me to keep my nose out of this before I got hurt. I stood there and got slapped and didn't try to resist. I didn't want to get hurt. Jack was on his feet again, winded and weak, telling them to stop fighting. They began punching at him again, so I rushed over and pulled him into the bar. The two sailors, both bleeding around the face, rushed into the swinging door; but we held it till the bartender decided that he didn't want any fights in his place. He came over and told us to get inside while he threw the two sailors out.

There was no harm done. Jack's face was bloodied up, but it didn't seem to be his blood. As for his head, he'd stiffened his neck and so didn't get hurt when they tried to beat it against the sidewalk.

Celine was all excited, and I began to shake my head at Jack for going outside at all. He just sat there, trembling; he looked tired.

We decided to go then. Celine was using my room for the night, and Jack had nowhere else to go, so we clasped hands, the three of us, and walked from the bar to my room without saying anything. When we got there, Celine sat on the bed, and then lay down. Jack sat down and put his face in her yellow hair and began to cry. I sat at my desk, turned on my small desk lamp and began to read Shelley aloud to them. When they seemed asleep, I put out the light and stretched out on the floor. But the bed began to creak soon, and I saw that they were going to copulate, so I crept out the door and took a walk by Riverside Drive.

I got back at 5 o'clock, just when dawn began to filter through the city. Jack had his seaman's cap on and was kneeling at Celine's side. She lay on the bed, her hair tousled up and her lipstick wiped off. He was kissing her goodbye and didn't seem to know what to say; she just smiled. I told him that it was time to go. He got up and we walked down the five flights of stairs. When we got to the bottom, I said, "When does your ship leave?"

"At seven, It's five now. I've got to hurry down to the dock." I kept quiet. I rode downtown with Jack on the subway.

"It was all very beautiful," I said, finally.

"It was."

We sat around in front of the dock talking about his trip. He thought that he was going to France. I hoped so and wished I could go.

"I won't see you for a year," he said, "please tell Celine I love her. I mean it."

He walked in, to the big dock, past a truck that had its motor running. Then he turned around and waved; and I waved. Then I walked around Greenwich Village to the bars that Jack and I and Lucien and Celine used to go to, till I was tired and melancholy and I wanted to go to sleep.

The Neurotic Personality of Our Time

I was sitting in my room at Warren Hall doing homework when I got a ring from downstairs. I went to the elevator and Sammy told me someone had just called in a hurry and said Jack was in Minetta's. I went back to my room and looked frantically at a chemistry book for a minute. I decided that art was more important than mismanaged techniques. It certainly was anticlimactic of Jack to return so soon.

Jack was sitting in Minetta's at a table in the corner near the john and he was already a little drunk on beer. He didn't take his liquor very well.

I rushed over and nearly knocked over his beer, I was so glad to see him. He didn't say anything for a minute and stared at me apologetically. I could see he was suffering. He almost began crying.

"I got back from Norfolk two days ago."

"Why aren't you in India?"

"I got into a fight in Norfolk. Anyway, I hopped a bus back to New York."

"What are you going to do now? You screwed up your chance to make money in the merchant marine." I knew he didn't know what he was going to do, so I softened up and asked him where the hell he'd been the last two days in New York.

"I had it all figured out. When I got back I decided I'd stay in the Village—get a job as a counterman, find a room and write. I wasn't even going to tell anybody I was back. Remember, don't say a word of it, or Edie will hear and come storming into town to know why I haven't been out earning money. Well I'm going to hide myself in the Village and work on *Galloway*. I wrote a lot last week on the boat. I also read the copy of Nietzsche you loaned me." He pulled the Modern Library edition from under his chair and opened it to read to me.

"Here is the idea. Art is the proper function of the human soul. Oh, that's the perfected statement of it: Proper function. Not a leisure activity. That's what's wrong with this civilization. I consider it a function like eating and drinking. You starve to death without the daily creative diet. You must have your aesthetic excretion—a function—properly and regularly. I'm getting a room here and directing myself completely to self expression. I'll bury myself here completely with no contact with the outer world until I finish *Galloway*."

I thought it was a good idea myself. He was really excited by the prospect. He began to ask about Celine, becoming more and more melancholy as the hours passed. He seemed to think he was really in love with her and maybe he was.

"Don't be silly, you laid her two weeks ago. Forget it."

"I can't. I can't and I don't want to." He began talking about her in Canuck French and I couldn't understand what he was saying, but it certainly was heartfelt. Then he took out his notebook and wrote a note for me to deliver to her: "*A propos de mon coeur de chien...Je t'aime comme un fou; comme une jeune fille sans orgueill, ne demandez pourquoi!* Unreasonable loves! *Je veux regarder tes yeux—encore! Ne me quittez pas / J'ai mal au coeur, comme toujours. Je suis miserable encore.—Jean*"

"Do you know who went to the opera opening? The new student down the hall," said Markham.[118]

"Yes, Arthur Rimbaud," volunteered Snow,[119] eager to purvey his information. Ginsberg looked up a bit shocked.

"Don't be absurd."

"Whattya mean? It's written on his door. Why not?"

"Rimbaud was a decadent poet of whom you'll never hear again in your life. The boy you're talking about is named Lucien Carr."

Markham resumed his tale. "Yes, he went to the opera and didn't like it. Do you know what he said when he walked into the lobby? In front of all these terribly delicate people in all sorts of frightfully expensive clothes he spoke up, 'When you put cattle in barns they copulate.' Poor Mrs. Cornwallis probably hasn't thought of copulating since the 1929 depression." Markham changed his tone to one of breathless wonder. "But he's allowed to do that. Some friends of mine know his family. They're all southerners with thousands of dollars invested in the slave trade or something substantial like that; Carr's just full of *noblesse oblige*. He's been kicked out of the best private schools in the country."

118 Richard Markham. Columbia friend.
119 John Snow. Columbia college classmate.

"I suspected that he's antisocial," laughed Ginsberg.

"Oh, have you met him?"

"Yes, he introduced himself by insulting me—he heard my name and practically called me Shylock."

Markham looked toward the open door of his room, for he heard Carr's lusty voice chanting down the hall: "Violate me / in violent time, / the vilest way that you know. / Ruin me, / ravage me, / utterly savage me, / on me no mercy bestow."

Carr, naked and waving a towel around his head, came from the shower. The three joined him, going to his room.

"Pied Piper and all the little rats," he chuckled. "But come in and violate. ...my room." He sat down on the bed without bothering to dress and lit a cigarette. "You're the one who thought he liked Brahms." He looked to Ginsberg. There was a hesitant knock on the door.

"Come in, Kammerer, come in! I have a nice group of plump little boys who want to meet you." The door opened, revealing a tall, hatless, red haired man, about 30 years of age, who immediately smiled and charmingly bowed to greet Carr's assembled guests. "Little boys, I want you to meet David Kammerer. David, this is John Snow of Teaneck, New Jersey, this Richard Markham, and this Ginsberg or something who has heard of Baudelaire."

"Well, Carr, you seem to have done well for such a short time." Kammerer fixed his eyes on Carr's and seemed in doing so to exclude the presence of others. He spoke, smiling softly, discreetly, communicating and omniscient mockery. "Haven't seen a more likely looking group of lads in some time."

"Yes, and they all seem to know how to read," replied Carr, continuing to indulge in what seemed to Markham a private jest at his expense. "But it's fortunate you called. I didn't have any money left." Kammerer glanced at Snow and smiled broadly.

"Well, you're in luck today. I picked up $10 in a bar last night. I had to roll a fag to do it. I had an idea you'd need it by now." His mouth twisted into a half ironic smile as he perceived an inquisitive dullness impressed on the faces of Carr's acquaintances. He was unconsciously compelled by his fear and contempt of them to pursue his game further. Their eyes on him, he attended Carr's dressing, helping Carr don his shirt. "When did you last eat?"

"Last night."

"What did you do with the money your mother sent you?"

"We spent that Friday night in the Radical Cafe. What I had left I spent yesterday on the two albums—Mahler's First and the Clarinet Quintet."

"Good!" Kammerer exclaimed to Carr, "I'm glad to see you took my advice and finally got them."

"My God," cried Ginsberg, "do you mean to say that you haven't eaten since last night?"

Kammerer leaned his long red rimmed face toward his left shoulder and smiled conspiratorially to Carr. "Ginsberg, a little fasting might do you some good, I think. It might nourish your soul."

Snow had finished examining a long fishing knife that was stuck by its point into the top of Carr's desk. "I'm hungry. Let's go out and get something to eat."

"Kammerer," Carr delivered definitively, seated cross-legged on the bed, "I don't feel like going down. Bring some stuff up. Bring some wine if you can get that too."

Kammerer hesitated. "Come down and shop with me."

Carr nodded a cold negative. "How much will you need tomorrow?"

"Oh," Kammerer smiled vaguely, "I can always get more."

"Then leave the change with me. Bring the food up and leave it at the door with the money. I'm too tired. You'd better crawl back to the Village."

Kammerer stood at the door. He masked his insecurity with an accommodating bow. "Goodnight."

"*Soit-sage, mon petit,*" jeered Carr. . . .

Ginsberg turned off the corridor into his room, ruminating suspiciously about Carr's friend Kammerer and his strange attitudes. Certainly he seemed faithful, perhaps questionably self-abnegating. Yet he appeared perfectly respectable, at least at first glance. He was marked with features of complete propriety: a handsome Roman nose, short, thick hair—though red—and an eminently weak chin. His manners were pleasant, in fact almost unctuous. He had a shy smile, though the shyness may have been a craven secretiveness. His speech was cultured and his manner of speaking almost retired. Yet there was something sharply superior in the way he pronounced his sentences— mumbling the last half unheard and gazing abstractly aside, as if to say ironically to the listener, you are not really worth communicating to; there was also an obscure mockery hidden in the attitudes of the eyes—he jested.

There was a knock on the door. Ginsberg walked to it and bowed Carr in. "I thought you were retiring."

"Not tonight. I merely didn't want Kammerer around. He does get boring after a while."

"Who is he?"

"A friend of mine from New Orleans. A fruit. He followed me from there to St. John's College and then here. He lives in Greenwich Village."

"What is a fruit?"

"A fruit? What mudhole did you emerge from? Well, life is various, a homosexual."

"This must go with my suicide note—Brahms Trio No.1, listen—." Lucien carefully placed the record on the turntable, adjusted the needle to the groove and the music began. "This is melody like wine!" He could not keep still, he was so moved by the music. He felt the urge to sing, to beat his feet, but he did not want to make too much noise and so he spoke softly. "When I play this, I have feelings of mortality."

"The suicide note?"

Lucien read: "Good creatures, I have no doubt that you can compose yourselves and that will not be too difficult for you are complacent beings to the fact of my inexistence. No doubt you will find yourselves smiling or pitying me. That you do neither I must explain my death; that you do neither I must justify myself. And if it be that I am merely indulging my self-consciousness in justifying myself, in inviting your attention to my misfortunes, then I must accept and espouse my egotism, for I find it my final pleasure.

I am lost, wandering, searching for all wombs which have crumbled since my birth. I am perverted! I am rational! I am obscene. Ah, I am insane. I love my insanity—it is my last womb. Yet, it too now crumbles! My sanity must be returning, for I wish to die.

Now I shall be whimsical. Here is a death mask. Look at my face: are you pleased? I desired many things—all have been denied. Most of all I have desired love. Yet I have loved twice. Marie Maechels[120]—her beauty roused my desire, her intelligence roused my love, my rapture was insane in my desire to possess her I corrupted her; she has caught my own infernal diseases. I shall kill myself—let her be cured. Another I loved: I will not pleasure your egos with a recital of this love though I might fling it in your face and defy you with it, you are too insensitive to know that I have mortally wounded you with it. It is my private love; I retain my privacy, unbroken by your boorishness."

Lucien rose and put on the record, feeling a queasy embarrassment in his flesh as he began to fear the fatuousness of reading a sincerely intended exper-

120 Marie Maechels. Possibly a pseudonym, Ginsberg couldn't remember who this was.

iment in communicative introspection to the object of its vilipend. Yet Ginsberg seemed sympathetic. Lucien waited his return.

"This reminds me of a Russian novel," chirped Ginsberg as he re-entered. "Here! It is my turn. I shall read a suicide note." By this time both were completely intoxicated in half dizzied exuberance. "Now mine has the advantage of brevity."

"Why Ginsberg," mocked Lucien, "do you mean to say that you write suicide notes between economic papers? Don't be absurd."

"Only when I'm in the mood."

"This is ridiculous. You have no right to commit suicide. You're not worthy of self-destruction." Lucien was almost angry. He waved his hand impatiently in front of him as if to brush away inconsequentiality.

"To all of my friends I present my rue and my disgust. I have no possession of value other than my soul. I do not owe it to earth; I will it to oblivion. I have attempted little and been satisfied by nothing. I desired much and rejected equally—all love is foul because it is compromise with hatred; all friends are fools and all fools are friends. All desire is hopeless, all dreams, dream; all faith, false; and all gods, faithless."

"As you say it has the virtue of brevity. But I think that your pen flew so fast your wits had difficulty keeping pace when you wrote that. It's confused, love-read, and in general doesn't rise above your natural mediocrity."

"*Eh bien, où pouvons-nous aller acheter plus!*"

"Rational Café."

"*Bon.*"

"*Allons.*"

They donned their coats and reeled gently down the stairs. But emergence into the bitter winter air gradually sobered their heads as they plodded along silently in the snow.

It may be now surmised that Lucien Carr considered that he was an artist. And, to tell the truth, it was not overly presumptuous of him to entertain this consideration, for he was endowed with a high degree of sensitivity and critical perspicuity of which he was, to be sure, aware.

"Every artist is bohemian as the deuce, inside. Let him at least wear proper clothes and behave outwardly as a respectable being." So said Thomas Mann's mature artist, Tonio Kroeger. On the other hand Jean-Luis Kerouac declared in his preface to *Galloway* that the young artist "is colored by his symbols. His hue is vivid: he postures." This because the artist is in growth, he has just grasped the idea, he has not yet absorbed it. In the fury of recognition he adjusts his physical aspect to the image of his ideas. Living becomes a symbol. He remains outwardly constant to his symbol in his youth. If, with maturity, he realizes that the physical symbol is a superfluous manifestation of his energy, if, in time, the current of his creation pours through his art, not his living, he may profit from the conservation of his energy. Yet it is perhaps proper that as preface to the development of his techniques of artistry that the artist should live his art. He is in youth a "genius of life." Such an artist—immature and promising—was Lucien Carr. His attempted suicide was a conscious gesture—and certainly it was self conscious: that is attested by his willingness to talk about it. His consciousness as to its origin and significance, rather than destroying its validity as a gesture, did but make it all the more profound. His awareness intensified his responsibility to the gesture. In recovery he was consecrated as an artist—or so he felt at the time—because his sensitivity had been proved. Thus he treasured his suicide note, partly – though perhaps he would not admit it – because it was a token around which clustered a variety of recollections, and partly because he considered it his first work of art.

1. Beginning:

Kammerer had left the groceries at the door. In the bag were two roast beef sandwiches, potato salad, pickles, a small can of caviar, a package of blue cheese, brown bread and two fifths of red Burgundy. Lucien bent down to examine the contents of the bag, and extracted the wine from it. He raised the bottle aloft and looked at the label. "Taylor's New York State Port. Humph. Too sweet, but effective."

He and Ginsberg walked into the room and sat down at the writing desk, Ginsberg a bit timidly, but unaware of any disapproval of his opportunism, chatting between gulps of roast beef about Toulouse Lautrec.

Lucien opened the two bottles of wine, he pushed one toward Ginsberg. "This wine goes well with the blue cheese."

"It should, Kammerer knows what to buy. He usually strikes good combinations." The two ate the cheese with the brown bread.

"Good pumpernickel," mumbled Lucien, vainly grasping at a large chunk of bread which he had torn from the loaf, as it fell from his mouth. He rescued it from the floor and spread the black caviar on it. He chewed energetically and vulgarly, wiping his mouth when he was finished with the sleeve of his bright red calfskin shirt, wiping his hands after that on his overall trousers. Ginsberg had been drinking the wine steadily, unused to it but enjoying its muted dryness. Now it began to go to his head. Lucien watched him as he slowly began to exhibit signs of drunkenness and to be sure, Lucien's inquisitive amusement was justified, for Ginsberg, who was more introspective than experienced, was drunk for the first time in his life. He had planned to experience this, but the coming of drunkenness on so extemporaneous an occasion had caught him completely unawares. Now he became conscious of his condition, and began to think of it as something immensely humorous. He laughed aloud and saw Lucien stare up amusedly from his wine; he had projected his attitude into a laugh, and this incongruously interrupted the diverse train of Lucien's thought. Ginsberg felt, with satisfaction, the inebriation becoming more intense. He did the things which were proper to the circumstances—moving his hands to grasp the glass, shifting his feet on the floor, looking down to his nails and then abruptly out of the window. But he felt himself doing these automatically—without reflection and anticipation. Occupied with his drunkenness, he was surprised to see his hand grasp the glass. His mind functioned, he thought, clearly, in fact even more precisely than before; his limbs functioned even more precisely than before; yet there seemed to be no correlation between the two. Still, his limbs seemed to be taking care of themselves, and so all was well—except that—ho?—a glass was on its side on the floor—well, he seemed to have brushed Lucien's glass off the table. This was not the result of drunkenness, he assured himself; it seemed more of a natural accident.

The West End Bar was a university replica of a Greenwich Village dive. The café was divided by a partition into two sides—in the evenings, Otto, the chef, presided over the lunchroom half. Otto was a nasty tempered and sharp tongued Dane who resented taking orders. Since he was a counterman he found much to resent. To repeat a request for a cup of coffee was forbidden; Otto could hear the customer the first time, he would have him know and he didn't want to be nagged eternally by a bunch of damned college boys who oughta go out and work a few years before they opened their traps. But Otto was dependable: his food, if not delicate, was digestible; his coffee was excellent; and he could be counted on for a free bowl of soup in an emergency. On the other side of the partition was the long, well-attended bar. There was a cigarette machine as one entered the revolving door, a juke box and a men's room at the far end. Bill or Johnny usually tended the bar. Bill was a well built, yellow haired man of about 30; he rather liked the students and served every fourth drink on the house. His motorcycle stood at the curb outside waiting to carry him away from the West End every evening. Johnny was an Irish Catholic—a great shouldered man with a large nose and a strong sense of morals. He thought that all students were communists (though they would protest that they were mere radicals) and he damned them all therefore. Though he did not like intellectuals, Johnny would stand above them at the bar lecturing them on Americanism, whenever he had nothing else of importance on his mind. An utterly humorless man, he insisted that they respect his past as a coal miner. Though Johnny was a Philistine—he espoused it, though he could not name it—he was not particularly well meaning, except insofar as all men are. He always ended his somewhat ill-tempered discussion with a stern and seriously intended admonition. "You'll all go to the dogs, and after the war, I warn you bastards, you'll all be hanged." Before he turned away, he would add grimly, "Don't worry, you won't be the one to start the revolution." Johnny voted regularly, for some inexplicable reason, for Norman Thomas.[121] Also he kept a mistress. He would have no part with any woman who drank or swore and he held his liquor magnificently for he had been drinking a quart of whisky a day for ten years. He boasted that he was a family man; he warningly boasted of how he was providing for his children. His mistress a black haired wench of about thirty two, ten years younger than himself, met him every evening at four to take him home.

The West End had a curious combination of patrons. There were two or three steadies. "Holy Mary," whose name no one seemed to know, had opened the bar in the morn and closed it at nite for ten years, as Johnny attested. She was a plump neat woman of about 40; she always wore a plain black dress with an ugly black hat; she used no make up and was not a loose woman. She merely sat at the end of the bar and looked into her beer. She seemed to care little for anything about her, and consequently said very little, except to "Aunt Jane," a yellow-haired whore in her late 40's, whose light, sloppily painted face, stared at the customers and the juke box for several hours each night. Mrs. Evans also came in regularly—she was a paranoid with an alcoholic twitch, an intensely dislikable old shrew. She had a tendency to disapprove.

There were also about a dozen men of middle age who frequented the West End. All were neurotic, all were financial failures, all were in the habit of addressing the bow-tied college youths as "sonny." All became either extremely ill-tempered or extremely sentimental when drunk. But ill-tempered or sentimental, they unanimously counseled all college youth to "forget this fucken' idealism you bin spoutin', take it from me" and "I don't want any of your damned back talk, when you get to my age you know a little about life."

The West End was the stage; on it each four years, the *dramatis personae*

---

121   Norman Thomas (1884–1968). American Socialist Party perennial candidate for President.

from the college was almost completely changed. It was traditional, since it was the bar nearest to the college, and also the largest, that it remained the meeting place of college intellectuals. The combination of liquor and proximity allowed the best and the freest thinking students in the school to drop in regularly each evening. These *Herrenvolk* preferred the quieter and more discursive life of the West End to the business of student affairs. Thus there was an intellectual hierarchy—the herd of students, the representatives of the herd, leaders and active men, and above them, the true intellectual. Tonight was Christmas Eve; all were home. The bar had a larger crowd clustering around it than usual. The booths that lined the sides of the room were almost filled. The revolving doors began to move, and Lucien and Ginsberg entered unsteadily. The contrast between the two was striking—Lucien's yellow hair was unbrushed; his clothes multicolored and dirty, his step vigorous, his glance at the crowd, contemptuous. Ginsberg entered behind him, almost timidly, neatly dressed, thin, Semitic. He started aside, as he saw Lucien screw up his face into a daemonic leer, push the hair over his forehead, pull his collar over his neck, and bound into the center of the room, shouting, *"Plonger au fond de gouffre, enfer ou Ciel, qu'importe?"*[122]

The drinkers in the booths poked their heads to the side curiously; Johnny the bartender guffawed; "Aunt Jane" looked up and cackled vigorously, clapping her clammy hands and hooting encouragement. Two sailors looked at Lucien angrily. Lucien sat down at the bar. "Holy Mary" stared into her beer. "She's the only wise one here," whispered Lucien. He ordered two pernods.

"I haven't enough money for that."

"Don't worry you close-fingered Jew, I've got enough."

"Your hospitality isn't particularly gracious, but I accept it anyway," replied Ginsberg.

Lucien looked around, "Let's sit down in this booth." They slid in, balancing their drinks as they bent their bodies to the curve of the table and chair.

December 31, 1944.

In Which Lucien Begins to Take Shape

The New York Philharmonic broadcast that Sunday featured Beethoven's Eroica Symphony. Ginsberg arranged the pillows on his hard chair and leaned back on them to listen. On his lap a new copy of *Anna Karenina* lay, opened. He

---

122 Loosely translated from the French, "To plunge into the bottom of the abyss, hell or heaven, what difference?"

picked it up slowly and began to read without interest. He still felt the lassitude which was the result of twelve hours of sleep. Meanwhile he felt a certain amount of impatience. Lucien had promised to meet him in the afternoon. It was already 3:30 and he had not yet appeared. Ginsberg continued to read, wondering vaguely when he could expect Lucien. It would be too bad, he ruminated, if Lucien did not show up. His first visit to the village in such company promised to be interesting. And above that, Ginsberg dreaded the dullness of a whole afternoon and evening reading the novel which had been assigned by his English professor. He lay down the book and picked up the *Times*, reading the Book, Stage and Magazine sections. He glanced at the News section, and then threw it aside, finding it boring. He glanced up at the clock again, stretched wearily, and plunged back into *Anna Karenina*, every few minutes emerging from it distracted by the music. When Lucien finally knocked on the door the night had come—it was 10 o'clock. "Well Ginsberg, busy at work?" Lucien asked roughly. Ginsberg stared in amazement at Lucien. His impatience had melted to incredulity as he saw Lucien slump into the room and stretch out in the bed. Lucien's face was splotched with blood; his yellow hair was unkempt and filthy; his hands were grimy; on his right thumb was an immense blister, covered with nicotine and dirt. His red shirt was ripped in the front. He had somewhere changed his overalls to a beaten and dirt streaked pair of white pants.

"What happened to you?" he asked, masking his curiosity with a faint smile.

"I don't remember everything," Lucien's voice was muffled in the pillow. Lucien turned over and looked at the radio. "What's on, more Beethoven? They've been playing it all day on WQXR," he motioned. "I heard a wonderful Brahms last night sometime."

"What happened?"

"Some of it's gone," Lucien shook his head. "I've got a horrible headache."

Ginsberg resigned himself. "I guess we'd better not go downtown tonight."

"Oh yes we will, it's OK. I'll take a shower and it'll go away. What happened after I left you?" he mused for a moment. Then he smiled sardonically. "Oh yes. I met Kammerer in Minetta's. We drank a lot until I was almost insane. Then Rubenstein began to..."

"Who's he?"

"Some artist that lives on Minetta Lane. Lived in England for about 20 years. He ghost writes novels for refugees. But he specializes in painting male nudes. He's a fruit. So he invited me up to his studio and began to paw me. Kammerer began to insult him, so Rubenstein pulled a knife and jumped on

Kammerer. Kammerer is weak as a fish, and I was drunk enough to get over and defend him. Really, it was mad. When I get drunk I become pathological. I kicked Rubenstein over and jumped on him, and then I began biting him."

"Is that where the blood came from?" Lucien did not seem to understand. "There on your face." Ginsberg handed him a table mirror.

Lucien looked into it for awhile. "I guess so, I remember that I began to bite his ears and then I bit off an eyebrow. He just lay there, with me on top of him, biting him. Oh, what a masochist he is. He just whimpered a little, and then I kicked him and I stumbled to my chair and fainted. He ran out and went into Kammerer's room on Bleecker Street and stole some whisky. By the time Kammerer and I got back to his room we were too furious to care any more, so we ran back to Rubenstein's room and tore it up. Oh, what a pleasure it is. No inhibitions and all sadism. We smashed a sofa and broke a vase on his table. Well, they weren't worth much anyway. Then Peter Genius came in and began to help us. We finished and went to Kammerer's room to drink. That's all I remember. When I woke, I was sleeping on Kammerer's bed covered by his coat. He was sitting in a chair staring at me. I borrowed a nickel from him and came back here." Lucien rose. "I'm going to take a shower, come on in." Lucien threw his clothes off in his room and flung them in a corner, wrapping a towel around his loins. He shook his head and looked in the mirror, staring at his body. It was youthful despite his constant debauchery: his legs and thighs were slim but well developed; the hair on his body was light and straight, and his chest was boyishly hairless, though it was well developed and muscular.

"Don't stare too long, Narcissus."

"There is no jest there," mused Lucien. "I do derive a sort of narcissistic pleasure from staring at myself. It's kind of amusing though," he added interestedly. "I'd better put on some clean clothes. I'll have to go down to see my mother to get some more money."

"Where does she live?"

"She has an apartment near Columbus Circle on Central Park West."

"I didn't know you had that much money."

Lucien turned and walked to the shower. "That interests you, eh, Semite?"

"I can't escape my conditioning."

"We had lots of money somewhere in the family. I'll show you the pictures of my ancestors when we get to my mother's apartment." Lucien entered the shower closet and flung his towel to Ginsberg, who sat back on a basin, silent. Lucien turned on the water and began to scrub himself vigorously.

"Who is the Marie Maechels you mentioned last night?"

"When?"

"In that suicide note?"

"When did I read that?"

"We were playing Brahms and drinking wine and you read it." Lucien scrubbed his hair and recollected.

"She's a little Renoir nude who goes to an art school in Philly. We knew each other in Saint Louis."

"You didn't seem too happy about her last night."

"Are you supposed to be happy about the one you love?"

"Oh, are you in love?"

"I only know that I languor when my beloved weeps and that I cry when she laughs."

"Is she intelligent?"

Lucien lost all of his solitude of mockery when he spoke of Marie. "Yes," he answered, "and a wonderful artist."

"You mentioned that you were corrupting her. How so—is she becoming a lesbian under your caresses?"

"If you remember I also spoke of artistic sterility."

"Meaning what?"

"I can write, of that I'm sure. I do critical work that is wonderful. And I've experienced enough to have material, but I can't bring myself to create. I sit down and become distracted, I begin to procrastinate and waste time or I drink. If I have no liquor I'll suddenly begin to masturbate. I·fell utterly frustrated."

"Don't be ridiculous. Just put your pen on your paper."

Lucien laughed derisively. "I'm sure you have no trouble communicating the emptiness of your brain to a blank paper."

Ginsberg smiled. "At least I don't leave the paper blank."

"No, really, I can't analyze it." Lucien narrowed his eyes in introspection. His face lost all of its harshness and mockery. He fumbled blindly in his mind. "It's impossible. I'm afraid to create. It terrifies me." He rubbed the soap reflectively over his genitalia. "And it becomes disease producing pathogenic."

"How does this tie up with Marie?"

"When I write I destroy it immediately. It terrifies me and shames me. It's so far below what I plan. The perfect unity in my mind becomes a shambles on paper and is so imperfect. And when I begin to criticize Marie's work by the same standard, she began to fear perfectionism. She was afraid to show her sketches to me, she began to be afraid to draw."

"You'll have to show some of her stuff to me." Lucien stepped out of the shower and began to dry himself. "In fact you'll have to show her to me."

"Come into my room." Lucien walked up the corridor with a firm, elastic step and strode into his room. He opened his desk drawer and produced four small drawings of himself, which he offered to Allen. "She made them last week. I visited her in Philadelphia." He began to dress. Allen examined the pictures—they were rough, sensuous, and lyrical portraits of Lucien naked, one lying on his stomach on bed, one sitting in a chair with a book, his thigh spread, the last of his head and shoulders.

"They're extremely well done."

"Yes, Marie is a genius. But, as you can see, she's terribly undeveloped. In two years she'll be a wonder."

"Does she do anything in oils?"

"No—she used to. Now she hasn't the patience and there you see, is part of the trouble. She'll be as sterile as I am before she attains any power. It's artistic leprosy. *Eh, bien allez mon enfant, nous allons.* Have you got an extra overcoat? I left mine somewhere in the village. My mother will be disturbed if I come in disheveled, and she won't give me money unless I pour some oil on our troubled family waters."

They opened the door of the taxicab, "Pay him, Ginsberg, I'll give you the money later." Lucien walked under the awning and saluted the doorman of the apartment.

"*Bon Jour,* M. Carr."

Entering he nodded to the elevator man, "Is my mother home, Charlie?"

"Yes sir, she is. Long time since you're home."

"A couple of weeks. Not too long."

"Still running around wild?" the elevator man laughed lightly at his presumption.

"Oh, not too wildly. I'm still alive." The attendant smiled good humouredly, and opened the door, "Goodnight. This way, Ginsberg."

Lucien knocked on the door and spit into the bowl of artificial flowers on the table in the hall.

Mrs. Carr opened the door. Her eyes lighted briefly, "Why Lucien! I didn't expect you." Then she queried. "But why didn't you call me up last week? Oh really, you were away so long I had no idea of what might have happened to you." Lucien waved his hand and smiled. "I've been behaving myself. Mother, dear, this is Allen Ginsberg."

"Do you go to college with Lucien?"

"Oh, yes, Mrs. Carr."

"Well, come right in. Oh, but Lucien you should have called! I was just going to bed."

Lucien raised his eyebrows and declared dryly, "Well, now you may sleep in peace."

He walked into his Victorian living room and lounged down in his chair. "Monstrosity isn't it?"

Ginsberg shook his head in a polite no. "Your home is remarkably richly furnished."

Lucien's mother rested uneasily in her desk chair. She was a nervous woman with a small, frail, almost wasted body. Her face was thin, her eyes bright and intelligent. She hesitated for a moment and then began to question him. "Well, Lucien, what have you been up to lately?"

"Innocent pleasure. Expensive though," he declared significantly.

She laughed inquieted, "Then I am to owe this kind visit to your bankruptcy?" Ginsberg rose from his chair, anticipating that his presence would prove embarrassing. He made himself as inconspicuous as possible before a large bookcase in the corner of the room.

"Oh, not at all, my dear mother, I decided to return to the womb for a few minutes."

"I warn you my womb is not lined with currency."

He laughed, "Perhaps if I explore I'll find an inter-uterine mint."

"Perhaps," she replied, defensively. "Allen, would you like something to drink?"

Allen turned innocently. "Thank you very much."

"Lucien, get something. There's some wine in the kitchen or would you prefer some ginger ale."

"Come on in with me, Allen. We'll raid the icebox."

"There's some roast beef in it if you want it." His mother resigned herself. "Help yourself. Oh, Lucien, how much will you need?" Ginsberg walked into the kitchen and stayed there, waiting for Lucien.

"I'll be right with you," Lucien's voice came to him from the other room.

"Now what is it to be, my little parasite?" she asked, smiling.

"What are you worth today?"

"To whom?" she replied.

"To your loving son."

"Very little, I must imagine."

"Ah, mother dear, I value you above riches. We've got to judge your worth by some other standard than myself if I'm to wheedle any money out of you."

"I wasn't sure I could persuade you to conform to any standard at all, Lucien."

"I'll bow down in obeisance before a fat check."

She smiled, unable to parry with Lucien any longer, and rose, sighing. "Will ten dollars do for today?"

"Magnificently." He rose, "Bully, mother dear."

She laughed submissively and went into her bedroom for her purse. Lucien joined Ginsberg. "Well, Allen, have a chunk of the fatted calf." Lucien opened the icebox.

"Were you successful?"

"Moderately. Mother is trying too hard to be moderate and progressive with me."

"She seems to be a fine woman."

Lucien raised his eyebrows. "Oh, thank you, *mon ami*. I feel highly complimented." He began to laugh. "She has only one breast." He bit a chunk of roast beef from a thick slice that he had cut.

They joined Mrs. Carr in the parlor, munching sandwiches. "Here you are Lucien." She looked at him with a delicately self-pitying humility.

"I'll see that he doesn't spend it all at once," volunteered Ginsberg brightly.

"Yes, Ginsberg has appointed himself my guardian angel."

"He needs one," she laughed.

"Well you just don't worry," Ginsberg continued lightly. "I'll restrain him in his sinning as well as I can."

"You must be a remarkably holy child," she laughed. "To attempt to restrain others from sin, as well as yourself."

The three laughed, as they moved toward the door. "Goodnight Lucien. Please call me up in a few days. I never can reach you at the dormitory."

"Certainly I will," he said with a smile.

"Goodnight Mrs. Carr." She stretched out her hand and Ginsberg shook it gently.

Neither of the two spoke as they rode down the elevator. Once in the street Ginsberg looked to the ground and then shook his head. "Lucien, you are a bastard."

"You've been echoing that friendly sentiment since last Friday night. Really, don't fall all over yourself in sympathy with mom. She's the self-pitying sort herself; she's the masochistic sort who revels in that mother-lay-under-the-cross feeling whenever she bawls me out." He waved his hand impatiently in the air to dismiss the subject.

"At any rate," concluded Ginsberg a little self-consciously, "I hereby register a formal protest." He was silent. "Where to now?"

"We'll take a subway to the Village."

They rode down to Christopher Street, Lucien leading the way familiarly. "In just a minute you'll see Kammerer's gutter paradise—a bookstore, a bar, and a funeral parlor standing next to one another."

They emerged from the subway, bounding up the stairs, and turned down to Bleecker Street.

"*Voilà.*" Kammerer's house was typical of the lower class of village residencies. There was no porch—a few steps led to an iron grated door. Lucien opened this and went into the dirty antechamber. He pushed the large glass double door at the other side. It did not open; he grasped the round knob which turned loose without moving the catch. Bracing his shoulder against the door, he shoved roughly. It opened with a loud crash. "*Viens-toi.*" Walking down the long dimly lit hall; he faced the low, wide white door that led to Kammerer's room. As there was no answer to his knock, he kicked it violently, opening it.

Kammerer's room was low ceilinged and large. On one end was a Venetian window that looked over a can littered courtyard. A small writing table leaned against the wall at the end of the window. At the other end was a beaten white icebox, with no ice in it; through its open doors could be seen empty soda and whisky bottles. Near the icebox was a sink littered with bottle openers, a loaf of half eaten white bread, a knife, and strands of red hair. The sink was separated from the rest of the room by an ugly black partition which wavered precipitously over a collapsed but comfortable single sofa. Against the adjacent wall was a large open fireplace packed with newspapers, half burnt wood, cigarette butts, and bent burned wooden matches. On the top of the fireplace was an open copy of Rimbaud in which was placed a small drawing of a dark, windswept, swirling sea with a whorled rock jutting out of the waves. On the lower right of the picture was a small scrawled signature "Peter Genius. December 27, 1944." A tall, white candle lay beside the book, a few curled hairs sticking to its base, its length streaked and finger marked. Above the candle was a bent reproduction of [Franz] Hal's *Bohemian Girl* much like the one that hung neatly in Lucien's room in the dormitory. A single, half filled bookcase stood beside the fireplace and across the room from the fireplace a low daybed, permanently opened, ran parallel to the wall. Above the pillow, above Kammerer's sleeping head, a gap of paint had cracked from the plaster. In the spot was the heavily penciled inscription, "Lucien-David."

Lucien stood over the bed, staring down at Kammerer who was curled up against the wall. Lucien shook Kammerer's shoulder violently. The sleeper raised himself slowly waiting for his senses to awaken, and then rose and stretched.

"Hello, Lucien."

"I've brought Ginsberg down. We have the honor of showing him through the Village for the first time." Ginsberg bowed respectfully.

"Well, I'm glad to see you Lucien. I see you've washed the blood off your face. I'd rather hoped you'd keep it on as a souvenir."

"Souvenir of Rubenstein? Ha! he's best forgotten."

"Rubenstein! My heart's blood, that was mine you had smeared over you."

"Yours?" Lucien looked at him without interest.

"My heavens don't you remember what you were doing yesterday?" Kammerer unbuttoned the white shirt he had on and let it fall from his back, his arms still in the shirt sleeves. He turned. "Look" he laughed, motioning to his shoulder blades. His back was bruised, though not heavily, and on his shoulders were the still unclosed wounds of teethmarks. Lucien leaned over to touch them; Kammerer winced. "Those are your teeth."

"Really?" asked Lucien in amusement. "Why didn't you defend yourself like a man?" Kammerer laughed.

"Here that isn't all." He stretched out his hand—there was a strip of flesh hanging from the fleshy lower joint of his fingers.

"Well, well, have I been biting the hand that feeds me?"

Kammerer looked in the mirror, an amused smile playing on his face. He half mumbled, "Well, I suppose we can dispense with recriminations." Ginsberg looked on, not quite comprehending, feigning an attitude of entertained tolerance. "But I'm afraid Rubenstein isn't going to let us get away with our antics last night so easily."

"What do you expect him to do? Call the police?" Lucien asked, restraining his laughter.

"Oh, no. Nothing so impressive as that," smiled Kammerer. "He'll probably break in here tonight and set fire to the place."

"I suppose we'd best visit him and patch things up before he takes things too seriously," decided Lucien.

"Oh, he probably won't. He's too ineffectual to do anything really decisive." Kammerer looked up and stretched himself, moving to the icebox. "I'm thirsty." Lucien smiled. There was again the same conspiratorial attitude that Ginsberg sensed when he first met Kammerer. Was this obscene innuendo in Kammerer's statement that he was thirsty? Ginsberg smiled in embarrassment. Kammerer turned to the sink, washing himself and then urinating into it. "Where'll we take our friend?" asked Kammerer.

"Is Louise home?"

"No, she went out of town for Christmas."

Ginsberg looked up, half alarmed. "Is she a whore?" Lucien and Kammerer looked at each other, then laughed in unison. "My heavens, Ginsberg," mocked Kammerer, "Don't speak so disrespectfully of our acquaintances. We won't break you in so violently and so soon…nor in such a manner." Kammerer leaned his head to his shoulder and smiled at Ginsberg.

"Ginsberg in Wonderland" returned Ginsberg, "after all, I am only a fledgling. But." he continued as coolly as he could, "give me a little time to collect myself."

"Come on," said Lucien, "we'll visit Burroughs."

"I don't think William is home either." Kammerer put on his overcoat and turned out the light in his room.

They walked down Sixth Avenue silently, both Lucien and Ginsberg enveloped in their drunkenness. Ginsberg suddenly found himself seated at a clean table in the spacious, well lit cafeteria. There was a smell of alcohol and urination in the air; this was not surprising, inasmuch as the Waldorf Cafeteria was used as an all night rest room by most of the homeless derelicts that drifted aimlessly through the village. "Stay there," said Lucien. Ginsberg nodded blankly. "This is Peter Genius." Ginsberg looked up, hiccupped, and extended his hand to a youthful looking westerner with a red shirt and a great flowing head of hair. Ginsberg sat staring at his face blankly. He felt he must speak. "I rather liked that sketch of the phallic symbol on Kammerer's fireplace."

"Do you feel like vomiting?" asked Lucien almost tenderly.

"Of course not," declared Ginsberg resentfully.

"Come on," Lucien helped Ginsberg out of the door to the curb. "Lean over." Kammerer's face at the window of the cafeteria broke into a wide grin. Ginsberg tottered over the curb, regurgitating violently while Lucien stood shivering, urinating into the gutter under a car. Lucien finished and walked back into the cafeteria. He sat down at the table and stared around silently.

The ladies' room and the men's room had permanent 'out of order' signs on them. Lucien glanced in their direction and smiled drunkenly. Peter Genius handed over a bottle and he drank, only half tasting the contents. He began to feel now much less heavily nauseous and he began to mentally record what he saw. The old men, whose hats always looked too large for them. Long gray black hair, curling moustaches. Someone who might be called Armand Picola, a small, angular mustache, a large head of black hair, fatuousness written all over his face, which is being poorly sketched at the next table by a primly dressed artist. All the fatuousness of the large nose is being left out—three Russian intellectuals sitting around coffee. One drinking, the other arguing violently with the third who sits white faced with Mongolian boredom. A woman with large bust and a pig face and beautiful golden hair. She looks familiar. An old man staring at her tits. He has a prominent nose, and alligator-like expression. There's Arthur Koestler or something. He looks like a copy of the *Partisan Review*—heavy built, black turtle neck sweater, political intellectual type. Another fat faced, young, boorish expression pipe. Hundreds of red faced Bowery bums—white hair, dirty white unshaven faces, one pours over a neatly folded copy of the *Times*, another digs among the ruins of a *Journal American*— man carrying a large tray with a single cup of coffee on it with his change in the tray, threading among the tables inquisitively examining what passes at each, presumably looking for an empty seat. Oh, that large negress with big breasts. Painted up like Salome. Long soft, black beautiful hair. Surrounded by Broadway Sam types—felt hats, creased suits, Jewish noses, loud ties, talking about horses probably. Sailors looking for their ass. The waitress picking up plates at the table—recruited from the gutter. Tall angular, old aged, unshaven, nasty smelling, dressed in clean white uniform. If they're going to work why pick this dungpile? What's the housewife doing sitting at that table? Snot-nosed little kids walking in, too. No hair and all thin voiced obscene laughter. Ugh! a bridge of saliva hanging between the old bastard's coffee cup and his rotting mouth. Dirty fingered fifteen year olds. He's falling asleep over his crossword puzzle. Here's Jesus Christ with a red beard. Looks almost like Kammerer. "Hey where's Ginsberg. Let's go home, this is getting dull. Nothing but people."

Kammerer helped him rise from his chair. He went out to the curb. Ginsberg stood near the window glancing at the editorial page of the *Times*. Lucien leaned over and found Ginsberg at his side, laughing.

"I feel better," said Ginsberg.

"Let's go." He had not thrown up. "I can't crack my supper now."

Kammerer led them to the Christopher Street station and rode uptown with them. Ginsberg had begun to sober and began to chat amiably with Kammerer. Lucien sat between them, his head bowed over, sleeping, disturbed only by the slow jolting of the subway.

"How often does he do this?"

"Too often," replied Kammerer. "He drinks much too much."

"Listen to Mephisto talking," laughed Ginsberg.

"No, at this point I become guardian angel." Kammerer stroked Lucien's head and withdrew it when Lucien mumbled indistinguishably. "I try to keep him from too much drink. But then," Kammerer added wryly, "youth will have its way."

"Will you stay around here tonight?" They were walking up the dormitory stairs.

"I don't know, Ginsberg. Is there an extra bed around?"

Ginsberg hesitated, and then offered, "My roommate is away on vacation. You can use his." He began to worry if this were not dangerous, considering Kammerer's character, but then decided that Kammerer was well controlled.

"Thank you very much."

Lucien was half unconscious by this time. They lay him on his bed and took off his shoes and shirt.

[*Although this is a fictionalized account, halfway through this section of his novel, Ginsberg began using the characters' true names, instead of pseudonyms. The editors have substituted the characters' real names throughout the story to help keep the identities clear.*]

Death Scene

They lay on the grass, brooding drunkenly to each other…"And when I get there I'll jump off the train or the cab or the ponycart and run like hell to *Le Rive Gauche*…And I'll sit there shouting Rimbaud to the Frenchmen," said Lucien. "Who never heard of him," replied Kammerer. "Then Jack and I will introduce Rimbaud to France." Kammerer was stony by this mention of Jack. "What ship are you sailing with?" cried Kammerer.

Lucien put up his arm and patted Kammerer's hair: "Don't be trite." Groping for words, Kammerer rolled over on his stomach and leaned his face above Lucien. "Don't torture me." His savagery had melted to bitterness, then anguish. "I am going with you," he intoned decisively.

"The devil will carry the angel to France," said Lucien.

"The devil will carry two devils to France. I shall go, I shall go!" Lucien smiled indifferently and added, "Hell."

Kammerer gripped Lucien's arm, "I shall go with you or I shall go to hell."

"You have no choice as to <u>which</u> hell you will go to."

Kammerer released Lucien's arm and knelt staring down at Lucien's face, blurred and whitish in the dark. "You have that choice," he appealed tenderly.

Lucien laughed "I am not God."

"You are," Kammerer smiled sadly. "I love you."

"Well then I order you to go somewhere and have your repression in decency," replied Lucien meditatively, closing his eyes.

"No, *petit diable*, I shall go with you."

Kammerer, balked and despairing, cried, "You deny me, you deny me! You are life; you deny me!"

"Then commit suicide," laughed Lucien, concealing his disquietude.

"If I did that," Kammerer sneered bitterly, "it would be murder on your part."

"I am not responsible for you. I'm not your brother."

"You are my lover," implored Kammerer leaning down to his Lucien.

"I do not love you," declared Lucien, grimly, pushing Kammerer's face away with his arm. The touch of Lucien's cold hand upon Kammerer's cheek roused his desire.

"I love you Lucien," he seized Lucien's shoulder.

"No!" cried Lucien in guilt.

"Oh yes, oh, oh, yes." Kammerer clasped Lucien, circling his waist with his arm, "Yes, you will be loved."

"I am beloved, but I will not be loved." Lucien rolled sideways to free himself. "Let me free or I'll break your arm." He half desired to submit, he was tired, he was more lonely,

"As you break my heart." Kammerer withdrew his arm, and cried passionately, "But free me!" And now he leaned over again and touched Lucien's yellow hair, "I shall be free tonight and you shall free me."

"I cannot," muttered Lucien, resigned. Lucien started, frightened as Kammerer grasped his thigh and reached his fingers into his back pocket. In Kammerer's hand was Lucien's knife, small, innocent. Lucien looked up wildly, "Kammerer give it to me."

"Give me yourself as I <u>shall</u> give it to you." Lucien's face hardened "You are a fool." There was an impasse, he sensed that.

"I am a lover, therefore a fool." He opened the knife and extended it, handle forward to Lucien, who grasped it greedily.

His fingers clasped blade and handle and pressed blade to its socket, sitting down upon the grass.

"Do not close it, for now you must choose my defeat or my triumph." Lucien stared up startled. He understood Kammerer's design.

"You have promised me that if I desired death...you would kill me." Kammerer knelt at Lucien's side imploring, "Now you must choose."

"Choose what?" Lucien asked, feigning innocence.

"Choose to love me or to kill me."

"Choose which hell," smiled Kammerer, running his hand up and down Lucien's arm. He was calm and undisturbed now. "Choose to present me with your pecker or your knife. Which blade?" Lucien could not speak; he stared terrified and drawn. Passion flooded into Kammerer's bones as he drew Lucien's hard body to him, murmuring and smiling, now almost grimly. Lucien held up the knife in warning, afraid yet to speak. Kammerer stared into Lucien's eyes, calmly, inevitably clasping Lucien to him; suddenly his calm erupted into weeping as he saw Lucien's eyes maddened in conflicting ecstasies of fear and desire, revulsion and attraction, hatred and love, wish and well, emotion and counter-emotion, open and close, straining their sight, blinking the confused turbulence of the body they mirrored. Lucien's eyes filled with tears; he didn't understand what was being done—he merely, waveringly, indecisively, raised his knife and pointed it to Kammerer's breast. Kammerer pressed on, crushing Lucien's body toward him, crushing the knife to his body, crushing death into his life. Lucien suddenly wrenched himself free, maddened with hatred and remorse. He drew out the knife violently and suddenly plunged into his lover's breast deeper than before, startled with himself, with his lover, with his knife. Kammerer still kneeled, his eyes closed, tears running down his furrowed cheek into his mouth. He lost his balance and fell heavily, attempting to sustain himself, face to face with Lucien. Lucien leaned over, overpowered by remorse, unable to speak.

Kammerer blinked, startled, at what had happened, all at once realizing that he was wounded. He had taken his death for granted once he felt the sharpness of the knife press back and enter his skin, and in taking death for granted he had lost all sight or consciousness of it, other than an automatic responsive sadness. Suddenly his mind grasped the idea that was in his heart, and his mind rebelled, shocked and frightened. "Lucien," he mumbled, "Why did you do it?" He heard a frightened voice somewhere reply, "But you made me." Lucien's voice and heart overpowered Kammerer and he lost all thought of fear; "I forgive you." Lucien was stroking Kammerer's hair red as the blood on his chest, Lucien's testicles enwrapping eternity, loving him, and hating him and at the same time dying of him.

Lucien Carr:

Sexual inadequacy leads him to assertion of artistic:

    1.) Compensation

    2.) Sublimation

    3.) Sexual assertion

Repressed artistry leads him to:

    1.) Further sexual inadequacy

    2.) Sublimation into life

    3.) Compensation in bohemianism

    4.) Fears of artistic sterility

Sadistic Tendencies:

    1.) Exploitiveness

    2.) Active hostility (not reactive)

    3.) Criticism

degrading

    humiliating

    enslaving

    parish-priest

    domination

    hurtfulness

    also: guilt

Today the Dean called my novel "smutty,"[123] and termed Jean-Luis Kerouac a "lout." The road to hell is paved with good intentions.

The thick Christmas winds wound around the corners, buffeting Carr and Ginsberg—two heavy, aged bums shivered in the doorway of the grocery on the corner. They crouched in the door, putting their faces out of reach of the wind. They shared a bottle of denatured alcohol between them.

    "Hey!" Carr turned. Ginsberg held back.

    "Have a gulp of smoke. Do you good." Carr bounded into the doorway.

---

123 Steeves, *op. cit.* Ginsberg took a writing tutorial from Steeves, who was also his adviser. Ginsberg had been working on a novel based on the Kammerer-Carr affair, but Steeves did not like the idea and discouraged him from continuing. He thought it would turn unwanted attention on the college. The criticism stung Ginsberg, and he quit work on the novel.

"Hey, Allen!" Ginsberg came forward.

"Is that all you've got? I'm not used to smoke."

"Well, we'd been saving this." The taller reached at a bottle of whisky that stuck out of his pocket. It was half emptied. He looked at it carefully appreciating the label and opened it. He worked his fingers on the cold bottle neck. He breathed heavily and constantly sniffed the nasal inhalation of the drunkard. He wheezed heavily and then coughed, handing the bottle to Lucien.

"*Merci!*" Lucien sniffed at the bottle and took a heavy gulp.

"You're welcome, son."

"Good stuff."

"Of course, I got it from a friend of mine." He smiled impishly and wheezed. "I got pull. Want some?" He looked to Ginsberg.

"Thanks!" Ginsberg took the bottle. He made a motion to wipe the top and then dropped his hand and took some of the whisky in his mouth.

"It is good," he said.

"Thank you, son." The bum looked at the label and took another gulp. Then he fastidiously tightened the cap and placed the bottle in his pocket. He stared silently in the cold at Lucien and Ginsberg and then patted the bottle gently.

"A man gets lonely."

"Goodnight," they all said.

He sat down, his back against the door and said, "You're welcome." They turned and walked across the lamplit corner.

1945

February 2, 1945.

[Dream]: Dream of first complete physical contact with beloved. I was active; she completely passive. I muff dived, taking the trinity in my mouth completely; she seemed to have adolescent organs, hairless.

Dream: Kerouac and I sat in booth in the center of Hamilton Hall hallway [at Columbia University]. Weaver[124] passed by. Kerouac engaged him in conversation, told him to bring a certain essay to him. Weaver recalcitrant, Kerouac aped Weaver's highly intellectualized infantile reactions. I was shocked to see

---

124 Raymond Weaver (1888–1948). Herman Melville's first biographer and one of Ginsberg's English professors at Columbia.

Jack Kerouac and Allen Ginsberg in the snow on Morningside Heights, 1945

Kerouac so cavalierly treat Weaver the sadist. Weaver smilingly obeyed him and came back with two manuscripts—an essay and a combination of *God's Daughter* by Kerouac and my turtle-ark poem. Weaver handed me the manuscripts which he had torn to scraps. I wanted to protest. Kerouac brow-beat Weaver who seemed to be under his power. I objected mildly.

Analysis: Fear of Weaver; dreams brought on by my taking Weaver next term. Wish fulfillment—that Weaver might respect me as friend of Kerouac.

Saturday, February 3, 1945.
Afternoon Dream. I was fighting with either an Italian or Kammerer or Burroughs—somewhat stupid, very friendly. He wounded me in the arm with a scimitar (somewhat in the spot where M[orphine] was injected). Blood began to gush out in a thin, wide stream from the wound. It was revealed to him that I was the son of God; I was not surprised. He held me in his arms proud to be chosen the instrument of my sacrifice. As the blood gushed, it became thinner and more transparent, till it seemed to look like white glycerin that was flowing from the bright red wound. Petroleum! So this was the way I was to benefit the world in death!

The two of us were in a dark little side room off a great big place, something like a cathedral or Pennsylvania Station. The petroleum flowed out of the side room and coursed through the back room down the steps which led from it to the main waiting room or cathedral. My friend exclaimed, "There'll be at least 20,000 barrels of this by tomorrow morning sunk in the ground around here."

As I lay dying, I heard the shouts of the vulgar multitude below on Times Square, celebrating New Year's Eve or Christmas, my holiday. They did not know of the portentous drama that was being played above them in the great lobby of the stock exchange at Wall Street, for this was what my cathedral-waiting room was. We would finally be vindicated for I was still the son of God. My mother, God's wife, was to approach. He picked me up, my friend and killer, and moved me from the spot in the side room, where I had been killed, to the spot where my altar was kept.

X = where killed
1 = my organ
2 = mother's organ
3 = God's organ
4 = entrance to Stock Exchange

We were hiding my sacrifice from Naomi, wife of God, my mother. She came into the chapel, went straight to her altar, which was a musical organ. We gods used the organs to direct and control, etc. She seemed to occupy a mystical position, had occult esoteric knowledge of the use of the organ which even I did not attain. She knew all and extricated me from my hiding place. I watched the bankers at the stock exchange arrive for a glimpse of the petroleum which was their salvation. I saw one banker whisper into another's ear, guessing with a gloating smile at the prices my blood would bring. I saw it as wonderful, hateful, irony.

A beggar cat knew me on the sidewalk and looked into my silent eyes, spoke of her melancholy in many muted whines. And when I stopped to touch her she first shrank and then, accepting my caresses, she gnawed upon my hand and wounded me with her claws.

Oh beloved! Tell me, why you maddened me with your mystical loneliness, and then as I caressed you with my love you left your claws in my heart?

Fetishes:
 The West End
 Pernod
 People
 The Rack
 Clothes (sweater, shirt)
 Shaving
 Music (Brahms, Mahler)
 The Face-mask
 Knives
 Greenwich Village—Burroughs at 48 Morton Street,[125] stores, alleys

[*Excerpt from a letter written by Ginsberg's father Louis to Lionel Trilling dated February 21, 1945.*]

"Allen, whom I am trying to appraise objectively, is a brilliant youngster, precious intellectually, but lagging, I fear, emotionally. He dramatizes himself as a writer, though he does have some potentialities.

At present, he is making clever but false verbal rationalizations that the

---

125 David Kammerer was living at 48 Morton Street at the time of his death.

immoralist way of life (à la Gide, I think) is a valid one. He thinks merely to rationalize some inner tendency proves a satisfactory way of life, harmonious with what we might term normal values. He seeks to philosophize abnormality into normality. I am not sure whether I make myself clear to you.

Since Allen holds you in high esteem and places great value on your dicta, I wonder whether, if it is not inconvenient for you, I might meet you. I feel that you could exert a salutary influence on Allen, who, by the way, has fallen in with some undesirable friends."

[*Ginsberg has copied a letter from his brother Eugene to his father Louis dated March 1945 into his notebook at this point.*]

"Your news about Allen was very entertaining, especially about his degeneration and reform. Tell him I'm beginning to wonder whether it might not have been better for the army to have knocked some sense into him. It's kind of silly to be frivolous, sloppy, and affected, when only the opposite qualities make for success no matter in what branch of affairs. But I guess he's sensible at heart."

This is a lesson to me! I shall no longer be childish and silly; I shall surpass my brother's realism. Henceforth I will be a jewel thief and be a success in life.

The basic virtues [and] the base vices (in order of importance):

1.) Consciousness	1.) Complacence and Madness
2.) Stoicism	2.) Sniveling; Base Prometheanism; Satanism
3.) Charity	3.) Niggardliness
4.) Love	4.) Neurotic Antipathy
5.) Action	5.) Quietism

Now: I am virtuous of 1, 4

I am vice: 2, 3, 5

Are Love and Consciousness antithetical? Are Action and Consciousness antithetical?

This is the second rough version of the "New Vision," finished March–April 1945. It is contained in poetic form, though somewhat bastardized by false sentiments, in the poem "Last Voyage."

The "New Vision" is in a sense the product of a strictly rationalized system. In it I affirm the power of the mind's reconstructed intelligence. The nineteenth century saw the agonized reaction to rationalism and its implications. The heart was unable to adjust its beat to the universal silence conceived by the mind. Morality remained sans theology. The morality, false as explained in the divisions between the ideal-mores classification and the archetypal naturalism. The first reaction to disillusionment took the form of Satanism. It was an affirmation of evil for its own sake; partly as an antidote to soporific moralization, partly out of confused tribute to the old ideas of good and evil: Baudelaire. The poetic Dionysiac, providing a faith of creation, was established for me by Rimbaud. He outgrew this gratuitous and confused infusion of principles into the universe. Nihilism followed the disillusionment of the poet, who conceived of himself as the amoral, creative, orphic deity! Nietzsche was a representative, with Rimbaud, of the anarchic poetic Dionysiac archetypal individual—the poet, or artist, or general superman.

The new vision lies in a highly conscious comprehension of universal motives and in a realistic acceptance of an unromantic universe of flat meaninglessness.

Kerouac is a romantic deluded poet. Burroughs is a realist, interesting himself in sociology as an entertainment. Joan Adams[126] has high consciousness—she chooses to live forsaking ambition and pride.

Keys: Supreme Reality—the real universe.
         High Consciousness—worthy thought.
         Dilettantism—action, life.

Rimbaud went through all of this, refusing to pursue art as an unconscious devotee. He preferred to live in the realities accepting them as inevitable. Art for art's sake is a delusion. The Satanist, the moralist, the poet, the politician are all poor fools. Only the dilettante is the exemplar of realism.

[May 10, 1945.]

Burroughs walks into 51;[127] greets Allen;

---

126 Joan Vollmer Adams (1924–1951). Intelligent friend and later the second wife of W. S. Burroughs.

127 51. Joan Adams' apartment at 419 W. 115th St. where most of the nascent Beats hung out between 1945 and 1946.

Joan Vollmer Adams, 1945 © ALLEN GINSBERG TRUST.

> Says "Hello [Hal] Chase," shiftily, and walks
> into the living room; Kerouac is lying
> on the floor reading; Burroughs walks over
> and taps him lightly with his foot; prods him
> to see if he is still perhaps alive or conscious.

Eating squids with Chase and Celine in Italian restaurant on 19th Street, Chase's description of "waiting maidens," sandstorms in Nevada, sand tornadoes, etc. on mountain, hearing voices in the valley.

Curiosity is the only thing that keeps me from suicide.

Factual information to be obtained:
1. Diseases: Causes—heart, cancer, death wish.
2. Neurosis symptoms in classes.
3. Physical effect of activity—burning out of active men.
4. Statistics on:
   a. Neurosis
   b. Drinking
   c. Gambling
   d. Sex
   e. Dope
   f. Criminals—from what classes / psychic state of

CULTURAL TYPES TO INVESTIGATE
1. Bars
   a. Queer bars: Main Street Bar, MacDougal's, Astor Men's Bar, Cerudis', Ralph's, Beggar's, Jimmy's (43rd), Tony Pastor's
   b. Sports, gamblers, gangster, hoodlum bars: Bar across from Madison Square, Tiptop, 43rd St., Sammy's, Chinatown
   c. Bowery bars: Sammy's
   d. Old men's bars: 8th Ave. near 48th St.
   e. Intellectual's bars: West End, Minetta's, George's, Beggar's, Village.
   f. Bars of chaos: West End, Paterson bars.
   g. Dilettante, rich bars, night clubs: Stork, night clubs.
   h. Jazz bars: White Rose, Vanguard, George's, Downbeat, Harlem, etc.
   i. Irish bars: Riordan's (60th St.)

2. People
    a. Newspapermen—wise guys
    b. Hoodlums (small)—hat up, morose, sadistic
    c. Gamblers—natty, wise, sharp
    d. Policemen—drunk, sadistic, Irish, foolish
    e. Gangsters (middle)—scars, alert, nasty, practical
    f. Jews—Brooklyn, rich, poor, West End Avenue
    g. Broadway Sams—middle aged, sharp
    h. Fags—aesthetical, ballet, social, literary, bums, village, parasitical, rich middle aged, Army colonels

May 12, 1945.

Dream in Paterson: I am in an apartment house, well-furnished and large and modernistic. The German war is over. My father and grandmother or mother are with me. There is an air raid alarm. Father gets his warden's helmet. I look out the window. I see the wooded earth spread out before my window; I am at a great height. It looks like a no-man's land, like Central Park in the night. Bombs descend in the forest, crashing and disturbing the streams that flow sinuously in the moonlight. Gas. I want a mask, but have none. I feel the stickiness of mustard gas eating at my flesh, and smell the acrid chlorine. I wrap a dishtowel on my face, and plan to wet a bed with water and crawl under the tent of soaked thick covers.

May 29, 1945.

[Dream]: I am riding in a car with Phil driving, others in back. We come to a railway crossing [in the dark]. Phil and I go under the railroad bridge, where he flashes his flashlight under a R.R. sign. I see half dollars. I pick them up, this is the first time I've found money, realizing the wish of my dream. I take somebody's girl (Helen Brody[128]) or Celine tenderly round the waist, lead her to the car.

Hal and I are talking about marijuana. He has half a cigarette, lights it, gives me a puff. I have the sensation in my dream. I invite him to my room. He says "How will I explain this to Celine?"

May 30, 1945.

[Dream]: I come to the party with the football. Lou Little[129] is sitting at his desk surrounded by attaché cases. A crowd is around. I throw the ball to those stand-

128 Helen Brody (*a.k.a.* Harriett). Ginsberg's eighteen-year-old girlfriend whom he took to cultural events, such as the ballet. At the time, he described her as having "overdeveloped breastworks."
129 Lou Little (1893–1979). Head football coach at Columbia when Kerouac was on the team.

ing in the room, which we are using as a football field. I get on one team. The game begins and at the first play, I run to the end of the field. The rest of the team skirmish properly. This is completely the wrong thing for me to have done; I feel embarrassed but defiant as I do when I pull a boner in gym. Someone on the team reproaches me resentfully. Just because I brought the ball for them to play I have no right to stick myself on the team. As I don't know how to play, I'd just as soon get off the team. But everybody's making a big stink. Louis [Ginsberg] is trying to explain things to Lou Little. Louis does not defend my integrity, but just pleads my youth. I tell Lou Little what's in my mind and scram the team. Somehow I feel injured; I make no motion to take back my ball; I do not even feel that I should have it back; I suspect however that they owe me something.

May 30, 1945.

Codeine Dream: Jack and I were waiting to meet Auden.[130] Then Jack decided to go without me. He walked out on the Ozone Park road. I picked up the baggage and ran forward, loaded down with Kerouac's weights, to his side. He looked down contemptuously and said nothing. I asked him if I could walk with him on the long road and he seemed to assent, but made no move to help me carry the weight. Finally we sat down at a little table on the chromium road. Kerouac said we were to meet Auden there. I was happy that he was going to let me meet Auden anyway.

Hal Chase came up [and began a conversation with] Kerouac. They each seemed to be drinking ice-water. Jack gave me their glasses and asked me if I would go to the cafeteria for them. I looked at him and nodded yes, feeling wounded. The cafeteria was a monster place and I got on the crowded line, which began on desserts. I remember seeing big soup plates of colored Jell-O. I picked a small dish with a little circle of Jell-O. I grab and eat some chocolate marshmallow cookies without the attendants' knowledge. Meanwhile, I rack my brains to remember what I was supposed to get for Jack and Hal. I reach the cashier's booth and present my tray, feeling that I've forgotten something. I give the cashier a half-dollar; he gives me 45¢ back, keeps a nickel. I ask if I can go back on line to finish my assignment. I explain that I want nothing much for myself, but have to make a second trip to get something for a friend. Then I notice my Jell-O has disappeared. The cashier tells me that it's merely turned into junket[131] in such a way as to indicate that though it's still good with changed color, I deserve it free.

---

130 W. H. Auden (1907–1973). British expatriate poet who spent much of his life in New York.
131 Flavored milk and rennet pudding.

Dream: Shipyard, Jack, poem. Tie poem on mast as he had done on mine.

> "Here I walked in shining terror and
> To view the city's shadow dance
> To wound the city with my glance."

[ca. July 28, 1945.]
Cher Breton:
... *A moi*—Tomorrow morning, all the preliminaries having been dispensed with, I shall sign into the Merchant Marine. *Incipit vita nuova!* Monday [July 30] I shall leave for Sheepshead Bay, where I hope to tutor myself anew in all these strange realities I have learned from the purgatorial season.

Your letter came to me after I returned from a fruitless journey into New York to recapture the grandeur of another time, and it came, almost, as a letter from the past, and conjured up in me all the emotions I had been seeking the days before.

But, Jack, rest assured that I shall return to Columbia. Bill never advised me to stray from the fount of higher learning! I should return, however, to finish college, even if it were only a pilgrimage of acceptance of former time.

I hear from Celine from time to time; I saw her two weeks ago. I'll probably see her before I leave. Hal has returned to Denver for the summer (a week ago.) Nothing from Joan or John. I still see Trilling from time to time, he's invited me to his house (yes, I received the invitation, I acknowledge, with my usual pleasure at such things.) I hope I hear from you from Paris; at any rate, please write when you get back to the U.S., before you leave for California.

[Excerpt from letter Ginsberg wrote to Trilling in early September (before the fourth) 1945 while training with the U.S. Maritime Service in Brooklyn.]

"I'm pretty well acclimatized to the situation; my passport to this corner of reality was a copy of *Batman*, which I purchased for a dime to insure my status as a regular fellow. This is a good place for contemplation and creative work, though, because each one here is almost isolated from the present chaos by his past, notwithstanding the initial hysteria of 'comradeship,' which runs the gamut of masks from a sort of hebetative obscenity to an equally obscene sense of bewilderment and all 'visions' and all values are suspended, at least temporarily, because they are simply and decisively out of place.

I brought here my beloved Rimbaud and an edition of Hart Crane, and a handbook of yoga, but I haven't much chance to read, though I do write a lot of prose now, my shipmates on this boat are much too friendly and interesting to forsake.

You have a copy of a longer poem that I gave you; since then I've written a number of more polished sonnets, and I'd like to send them to you if you have time to look them over. My father and I differ so violently on poetic method that I hesitate to ask him for advice and criticism.
Meanwhile, I am very happy here."

[*This excerpt is from a letter that Ginsberg wrote to Trilling from the Merchant Marine Training Center Hospital, Sheepshead Bay, Brooklyn, on September 4, 1945.*]

"I have been confined to the base hospital here with pneumonia in my chest for the past few weeks. Thank you for your criticism of the poem with the portentous title ["The Last Voyage"]. I must admit that it pleased me to read all those nice things you wrote about it, but to tell the truth I have only a hazy idea of what you mean by 'the voice and its tone', which you admire in poetry. As for rhyme, I usually try to make an extremely loose rhyme do if necessary where I can and find one that fits, and that I have no compunction about this because I'm increasingly pleased by the effect of the sort of 'muted' rhymes of Auden and Cummings. So I would rhyme 'touched' and 'watched' and 'flesh' and 'death' or even 'birth' and 'death'—to use some more obvious situations. I wasn't aware of Shelley while writing, though I aimed at a violent semi-cerebral rhetoric. I found a copy of Shelley here (incidentally I have been reading *War and Peace* during my convalescence, with great pleasure) and on re-reading *Mont Blanc* I found the language much akin to my own desire.

That you are unable to understand why I make so much of Rimbaud, dismays me somewhat. Though I should dislike to be over bumptious about it, with your kind permission I must witness his defense. I think of Rimbaud as a hero in the sense of having a violent, varied—and finally mature—response to a fairly representative social situation. I admire Rimbaud not as the *poet maudit*, the decadent, but the representative hero, the sociologically concerned, and in the highest manner politically minded poet.

Season In Hell seems to me the most individually expressive poetry I have run across—more than any poet, I can understand the personality—half childish, half sardonic, somewhat sentimental, furious, jealously personal and strikingly dispassionate—from the poetry. I mean, it is so compressed and flexible that it contains whole visions in a single line. To me it is pretty clearly the work of genius, and so despite your lack of enthusiasm I continue to admire Rimbaud unabashedly.

Batman is second on the best seller list of semi-literate America. He is the sustaining feature of *Batman* magazine, a rival of Action Comics, in which Superman hangs out. Everyone here reads comic books, it is a fixed part of the mores."

1946

[*The following is from a letter Ginsberg wrote to Trilling on January 7, 1946, while on board the* S.S. Groveton.]

I enclose a poem ["Ode to Decadence"] I've been working on for about three months which has absorbed most of my literary energy in the time.

I finally pushed myself to sail again after the first abortive Venezuelan journey. The ship I am on is a new tanker with a type of romantic young captain—a sort of narcissistic Nietzschean, aristocrat and master of his ship, a man of silences. The chief steward (under whom I work) is also rather interesting—a kind of weather-beaten Prufrock with a predilection for pornographic literature (I had a long talk with him about the Marquis de Sade and another little volume I'd not heard of before called *Lady Bumtickler's Revels*) and scatological anecdotes. The rest of the crew is half negro—all of whom are dope addicts of one sort or another. Then there are a few Texans, sturdy Westerners, and a sprinkling of Cubans and multilingual Swedish seadogs.

The vocabulary of the part of the enclosed poem beginning "Right around the block is Huncke's[132] pad" may be unfamiliar to you. It is a sort of jive talk I found in use among the "Hepcats" and dope addicts on both of the ships I've been on—and it is also prevalent in the "Underworld" of New York, especially around Times Square. I was first hesitant to use it, but in the last few years I've heard it from so many various lips that I think it is a very wide-

---

132 Herbert Huncke (1915–1996). One of Ginsberg's close friends, Huncke was instrumental in introducing the Beats to the drug and underworld scene around Times Square. He later wrote several books including *The Evening Sun Turned Crimson*.

Ginsberg in the Merchant Marines

spread and semi permanent in an extremely complicated culture. As such it is in a way—the use, that is—formally justified by the Wordsworth essay.

I'm bound for Louisiana (*sans* banjo but with a lyre)—possibly New Orleans. Right now I'm in the middle of the Gulf of Mexico, in Hart Crane seas, amid "adagios of islands" and proverbial sunblue seas. Really, I do enjoy sailing in these tropical waters, in watching the stars, in inventing fabulous romances on the prow of the ship as she bounces forward. I did get seasick about three days out of New York, at which time I experienced what must have been at least one of the most agonizing depressions known to man— the universe dwindled to a succession of trivial absurdities, chief of which was the pointless voyage of a group of useless men on an empty ship, not yet sure where they were going and having no real interest in destination—all of this involved in a seesaw nausea and a desire to return to the womb.

> I buy a copy of *Batman*[133]
> which is my passport to reality
> and costs a dime. I am one of the Boys.
> Visions and values exist
> but are mostly gratuitous, inoperative here.
> Each head can circumscribe a separate universe,
> and Berkeley has come true.
> The metaphysics of the petty officer
> outranks each isolate cosmology.
> Yet one must talk: to bitch, to gripe,
> to find a refuge from a premonition of reality.
> Obscenity is false but necessary.

[*The following note in Ginsberg's notebook is in his father's handwriting.*]

April 25, 1946.
Dear Allen,
Meet me and Eugene Sunday night at 5:30 P.M. on the corner of W. 18th St. and 8th Ave.[134] We'll go for supper to a good Jewish restaurant on the East Side.
Louis

133 *Batman.* Popular comic book character. Ginsberg refers to the "Boys," his fellow shipmates, who accepted him because he read comic books just like they did.
134 Ginsberg's mother Naomi had separated from his father Louis and was living in an apartment building at 319 W. 18th Street. Both Allen and his brother Eugene stayed at her apartment from time to time and it is obvious from this note to meet on the corner of the block that Louis didn't feel comfortable meeting his sons at Naomi's apartment.

March–April 1946 [Reading List].
Rimbaud, Arthur. *A Season in Hell.* Buy

Aiken, Conrad. *Preludes to Memnon* and *Time in the Rock* and *Brownstone Eclogues*

Ransom, John Crowe. *Selected Poems* and *Chills and Fever,* 1924. *Two Gentlemen in Bonds,* 1927. New Criticism (skipped over)

Jacobson, Edmund. *You Must Relax*

Freud, Sigmund. *Leonardo Da Vinci, a study in psychosexuality*

Kafka, Franz. *The Trial*

Muir, Edwin. *A Kafka Miscellany*

Crane, Hart. *The Bridge*

Horton, Philip. *Hart Crane, the life of an American poet*

Transition Magazine. 1928–30 (reviewed)

Crane, Hart. Prose in *Twice A Year,* no. 12/13 (1945) p. 424–452

Spender, Stephen. *Ruins and Visions* and *Vienna* and *The Still Centre* and *Destructive Element* (looked over)

Tate, Allen. *Selected Poems*

Thomas, Dylan. *18 Poems* and *New Poems 1942*

Roberts, Bechhofer. *Paul Verlaine* (p. 73–152)

Rimbaud, Arthur. *Lettres de la Vie Littéraire* (Jean-Marie Carré edition)

Rimbaud, Arthur. *Lettres de Jean-Arthur Rimbaud* (Berrichon edition, 1898)

Finney, Charles G. *The Circus of Dr. Lao*

Capek, Karel. *War with the Newts*

Auden, W.H. *Another Time*

Rilke, Rainer Maria. *Sonnets to Orpheus*

Mallarme, Stephane. (Roger Fry translation) *Poems*

Butler, E.M. *Rainer Maria Rilke*

Lewis, Alun. *Ha! Ha! Among the Trumpets, poems*

Eliot, T.S. *The Family Reunion*

Connolly, Cyril. *The Unquiet Grave*

May 1946 [Reading List].

Camus, Albert. *The Stranger*

Sinclair, Jo. *Wasteland*

Eliot, T.S. *Four Quartets*

Rilke, Rainer Maria. [*Sonnets to Orpheus*]. Translated by M.D. Herter Norton

Williams, Oscar. *The War Poets*

Welch, Denton. *In Youth Is Pleasure*

Perse, Saint-Jean. *Anabasis, a poem;* essay by S.A. Rhodes / *Éloges* (translated
    by Louise Varèse); *Exile* (limped thru); also his *Pluies* (translated by Denis
    Devlin) Bibliography

McNiece, Louise. *The Poetry of W.B. Yeats*

Isherwood, Christopher. *The Berlin Stories* and *Prater Violet*

Howe, J.B. *William Butler Yeats* (biography)

Menon, V.K. *The Development of William Butler Yeats*

Yeats, William Butler. *A Vision; Collected Poems; Last Ideas of Good and Evil; The
    Autobiography of William Butler Yeats* (parts)

[*The following are excerpts from a letter from Ginsberg to Trilling dated June 27, 1946.*]

I have been shipping again on a collier—carrying coal between Norfolk, New
York and Boston. I am sailing for the Mystic Steamship Co., incidentally,
which is pleasing, though it doesn't make the coal dust any less filthy.

   I finished another long poem—30 pages of hexametric elegies (eight of
them) topped off by a "celebration" and an epilogue ["Death in Violence"].
I've hacked and revised sufficiently for typewriting but the more I consider it
the more it strikes me as a sort of white elephant. I think it's the best poetry
I have written but the whole affair fails to satisfy me, or rather, depresses me
when I reapproach it. I haven't written anything for the last two months, and
I don't think I shall want to write very much in the future, which may
explain my feeling toward the last poem. In a way of speaking, I am closing
my accounts with poetry.

   I have been rereading [Yeats' "A Vision"] in the last few weeks. Studying
the "Vision," which has been difficult for me to assimilate and it is a book I
should like to master completely.

June–July 1946 [Reading List], Aboard S.S. Jagger Seam.
Céline, Louis-Ferdinand. *Death on the Installment Plan*

Yeats, William Butler. *The Vision* (from Jerry Rauch)

De Stendhal. *Rouge et Noir*

Trilling, Lionel. *Matthew Arnold*

Dostoyevsky, Fyodor. "The Thief" (and others, *One Hundred Best Short Stories,* Vol. 8)

Mann. *The Beloved Returns, Lotte in Weimar* (from Joan Adams)

Vercors. *The Silence of the Sea* ([from] Bill Burroughs)

July 13, [1946].
A Dream, aboard *S.S. Jagger Seam:* I am on a ship, white, going to college in the South Seas, preparatory to returning to Columbia. I am in a round bed with my father and some young woman (Jerri Lust). We talk, then surprisingly, under my father's <u>nose</u>, she either passes me a note or says: the context "Shall we now abandon ourselves to the lusts of the flesh and the freedoms of satanic delight?" I look upon her cynically and say, "Don't be ridiculous." [In the left margin Ginsberg has written: "The deaf and dumb aggressors at Bickford's[135] last night. Invitation to fight. My reply to the blind."] As I move in to her she responds surprisingly quickly. I clasp her and she rolls over, undulating, in a smooth bump. In her embrace I am impotent, though I kiss her breasts. My cock is on her pubic hair, limp. I do not particularly feel ashamed, but I am a trifle disappointed. Then the dream becomes a curious technicolor opium-type *rêve* of an oriental dance between us, our bodies meeting, curving and gliding slowly and evenly about each other's. The postures are impossible, as if I slid headfirst between her legs and came up to meet her face; and as if our faces met side by side and glided off in a curve intertwining with our arms in symmetry and continuing so with many variations. [In the margin beside this, Ginsberg has written: "I am penis in white body. She has none, head in place of penis. woman castrates man. Like the English documentary [film] short of plants growing (accelerated)"]

I leave her and end the dance to join the company of young [John Crowe?] Ransom and Walter Adams. Ransom wants to know if I've heard from his

---

135 Bickford's. Popular cafeteria near Times Square. Ginsberg worked there for a few days and was a long-time patron.

father lately. (There is a confusion between the letter of Ransom's and those of McKnight).[136] I see he has some family reason for wanting to know: perhaps he wants news of his father, who doesn't write to him. I offer to show him the letters and invite Walter along. I am proud to be of intimate value to Ransom: as I say to him, "Nothing like making a member of the Adams family," with an intended slip-jest on 'making'. When I woke I realized that the other slip was substituting Adams for Ransom.

July 16, [1946] at anchor Kearney [New Jersey]. S.S. Jagger Seam.
I visited Columbia last night, by passing my brother's room on 18th Street. Searched around for someone to be sociable with, finally met Ann de la Vergne on Broadway. She told me that a mutual acquaintance had seen L.C. [Lucien Carr] in Chicago. I was frightened and incoherent for a while. Then I forgot it mostly until this morning, when I tossed in my bunk for an hour in melancholy rumination. This is the real testing point: the climax of cure and the downfall of neurosis. I resented his being at large without my knowledge. I must write a pretty note to Mrs. Carr inquiring about L.'s fate. My impulse was to write some poetry to be published where he could see it, if in Chicago, and communicate to him thereby. Perhaps he would respond. Poem: "Address to an Old Friend." What are you doing, waiting on the street corner of another city, attending a vision? No, waiting in ennui for a streetcar. Ennui is an overused word.

The breaking point of the neurosis is in these present intentions—how will they arise? The conscious mastery of the soul which I have achieved strikes me as here being artificial; a suppression of desire rather than a change. Is this mastery or an alteration the desired end of analysis? I saw myself relapse into the masochistic fantasies of yesteryear. Also I must write Bill [Burroughs] in St. Louis. What shall I ask him? What do I want? Either the poetic somber lover, or the self-contained, flexible, spontaneous picaresque "man of action."

I think I must try to write the end of the summer. This journal is, at least, a beginning in prose; although it has no literary value from a technical point of view. I allow myself slipshod expression and confused motivation, which should not do for a novel.

Also I must continue to study psychology. Neurosis is a <u>serious</u> affair. "He can be a serious danger to mankind." After complete exhaustion of neurosis, the renovation of the personality, I shall be free to continue to strike out in new

136 Nicholas M. McKnight. Assistant Dean at Columbia.

objective branches of psychology. As it is, I assume that the more esoteric func-
tions of the mind cannot be controlled without control of the simpler moti-
vations of personality. But upon attainment of "grace, as the psychoanalyzed
man, I shall have to extend my knowledge of the processes of mind: relax-
ation, levels of thought (visual, auditory, sensual), memory, dreams, hypnosis,
telepathy, and the states of the soul.

I returned Yeats' *Vision* to Rauch, having at last finished it. I must master
this system.

The dream that followed perturbation is lost mostly. I only remember
being in Chicago or somewhere with someone who was supposed to be L.C.
[Lucien Carr]. In this, I remember as I noticed when I awoke, I was a young
girl, such as may be found in the nineteenth century writers: Tolstoi, Austen,
Mann—dressed in a white frock. [In the margin AG has written: "Lottchen in
The Beloved Returns, a portentous title"] This is indeed an unpleasant reversal of
what I have assumed to be my psychic change—am I crossing the bridge,
descending the tower? Or are these other dreams merely artificial vanities flat-
tering to conscious desire?

There was also some reference to my father. Carr as father image was the
only thing I can get out of it, and that is so vague as to be useless.

A Reading Schedule:

Ezra Pound—Poems and "Culture"

T.S. Eliot's *Essays*

O. Williams. *Golden Treasury of Modern Verse*

Hoffman. *The Little Magazines*

Bill's letter to Jack: He sounds almost grey and desperate: Kells Elvin "For
my share in this $1,000,000 project, I would take $5,000 cash." His letters con-
tain long tireless instruction on how to send the stuff (junk). The feeling insists
on the fact that now I am sure he should stop or be made to kick the habit. Joan
tells me the story of Phil White's[137] friend who went to Washington to kick
the habit. Phil immediately received money and a letter asking for stuff. Phil
didn't send it for some reason or other, and the character in Washington was
so sick he committed suicide. Bill has avowed in the past that such a thing as
suicide would be unthinkable for him—as something of spontaneous origin in
the soul—except under circumstances of prolonged physical torture. He is not

---

137   Phil White. Junkie and thief, one of Herbert Huncke's associates.

impressed by the likeness between psychic despair and physical torture, since the despair, briefly, is usually of a neurotic origin, that is, is not an authentic, but an imposed reaction, to externals. This is true in most cases of contemporary madness: angst is encouraged by the culture. Where is the man free and healthy who will create his own world?

Ezra Pound's poem (1907) *Endurance*: "I am homesick after mine own kind."

July 18, [1946]. At sea:

Last night encore I visited Columbia. Joan is looking more starved and is slightly battier. I walked in and found her at the window in Sal's (the roomer's) room listening for noise, lest Julie [her daughter] be awakened. The hallucinations (paranoid) as the effect of a long overdose of Benzedrine—much the same on a grand scale), imagine, as the paranoid reaction after the first dose in depression. Also, Joan sat in the same room later, knitting on the bed in company with Sal. Though she is aloof she has need of some company and this is rather pathetic.

In need of company myself I sought out Jerry Rauch. He was writing a paper which I had to read—on anthropology, which began to get itself involved in all arts of academic verbalisms and dichotomized ideals: Individual and Society, History etc. He came to the somewhat sensible conclusion that there is a mutual cause and effect or something like that. What other conclusion can be reached along such a cloudy road? Began expounding psychodynamics to him, for the fourth or fifth time, since he is a sympathetic listener, and he countered with some sort of book on morphological psychology—endomorphs, viscerimorphs and cerebromorphs, or something like that. This introduces an element of dual cause in formation of personality,—the Freudian structure of guilt, conflict, and anxiety competing (in the cerebromorph) with the physiological structure implying the same types of anxiety, physical tenseness and castrate ineffectuality or demoniac possession. The questions that arose were confused in my mind but run somewhat along the lines of the difference between spontaneous and neurotic personality. Is the morphological the spontaneous personality with its particular openness to certain types of environmental neurosis? Would analysis of a cerebromorph turn him into a psychic equivalent of the endomorph (athlete)? Involved in this is the archetypical personality which presumably does not exist. Nonetheless are there not archetypical needs and motivations; anti-Oedipal, and need for action and change? Presumably the visceramorph does not spontaneously desire activity, etc.

Picked up Fitzgerald[138] and, walking to the West End, met John [Kingsland], who was swaying on the street behind John Jay Hall, greeting us with shrieks of despair. He has developed a quite sinister ill in his leg. "First my mouth and then my rear end and now my leg." It seems to be rotting away or something and he's quite embarrassed at the whole business.

"Rauch, what are the symptoms?"

"None particularly, it just seems to be sort of gushy and it smells."

"Well, you don't mind the smell?"

"It isn't myself I'm thinking of, but my dear, the downstairs neighbors!"

Then he vented his other ills—a stomach ache (ulcers or a strained muscle. Here he gave a delicate obscene illustration of how it might have become strained—an invitation ecstasy). His doctor gave him cocaine for this. It doesn't take away the pain but, "it makes me feel ever so much more cheerful about it all."

John, since analysis, has made no false effort to be good and has gotten stouter and queerer and more indulged in appearance—more desperate of mind. It occurred to me last night that when I first knew him the elements of his mask were present—the social taste, the *chi-chi* sense, the simulations of the queer and the old dowager and the Thurber characters—the Waugh satire. But then he was more allusive, delicate. He's become open and "screaming" in mask, not buffoonish ever, but fauve and queenish. His conversation is less about trifles, odds and ends of social affairs, but directly allusive to homosexuality in almost any consideration. So wrapped up has it become that while more comedic, it is also more starkly relevant, more compulsive and neurotic—in the sense that it is now no delicious play but a necessary attitude, something not of choice nor even of pleasure. He must be more melancholy than ever, living in enforced servitude to his castration. Also it is something no longer of a perfect attitude (which it seemed more nearly once) but of a "character"; something not designed to mask himself but to reveal himself. There is no coolness, dexterity and *savoir faire*, but demonism, slavery, and disgust. This the result of the knowledge of self, and meeting the self on its own terms.

Burroughs would justly laugh at my description above: romantic, literary, overserious, without literality and clarity amounting almost to shrewd clairvoyance.

In the dream of the evening (or morning) which was interrupted by a rude awakening, I repeated a situation which is familiar to me in dreams: a carnival.

138 Jack Fitzgerald. Columbia student and jazz aficionado.

There is a circus parade passing through town (Coney Island). I go to a sideshow (peepshow). It seems that normal people, or virile, or just most people, in addition to standing outside go inside to a sort of guided obstacle race to see the real wonders. On awakening I remembered also that there are two strong, half stripped (bathing suits or shorts and T-shirts) men as "guides" who run you through the mill. I am filled with horror at the course (cunt, vaginal tract, etc. in association) and I am afraid to enter. I know that it is the masochist's track where I will be beaten, mocked, and possibly castrated. [Ginsberg has written in the margin: "Incident with the old drunkard at Revere Beach sideshow."]

July 20, [1946].

My morning (yesterday) was filled with deep disgust and irritation. No lonesome homesickness for "mine own kind" but a paranoiac hatred for everyone that approached me to inflict their ration of aggression upon me. I am usually more passive psychically, but the steward annoyed me with his stupid gruffness, and the cook with his frustrated complaints (someone orders sandwiches and he raves for a minute etc.—wasting time—about children who have to eat sandwiches or something incoherent like that). I was once proud of tense moods of Rimbaudian hatred—and properly so since they are at least an evolutionary step from "philosophic" acquiescence. But they are the reverse side of the coin. Ennui, Prometheanism, aesthetic rebellion, sea lawyer liberalism and moral jeremiadism ought to be properly understood—external causes and sociological causes, surround us and basically motivate us. But the moment of hatred is filled with psychic frustration and the hatred is not the authentic emotion of a free man, but the desperate neurotic reaction of the maladjusted. Shakespeare has something informative to say about this, and the Bible comments wisely thus, and so does any personality which is serene and accomplished. What the spontaneous reaction of the psychoanalyzed man is I am unsure as yet.

I mailed Hart Crane to Ransom yesterday and today I am filled with pleasurable fantasies about my literary life—beginning with *Columbia Review* and continuing to my introduction to the literary world at a cocktail party. I must get W. Gilmore[139] to introduce me to Auden there and not have a formal introduction engineered by my publisher. It certainly would be a social triumph to get T.S. Eliot to put in an appearance.

---

139 William Gilmore. One of Burroughs' friends from Harvard, who had earlier introduced Burroughs to Auden.

I find myself drifting more and more into the web of poetry. I am not exactly powerless to prevent myself from these fantasies but they enlighten the heart and make great pleasure for a moment. They are so strong that the return to reality is accompanied by a sense of dread; and when a fantasy of this sort is interrupted, my mind retains the pleasurable anticipation of resuming the fantasy, even if it is forgotten—so that it is as if I were trying to remember the prospect of a treat or a surprise. Sexual fantasies as well have been amusing me. I imagined the boarding house in Boston, the rainy night, and Hal Chase masturbating Kerouac. Thus, unconsciously, I place myself in Kerouac's body and place, and take the responsive initiative; overwhelming Chase with somewhat brutal caresses. Experimentally placing my own body in the bed I experience a let down, a sense of indignity—the cerebromorphic stomach rut Chesters, huge genitaled self makes me fear the aesthetic anachronism, or plain sexual vulgarity of the routine. All this I see is mere castration sense. I have taken over Jack's virility thereby to castrate the inferior Chase. Reversing to myself, I am afraid to try or dislike the attempt even in fantasy. A sort of vicarious "sacerdotal" pleasure, in seeing Chase castrated or loved up by Jack, even in fantasy. How many times removed from the archetype this is!

The Freudian language must be revised. Does the self that rises out of the oedipal situation feel itself literally castrated? Is the genital a symbol of the whole personality to the psyche; that is, does the paternal intimidation, the consequent passivity and insecurity and confusion of the mind manifest itself (other than in incidental importance) as the removal of the genitals? Which precedes which—or, better, and finally, is the literal castration a symbol of the mind to express the whole intimidation, or does the intimidation proceed from the sense of literal castration, not meant as symbol? Or is, as I assume, the mind unconcerned with these generalizations and dualities—in what way does it respond literally? In association I can quickly trace almost any neurotic act back to oedipal castration. Is this tracing back to first cause, to generalized subconscious symbol, or cultural (acquired) symbolism for crippled psyche—: choice of image cripple, i.e. castrate?

Think, apropos, of the horrible result, the traumatic response, the shock, when the neurotic citizen, in the army, suffers a limb to be amputated. How this symbol must echo and reecho in psychic caves. What an opportunity for the oedipal castration sense so invariably educated in the poor yokel to assert itself. Al Capp certainly has a job on his hands.

I see by the papers the army is working on radar vision for the blind. One of my great dreams may soon be possible, vision recorded of dreams and thoughts. Then shall we see the horror! I must learn electricity and physiology. This last requires, as I said, psychoanalysis, relaxation, garden variety yoga, and esoteric yoga. I must find time to spend a season in Tibet.

Finished Pound and Swift. Delaying *Bovary* as usual.

July 22, 1946.
Waiting in mess hall for the morning, reading Fowlie's Rimbaud.

Conscience: "Well, my late sleeping bedfellow, my neurasthenic dreamer, the time has come for a reckoning and no frivolous or incoherent passion, no sly attitude, no metaphor will suffice. We must have it out here and now."

The Muses: "Have what out? (Sleepily) That presupposes a problem at this hour?"

Conscience: "The problem is most relevant to the hour, inasmuch as you are so crowding me in this bed that I have been forced to pace the floor these last hours. Besides the bed is mine anyway, you have been my guest, now that our cohabitation is no longer pleasurable, it would be sensible for you to leave without making a scene. But since you have been in bed this evening you have seemed to me particularly a loathsome creature, a woman of no true leisure, no beloved, but a gutter whore, a painted lady, and a diseased one at that."

Muses: "So far you have indulged in structureless metaphors, and tropistic chatter. You pass yourself off as reason, clarity, not false scientism, theoretic casuistry. You are assuming what you would like to think are my own characteristics, and your similes are as the sores of my diseases. You are shilly-shallying, afraid to face the problem, and so far all this talk has been useless. Unless you get down to facts I'd prefer to sleep on."

Conscience: "Facts then it shall be; I'd have preferred to spare you the scene."

Muses: "You'd have preferred to spare yourself the necessity of clarifying your thoughts."

Conscience: "In any case I proceed: What do you offer? We two have wit enough and sufficient sensibility to continue to write and achieve what you might call aesthetic success. I tell you this aesthetic success is a delusion; it is not a success of spirit, a perfection of the soul; an accomplishment of greater potentiality, it will merely rhyme and glorify our—shall I say incestuous relationship?—which, as we both know by now is not the product of our aesthetic desires."

Muses: "Do we know this as definitely as you insist? With unity of vision, clarity, grasp of reality, with the gestalt of life which we boast of and grow more familiar with, I tell you our love is compatible."

Conscience: "No true relationship is possible, no joining of our desires. I know that what will give me true life is authentic life, life of activity, self-contained, unified as the man of Dante's perfect parts. What is true beauty but in virile, socialized action, self-assertion, conscienceless play with existence, picaresque adventure?"

Muses: "Do you mean to appeal to the appetites of the muse or the appetites of conscience? Beauty is my own angle."

Conscience: "It was a slip, revealing my sibling relationship to you. But I may say there is aesthetic beauty comparable to your own in activity such as St. Perse's. But what I really meant by beauty is harmony. And the virtue of harmony is not its beauty, but in its fitness and justice."

Muses: "You still can't say what you mean in real terms."

Conscience: "I have been struggling to give verbal form to physical fact and spiritual necessity. The needs of the healthy soul (and since I have fallen out of love with you and your human forms) include activity. More precisely, the soul is active in nature—uncorrupted by neurosis—the soul demands action and change, it is dynamic, flexible, amoral (though this is the affair of neither of us): Faustian, though not Promethean, vigorous, though not bumptious. I think the emotions I have listed might be called authentic, in contrast to the passions which you state which are perverted. Only when the soul discovers its weakness, and submits to the interrelation, the imposed pattern, the trauma, the castration, the guilt, need it take demand. *Il arrive que l'espirit demande la poesie.* You now serve as a fetish; a neurotic, defined by substitute phallus; a catch to the weak sister art the soul has been putting over. I know very well what it all means, this mask of intellectual activity, oh hypertrophic deceased sensibility. It is only a mask to hide the face of the pederast, the invalid, the child who has surrendered. You are afraid of life not because it is varied but because you fear vanity where it touches you in non-symbolic form. You fear enterprise, activity, responsibility, clarity of thought and action which is unintimidated, you actually fear to understand beauty because it, like any other phenomena, requires decision and courage. You have no true courage, only spurious symbolic nonsense. You worship the child of the rainbow because he is free, authentic, courageous. You cannot hide behind the veil of dualities, Hamlet fears to kill because he is oedipal not because he is philosophic. Duality would disappear for you as it has for me were you to become coherent and integral. Psychoanalysis has taken us too far to evade the knowledge of your function and your falsity. It is because you are incompatible with life that you must go, lest happiness be denied the soul in the pleasures of actual existence, in the sensual and intellectual delights of natural life by this do I champion beauty and justice and life, all in one, delivered from dualities, trinities and questions."

Muses: "One thing which you will not face is the fact that poetry can be an harmonious and active life: Homer, Thucydides, Herodotus, Plato, the dramatists, Shakespeare, Beethoven, Thackeray, all the greats. Our modern aestheticians are fools as we know; but give me leave and perhaps we shall join the company of immortals—not as an honor do we seek this, nor for reward to our avaricious vanity; but gracefully and energetically, shall we not be their equals, knowing one of their essential secrets—the nature of life, and its relation to such poetry as you have just denounced."

Conscience: "Truly, if you were a free agent, if the soul was whole and healed, if we subconsciously used poetry properly. But I flee to you in moments of despair and melancholy. You are the *galiante* of my invalid moments, not the mistress of my pleasures. After writing I feel as if I had spent the night in a Turkish bath reminiscing over *"des saisons anciennes."* The point is that though under certain circumstances you might be a manifestation of health and prowess and virility, you are now in reality—I repeat—the panderer to my perversities, one who gives no real satisfaction—because my appetite being perverse is not evil but unreal, unsatisfiable, wretched and self-destructive. Let us be St. Perse, then you may have what license you chose."

Muses: "Well, I think I could maintain that even if we were whole, the soul would be still poetic—it has been so rehearsed and trained to aesthetic response that it would be impractical to change horses in midstream."

Conscience: "The rider could do it if he could ride; the business of poetry being a healthy, natural calling, however, may be true."

Muses: "Look at yourself: it may be true, you don't know for sure. What kind of discipline and clarity is this?"

Conscience: "The perfection of the soul is still incomplete, analysis must be continued, and a sign of the progress is your anticipated exile."

Muses: "But how can you say I am unnatural when you still can't tell yourself what your spontaneous personality is like."

Conscience: "If it were spontaneous it would demand..."

Muses: "This is all too theoretical for me; you really don't know, do you? What do you want—to be a neo-Rimbaud—a St. Perse? A businessman? A Hollywood producer? A book publisher? A diplomat? An anthropologist? A psychoanalyst? All these are beyond your reach for one practical reason or other. You are not of the aristocracy so diplomacy and politics would not be your field, nor is the culture sufficiently unified for you to be really interested. Decadence, things fall apart, anarchy, etc. Do you want to be the supreme savant, the criminal? You haven't the guts!"

Conscience: "That's your fault."

Muses: "It isn't mine, it's the crippled soul which you can't evade."

Conscience: "Defeatist!"

Muses: "Be realistic! Will you ever be Jack, handsome, virile, aggressive? All the psychoanalysis in the world wouldn't give these things to you, because I don't think that social aggression is really a spontaneous function of your soul. It would be really impossible to restore such power to your soul, even if that particular manifestation of power were innate in all human beings—which, as you may guess, it is, probably, not. You are too theoretical, setting up one of those meaningless compulsive archetypes, which you never can attain, which you really don't want. I mean really, *sans castration sans neurosis.*"

Conscience: "This is all theoretical at this point I admit. What I think, now, that I want, are activity of some sort, love which is casual and consummated and not demonic and frustrate, social prestige or as an equivalent (since the prestige is in lieu of activity friendship and love) some social stability; intellectual excitement, physical unity, and money which involves all."

Muses: "Somehow all your desires sound fishy to me—as if they were the reverse side of the coin of aestheticism."

Conscience: "I don't think they are essentially, though they are still hinged with the purgatorial fires of frustration, penuriousness, servility, and vanity."

Muses: "Well, make up your mind."

Conscience: "It's all so confusing. But the same difficulties exist in your own mind for your equivalents."

Muses: "Then it's a draw."

Conscience: "Mostly, except that you'll have to mend your habits and transmogrify into true femininity with the hard core of shrewd practical knowledge, including a knowledge of your place. For the duration that is, the duration of the analysis."

Muses: "I think your 'solution' is confused. Come to sleep."

Conscience: "I think I have not succeeded in this affair at all."

Muses: "Then sleep on it."

Conscience: "That's what you'd like me to do."

Muses: "You have no other choice."

Conscience: "I shall dream of Rimbaud."

Muses: "In an oedipal manner, no doubt."

July 1946 [Reading List].

Flaubert, Gustave. *Madame Bovary* (unfinished) will I never finish this!

Pound, Ezra. *Collected Poems* (introduction by T.S. Eliot, Faber, 1935)

Hasek, Jaroslav. *The Good Soldier Schweik*

Miller, Henry. Essay on Rimbaud (in *New Directions No. 9*)

Lautréamont. Preface to Poems

Empey, Arthur G. *"Over the Top"*

Fowlie, Wallace. *Rimbaud*

Williams, William Carlos. *Collected Poetry 1921–31* (preface by Wallace Stevens)

Williams, William Carlos. *The Wedge*

August 3? [1946].

For, in the end, our will becomes our destiny. What shall rise out of the violence, this embroilment. Fitting to it, its creator, to the starry world created. But words and deeds in words, and dialectic. Words and dreams, and death in violence.

August 1946 [Reading List].

Williams, William Carlos. *Paterson, Book 2*

Oscar Williams. *A Little Treasury of Modern Poetry, English and American*

Thomas Wolfe. *You Can't Go Home Again*

Steeves, Harrison R. and others. A College Program in Action (Columbia)

Hoffman, Frederick J. *The Little Magazine, a history and a bibliography*

Warner, Rex. *Poems and Contradictions.* (thumbs down)

Pudney, John. *Selected Poems*

Sitwell, Edith. *The Song of the Cold* (still fell the rains)

Todd, Ruthven. *The Acreage of the Heart* (nice, but thumbs down)

Tennet, Sean. *Cloth of the Flesh*. T.D. except Cycle.

Durrell, Lawrence. *Cities, Plains And People* (good poetry at last)

Toller, Ernst. The Swallow Book

Wylie, Elinor. *Black Armour*

Haire, Norman (ed.). *Encyclopaedia of Sexual Knowledge*

Haggin, B.H. *Music on Records*

Turner, W.J. *Mozart, the man and his works*

Barnes, Djuna. *Nightwood* (repeat)

Tyler, Parker. *The Hollywood Hallucination,* half

Chisholm, A.R. *The Art of Arthur Rimbaud*

Gorman, Herbert. *James Joyce*

Mann, Thomas. *Death in Venice, Mario and the Magician* (repeat), *Transposed Heads*

September 3, 1946.

Have typed "Death in Violence" as "Death of the Voyager" has been titled. Also thought of "The Character of the Happy Warrior" as title (a work of instruction for the young). Up in Buffalo. Also wrote a review of Steeves/Barzun book on Columbia education. Home again, finished an introduction to "Death in Violence" using benny (Benzedrine) for inspiration. Prose is getting more Joycean, Aristotelian or whatever quality it is that Joyce and Carr have got. No new poems in months and months.

Bill's [Burroughs] letter to Joan [Adams] last week the best of them all. Off the habit. "Kells wants to associate only with 'dynamic' people, and I am forced to admit that junk seriously hampers my dynamism." He has invented a new character greater "and even more uncontrollable" than Luke. It seems this character has as his intention to "put everybody out of business." Fluorescent mouth washes for dentists, home dry cleaners for dry cleaning, monopolies, etc.

September 3, 1946. 11:15 P.M.

I have for this evening's entertainment, to write a review of William Carlos Williams' *Paterson* (Book I) for the *Passaic Valley Examiner*. I was foolish to have volunteered for the job, expecting to catch the eye of Williams[140] whose eye I am not so sure I want to catch very much. At any rate my intention to interview Williams *vis à vis* the review fell through last month, and I am left holding the bag—an empty one in this case as the book and I have little in common. I might as well rehearse the review here: "Mr. William Carlos Williams, promi-

---

140 William Carlos Williams (1883–1963). New Jersey poet and physician who became a lifelong influence on Ginsberg.

nent Passaic County physician and a resident of Rutherford N.J."—this is hopeless!

[*The following are excerpts from a letter Ginsberg wrote to Trilling dated September 7, 1946.*]

I had an unexpected turn of events in my trial. While delivering the manuscript [of "Death in Violence"] to your box in Hamilton Hall I met Fritz Stern[141] chatting in his usual fashion with Dean Carman.[142] I was as charming as I could be under the circumstances. Carman suddenly asked me if I were returning to school, and after I explained, he invited me into his office (at 3:00) and undertook to handle it all personally—taking over from Hance. So while I was there he arranged for an appointment at the medical office for next Tuesday. Providing all goes well with Dr. Adams, I have Carman's assurance that he will send a note to the registrar admitting me by the end of next week. Although I suppose that everything is set now, do you think there would be any point, if you were so advised, in speaking to the Dean on the matter and strengthening his resolve? Incidentally, I enclose a copy of the "testimonial" from my psychiatrist which I presented to McKnight. It may amuse you, for I wrote it myself; but it is kosher, for Wassing signed and approved.[143]

The poem you have has also a five page critical and exegetical introduction—which would be pretentious if the poem were not at all successful, so I am holding it back for the time.

If you finish the poem, and have time to receive me before the term starts, will you send me a postcard to Paterson? If not, I'll be around school next term, it appears, and will see you then.

September 14, [1946].
I wrote the review [about Williams' *Paterson*]; a neatly balanced, delicate essay in restrained burgher style complaining about Dr. William's uncharitable position in regard to Paterson's attempts to spread education to the masses. Published today in the *Passaic Valley Examiner* and edited by poor Mr. Zimel. It reads juvenile and blatant due to changes, deletions and—mercy me—additions! I should have known better; there is an issue of reaching the masses involved here, perhaps, but really, Allen! This will be a lesson. I better get a

---

141 Fritz Stern. Another of Ginsberg's early Columbia friends and one-time roommate.

142 Dean Carman. Dean of Columbia College.

143 Ginsberg had been suspended from school in March 1945 for writing obscenities on his dorm window and allowing Kerouac to stay overnight in his room.

hold of the review of Columbia that I gave [to the *Columbia*] *Review* and tuck it away evermore or send it to a magazine. But the style is too rough and the essay has no real dignity.

I have been thinking as before, of writing a novel. I recounted the charades of Luke and the well-groomed Hungarian to Eugene, and worked up a vision of a *Walpurgisnacht*[144] scene in which the three of us, Jack, Bill and myself would charade spontaneously and be transformed into our alternate personalities, our cultural equivalents or alternates anyway. This has not often been done in English: the interchange of roles, in a way, or of clothes and time, retaining the nature of the player and I suppose his body of fate to signify the natures of the people written up. This here is such shoddy prose it bodes ill for anything formal. Relaxation is right, complete disintegration, boy! Boy! bring thy lute, and play for me.

September 16, [1946].

Have been teaching Arnold Rosenberg to write. I wish I could communicate to him the honor which is accorded. Of course, $30 fee for twelve hours work. Also, have been latching on to Joe Moony Quartet at Sandy's [bar] in town (Paterson). They are undiscovered at present, except for a few laudatory notices in N.Y. columns. Saw: Alan Ladd [in] *This Gun for Hire, OSS, One More Tomorrow, Diary of a Chambermaid, Centennial Summer* [and] *Anna and the King of Siam.*

September 20, [1946.]

Readmitted to Columbia.

Whether The University Is The Wasteland Of Mr. Eliot Or The Sandpile Of Mr. Cummings

> To college then I came...
>   and in my ears jug jug is sung
> By those who squat upon the sandpile and romanticize.
> The metaphor is real for them,
>   so rudely forc'd, their dung.
> (I shall not spend my passion on these isles.)

---

144 *Walpurgisnacht:* May Day eve, when witches gathered and reveled according to German folklore.

This was to be a long and serious reflective poem, but my failure to turn out anything but a warped and somewhat pointless satire (pointless = vague, semantically undecided) is significant.

"I thought of Lucien..." *à la* Yeats' McGregor is the idea, partially or, "Here, to abstraction, flee the children!!"...like Ben Maddow—David Wolfe! or "and there the toothless mastiffs give them suck"—thinking of Steeves and the dry udders of his pedantry. Or is it dry teats for a female dog not a mastiff? But I meant to suggest the castrate bisexuality of pursuit of abstractions. Or "I saw them once as juveniles but now they fall like rotten fruit" the students. There is a difference between Stern's former childishness and Bass's lack of profundity, and their present senile urbanity or testy perplexity. No, Bass has not enough beauty to be perplexed like a child of the rainbow. He is merely desiccating in mind.

I have not said what I meant. "Words slip, slide, decay with imprecision, will not stay in place." I cannot yet tag the vision with a vocabulary, nor illuminate it with a stripe of natural metaphors. Perhaps I am not serious enough: I don't do anything with my life but romanticize and decay with indecision. I am losing my virility: I don't know if I can even write poems now. I have fantasies in which I pursue a business course and lose the power of (elegy? eternity? speech?) poetry. Lose practice, ability, I am almost becoming haunted by sterility. I cannot yet face fictional prose, and I procrastinate with fantasies of scenes and plots and ideas and structures of the epical novel. "Disconsolate chimera." This book is an excuse to daily creation. But do I want to create? (I am using creation as a simple descriptive term, neither in irony nor orphisms).

I see my trouble comes from this confusion in the will: my difficulty in choosing an attitude and style is the difficulty of finding one. I choose too much. So rudely forced. Spontaneity! of being impelled unconsciously to an attitude. Inconclusive psychoanalysis. I need a frame of mind that serves me, suits me, is me. How can I write when, looking thru Bill's analytic eyes, I see that what I write is not me: is self piteous, or pretentiously hyperbolical (not like Rimbaud's acid hyperbole), or afflatus—romantic, but just silly despite the blowsy rhetoric. I <u>must</u> reform. *Il faut etre absolument moderne.* (Rimbaud meant such a situation as this: I must become pagan, thought he, and not jejune and bohemian.)

Really, what is there to say when we reduce poetry to essentials and useful values—real beauty? We shall have Shakespearean drama again, and such toughness as Molière. That is fit for a really shipshape mind. [in the margin Ginsberg has written: "Stupid Verbalisms"] The mind is like a muscle; even after the sickness is cured, it must be exercised before realism becomes habitual. One must develop muscles, not of intelligence, but of self interested thought. (see "Death in Violence" Section VII)

Until I am a man I shall never write good poetry, poetry which is tough in mind, poetry of which I approve: is spontaneous (should be) rejoicing in beauty, sensuality, sensation. (Rimbaud's Illuminations in part). Baudelaire's spleen is tough poetry for his intention which was not that of the whole man, but a possible reaction that one might have, though healthy, under the duress of the decadent society.

September 30, [1946].

Today I have been raging pitifully on myself. First an argument with a fool named Pierpont in which I was impotent in dialectic. Then a meditation on Carr, with several conversations with some incidental acquaintances of his. Then a stupid interview with Trilling in which he refused to let me become dependent on him. Then (or previously) a disgust with Arabic.[145] Classical. It is different. I'd forgotten that this Arabic kick was real. I'll drop it. Still it is the only real subject I am taking, as Joan says, all the rest are discussion courses. I'll take Chinese civilization instead. Anxiety and frustration and perturbation unreserved. A decision, any decision, I must make one. One must take steps.

Psychoanalysis is for me only an escape from decision. I must be serious in it. I am beginning to suspect Bill. Joan said, "Of course there are certain things he can't do. I don't suppose he could really analyze anyone's sex problems. He'd be too discomfited (or uneasy or embarrassed)." So I see Arabic, Bill, Joan, sex. My sex life has atrophied. I must be strong! I feel more at peace now. Reading Donne.

September 1946 [Reading List].

Yeats, William Butler. *Last Poems And Plays*

Devlin, Denis. *Lough Derg and other poems*

Wilson, Edmund. *Memoirs of Hecate County*

W.C. Williams. *Paterson I*

Connolly, Cyril. *The Condemned Playground, essays*

Forster, E.M. *Aspects of the Novel*

---

145 Arabic. Ginsberg had registered for an introductory course in the Arabic language that term.

Wilson, Edmund. *The Wound and the Bow*

Stevens, Wallace. *Harmonium*

Lawrence, D.H. *Look! We Have Come Through; Amores, Poems*

Lofting, Hugh. *Story of Dr. Dolittle*

Started work on *Finnegan's Wake* [by James Joyce]

Forster, E.M. *A Room with a View*

Virginia Woolf. *Mrs. Dalloway*

Daiches, David. *Virginia Woolf*

Spencer, Theodore L. *A Garland for John Donne, 1631–1931*

Donne, John. Poems (in *English Poetry of the Seventeenth Century*, edited by
    Roberta Brinkley)

October 14? [1946].
Much has happened, obviously Carr home; still potent, disturbing. Sometimes
I feel emancipated, sometimes not; always, intellectual rivalry. Unsatisfied with
my demeanor, as he remarked; I "always seem to be giggling." Tee hee.
    I am starting work in school more in earnest now.

October 25, [1946].
Burroughs in N.Y. Dr. Burroughs' Vital Juices: The spiritual fact of herbs and
snake oils. A chart:
Vitamin A—Specific for cold large doses 200,000–500,000 units—take every
    day about 30,000

Vitamin B complex—for hangovers—for lack of energy—for melancholy

Vitamin C—for gums, for piles. 250 milligram per day—other (normal) 100
    per day

Unicaps—(1)

Euziflem tablets—for teeth and gums

October 31, [1946].
Conversation at Clendenning (103rd Street and Amsterdam Avenue) evening
12–2 with Joan and Bill (Thursday Evening). On speech—hieroglyphs, expres-
sions of nonverbal psychic situations, impulses and understandings. (Mayan
and) Egyptian and Chinese character. Visual thought. For (hypnosis) rather, for

telepathy, perhaps visual communication possible, not verbal. Egyptians and Mayans magic based on language differences, etc.

Bill's description of Mayan drawings—men turning to crabs, eyes extended, fingers in eyes (vice versa—eyes on fingertips, etc.) normal, bourgeois standard of art there.

"I won't take any more shit from no one."—and immediate (telepathic) epidemic of aggression—defacing of idols, revolutions that started after centuries of "security" and last centuries at a time started by someone suddenly becoming violent, etc. Result in America—all technicians and bureaucrats suddenly killed overnight, culture disrupted demechanized and decentralized anarchy after a brawl.

Two types of telepathy—hysterical call, and "slipping" casually and accidentally in unimportant strains of thought.

Suggestion: Aiken's "Silent Snow Secret Snow" and Mr. Odopolus; F. Scott Fitzgerald's "Return to Home?" a horror tale. Kafka, Gogol's stories.

1. The Dreamer
2. Anxiety of letter written leading to murder
3. Benzy drag
4. "I won't take no more shit" leading to disintegration of culture
5. Joke "Ever see material like this?"
6. Philosophers and Supreme Reality.

Write to Indiana Botanical Garden, Hammond, Indiana, For Yohimbini [and] Quehelrachel. Aphrodisiacs 25¢ pack, $1.00 minimum.

October 1946 [Reading List].
Burckhardt, Jacob. *Force and Freedom*

Eliot, T.S. *Four Quartets*

Partisan and *Kenyon Reviews* (Fall 1946)

Sweeney, James J. *Marc Chagall*

The Partisan Reader (parts)

Carr, Edward. *Conditions of Peace* (p. 1–128)

The Song of Roland. Translated by Merriam Sherwood

Rimbaud, Arthur. *Illuminations* (translated by Louise Varese, 1946 ed. New Directions)

Jonson, Ben. *The Poems of Ben Jonson* (edited by Bernard H. Newdigate)

Beowulf. (introduction by Charles W. Kennedy)

English Poetry of the Seventeenth Century, edited by Roberta Brinkley. (selections)

Levin, Harry. *Stendhal*

The Rule of St. Benedict

Bede, The Venerable Saint (selections)

Geoffrey of Monmouth (selections)

Feneloso, Ernest and Pound, Ezra. *The Chinese Written Character*

Korzybski, Alfred. *Science and Sanity*

November 13, [1946].
Scatological Trimmings:

1. Earliest: Experience with boys in School No. 1 or 17 ties in with confusion of age 4 (Fair St)—no—before. With age 7 (1933) in the bathroom—"Can I help you button your pants?" [Ginsberg has written in left margin: "aroused infantile homosexuality—Earl: Pearl Oil Italian."]. Shame of pants; aversion of buttons; crib Fair St. (aversion of enclosing, buttoned night dress). Involvement of castration and shame at not knowing multiplication table.
2. Pissing behind piano in Newark (1933). Association with dark hallway next door.
3. Exhibitionism at 155 Haledon Avenue.
4. Masochistic dream at 155 Haledon.
5. 72 Fair [Street]: Stamp wrong on envelope. Shitting on floor and carried in.
6. Visual image of oral sucking and masturbation synchronized movements.
7. Visual image of forcing out feces and masturbation (flexing penis muscles). This to do with defilement and fear of pants with buttons which kept shit in near me, against me.
8. Appendix: Dr. Weinstein!? and rubber finger up anus: aroused anal sensuality, fear, repression of feeling.
9. Dutch Boy uniform buttoning up.

November 14, [1946].

Blake's little black boy—This was my conception of self romanticized with happy ending with child of rainbow:

> "And then I'll stand and stroke his silver hair
> And be like him and he will then love me."

November 25, [1946].

Things going ill; poetry stopped, reading desultory, neurasthenic sleeping, loneliness, splenetic moods, boredom, fear, vanity.

Written: Page on Marianne Moore (stylized)—Paper on Korzybski (sloppy)—Paper on Vico (inconclusive)—Ballad for English course (bad).

November 1946 [Reading List].

Dunne, J.W. *An Experiment with Time*

Sinclair, Upton. *Mental Radio* (1930)

Tischner, Rudolf. *Telepathy and Clairvoyance*

Journal of Parapsychology

Boston Society of Psychic Research—Bulletin

Proceedings, English Society of Psychic Research

November 8, [1946].

Ouspensky, P.D. *Tertium Organum*

Have begun to put Korzybski, Spengler, Freud and Kardiner together.

November 10, [1946].

Meyer, Adolf. *Psychobiology*

Rosett, Joshua. *The Mechanism of Thought, Imagery and Hallucination* (Columbia University Press, 1939)

Pavlov, Ivan. *Conditioned Reflexes* (1927)

Pavlov, Ivan. Lecture on (International, 1928)

Rhine, J.B. *New Frontiers of the Mind*

Milton, John. *Samson Agonistes*

Lowell, Robert. *Lord Weary's Castle* (ok)

Weaver, Raymond. *Black Valley*

Aucassin and Nicolette

Flint, Robert. *Vico*

The Autobiography of Giambattista Vico. (preface by Max Fisch and Thomas Bergin)

Croce, Benedetto. *The Philosophy of Giambattista Vico*

Eliot, T.S. *Selected Essays 1917–1932* (parts)

Tate, Allen. *Reactionary Essays on Poetry and Ideas* (parts)

Eliot, T.S. *The Waste Land*

Beerbohm, Max. *Zuleika Dobson*

Gray, Thomas. *Letters*

Merton, Thomas. *A Man in the Divided Sea*

Petty, Mary. *This Petty Pace* (cartoons)

Kafka, Franz. *Metamorphosis*

Durrell, Lawrence. *A Private Country: Poems*

Stevens, Wallace. *Notes Toward a Supreme Fiction* [and] *Parts of a World*

Lowell, Robert. *Land of Unlikeliness* [and] *Lord Weary's Castle*

Rank, Otto. *Art and Artist* (begun)

Boas, Franz. *The Mind of Primitive Man* (skimmed)

O'Neill, Eugene. *The Iceman Cometh*

Harvard Thesis—Pound's Poetry

Petrie, W.M. Flinders. *The Revolutions of Civilisation*

Henderson, Lawrence J. *Pareto's General Sociology*

Gold, Ivan. *Fruits of Saturn*

Melville, Herman. *Selected Poems*

Isherwood, Christopher. *The Memorial: Portrait of a Family*

December 1, [1946].
Got some pantopon of my own (two grains) and shot half a grain last night, lay in bed and read Baudelaire's "Spleen" and Yeats' "The Gyres". One can understand Baudelaire's "Ennui" and "Spleen" only if one has similar experiences with drugs and compulsion to them. Have been wasting time: Hilda

Banks' recital night before last, cocktail party afterward. Set out to impress Jack Brimberg to whom I was introduced then, and worked right well. Schnabel students, a good group to watch. Last Thursday night I spent talking to Walter Adams and Ted Hoffman whom I hadn't seen for a year, and Diana, who is rather pleasing. Also set out in earnest to get psychoanalysis. Trilling amiable but not too helpful practically. Called Carr; he's busy and I haven't patience any longer to chase him down, though I might want to; called Jack Kerouac, and also was rebuffed over Thanksgiving arrangements. Chase and Fitzgerald invited over, not myself. Started to get jealous of course, and then censored the reaction. My analysis is half-verbal and, as Korzybski says, has not reached the thalamus level with regard to such things as this.

Spent an hour Tuesday talking about "Death in Violence" with Trilling. He said he was beginning to wonder when I was going to purge self and rhetoric of self pity; I was later dissatisfied with reaction, since, as I tried to explain, that was the whole point of the poem, I don't think he really understood it, though I admit duplicity in the intention (as shown in the rough preface).

I keep wavering now between absolute dislike of writing, and a desire to write well and "in extension" as he calls it, or "objectively" or as part of unity of being à la St. Perse. I gave Trilling a copy of the "Anabasis" to look over to illustrate the point.

Idea for short story: Talk with Edmund Wilson—Scott Fitzgerald—Trilling types (Adams and Hoffman), advising them in the end to rob a bank ("get off your ass and go out and etc.") instead of this dualistic humanistic multiple consciousness of social form, conduct etc. Hoffman's characterization of the world of the boys (and Jethro Robinson's) "makes you worry a little about conduct," etc.

December 2, [1946].
Out to Rudley's for juice, toasted English muffin and coffee at 4:30 AM slept from 9–3, read from 3–4:30. Kerouac in town, I stopped at Chase's to inquire, but Chase slept all afternoon and morn, and Jack hadn't shown. In Riker's [cafeteria] I meditated on the different outlooks of these last years. Once I would have gone in there with a sense of longing and juvenescence acquired from atmosphere of Carr. A terrible beauty is born: all is changed, changed utterly. Whatever the feeling was that persisted then. I can only remember it vaguely in fragments and abstraction now—in association with the frequented image of phase 17, or with the rooms at Hastings, or with recollections of nights in the Village. It is very sad and I have received little sense of gain for the loss thereof. Is this the gift reserved for age? Analysis has made me healthier,

and I have lost some of the more childlike feelings of poetry. Alan Temko applying childlike to the prewar years at Columbia, describing his former friendship with Chase. Even Carr does not give me that lift anymore.

December 3, [1946].

Fantasies encore (as once before on death of Burroughs). This time on death of Kerouac. He didn't show the last two days. My imagination dwells on his death in recompense. Always, of course, the elegy (Memorial Elegy, etc.) to be written à la Otto Rank's thesis of inspiration of elegies and process of creation. One good line springs up, "The kindled bough (showers) is ash again." Freudian conjunction: Kindled boughs, aroused genitals / Ash (ass) impotence again. Showers is sinister (original masturbatory ritual).

I put the best foot (!) forward and went up to Kardiner's psychiatric clinic to ask for analysis. Come back after Christmas.

December 4, [1946].

Of course! Dualism. Was talking in university bar to Fitzpatrick about his queerness (he suddenly has been bursting out, in his own queerest way) with "revelation" about that l'affaire passionel he seems to have been conducting with Don Kahn. Horrors, what splendid taste he has, and to dare mention it publicly! Then to Henry James (he paid the check)—it boils down, I am told, to stylization as an indecision. Conflict and guilt—confusion in ethics and conduct—failure of decision—refuge in manners and reading James. What stupidity. So I told him demonically that one must dispense with dualism and learn to live. Which is true of course, but I fear my conduct was there at fault, I had no right to be interested in converting him, I should have been talking to him with clinical aesthetic interest in his type of moral trouble. He has guilt over affairs of personal conduct, he declares.

Time to codify vocabulary. My words this season:

1. Confusion in the will—neurotic contradiction of motives.
2. Calvinism and Freudianism. Freedom (metaphoric) / Responsibility (to self)
3. Spontaneous personality (idealization of free man's mind with neurotic conflict removed).
4. Psychoanalyzed man, emergent figure of.
5. Death in Violence
6. "Attitudinal," "Stylizations."

I also told him that it made me feel so sad to read people like Thomas and Lowell, who are so sweet and sick. And of course, theology. He's reading St. John of the Cross, and can't dispense with stylistic sentimentalisms about the possibility of God, "which one mustn't ever lose the sense of."

Pantopon: This is fire: to be craving for. It is the answer to the anxiety of boredom, to ennui, depressive cosmologies and sociological emptiness—senses. I find it less helpful now for visual imagery and dreams (I now half sleep instead of constructing hallucinations) and it is thus disappointing: But it relieves the pressure of solitude upon the conscience. There is a sense of achievement after a shot, a satisfaction of vanity, and a satiation of need; a relaxation of compulsions. I'll never forget the first shot on 60th St. over Riordan's [bar][146] and the subway trip home: the elation, the feeling of mastery: like Stephen Dedalus, in the *Dubliners*, when as a child, walking the streets, he felt as if he were bearing aloft, protecting, a sacred cup among the crowd.

The struggle tonight is not physical yet, and may it not become so! But (having shot two pills Saturday) I felt (as it was the middle of the week) that I might safely take more, and I wanted to, or was so involved in the desire, that I did not feel it was safe. Then I took out the apparatus [Ginsberg has written in the margin: "Apparatus = works (needle, pills, eyedropper, etc.)".] and then forced a negative decision out, one which was no real decision, because it did not come of itself (as a choice to take the hop would have been), but one seemingly imposed from without, yet not definite or strong either, for all its external authority. Then I thought of writing about it, and in writing I remembered an earlier observation that the spacing which my mind had made (of twice a week) was similar to my first self imposed spacing of masturbation. Of course, last Saturday evening, I could not come, whether I masturbated, *ce cause de l'Hop*. And now, as I have been jerking off seven times a week, that's a sinister thought, to think of developing a hop spacing similar to onanistic habits.

Wrote paper on Vico today in Fitzgerald's room on typewriter there. I must look up a *Messiah* this Christmas; and also hear some of the new Bartok.

December 7, [1946].
Pearl Harbor Day: Jooss Ballet last night with Paul Goldstein (that shit). Thursday Evening. Walt Adams came with me to Kardiner's class. Got to discussing the deficiency of Kardiner as philosopher. Walter's philosophical problems are results of confused S.R. That is, the ones Walter used that evening. Saw *Blithe*

---

146 This was the location of the apartment where William Burroughs was living at the time.

Spirit with him, came home here to 200 W 92 and shot some pantopon. I fumbled my vein shot, so had to shoot the bloody mess in arm. Walter got effects well enough for first try. I then set out to hypnotize him and did poorly at it to be sure.

Today I was roused by Huncke: met some characters living at 89th and West End [Avenue]. Vicki[147] the incomparable is there, but was not home, so I did not meet her. We blasted some tea—good shit. Thence to Elanor's [Ginsberg's aunt], where I fell to thinking sourly about Eugene's drunken hysteria that one night there. Heard *Boris Gudinoff* and *Castor Dina* sung by Ponselle and Mugio. No choice. Wrote on returning, to Lazarus and Kingsland. Told Kingsland about Fitz, and invented a tale about Schnabel at Hilda Banks party, and a cellist named Carroll. My writing of letters and papers becomes more sloppy and inaccurate. I lose all style half purposely and go to pot etc. like here. I wonder why? Then two goofballs to put me to sleep. Have them in me now. This is the noblest literary style man is capable of. I must write a novel like this. Dead, broken, direct.

December 8, [1946].

And so slept 14 hours! After the surprising conversations: "We who several years ago / Talked of honor and of truth, / Shriek with pleasure if we show / The weasels, twist, the weasel's tooth." Meant the conversations in apt. 51 on people we knew, movies, newspaper stories, hip doings, queers, liberals talking, etc. This strikes a responsive note and yet is inaccurate. I wonder if Yeats is (of course) romanticizing it all. The first two lines are rather sentimental and the second, overdramatic. One takes a sadistic pleasure in analyzing folly nicely.

Later: 2:00 A.M. Took one strip benny and whisky and four vitamin B and two of Rauch's fish oil tablets and have been facing the night. Began to read scatological frontiers of society, and rehashed Petrie, taking copious notes and commenting. I will write my next paper on fortune and misfortune in history: Treating force and freedom, Petrie, and Otto Rank. I'll begin—(much pleased with the benny. Real zest in me now)—with a description of different types of history—progressive liberal H.G. Wells, vague liberal, "objective" meaningless Chinese record, Marxism, Theological, Ethical, Mechanistic, etc., and speak of

147   Vicki Russell [*a.k.a.* Priscilla Arminger or Armager]. Friend of Herbert Huncke's, who became close to many in the Beat circle. She was a six-foot tall, beautiful redhead, the daughter of a prominent judge, who supported herself and her drug use as a high-class call girl and a petty thief. In Burroughs' book, *Junky*, she appears as "Mary."

Burckhart's essay; then to considerations of what is progress (or health or power or virtue) in a culture. Then a short description of our state à la Petrie's theory of the *ausgespielt* spirit and conflict. Then his point on our art. Shifting I will speak of Rank, and use Rimbaud and Kafka as examples of: 1. The function of art in our day, 2. The type of art. So then to the exhaustion of the "creative impulse" and aesthetic participation nowadays, its perverted form. Then try to build a psychodynamic bridge: an explanation of why the psychology of the artist today which makes him leave art or practice it in disease and sterility—why this psychology fits Petrie's description of decadent art: then how the two systems are different notations of the same fact: our own cultural decline.

Petrie—The event
Rank—The explanation
Kafka—The whipping boy: an illustration
Rimbaud—The hero: another illustration

Meanwhile, since the spirit calls me, I shall write a poem beginning with some variant reading of (as previously explained) that most diseased of all lines: "The kindled bough is ash" and ending "and this be the end of all," and quoting in beginning, the magnificent, shining image of annunciation of doom from Petrie, quoted from Plutarch's "Sulla." I quote the passage and comment in full here, not elsewhere. Incidentally, it also sheds light on Yeats' sources.

"We have used the simile of summer and winter for the growth and fall of civilization. This analogy of the Great Year was familiar to the ancients; in the east, Berossos, the Babylonian, writes of the summer and winter of the Great Year; in the West the Etruscans also spoke of the Great Year as the period of each race of man that should arise in succession. When their own Great Year, of 1100 years, came to an end in the turbulent time of Sulla (87 B.C.), we read: One day when the sky was serene and clear there was heard in it the sound of a trumpet, so shrill and mournful that it frightened and astonished the whole city...The Tuscan sages said that it portended a new race of men, and a renovation of the world, for they observed that there were eight general kinds of men, all differing in life and manners; that heaven had allotted to each its time, which was limited by the circuit of the Great Year; and that when one race came to a period, and another was rising, it was announced by some wonderful sign from either earth or heaven. So it was evident at one view to those who attended to these things and were versed in them, that a different sort of man was come into the world, with other manners and customs, and more or less the care of the gods than those who had preceded them. Such was the mythology of the most learned and respectable of the Tuscan soothsayers." (Plutarch in "Sulla"). Apart from the innate belief in divination, we see the broad idea which the Etruscans had of history, that each successive race had its period of a Great Year in which it sprouted, flourished, decayed, and died, etc. This is quoted in the "Vision."

December 11, [1946].

Suffered drag all next day after benny—like a fool I wasted my kick in the last pages written above, and all the way sliding down tried to write the poem—and started with an out of this world conceit (now somewhat vague in my mind) concerning the "savage carol" the "Ah silver, sad, magnetic carol" the "magical clarion," etc., its awaited noise; its noise being drowned out of the imagination by noises in the air, voices speaking to no one, (radio voices, etc.) or a self beside me "shadowy, ubiquitous, a citizen." etc. and then wandered off in typical benny drug style with incoherent and mediocre complete describing these noises and the possibility of a place of light which is silent, where only the luminous annunciation would be heard, where I can regain my ears. The trouble was that I went off, strangely enough on the importance of ears—deflected from the point of the poem. The image in my mind is of Gabrielle atop Riverside Church down the street, and its presentation in a poem by a Barnard girl that I read some years ago in a collection of undergraduate verse, a sonnet, not very good, but striking ending, "da dum da de dum dum angel seraphic, / But will he be heard above all the Traffic?" I might as well bring in Gabrielle for a classic reference; and then shift in the development of the clarion to the "jazz syrinx" idea. The hot trumpet of disintegration. I have become entangled lately (by Pippin[148] and Jim Fitzpatrick) in anxiety about breeding, consciousness of manners, etc., with the Jamesian-Forster worries. They overextend the attitude, confuse the metaphor, and the tensions they perceive are self created to a degree, but since I am not free of such anxiety nor have I found a personality properly myself and the situation, I must have recourse to study the artificial solution presented, temporarily. I think I can know my way about the difficulty without much fuss. I must reform my approach immediately—the Barzun papers were written improperly under the circumstances—true he lacked perception of their merit, nonetheless the riot of vocabularies,

148 R. Gene Pippin. Scholarly, literate poet and classmate.

the obscurities, crudities, casualnesses, undisciplined sentence structures did reflect confusions of my own mind about meaning, did hint of ignorance of the subject (but what is there to do for that?), did cover up for attitude-anxiety. My next paper will be more formal—yet that is no solution, though as we see, it is the one that the society tends to precipitate; I wonder what the true talent would live and write as? Would there be a formalism and control of self and thought at the same time, the formalism being a manifestation of control and understanding, yet not preventing expression? or would the style come of itself and obviate by its verity, pointedness, and generosity of intelligence, the need for the usual types of style. Would there be incompatibility of subject matter and polite style? In what ways? (style as necessary hypocrisy? style as mask? or style as purposeful obscurity, another mask?) But of course, the style would be unsynthesized, rise of itself, with clarity of the mind: the manner would not be too precious, there would be direct statement and regard to structural refinements. Precocity is always a result of anxiety, and not control; it comes with hyperaesthesia of consciousness, a false self consciousness, being conscious even, I hope, inaccurately. It does when there is fear of understanding the situation; for when tension is noted (and brooded upon but not understood to its roots in personality and factual issue) merely, there is refuge in manners to ward off decision, as an escape, from both understanding and activity therefrom. The style and breeding become fetishistic in society—they represent the immediate sensitivity, the consciousness of the problem (as opposed to vulgar, stupid lack of self knowledge and insight). But it is as a fetish mere sensitivity; the defeat in living is acknowledged, and an artificial code—that is synthetic, formal, universal, acknowledged—of safety measures is set up as both self-preservation in irritating situations, and self-ignorance, idle men, idle minds, invent these problems, and it is a sad season of the great year when they have become obsessive.

So I must familiarize myself with all of this in practice by practice, and not allow the temporary 'hip' and superficially direct and self possessed informalisms and purposive sloppiness control me compulsively. All well and good to act hip when one is, and non-compulsive and all wise when one is, but I am not, and the act is a sham—till now, really, I formulated this even more vaguely in my mind.

One must create one's personality, discover it, find its spontaneous delight, develop it and know it. One must, as Pinchwife says, "know the world town." Then an adjustment will be made of itself. Too many adjustments of style are made by half-knowledge of the self, and such an idealized style resulting

(Kerouac) or half knowledge of the world and self—Fitz (inferior), Pippin (superior)—or half knowledge of the world; (Eugene: a crude one) [and] by association myself. But a whole knowledge of both, as near as is possible—as in Kingsland, Burroughs, Joan or struggle for thalamic understanding where raw material is present for both—Self.

Today I met Vicki. Last night I wrote a paper on Milton's "Lost Brother" poem in a clumsy Donne style (quoting Pippin's letter in conclusion) and a clever but unpolished paranoid type letter to Pippin in reply to his theological type. My style suffered from being such a mélange. Laughed so hard with Pippin and Fitz at Philolexian meeting[149] tonite that I think I strained my back.

December 13, [1946].
Wet dream this afternoon. First time in months and months. Opium last night. Its effects are more and more dull, yet still strangely satisfactory. Do I need to step up the charge? Interval—one week. Next shot projected: Saturday the 19th. Stole Dylan Thomas *Selected Poems* and sent them as Christmas present for Louis [Ginsberg]. Dislike Dryden or rather, indifference mixed with impatience.

December 16, [1946].
Met Vicki again. She's unattached and as attractive as any woman I know. Too bad I'm not ripe for one such as her. Another wet dream this afternoon, forgot over what. Saw Lucien last night with Joan and Bill (again in town) and talk was amiable. He asked me about my sex life and so I told him I was queer. He seemed surprised. "So that's the set up!" He talked about it and made it sound almost 1943 romantic, but I couldn't get in the mood for bohemian-morbid reactions. I couldn't make myself sound amused and etc., but just was ill at ease and objective. I suppose the conversation was a sort of memorial landmark, after all these years, but I can't feel very historic about it. As he talked, he sounded technically naive, I must say.

December 18, [1946].
Picked up on Vicki last nite. Picked up on carny [carnival] talk from Huncke. Heaze teazold meaze alzall alzeabeazeout iszit.

    Bill: "Why, you can't even get a heazard-on!'

    Joan—Giggling, "It's his innate sense of delicacy."

---

149 Philolexian Society. Student literary society at Columbia, of which Ginsberg was a member.

magazine = ma ga zine =maezgazezine (a variety of pig Latin using lazi or azi) seazunreazise—sunrise.

December 18, [1946].
Went down to look at the Mayan Codices today—Madrid Codex with Bill, Joan, Huncke at Museum of Natural History.

December 24, [1946].
Christmas—rather lonely but not unpleasant. I every once and a while set me down a lyric, but do not try to polish or perfect them, or make them complicated, because I do not need them, and trust my own emotions, caring not how they are expressed or if they are expressed at all.

I took pantopon—heroin six nites in succession with Bill. No habit resultant, but habit would not now be unpleasant. No more anxiety associated with it. Began to work up a liking for Dryden.

December 28, [1946].
False Rhymes:

birth / earth / breath / seize / etc.
Retaining vowel-sound: Breath / Seize
Retaining consonant sound: Birth / Breath

When I discovered them (by myself) I named them muted rhymes, for such is the effect. Dryden's: "If they may give and take when'er they please / Not kings alone, (the godhead's images) / etc." *Absalom* (lines 876-77). The effect of please and images rhymed is not to mute the sound but to make the rhymed words discordant, as it were, expand the sound, stretch the meaning, extend or explode the metaphor. Dryden's "sterile" vocabulary, such as it is, is given a sort of physical—symbolic quality by this rhyme, so that it approximates the charged "images" of Yeats.

Find other rhymes like that. Also: write poem with rhyme scheme a b a1 b1 a1 b1 a2 b2 a2 b2 in which first false rhyme a mates first rhyme a1, second false rhyme mates first false rhyme a1, third false rhyme a2 mates second false rhyme a1 but is muted or changed, so that a and a1 rhyme, a1 and a2 rhyme, but a2 does not rhyme with a.

Auden has:

> "Let the florid music praise, (a)
> The flute and trumpet, (b)
> Beauty's conquest of your face (a1)
> In that land of flesh and bone, (c)
> Where from citadels on high (d)
> Her imperial standards fly (d)
> Let the hot sun (c1)
> Shine on, Shine on. (c2)

December 1946 [Reading List].

Sitwell, Edith. *Aspects of Modern Poetry*

Selections from Herbert, Pepys, Butler, etc. for Krutch

Van Doren, Mark. *John Dryden, A Study of His Poetry*

Wycherley, William. *The Country Wife*

Noyes, Pierrepont. *Gentlemen: You Are Mad!*

Dryden, John. *The Best of Dryden* (edited by Louis Bredvold)

Chaucer. *Canterbury Tales*

Burney, Christopher. Book on Buchenwald [*The Dungeon Democracy*]

West, Nathanael. *Miss Lonelyhearts: A Novel*

Walsh, Ernest. *Poems and Sonnets*

Fox [William]. *The Super-Powers*

Slater, Montagu. *Peter Grimes [And Other Poems]*

Rimbaud, Arthur. *Illuminations And Other Poems* (translated by Louise Varese)

Gregory, Horace and Zaturenska, Marya. *A History of American Poetry, 1900–1940*

Moore, Marianne. *Poems* (selected) [and] *Nevertheless*

Graves, Robert. *Poems 1938–45*

1947

January 2, 1945 [sic: 1947].
As to New Year's Eve:

I missed out on any parties that the Adams-Hoffman, Lazarus-Stern, Kingsland-Caswell groups might have given, but dropped up to see Vicki—no one was home in her place, she had gone out (I found) with Jack and Lucien and Celine. Celine had gone to the movies with them all (*Karamazov* and *Punishment* at Thalia) and left for home at 10:00! Some difficulty with her mother, it appears. They went on to parties that Jack knew of. Lucien drank, got all upset about a hat and scarf that Jack carried away.

Well anyway, I drank a lot of wine at the Frank's who were to leave for California. I met this dull Michael Scott character, who seemed to think he was going places; a lot of chicks came in, etc. Then we all picked up on charge when Norman (Schnall) and Bridget O'Reilly came in. After we were all high, Bridget, I, and Norman went out to Stark's for a meal (I wound up with cherry pie with ice cream and whipped cream after a ham dinner). Then we went to Bridget's place (232 W90?). She has a few rooms newly painted, one light solid blue, one light pink. The ceilings are low with a miniature Christmas tree in one window, it all looked like a doll's house. I got undressed and stepped into the "accumulator" which she rented from the Orgone Society or something of Reich's and sat there.[150] She gave me some "literature" as she called it but I was too happy with charge to be able to read. After a half hour or more I got out—without having felt any result. Norman said at that point that in the beginning one doesn't usually feel anything till a few hours afterward.

They were drumming on Bridget's muffled drums; playing records etc. Norman and I went back to Frank's and gave them some charge and went out to Elmon's with Frank's wife and a little cutie named Helen. We shook them and went back to Bridget's. She was finished a bath and stepped into the accumulator. We sat around and chatted and had more wine. Then we got more charge out and blasted, and all of us sat down at the drums. We would each

---

150 Orgone Accumulator. Wilhelm Reich (1897–1957) claimed to have discovered a universal cosmic and biological energy, which he called orgone. He believed that a box built with organic material on the outside and metal on the inside could collect and accumulate orgone from the atmosphere. He further claimed that exposure to orgone, particularly through sitting in the accumulator, promoted health and vitality and was even an effective treatment for cancer. The FDA charged him with fraud and a discredited Reich died in prison in 1957.

beat some rhythm—mine not very complicated at first, and try to synchronize all the varying beats to make a pattern. I began going off on more complicated rhythms—off beats, etc. and Bridget started talking about them, saying they were intellectual beats. We beat on, "blowing the drums," Bridget on the couch, I facing her, Norman on my right. After a while I got in with the rhythm and began to have strange sensations. The beats we exchanged seemed to carry messages; it was as if the beats we each made formed a personality pattern, and we synthesized, exchanged rhythm, got effects, talked to one another thereby. I felt a lot of energy in my chest and abdomen, very sexual, and it pushed itself down to my genitals whenever we seemed to particularly agree on a beat, we were all "sent" simultaneously, and I suddenly felt, at one of those moments, an orgasmic sensation, though I had no hard on, I think. It was as if the semen just coursed out, as in a dream. I was surprised at this, but they seemed to be hip to what was on with me. As we beat on we reached a point of clairvoyance, I had an out-of-this-world, short, mystical, visionary sensation of telepathic communion with Bridget (and sometimes, not often, with Norman). We held long conversations. I remember once or twice I faltered in beat, afraid of my orgasms, which then were coming steadily, but when I looked up Bridget was nodding "Yes, go on, it's supposed to go like this, latch on to it." Some of the beats between Bridget and me had a strange, dreamy complementary pulse; some were very funny—with the music I put into mine—and we would suddenly burst out laughing in recognition hysteria. I kept to one and varied that with Three Blind Mice and a conga rhythm and our beats we noticed, came out together as queer "gallops," or funny bumping joggling (but patterned) rhythms. The most striking thing was the sense of complete understanding—at one point just Bridget and I were playing, and I began to quit because of the orgasm sensation, but we were on a neat little gallop; my beat got more eccentric and slow, this sent us and we concluded together simultaneously, in perfect comprehension of my feelings and my beat. I gave a sort of last rattle on my drums, an *ausgespielt* clatter, and at the same moments she gave a slow little bump—and we simultaneously stretched back and roared and screeched away in pleasure.

The sexual situation blocked me; I was restrained; fearful of giving vent to my queerness, at the same time perplexed about my relation to her. She and Norman had a telepathic rhythm conversation in which I read comments on my "coming," my failure to mention it, my queerness. They understood and winked. I would begin a dominating beat and push Norman out of the picture, and a sensual one to her. This went on till six in the morning. I asked her what was going on, and what she said substantiated my feelings. Though I called it telepathy, she said it was "vibrations."

We played some Mary Lou Williams record, with Bridget on drums *Humoresque* and I got the same sense out of the record. Also *Scythian Suite,* which she said was "gone" and "so far out" neurotically (like Dali) that she liked it.

My orgasm's weren't real. I went to the bathroom to investigate. I had discharged (I think) drops of wine; I then pissed violently as after an orgasm. Norman and she said the orgasmic sensations come simultaneously. He said he'd been frustrated, and of course he had felt my hostility toward him, that "I'd drummed [that] thought to Bridget." At one point (several times) during the sent moments, with my eyes half closed, I looked at Bridget. Her face seemed to be several faces; when she turned her face to one side the second visage stared straight ahead. Then I saw her face—minus hair and neck—floating as a perfect Greek type, and it looked like Lucien's. Then her face divided—one part was dark and female, the other part light and male.

January 5, [1947].
Having blabbed and investigated I make mine conclusions:

1. Vicki reports the vibrations. Everyone who goes down to Bridget's gets them.
2. It seems to have nothing to do with the accumulator, it can be got without tea, and without drumming, it is simple telepathy. I have since gotten high on tea (particularly last nite) and had it happen again, in minor form.

January 7, [1947].

> Whoever comes, henceforth, for thee
> Thou wilt in fear and anger flee.

January 8, [1947].
Got high on phons [pantopon] and charge last nite with Norman, Jack, Vicki, Huncke, who made a doctor for a scrip with my money! Told Lucien my mystical experience.

The sense I have with charge is like the sense in a dream where, with or without verbal conversation, we understand the meanings of whoever is talking to us.

I did not regain (as yet) the pure communion of New Year's Eve, but what I have felt since with charge makes me think that it is partly an illusion—the illusion of understanding motives and intents. The understanding is of our/my projections into the situation, and not of other's real minds. I kept checking up on Vicki and Norm last night and found that often my interpretations varied from their meaning.

January 13, [1947].
Tried tea and junk tonite for second time.
    Hip conversation:
    "You bug me."
    "I bug you?"
    "Yeh, you bug me."
    "I bug you."
    "You bet you bug me."
    "Well, you bug me."
    "So, I bug you."

January 18, [1947].
Wrote a poem after feeling Caswell's vibrations:

For P—

I know my love as well as he, etc.

January 20, 1947.
Dream: I forgot it all, but, there is a grasshopper a foot long beating around my room. I rush out of the room and it blunders out of the window. It goes thru difficulties, getting in people's ways. It flies in the air, past a cigarette lighter, burning above. It freezes after firemen? put out the fire. I take pity on it, pick it up (like a stick) and it wakes up, begins flapping, and terrorizes me.

Dear Bill:
I feel as if I am at a dead end and so I am finishing the situation off this way. All your preachments and "spiritual facts" I realize as true, but joy or pleasure or whatever it is, while I think I understand them, have not helped me very much, or I have not helped myself to them very much. I never escape the feeling of being closed in, the continual relentless anxiety, the frustration, the sordidness of self, the uselessness. All my pleasures are melancholy, and

liveliness has only been a weary promise, gratifying, but somehow escaping me. Maybe if I continued things would please me more, but as it is I feel no hope and I am tired. You have my love, and pay my last respects to everybody else, if you have the opportunity, but I wish I could curse everybody involved and drag them all down to my level. —Allen.

[*Late in 1946, Neal Cassady arrived in New York City from Denver with his young wife, LuAnne. Ginsberg and his friends around Columbia had heard many wild stories about Cassady from Hal Chase, but no one was prepared for the dynamic Adonis who swept everyone, including Ginsberg, off their feet with his rugged charm. From the moment Ginsberg first saw him in the West End Bar, he was head-over-heels in love with Cassady. LuAnne and Neal often quarreled, and before long, she returned to Denver leaving Cassady on his own. Within a few days, Ginsberg and Cassady began a sexual relationship, which would last for many years.*]

January 21, 1947.
Having spent a wild weekend in sexual drama with Cassady, I am left washed up on the shore of my "despair" again. It is after such pleasure that I get a full knowledge of what I have slowly closed myself off from. The kid calls me ascetic; which is amusing, but pointless, vague. Here I have sat for two days, my emotions slowly subsiding, irritated, pettish, splenetic, depressed, nervous, bored. I fear that I shall have to enter into Hell again, and it is not sorrowful nor tragic but uneasy and depressing to me. I have lost the ability to really feel any but extremes of pleasure; for the rest it is only a dull, slowly lengthening pain. The sickness is that I cannot even love or respect my pain and my failure, but merely gaze on my "agonistic travails" with nervous displeasure. I wish that I was in despair, or fright, or love; but I am in no state of clear emotion; just turbid, vascular lethargy and slow fear. I spend my life rushing out meeting people, connecting with facts and dramas; I do not need to know the facts and I am not a good actor. I want a life of repose and solitude. I want a life of power and exuberance. I think that I should approach Neal and propose to him that we live together for a season, short or long as it may be; I need to catch the ways of his personal power, his lack of some fears. I have not much to offer him in return except what he seems to think that I have, intellectual polish, learning, subtlety of thought. All of this is so childish and useless. Everything that is dust and ashes in my mouth—and everything that I do not possess: I shall offer these to him in return for the secret of existence?

Now to get to the point. I am frustrated and, I suppose, too helplessly

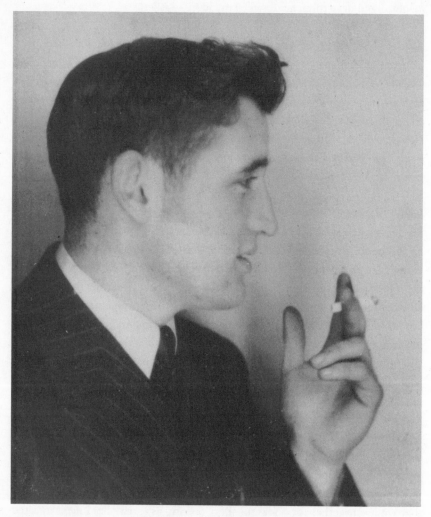

Neal Cassady

caught in the web of my failure to rescue myself; and at the moment I could be satisfied, if at all, and, if only temporarily by a physical union (intermittent) with Cassady. This pose, this prose, its afflatus and stupidity. How can I ever save myself from all this sordidness. Stop!

I am really at a dead end. And no commissions. I have seen unleashed (!) the last two days, all the latent suicidal mania that I have refused heretofore to recognize. I keep returning to the feeling that I will never really do anything to satisfy myself. The thought of living like this for a lifetime is enervating. I keep knowing that someday I will get up enough vitality to commit suicide.

Let me go!

God damn you bastards all! Let me fuckin' go out of all this! I'm tired, I'm tired, I'm tired, I'm tired, I'm tired. I can't stand the stupidity any longer. Returning then, to the frigid beauties of lake placid. The childishness of sitting here writing. I don't say what I know and mean: Someone is looking over my shoulder! Fuck it all.

The frigid plasticity of the craven image. The futility of all that I have seen and done and said. Now, complete, chaotic, disorganization. Everything drops out from the bottom. No wonder I can't write.

Strangely (one hr later) I read Donne and understand him for the first time tonite. Why is Donne so good? He is not the ascetic poet, in his examinings of passion. He is not the frightful romantic glorying in the agony. He has a subtle, balanced mind—which "subtle to plague itself" is expressing in controlled form, stark, sharp imagery, passionately, and with clean intelligence, the confusion in his emotions. He catches the point where he knows what is perverse about his desire, analyzes it, purges himself not of desire but of confused and contradictory desire. He is a tragic poet, his muse is tragic; because in his poetry is the free will and the objective intelligence opposing the inevitable emotions which are fate.

January 23, [1947].
I have been writing love sonnets and lyrics like mad. None of them, at the time of writing, seem to be very sharp, distinguished, stark.

> "The romance of the wild kingdom,"
> "Tomorrow's Thursday and I'll see my love."
> "God knows how many bells would ring."

January 28, [1947].

Strangest psychic upheaval this week: affair with Cassady and rejection by psychoanalytic clinic in free analysis. This means Reich I suppose. I can't work intensively or extensively—no reading, no writing. I can't write proper exam papers (this is exam week) I can't think of discipline and order. Just wildness, anxiety, stubborn disgust.

Dream: Recurrent dream sense of consciousness of dream in process. I look at Lucien (create him) and from profile he changes into Aunt Edie—strangely—an Aunt Edie of childhood feelings. Her face is double and then into Naomi. I realize that there is important traumatic experience uncovered here, while dreaming. My body is pushed in and tense, my abdomen feels as if it must burst out. Stiffness, rigidity, as if held in place by vise all over. Suffocation, heaviness on chest. I decide to plunge on into dream, and do so—knowing that it will hurt, having the material brought up. I move towards Naomi—I am not corporeal—and feel very sexual—anticipate orgasmic feelings. Then I realize that I am thinking about her black breasts, and choking and clucking and gasping like an infant. Under what circumstances—deprivation of milk? Birth and breathing commence? [In the margin Ginsberg has written: "Association with last nite. Gene's remark about wanting mother's milk. His 'joke.'"] Do I think of Lucien as a mother? A surrogate—Aunt Edie? Why Edie? Something important.

January 29, [1947].

Complaining to Cassady, conferences with Trilling, phone calls to Kardiner,[151] perturbation paralysis, and finally physical sickness over dead end at analysis. Cried over seeming impossibility of saving self (made suicidal fantasies) for first time in a year.

Dream: I am on *Normandie* or *Queen Mary*, going to Europe (association heter or homo boat?) Long open top platform, exciting N.Y. harbor. Much excitement, people all about, etc. I am standing next to a girl who I talk to, not recognizing. There is something high school like about her, but she is someone I once knew when she was young, a cousin (Pearl? Gil?). She reproaches me for not knowing her. I am below, wandering the corridors, and meet Justin Brierly of Denver. He is silver haired, looks like Otto Kruger. He greets me: a situation is here, we are antagonistic. He shows me his protégés—five little kids, "of all ages, 9–15 for my taste." They are playing half naked in the corridor, some

---

151 Abram Kardiner. Psychology professor who ran a free clinic, employing his students as therapists.

embracing one another. He shows me them with pride as his possessions. I think, or I ask, "Well, how about fixing me up while you're at it. You won't need all at once." He suggests that we go to the dining room. He is dressed, and I am only half dressed, and I see that he is trying to embarrass me, put me at ill-ease; so I stop the whole conspired situation by considering a moment, then saying pre-emptorily, "Meet me at my (or your) stateroom in an hour," and I walk off without waiting for his reply. I feel as if I have enforced my will on him, that he will not dare not to come; at the same time I wonder.

We are in a Museum of Modern Art atmosphere all the time. I am very pleased to be off to Europe. I ask someone, "Where do we stop?" "Le Havre"— "Oh, I would prefer so much to make Marseilles." "Yes," she replies, "it would be grand." I consider the food: or is it only on those French lines that the enormous dinners came as part of the ticket? Charges. There is ambiguity about my own position on this boat: I don't know who paid or if I am paid. But I am here: This makes me think that this whole business is psychoanalysis.

Another boat, after, as in another dream, half in the museum, I meet the family. We are all about, eating. I have a guilty feeling about them: I have not seen them in a year, all the children are grown and do not half-recognize me. Lou looks older and tired. I weep a little at my own neglect of them, and their answers, and indestructible piteous state; and the change. Eugene: he is older, married, has a kid (I inquire about that) and is in a commercial uniform. He has finally settled down as a pilot between Canada (where he now lives) and France or England or U.S. He takes planes back and forth. (Museum now) He seems to have fallen: his ambition (legal) is thwarted; he is piloting, which is a unique and paying job, but it is an ethical and aesthetic and personal dead end. I am affected by the air of him, of frustration, sadness, mellowness, resignation, mediocrity, impotence. He is not much enamored of his family (wife and kids) but they are there as an easy way out. I am in bed with him (as if in resolution of our youth's misadventures) and I realize suddenly that we are moving together sexually. I decide to go thru with it, though once I had suppressed such knowledge and we jackknife and move. Then I take his genitals, they are small, erect and soft. However the sex play is unfinished or something happens: I remember no more.

January 1947 [Reading List].
Pareto, Vilfredo. *The Mind and Society, vol. 1*

Lowes, John L. *Geoffrey Chaucer and the Development of His Genius*

Sir Gawain and the Green Knight. (translated by Jessie Weston)

Donne, John [in] *English Poetry of the Seventeenth Century* (edited by Roberta Brinkley)

February 4, 1946 [sic 1947].
Tea [marijuana]: Well, the picture of complacence: I recline here, an ounce of charge in the desk, an apartment waiting for me, a young man out at work. Last night got high, rolled three sticks with Neal (bombers) and blasted them. Then listened to music and ate. In Spanish restaurant at 105 St., proprietor got into fight; there was an air of oppression in the room, I became panicked. Great waves of fear in my mind and/or in the atmosphere. Childlike terror.

Listening to jazz, then: the jazz kick. With tea one is permitted to enter a world of rhythms of ideation. Listening to a good record, you hear the whole orchestra working in a repetitive pattern, pick up on each different kick in the music, are the music. Then some man gets sent, the whole orchestra works together to get a strange, out of this world, orgasmic, spontaneous hysterical, kick. The listener hears; if he is sent he shares the kick and goes wild.

February 17, [1947].
Jazz records.
Lester Young—B.B. Blues (VV)

Cozy Cole—all star 9–12 in Keynote

"That's all for tonite"

Jazz at Philharmonic—Illinois Jacquet. Vol. IV, Sides 2–3

also "How High the Moon"

Part 3 ask

Krupa on this—Fell off chair, interrupts record in end of wild drums solo

Illinois Jacquet—Bottoms Up

Dizzy Gillespie—Things to Come

Lester Young—Lester Leaps In

Basie, Count—Muttonleg (VV)

Dream: A lot of people in Ted Hoffman's hallway. Lucien has to go somewhere with someone to home to be taken care of. All families reject him: his own, mine, Jack's, Hoffman's. I want to give him shelter, take him home with me, but something frustrates my plan. (I am evil in creating the situation where I can get my claws on him by the fact that he has no one else to turn to: that is what I'd like to see. The sordidness of my desire, so small is my self that the only way it can submit to or love the beloved object is to wish it ill that I may dominate it, and at the same time I cannot really dominate it/him, because I am really too little to do so. So no matter how "favorable" the external situation my plans and life are doomed to sterility and failure.) The dream breaks off at that point. Anxiety that, after all, I really won't be able to give him shelter and love no matter how much he needs it and I want to, because anything would be preferable to me.

February 21, [1947].
Lester Young—Jumpin' at Messners, Savoy Jump.

Turning back to study in Johnson, Pope, and Swift, peace sort of descends. By discipline I avoid subjective embroilments, discipline and work. But this solves no real problems, just relieves the monotony of despair. Suddenly, in a few weeks, I will feel the pain of sterility and narrowness of emotion, and will turn inward again. You never lose yourself in work, you try to forget, but you can't and you never will, you'll remember, if at no other time, with sickening dread and pitiful regretfulness, on your deathbed. Saw Lown today, got [Wilhelm] Reich's address: will write in a few days.

February 22, [1947].
Talk with Cassady: He has a highly developed situational imagination and an even, clear mind as far as emotional entanglements are concerned. He can act to his interest, at the same time carefully considerate of all emotional angles and will do no wrong. I trust him.

February 23, [1947].
Dream: I am in a restaurant, don't have much money. In the revolving display window I see a lobster. It is undergoing a strange, magic, evil operation. I (and others) see it viciously lopping off parts of itself—with its claws?—at any rate, I think, this is evil, this is neurosis. The lobster continues till it has chopped itself to bits; the window revolves to the end of the revolution, where all sections of the panorama are revealed at once, and I think and ask, "Is this going to show us the evil?" The broke lobster? No, the panorama is there, (buildings) a street perhaps, but no lobster. I breathe a sigh of troubled relief. [Ginsberg has written in margin: "Associations. Waitress in Old Salt 8¢ tip his remark 'It's

terrible.' Preying mantis of other dream. Crab of castration. Snake eating self. Mechanical lopping self mutilation. Like mechanical jazz ecstasy."]

I leave and go into the next room, which is an antechamber, sort of, a lobby to the restaurant. It's a classy place, and has some Japanese sumo wrestlers toying around. A crowd gathers; they put down a little rug and are going to wrestle. There is a phallic, spiteful, efficient woman there, the manageress, sitting overseeing. I am there, but I have no money. I am therefore, in my debility, moved to make sincere suggestions in general. [Ginsberg has written in the margin: "1920's in Lynd Ward. Thalia Lobby, waiting for seats to Malreaux. Argument of Louis with usher. Unpleasantness similar to Old Salt. Woman teacher and Chem. Boss at Academy Bookstore on Times Square with Makin. Sumo Homosexuality. Eugene's roommate. Think of Lobster Supper, Eugene crying, teeth mutilated, corn on instep torn, great blood. Who?"]

Then I leave, noticing that I am wearing only a few layers of underwear (above my waist). I have difficulty now, trying to explain that I do have regular pants and shoes, etc., that my trouble is above my waist (wrists—slip). [Ginsberg has written in margin: "Childhood dream of exposure. Downtown in only underwear top."] A chaos of associations. Do you know what happens to people like you?

February 23, [1947].

I will try to think on those sexual positions with Cassady which would please me. It is unfortunate that as yet I am unable to woo him with speech, but, in bed, merely discuss things with earnestness. Try him laying me again; try breast to breast position. Try 69 again, coming both at once. Try sitting on his chest and making him blow me. Try laying his mouth. French kissing, etc. Make him give me a trip around the world. Try (this requires real passion) browning him. Also a good massage. Laying his anus. Laying him backward— thighs—kneeling and blowing, both ways. Wrestling—Whipping? Have I guts? Trip around world, complete, winding up with blow job. No, I want some real hip sex, what is it?

February 1947 [Reading List].
Trilling, Lionel. *E.M. Forster*

Pope, Alexander. Essay on Criticism, *The Rape of the Lock, with the Epistle of Dr. Arbuthnot* [and] *Eloise et Abelard,* etc.

Sitwell, Edith. *Alexander Pope*

Marvell, Andrew. *Poems* (Vol. 1. Straight poems), Eliot's essay

Krutch, Joseph. *Samuel Johnson*

Johnson, Samuel. Life of Pope, Swift

Baudelaire, Charles. *20 Prose Poems of Baudelaire*, translated by Michael Hamburger. (Editions Poetry London, 1946)

Swift, Jonathan. *Gulliver's Travels*

March 2, [1947].

Tea can have real disturbing influences on a neurotic or on personality anyway. Some visions: Cassady and I talking, plumb such strange depths of insight, and yet never so convincingly afterwards: at the moment they are tremendous, the frame of reference is understood, but later, retaining some of the sense of insight and, perhaps, having lost the identity of the frame of reference, we are or I am, skeptical, or, rather bewildered, and run away from the problems. This is in measure of pursuit. This ties in with our conversation of the other night in a bar: Norman, Vicki, Neal and *moi*.

Sometimes it seems, as to Neal, that he has a special way of thought—retiring deeply into himself, except that rather than retiring he has simply left himself open really to experiencing things—as if under whisky. The quiet "stoned" feeling, partly, or complete loss of consciousness in looking and listening, perhaps in responding. Going off the deep end to impulse. It is this quality, extended to such a length, that makes me inquire of him, "Are you really down there?"

For myself, I pursue the limited understanding of each situation, analyzing it before going on. The vision we had of me was of demonic, neurotic will pursuing (in sterile ways of thought?) on and on trying to "understand" a situation which 1) I perhaps don't really want to understand 2) or, understanding, I find that I am emotionally unreceptive, sterile, shallow in the situation. Also there is the sense, that "understanding" or formal mental arrangement of the situation is an "anthropomorphism," a neurotic defense against it, so that if one saturated oneself in the situation, one would <u>need</u> no formal understanding, but would live in <u>complete</u> projection, feeling, identification with things. To this is added Walter's observation, that one need not worry, it seems that "everything will take care of itself." To this is added the difficulty, which Neal brought up, that on his "level" <u>down there</u>, there is constant long range thinking ahead, rapport, and association and understanding. That I think things that occur to me, and think to say, four associations, or think within the limitations of the structural idea of the world. Automatic thinking as it were, relying on fixed ideas and responses to carry me along after having "analyzed" automatically to that superficial, shallow fourth level. And when I pursue the *idee fixé*, the situation in analysis or thought, I pursue on this shallow level, continually evading plunging on down to what Neal calls his "sixteen thoughts down" or sixteen associations, or saturation thought (naive conning) so that my moments of real insight and understanding are bewildering—when I really understand, I feel bewildered because it is not like formal understanding (four thoughts down)—understanding that one can verbalize and argue (see Jack's objection to my mind)—but the real understanding is a different kind—it is a feeling, a response; ride with the response and <u>everything takes care of itself</u>, there is no need for the "unbewildering" "verbalized," "conscious" understanding. Neal's is awareness, mine is consciousness. The consciousness is shallow; awareness is all embracing.

But I do not sometimes believe (on my conscious level) in the <u>existence</u> of the awareness level; or if I believe, in bewilderment, in the awareness level, I don't trust it. So I ask Neal, are you <u>really</u> "down there?" He says, "Yes." I say, "Do things take care of themselves?" or "Does it work?" And his reply is disconcerting as far as the system is concerned. He lives on a rational level as far as things are concerned; but with personality, in social relations, he descends completely.

Then I wonder "but to verbalize" you have to come up. I continually verbalize, continually "pursue the understanding and analysis" so that pursuit distracts my mind from full feeling, as it were, forces me to think on a near surface level, with consciousness; that in turn prevents me from pursuing to the bottom, to real awareness and satisfaction, I pursue on a shallow level. If I would stop verbalizing, stop surface identification, stop acting on the neurotic surface to protect myself from the real awareness which disturbs me— moments of deep awareness are "bewildering," perplexing: I wish to verbalize them, bring them up to consciousness. Why? So that I know what to do with them? But that is the neurotic way of living. You don't arrange and deal with things so, you let them come in and out, let things happen, not prevent them. Besides what do you really need to do with them? By doing, you only mean fitting them into the useless, sterile structure, or categorized thought. Anything that is beneath the surface of the structure, that you can't intellectualize and identify, you fear.

A question: on what level, or how, does Neal think about things other than social relations? If I understand, he does not do the same thing, feel "down there." But he obviously does not think on my fourth level, according to consciousness and law and structure. He spoke of a continual mixture of levels. When he verbalized, he verbalizes with 16 modifications, or as many as rise to the surface varyingly; I verbalize with a continual unvarying pace of four modifications. That is "sterility," hardening of the psyche, shallowness. I want to understand all things on the same level, related to one another, so there is no confusion when I work from one idea to another: they all fit in in the structure. So I think about most things on the same level. Neal thinks on many levels, so that one thought means nothing to another, in a sense, is not ordered to another; but there is no need for that conscious order, which is only "defensive?" Meaning? Merely, that I am perturbed by bewilderment in natural varying thought. All must be within frame of reference. (True art is where you jump from one to another? Stay consistent.) Conversation, then is difficult, when I pursue: If he responds he responds with a statement, and then modifies in a chain, getting more and more complicated: I don't follow his chain, I interrupt and ask for modification of each link: as it were, for every modification he explains, I have a whole series of modifications: I try to clarify, more [in the margin Ginsberg has written: "and/or associate"] deep, in addition, to each of his chains. Or is it that for his enormous structure of 16 thoughts, I can't follow along, it is too big and deep, so I ask for a halt for each one: and it is that halt then, that prevents my understanding of his whole thought? Those times he talks without interruption, explaining his personality or mine, I emerge with a feeling of an awareness of a sort, really unverbalized; a sort of gestalt without consciousness, but bewildered by it, not "knowing what to think" or "how to act upon the awareness," or not really knowing what the awareness is. I can't remember or see the whole structure clearly. I feel it merely. I am feeling guilty 1) about not having a clear understanding but only awareness. 2) at the same time if I attempt clear understanding on "my" level I feel quietly of disruptry and losing the true awareness. But is my bewildered "deep" thinking "true awareness?" Is it the same thing as Neal's? Now is his awareness, 16 deep response, responsible for his "con" success, his vibration? He spoke of formalizing for people that awareness of lack of awareness. That's it—they all fear him because he is so aware of them and their level of thought, and so unjudgingly, unverbally responsive, that it frightens them. My own life on the other hand, depends (in its social phase) more on mere verbalism than his, on conversation. He and Jack go out and experience together; I go out and analyze with people, or against them; and since the conversational analysis is "protective," covers anxiety, fear of "responding with awareness," or moving with them, the analysis soon (as with Rauch today) becomes personal: and after a while embarrassing and shameful to me because I realize my own anxiety, posturing and hostility, masochism, aggressiveness, and superficiality. This also, leads me to say the obvious. It strikes me that I attempt to integrate my personality by making up my mind, making decisions as responses, analyses of situations, identifying that singleness of mind with integration. This leads to the thought that at home, I received and submitted, with awareness of a true nature, to my mother's paranoid emotions: this identification with my mother's feelings. Then, listening to my father's complaints, I identified myself with his emotions: the result was that in one hour, I was on her "side" and "his" and continually felt called upon to make a decision in who to think with: this decision, when conscious, is the neurotic mask, when unconscious, without decision, I am flying from pole to pole: whoever I'm with I understand and identify myself with: at the same time I fight consciously against that understanding and awareness because I am conditioned, habitually forced to make an independent decision and take a position of my own, and act on it—So that with Jack, I can let myself go and feel with him; I do consciously analyze him also: so that with him I am of a double nature, grouchy, superficially quibbling, varyingly responsive and hostile. Repetition of traumatic situation in the Joan Bill vs. Hal Jack feud. I understood both, sympathized with both, made an intellectual conscious decision for Joan and Bill, but loved and was aware of both sides so much that I was loathe to abandon the emotions of either side so I am continually forced to act, and my actions must be my own, with integrated self, but how to act without some decision? And where else do you make decisions but in the mind, which counts and tabulates the emotions, so that I won't act the way I don't feel. But then, I so often feel neurotically, feel emotions (say, love) that aren't mine—learned conditioned emotions—that I can't successfully, practically respond to them without fucking myself up and making myself unhappy. So I relax and interpose consciousness between "awareness" and "action" and muddle through, deciding as best I can. If I follow "emotion," respond automatically, I fear people, work, sports, etc., get into school troubles, become eccentric and disordered, melancholy, suicidal, ingrown and *jejune* and "juvenile" emotionally—I become morbid and "romantic." If I think, I become mechanical and sterile, shallow, embarrassed, conflicted.

Now to speak of a way of awareness of Neal which I recognize as my own, of his strength of mind. He was aware of me, my emotions, sympathetically and objectively; he responded, and at the same time aware (as Jack and Hal and

Lucien are not; as Joan and Bill are to a great extent) of his own interests and needs. So that he took pains, naturally, to try not to hurt me, to arrange a solution to our emotional entanglement which would not rebuff me or reject me; he was secure enough and wise enough not to need to respond with hostility to my emotional demands. This double awareness I have always also—though whether his and mine are the same is in doubt: here things are ambiguous.

Nevertheless, the point here is that above my objective understanding he has a subjective understanding and integrity—the strength of mind—that allows him to act with sympathy and pity, but without confusion and guilt, in his own interests. I can act so—as, politically—in school, with regard to poetry etc., and to some personality (this is Neal's straightness and mine). But as regards real subjective strength of mind, I have a blind spot. I don't know what to do, so I fit my personal decisions into the 4th modified structure of reality that I consciously apprehend—and act on the conscious level always—so that my actions are really confused, sterile, as is my thought. See clearer now, I think. Wonderful!

Now, for instance, discussing [Jerry] Rauch's liking for Lilly and Fast: on a 4th, conscious level, I wasn't interested and was cleaver and belittling; as soon as I heard that Jerry was ready to join the party, I was aware, and understood: so that I felt benevolence and sympathy to his joining the party, and towards the magazine: "Oh, that's different, I said to him." But on a conscious level I felt the sterility of the party; I sympathized with his interest. Now the crux: I identified myself with his emotion, and felt drawn to the party (drawn to his impulse) on a conscious level, I knew that it isn't right for me, that I don't want the party myself, but I felt guilty about liking Jerry's party (and disapproving) or being indifferent of my own party. So then I became confused. I identify: if he joins the party why don't I join? or, if the party is wrong, or sterile, or useless for me, why should it be right for him? That is, on an objective level, the party itself, I felt called upon to make a decision, and became bewildered. Same as mother father—sympathy with each, yet "called upon" for decision for or against; and since my decision must violate some sympathy, I feel guilty about decision. Question. Does one, then, go thru life, "letting things take care of themselves?" Really, is one called upon to decide; does action really need that kind of decision? Doesn't one really just go thru the world responding? So, asking Neal, "Are you really down there?" He says, "Yes." I say, "How do you deal with practical things?" "I get up to the surface and stay down only for social relations, where it works."

But, really, what difference is there to the mind between responding and

personality, and to things; particularly consider, that in action, things and per-
sonalities are always mixed, practically the same. How does the mind decide
between the two, and go into its right act at the right times? But this is fine
spun and silly; but it is. It seems now as I think, the inevitable question to
which I always return—it seems almost an unstructural, an impossible struc-
tural position; at the same time a position improbable in awareness—so that I
conclude—? that my understanding, here, of the whole problem, on whatever
level this is being thought is incomplete or inadequate: ask Neal about all of
this. "Perhaps he has secrets to change life?" We are really, if I can iron out
my emotional shallowness, and if he can do whatever is necessary to him—I
really don't know what goes on in his mind—a satisfactory couple. We could
make great music together. After all (petulantly) I'm not so bad, really. What
annoys me, is that in all this embroilment—I, guiltily—assume all the blame
for all the trouble, feel unworthy, sordid, sterile, shallow, etc.—when I might
be merely—by strength of will—realizing what is wrong with me (awareness)
without realizing, really, what is wrong with others, and taking all the blame.
Really, I may be vibrating and aware, so much for others, and not vibrating and
aware of my own soul. Or perhaps this is all a really mad illusion, which obvi-
ously it isn't. But none of these are really satisfactory. I am mostly prepared to
abase myself and take judgment, penance. I am really the lowest of the low,
really, no one is as useless and unlovable as myself; I really can't escape that.
Now I am Dostoyevsky, but I really am and know it; now things are peaceful,
but look at me. Or is everyone the lowest of the low? or now, am I conscious,
excusing myself. No, I must take my blame, receive it, saturate myself with it
till I can live with it without disgust of myself. Where am I? Surely no one else
goes through this? Either I am the lowest of the most shallow and decadent
and I degenerate, vain, really stupid human, or the highest, the true crucified
Christ. Or neither, or nothing. Who am I? I must ask someone. Yes that is the
solution! Accept someone's answer. No, I will believe them, I am so naive and
credulous, and then I will be any number of things and selves, all different, all
horrid. I will be wonderful with Neal—he'll tell me that; or else sometimes, I
must take the blow and accept the fact that I am nowhere, that I can't profit
him. I will be stiff and bright and lovable but overdignified, by Norman, by
Lucien I will be superficial and really sick and repulsive; I will be sweet to
Trilling; sharp and unfathomable to Bill, cute and annoying and superficial and
profound and overrational to Joan; insignificant to Jack; mad and confused to
Rauch; deep and soulful and brilliant to Harriet and Paul; reserved and smart
to John; soulful and stable to Pippin; mad, manic, strange, naive to Walter;

sharp and disciplined to Ted Hoff[man]; childlike, amusing and stubborn to Fritz and Bass, etc. Of course I am all of them, except really not the good ones or the frenzied ones. But I am frenzied really. When will this end? Where will it lead to? Follow. Follow! *"J'attends lieu avec gourmandise!"* Well, Lown, advised me against tea on horse, my kingdom for a horse. How much of this does Cassady understand? How much more or less does he know? Or, as Norman said, is it, really, that, with tea, nobody really understands anybody: and maybe that is the state of nature. The only conclusion that I can draw from all, is that I should descend lower, feel people more; and I have begun that a few months ago and I began that a few minutes ago. As to Cassady, today, this afternoon, I found myself bored with him; or else, (answering guilt again) afraid I was boring him. Certainly my sexual advances are not pleasing? or are they? No. I have had an increased feeling that the nearer we come to understand each other, the less he is attracted sexually, whatever the fluctuations of brotherliness; so that the last week I have felt no little response that I have necessarily made my own comings perfunctory, sort of taken from him, and, feeling so little response, have stopped really trying to seduce him and working on him till he comes. This is partly the boredom; he doesn't seem to feel me sexually, and I feel him less because of that, so that my sexuality has become mechanical, impulsive still, because it is so pervasive, I am so sensual; but I am become sensual without love emotion, more with boredom; I feel as if I were jerking off or him; and do so. So, for the moment, I am glad to see him go, it's a relief; but when he is gone how I shall need and miss him; wish that I could have been satisfied with the few crumbs of emotion he delivers up, and not so demanding and irrational as to wish more. The fault really is mine here; I can't adjust my hot emotions to his. But then, why should I? or why shouldn't he adjust to mine? or why not a compromise? But that would be in form only; it would be unsatisfactory to both. New lovers compromise. They are made alike—that's why they are mated; Neal and I are not evenly mated. And the fault is mine thru excess of love and need because, after all, his is straighter than mine. The "inevitable conclusion" is that we should part; or adjust ourselves which is his solution, the adjustment. I see his reason: yet I will never really adjust, and I don't know if he will. So where are we? Then I feel bored, knowing that we are not true lovers. Yet here an impulse comes "irrational, neurotic" saying that I love him; and that in his way, he needs me as much as I, etc. Following this impulse I should be joyous and mournful at his departure; but, really, with awareness—of his kind, I think—he does no longer excite me, I've almost used him up in a way, learned as much as I will from him, loved him as much as I can, to no end, except final loss of real feeling and love, and want no more of him. But of course I do want more of him, it's just that I haven't got enough? And, then, have I really given myself to him? Have we gotten anywhere on each side, *ad infinitum*? At this point it is useless meanderings and I have things to do. If I can feel—really one doesn't solve and theorize and conclude—really, then I finally feel him, we will move together, tonight, tomorrow, next year, or never. Or, perhaps, we will be most penetrated with grief for each other when we are apart.

(To Cassady, Given: Elegy of Ruins, Death in Violence, Sonnet: Jan 22, 1947)

March 1947 [Reading List].
Pound, Ezra. *Personae* (repeat)

Vayakas, Byron. *Transfigured Night*

Sidney, Philip. *The Defense of Poesy* [and] *Astrophel and Stella*

Spenser, Edmund. *Amoretti* (in Potter) [and] *Faerie Queene,* part 8

Legouis, Emile and Cazamian, Louis. *A History of English Literature.* (on above reading 50 pps.)

The Kafka Problem (selections) edited by Angel Flores

Deutsch, Babette. *This Modern Poetry*

Defoe, Daniel. *Robinson Crusoe*

Malory, Thomas. *La Mort D'Arthure,* books 11, 12, 17, 19, 20, 21

Norman, Charles. *The Muses' Darling: Christopher Marlowe*

Marlowe, Christopher. *Tamburlaine,* parts I and II; *Doctor Faustus;* [and] *The Jew of Malta*

Preston, Raymond. *'Four Quartets' Rehearsed*

Spender, Stephen. *Poems of Dedication*

Gay, John. *Beggar's Opera,* and a few lyrics

March 7, [1947].
In bed, then, we dismissed such things, and understood one another well. He has awareness! How much that has come to mean. More than dignity permits? But a working proposition. I spent the night, last, with Jack and Neal. I came out and talked soberly (and severely) and straight and vibrant to Jack, *à la* Cassady—and it worked! Jack and I in an unofficial rapprochement, Neal off to

Denver this evening at 6:30. I stood by the bus and said goodbye and walked home. No tears, some melancholy, but mostly a peace and grace which I attained with Jack last night. We are going into Garver's coat business together.[152] Home, empty but not too dragged, afraid of what's to come, I went to Vicki's for a while. So Maureen and I began playing games (or she did, with all).

Allen Ginsberg—hate [Letters of words crossed out as per a game.]
Neal Cassady—marriage?
(Like love hate marriage)

Our's (Maureen's) turned to M M (marriage with marriage). She went on with fuck shit piss suck etc. She told me she had her cherry. I expressed surprise, pain. Offered to fill in. Surprise, coyness, acceptance—so to the flip delight of all we retired from Norman's to Vicki's room, and made love. I blew her, half jacked off. She gave me a hickey (suck blood in neck to surface to leave red badge of honor). What a surprise. I was enjoying much of it, I suspect I'd really get a rise by being passive. (Rise out of self) Anyway, to be continued, etc.

March 11, [1947].
[Someone's name has been heavily crossed out at this spot in the journal.] or blew him, momentous occasion, bored, (salty) but straight pretty much. Walked together through sunshine and shadow. Phrase from religious pamphlets. Talk with Carr. Vibration with Kroner, Rauch, L. Kurke, Bridget O'Reilly. My Sea Voyage Vigils. Met and heard Sylvia Simms. Talk about Re bop language and literature. Mar ? Example of Re Bop perception: Cassady's characterization of W. Wager as Big Stoop. Then, I think of Bill Burroughs' sometime neurotic mask: Wallace Beery, he plays and Frank Morgan.

March 20, [1947].
To use in Poetry—

"From Mohack and from Hawkubete
Good Lord deliver me,
Who wander through the streets by night
committing cruelty" —[John] Gay.

---

152 William Garver. Petty criminal around Times Square, who stole overcoats from restaurants and sold them in pawn shops.

March 29, [1947].

Met Dr. A.A. Cott;[153] met Justin Brierly in N.Y. and dueled with him over authorship of "Death in Violence" (asserting Cassady's powers, etc.)[154] Long talk with Jack Kerouac about his "neuroses" etc. If one perceives the aesthetic beauty of Jack's tableaux, how can one shut the mind to them and analyze?

Dream: I am on train to St. Louis (Denver). So is Chase. I see him. We avoid one another unknowingly, or he avoids me. I have a lot of books I've accumulated aboard. Lenny (tea connection) is there. We discuss Chase, he suggests knowingly that Chase really doesn't want to cut me, offers to take me to him. All is well. Dream ends. That is a shame: I realized on waking how little I'd forgotten Chase and how much he had wounded me; it is a permanent sorrow which remains with me but only subconsciously since I continually censor it and assume some strength and rationality in it all. The compulsive trying not to feel rejection. I don't however really love Chase in the sense that I do not think that I could get along with him in his real masks as well as others. I have little use for him and vice versa except for interval personality combinations, not long range work or play. Yet I mourn the passage of this season as it has ended with no reconciliation; that is one of the major fuck ups of personalities I have experienced. Why did it have to happen, I mean?

April 1947 [Reading List].

Tillotson, Geoffrey. *The Moral Poetry of Pope*

Stevens, Wallace. *Esthétique Du Mal: A Poem*

Shakespeare, William. Sonnets, *Romeo, Richard II, Midsummer Nights' Dream*

Fielding, Henry. *The Adventures of Joseph Andrews*

Durrell, Lawrence. *Cities, Plains and People: Poems* (rehearsed)

Fielding, Henry. *The History of the Life of the Late Mr. Jonathan Wild the Great*

Boswell, James. *Boswell's Life of Johnson*, edited by Charles G. Osgood (Scribner's, 1917) 550 pp.

Drew, Elizabeth. *Directions in Modern Poetry*

Nims, John Frederick. *The Iron Pastoral*

---

153 Dr. A. Allan Cott. Newark psychiatrist who used orgone therapy to treat Ginsberg for a very short period.

154 With Ginsberg's complicity, Cassady had been telling people that he was the author of several of Ginsberg's poems for the purpose of impressing them with his abilities.

Greenberg, Samuel. *Poems*

Rodman, Selden. *A New Anthology of Modern Poetry* (Modern Library)

Auden, W.H. *New Year Letter* (*The Double Man*)

(Met Auden and Kallman)

another time: Poems (*The Orators*, [and] *Sea and the Mirror*)

April 29, [1947].
No news for you, lots elsewhere. Trouble with Cassady; lain with Carr; argued, affection, split, his angst. Seduction of Lucien to human perturbation; near Bill's view of him now. Naomi, Bellevue, radio back. etc. etc. Depression, relieved, but settling in; sexual stasis again.

> More jazz
>> Out on a limb—(Trio) Lenny Tristano
>> Walkin' Boogie—L. Hampton
>> Holiday—Brown Eyes, Lover Man, Man I Love
>> House of Joy (Cozy Cole) or (?)
>> Sunny Side of Street—(Dorsey?)
>> Miller—String of Pearls
>> James—One O'clock Jump
>> Pearl Baily—Tired
>> Dinah Washington, Hamp—Blow Top Blues
>> 3 Bips and a Bop—La pi da pickup—Haba (Scat)

April 30, [1947].
Met Auden (second time) at Boar's Head, read seventeenth century style poems before him, received some approbation, conversed in Gold Rail about teaching, Céline (whom he dislikes), St. Perse (who leaves him unsatisfied), subways, weather, jazz, Mozart, etc. Sterile silly conversation, I aggressive, distracted, impulsive. Auden, aloof.

Chester Kallman in Terry's. Chester walked in, was introduced by Gene to me. His conversation (anecdotal tale of walking into bar near his house, meeting the sailors, burlesquing his proposal in the urinal): "I suppose you have to be back in the morning?"

"No, we got ten days."

(To self: "Chester, no. Chester, no. This will never do, etc.") "I suppose you have some place to stay?"

"No, we just got in town."

"You <u>don't</u>?—Well you're welcome to share my apartment."

"Are we? Where do you live?"

"Just three blocks from here."

Chester continued with—he wanted another drink, so he appointed to meet the two sailors outside in a little time. At the bar he drank on while they were with some bitch he had brought. He nodded and winked to one, to see if they forgot. The one whom he talked to shouted back, "Hey don't forget, we're sleeping with you tonight."

To preface, he saw them in first bar he went into. "What did I see but two stunning sai-lors." Went on to next after saying "Chester. No. Not two, Chester, No."

So they all go home etc. next morning one paid him "the nicest compliment he ever received." "Man," said the sailor, grasping his arm and squeezing looking him straight in the eye, "you're great."

To this I said a stupid thing, that this was actually a <u>real</u> comment. Kallman confused me, I am having a recidivist perturbation, thinking that he is big time. As to Wystan, "Yes, Wystan said that it (the opening) was dreary. *Les jeunes* have a new idea about the artist going back to life."

May 1947 [Reading List].
Tempest—Read and reread for a week—Shakespeare

[*Ginsberg spent most of June in Texas with William Burroughs, Joan Adams, and Herbert Huncke on their farm near New Waverly, where they were attempting to grow a crop of marijuana. In July, he left to visit Cassady in Denver, believing that Cassady would return to New Waverly with him within a few weeks.*]

[written in] Denver:

> N.Y. Scraps / And my mind presides / on what my will prophecies.
> Loneliness: Liveliness is a weary promise, / My pleasures as all
>   melancholy.
> Whoever comes, henceforth, for me / I will in fear and anger flee.
> So in this 21st year I praise creation.
> Someday finish the great sonnet: / Lord, forgive my passions, they
>   are old / and restive as the years that I have known.

<u>Tea Leaves:</u>[155]

I am alone in a room in Spanish Harlem high on weed, and what a
 kick—note the eager youthful style. Tomorrow who knows what? /
 "I was never born; there is no yesterday. And no tomorrow, neither. /
 I wuff Beethoven."
Take her in the arms and kill her / assuredly with my permission and
 then / open...

July 28, [1947]. Denver.

Carolyn[156] to Neal: Whispering bedtime passion: "I love you, I love you." Self-
humiliation, over with for myself: Colburn Hotel Apts. Such terrible nights.
Denver Doldrums.

 Suggest to Neal that he keep a diary like Edouard's in *The Counterfeiters* [by
Andre Gide] or this or Jack's. His would be the most intelligent and perceptive
and touching of all in all likelihood. I should be all too curious to read it. This
is a problem, he must keep a personal one. O.K. He will buy his own.

July 29, [1947].

Some dreams: Yesternight—at a play (night after another concert in Central
City). I have an $11 ticket presented to me by Brierly (slip) Lancaster. [In the mar-
gin Ginsberg has written: "Talk to Neal about Oedipal mothers. Mrs. Carr. Mrs.
Lown apropos of Mrs. Chase."] The play I suspect I wrote—a surrealistic
Kafkian scene on a bare stage with character out of the fiery tales milling around
the proscenium. Played by the Marx Brothers, though there are six characters or
eight, including Santa Claus for sure, and John Rockwell playing a cross between
Uncle Sam and the Mad Hatter. Their dialogue is earnest and trite and profound,
yet irrelevant—not profoundly irrelevant at all, don't get the sense wrong, but
saturated with cosmic significance, and highly comic probably. Like that last sen-
tence—"saturated with cosmic significance, and highly comic probably." (ba ba
black sheep, baby) I wander on stage with them, so what, it doesn't bother me.
I think, but I'm really looking for a seat. I wander off, and hesitate to cross the
stage when suddenly I espy Lucien C. and his mother. Well! I hesitantly go up,

---

155 Tea Leaves. Marijuana notations, a heading that Ginsberg adopted around this time in his
notebooks for random thoughts, etc.

156 Carolyn Robinson (b. 1923). Later Carolyn Cassady, Neal's second wife. Ginsberg would fre-
quently misspell names, especially Caroline's [*sic*]. The editors have corrected the spelling of names
throughout the journals for the purpose of clarity.

and they very kindly move over so I can sit down. Strange, our different sets of (motives) emotions in appearing at these chic affairs.

1.) Motives
    a. His—In his milieu, high social atmosphere, naturally he turns up (doesn't plan to go) to these things.
    b. Mine—I go to them for work or duty or meaning, or seeking after innards of chicness and culture.
2.) Emotions
    a) His—amusement, then, at my Jewish presence. Casualness and competence and ease at play, sweat sardonicism at whole affair.
    b) Mine—Eagerness, earnestness, judgment, anxiety, bewilderment, seeking.

Later Lucien drifts off. I am together with his mother. She says, very gently and warmly, "You don't think, do you, that I've dropped out of the race for Lucien?" [In the margin Ginsberg has written: "Race: association with (Speedboat) (motorboat) midget auto races."] I am surprised at the generosity and competent adjustment of her to Lucien's needs and mine. She is as good as I could profit a fantasy of her developing. She offers me liquor at the bar, but I refuse, taking a small glass, $1/3$ full, of 7-Up.

Analysis: Worked out from above slips [of the tongue]
    Relation to Cassady. Relation to my projection of self to Oliver's mother in Gide's *Counterfeiters*. I have projected and transferred or whatever the technical word is, my own sense of adjustment to Cassady into Mrs. Carr. I ask Mrs. Carr's "sweet, you don't think." This applies to Lucien, but in the present set up, in relation to Cassady. The play of my making suggests the Denver situation. Santa Claus as Big Brown Sex God.
    Obvious derivation of race from Cassady's midget racing.
    I was pleased, afterward, to have dreamed this dream, as I said to Cassady, before analyzing it, so, I see that this is all good; nonetheless, realize here the ambiguity of my adjustment, my and Cassady's knowledge of Mrs. Molinier's lack of real adjustment, etc.

Dreams Last Night
    Early at night in dream I met the Mad Hatter walking under the Third Avenue El, talking to himself, mumbling. I have seen such people already in Denver.

In the late morn (8:30) I dreamed that, now that the war was over, I might as well register for declassification. [In the margin Ginsberg has written: "Remember this week angst—about queer classification."[157]] So I went back on my path, backward thru the alleys and buildings, climbing by rope and sheet, thru N.Y. windows high up from tower to tower. I wind up in the lavatory overlooking the bay and the city, a sort of 42'd St. towers and Benjamin Smith town of Empire State combined. It is the head where Chichuahua read his Nicaraguan mother's letter to him, and wept, the noble Castilian. [In the margin Ginsberg has written: "Return from homosexuality or this situation trying to retreat back to pre Carr, pre-War."] I get back on the green lawn of the draft board. The lady gives me forms to fill out. I think, as I fill them, what have I really to declassify my self from? [In the margin Ginsberg has written: "queerness?"] I was only in the U.S.M.S. I have no benefits to gain. Everything is so anarchic and confused. This is just one of those senseless gratifying bourgeois formalities that appeals so to my nature. So I don't register.

I am walking down the street and there is the Mad Hatter again, in light brown tall hat and coat. We're (now, at least, if not before) under the El. He's mumbling about marihuana, talking too loud. His tale, "I never had any myself, but once a rabbit I had or caught got a whiff of it, I think was the end of him. So I ate him, and it was good eating, all except the leg, the right (left?) leg. That was so full of smoke, I never got so high in my life." [In the margin Ginsberg has written: "White Rabbit. Thoughts last week of Allen in Wonderland.] The phrase about Greenwich Village I used first with Lou [Lucian Carr] and Dave [Kammerer] in 48 Morton St."] I was so annoyed and irritated with him that I pushed him, or fearing that he would engage me, I pushed away from him. He got angry, made a scene, I was furious and frightened. He threatened me with the police.

Next thing I know (in the dream) there are the police, two of them in shirts blue, with caps, and they have this tough guy, a wop or an Irishman who's got raven black hair and is drunk; he is cocky and desperate and really rock bottom lacerated of mind: he offers to take the two of them on. They laugh sadistically—a crowd joins. They have [Bob] Burford (Denver Jack) between them. I can't see any of him but head to chest: the citizens have joined the beating and are holding his head still in a blanket or something (on a blanket). The cops apparently have his pants down and are torturing him (castrating probably) and I can but watch in horror and anger and dread and disgust. [in the margin

157   Ginsberg was classified 4-F by the draft board because of his homosexuality.

Ginsberg has written: "The track of other dream. Lucien's tale of beating in jail of his roommate."]

July 30, [1947].

This was to have been written a night ago, last night, which I might well have, having carried it in my head a week or so vaguely till it appeared inevitable and no longer strange. But I got involved in dreams contradictory to its sense and did not want to mix the two. So I shall write it down, write it for no reason other than that I am bored and that there is no opportunity for true expression, or truer than writing for the moment, of my energy.

In *The Counterfeiters*, Edouard says of Olivier's attempt at suicide, that it was a resolution of the evening, not one of the stable more powerful harmonies of morning. So, too, last night, Neal was to call me and did not, which I no longer know how to deal with other than outright disgust. And yet my weaker nature would tell me to be hurt! and so I am, effortlessly. At night it is easier to be hurt than early in the morning. When he did not show up in the morning, then there was disgust, surely. And yet disgust, ennui, weariness of emotional violence, of pain, is such a sterile feeling, so unsatisfying. It is not rife and ripe and fruitful, almost, as pain. Yet pain is not the word, nor grief, though grief, despite its connotations is nearest. Melancholy is too languorous, heartache too banal a word. "It takes your heart away" and "The thought of it may make thee catch thy breath!"

So much for poesy. Yet at the present moment I can feel this *weltschmertz* only dully; it is there, and will rise spontaneously later on, I know, and I almost wait for it with anticipation, to free me from the coldness of this present moment. So I write on and on, not attempting, mind you, to summon weakness, but seeking another way—working out in words, so be it—then either of these two feelings. It strikes me and has always secretly done so, that all my personal strength, such as after all, that of this moment (for I do not really suffer, am just—what?) Irritated, angered? No, there is no rough jaggedness or strong antipathy, first a sort of weariness of emotional violence, and not a lonely or solitudinous one. I feel whole and complete. As last night, when I entered the room—yes, I had fantasized a sudden flood of the intelligence of love in Neal, and half expected, yet knew otherwise, that somehow (like Ingeborg in *Tonio Kroger*) as he stared on the blind window. Will Inge come to him and say, as Mann, "Ah! She must come. She must notice where he had gone, must feel how he suffered! She must slip out to him, even pity must bring her, (Oh!) to lay her hand on his shoulder and say, 'Do come back to us, ah! don't be sad. (Yes, sadness is about the word, but not Whistler's Carlyle's sadness)—I love you Tonio.' He listened behind him and waited in frantic suspense. But not in the least. Such things do not happen on this earth."

Do you know a secret? It is Tonio, I have discovered, that is "in the right." Mann's last sentence is all wrong. Tonio has the right to expect this, life is made this way, he deserves it, it is only the close stupidity and lack of perception that Mann has into the heart of his bourgeoisie that blinds him to all that Ingeborg would come if she knew. If she knew. Is she not made to know? Really, he does not see that the "naturale" are almost as perceptive as Tonio but just fail. They long to join Tonio at the window.

What I have said above is not wrong, not right, just ill expressed. It is not an unnatural demand I am considering really. No miracle is necessary, is what I mean. The happiness of Tonio may be not in his destiny at that moment; but I think it is nearer than Mann knows. But perhaps he does, for I see, thinking, that Tonio has written with the same coldness of mind and "icy ecstasy" as I do now, and with the same thoughts. That is why he does not continue to love. If it were really hopeless, he would love on. But what does this all mean? I only half know now, yet I remember I meant no simple paradox.

Yet there is an even more touching moment in the story. It is where Tonio, worn and middle aged almost, sees Hans and Ingeborg together. He does not approach them. Perhaps he should, but why? But I recognize Tonio in his retirement to sleep: "He looked back on the years that had passed. He thought of the dreamy adventures of the senses, nerves, and mind in which he had been involved; saw himself eaten up with intellect and introspection, ravaged and paralyzed by insight, half worn out by the fevers and frosts of creation, helpless in anguish of conscience between two extremes, flung to and fro between austerity and lust, raffiné, impoverished, exhausted by fright and artificially heightened ecstasies; erring, forsaken, martyred, and ill—and sobbed with nostalgia and remorse." The magnificent thing about this is not that Tonio in his solid age is suddenly overtaken by self-pity—which for the most part, this of his and mine is not—but simple, rock bottom understanding of his human condition. The sudden flood of knowledge of his pain and sorrow as it really is, of the inadequacy of his masks and motives, the knowledge that he has nothing more to do, that there is no person and nowhere to turn to, except himself, and that this self turning will only begin him again on the same road of ambiguous, futile introspection, that, actually, his destiny is unhappiness, and however strong of intellect and however he try to summon his will to an effort at unity, he knows that he will fail. He does not love his destiny (at moments he does, moments of creation and forgetfulness not moments of knowledge). He is really, truly damned, there is no salvation, and he has only to face Death, which he cannot, or the suffering "in perpetual labor, of continuously and idle residence."

It struck me consciously, last night, as before that there was really no way out, for me, but for the first time I realized that the intellectual fantasy of unity of being, slow development to strong happy will, psychoanalysis *et al*, which I <u>really depend on</u> (I knew that before) to keep me forgetful of my misery, is a fiction, perhaps, an impossibility. I had never really consciously doubted any of it, yet this morning, for a moment, I (only half) know that it is the simplest of wish dreams, really, too much to expect, too precise and planned, yet, eventually, I will find it, not unsatisfying, but mechanically impossible of attainment. I keep wondering after my 23d year. It seems now as if that is my last, because I have failed and know it by then, and have so stripped myself of all illusions but guilt, that I can no longer suffer perpetual labor, continuance, and idle residence. I never really reasoned that at the back of my mind I had real unromantic death, simple suicide from exhaustion then. Two years from now, which is just enough time for me to have accomplished the first great prose work, and a small body of perfect poems, which were of no use to me, and to have attempted some happy labor in the world, and failed, and to have gone all the way thru analysis and come out the same as before, only with different problems and different people about me.

So it's now three o'clock, Neal has not come to me, and I think that if at this moment he came, if I were not to throw him out of doors, I would let myself play love with him, out of sheer boredom, having nothing else to do, knowing that it was futile, I would no longer care, knowing that I would leave him in a week to try another way alone or with someone else, I would please myself with an Alice in Wonderland emotion, an act *gratuite*—love, energy, the one ungratuitous destined force, assumed finally in sheer freedom, because there is no real love or energy, sheerly gratuitously. And perhaps out of a perverse desire to move myself, I would explain to him what I was doing.

I thought, yesterday, as I walked on the streets from work of what I had said of Carolyn. Why doesn't she say, "Now look here, I've had enough. If we're going to live together there are certain things I expect and I expect you to live up to, otherwise that's all." [In the margin someone, not Ginsberg, but quite probably Carolyn, has written: "Oh Alyosha! go and get married!" Beside this comment Ginsberg has written: "Feb. 7, 48 This is beautiful."] And then proceed to list them and demand with ease and lucidity. Neal would fall in with such a woman. So he thinks, possibly truly, yet thinks not, and knows it at the same time. Now why don't I do this myself? I won't answer that, it is always easier to solve other people's problems than your own.

Stop now for coffee. Will he come in when I return? No. I will begin writing more to the point when I return.

After tea at 3:30 I went out, elated, leaving this note:

"Neal: If you have anything on your mind and want to talk to me, wait here and I'll be back at 4:15. I have gone over to 1830 to get mail. If not, run along, and don't worry. Come and see me when you have to. But do take care of the Business tonight. Here is $1 for the stuff. Allen."

To resume: Why don't I do what I advised Carolyn? Many reasons. I thought last night—and my thoughts on this subject are almost always in the form of a dialogue, with myself addressing Neal. The action is hampered by the division of my own thought and lack of real knowledge of what his thoughts and responses would be to what I say. So I fantasize a sweet reaction, and an alternate cold one, and a true one—an ambiguous sort of negative agreement with never any action taken. I said, first you must realize the trifling nature of such an approach. It would take a good woman (or a really whole one) to react so. But you must realize and you do as I do that I am beyond simple craving and capable of strict demand, but beyond that, too, to a search for inevitability, and a vague hope that I can control my destiny and you yours to the extent that the fate working out will bring more than a masked armistice, that we should move together in a sort of complete responsiveness. The good woman would be superficial, she would really not touch deeply, would help you little except for imposed, external order. I could sustain the mask, further, but it would be at the expense of deeper, if sick, emotions, and the balance and harmony of such a block of other feelings and a shutting off of the mind to its inner secrets is not what would profit, please, or in the long run, satisfy me, (perhaps as well, you). Is it clear to you that my sense of what goes on would penetrate beyond the artificial inhibitions I would impose on myself, beyond the superficial reaction in compliance that you would bring. And is it clear also, that despite the seeming balance and apparent straightness of such a deal as that, it is not the real play in freedom, which may (even for us) possibly take that form? Further, is it clear that I am straighter than that so-called straightness of my suggestion for Carolyn, that, you see, I trust my weaknesses because I know them and do not want to eliminate them except by honesty and basic purging. This cannot be done unless they are given out, and exercised, and accounted for. You seem to expect, with trust and sincerity, a waxing and developing in me of self pity, dissatisfaction, weakness. I expect a slow release of them, a comfort and a stability and a security and development which will free me from them; as I account and love your intellectual and emotional *naivetés* because they are a part of your character. And I love the whole, and want to see it flourish and strengthen itself—not thru disillusion and disappointment and hardening and irony—but through love and care and awareness to true harmony; so I would wish to be in your eyes, emotionally, taken whole, weaknesses and all; I would not wish an emotional hardening through frustration and an idea endured thru despair, but strength thru joy, consummation, surfeit, acknowledgement, experiment and love. So you see I have said again as I have thought lately, I trust myself even down to my weaknesses because I have come to a half-timid love of myself, as I have a more objective and complete love of you. And I would wish you to care for my sickness and cure me—as such cure must always be effected—not thru deceit and manipulation, but thru acceptance and whole consideration, meditation, awareness and action. I keep listing verbs one after another because one series is not in itself enough to express the fullness of being, the way and structure of an organic process.

Yet increasingly I have found developing in me that strength of the kind I advised for Carolyn, which you think superficially will solve our problems. So now when I fantasize any sexual union for us I sometimes, infected by you, do so in terms of free play, laughing hard amusement. All well and good, perhaps better than none; perhaps if I fully accepted such I should be happier and harder and stronger—I don't know for sure. Yet I doubt it, because I know underneath is craving, sadness, loneliness, hopelessness, defeat, desire, mixed emotions. Yet you have destroyed these in me, to the extent that I cannot without (not embarrassment but fear) horror of rejection or incompetence. If you think this is good for me or you, you are wrong. Unless I am given freedom to pour myself out to you, guts and grease and all. I shall never develop beyond inhibition, sexuality will be mechanical. For you, my intellectual labor on your mind and soul will be one not of love and fullness and so, real truth (I am speaking in concrete terms if you can understand them) but a labor of craft, idea, abstraction, it will be incomplete, and so you will be incomplete, and the whole point of my own genius, and my fitness to work with you, the appropriateness of my personality and intellectuality would be destroyed. The qualities of profundity and complexity and structure and usefulness of my intelligence would be negated, and all communication (if only in formal terms of them to you) would be crippled. In other words, we need a real equality;

because the fullness of my devotion to you springs from knowledge, or if not knowledge, desire for knowledge and consummation in action there from. And your present need for me is a vague quasi practical sense of usefulness mixed with a little respect, but not knowledge of me, because you are either incapable of it, or, if capable, fear the responsibility, or, if not fear, lack of interest in that responsibility, disguise, perhaps contempt. I have hoped all along that it was lack of knowledge because if that were so, much more care for my personality (care and attention and desire to help) could develop with knowledge. But as I suspect, and as I think you would maintain you have that knowledge—that is sympathy of love, which is what would be required for that knowledge. Yet you do not act with simplicity of acceptance and love upon it. So that we come to the realization that the knowledge may be full and at the same time uninterested, which, I continually suppose, may be so, and I think you secretly know that that is the case. At this point I find our relationship destroyed—not thru any blame on either or guilt, but, as I have spoken of before, a mutually antipathetic set of desires and uses on our part, a mechanical difficulty, a true inevitability of separation between us. That is, you know and love not, and I know and love. This is on the point of realization of our incompatibility in its full complexity, but that last sentence "you know" is an obvious oversimplification I will explain: That I am weak in such ways that my desires for solace and development are impossible for you to fulfill for they demand from you an acceptance in complete sweet sympathy, not inhibited, and <u>there</u> spontaneously and deeply, and not momentary, greasy and forced or demanded or merely desired. You are really unable to be as good to me as I want—because, perhaps, you think it is not for my own good (psychically you have an antipathy into indifference to such demands because you are strong enough in the ways I am weak not to be affected by pity, which is self pity. Or perhaps you are affected truly with self pity by such sufferings of others (which, after all, you court and cultivate in others), or with sadistic pleasure concealed in masochistic greasiness etc. on and on with alternatives.

Yet I always reduce such ambiguous complexities to the simple knowledge of the validity and desirability of a full basic acceptance of me by you, and the near possibility of it because of awareness. And now I come to a defect in your character, the coldness of your knowledge in its way. I call it a defect because I do not see you as perfect without warmth, and I almost now come to a point of rationalization of trying to teach you to love me for your own sake. And also I know that that awareness is not sweet and warm because it is not complete and full, it is imperfect.

To be continued. Off to work. Will Neal come to me tonight? Imagine that as the possible, yet so pitifully improbable revelation of his sense and honesty and real desire for service, understanding of the situation with me, spontaneous desire to act. And if he comes not, shall I attribute that to an even greater knowledge than mine, or an even greater sickness and misery, which I must allow, and let him follow till he is well, without demand on him? That requires a self-sacrifice and a suffering on my part—real and not imagined, not mere self pity—which, as it is real, I must, I think, be forced to reject as a choice for myself. So it was that half a week ago, I had a sudden luminous insight, and relief, and pity for him, and sorrow for all, yet all in great joy, and knew that I had decided to wait a little longer, and must leave Denver, and Neal, and all, in a week. I knew then—with great pleasure that that, as the alternative to a complete union with him, would be the inevitable choice, the destiny, the necessary strength.

1:45 A.M. After work: how heavy and meaningless this prose is and this thought above. I was trying to fix a delicate idea, and I did not even know what my thought on it was, that of destiny. Yet on rereading the last pages without bothering to go back on it all I think that it is well balanced and sober and that surprises me since I have the memory of the last days as one of continual hysteria. No, Neal didn't show tonight, yet I am less disappointed, and at the same time I am more sure he should have, than last night. I do not know where to begin to recapitulate these last two nights, and I have just begun to write of them. For the moment I shall bypass last night alone for that was too sad and too sick, I wept steadily again, the second time I have done so in Denver, and the third occasion of personal weeping in months; that is, I have not done so for a long time, but I suppose I do so often by comparison with others; yet at the moment I think it—what justified? Good? No. But simply a fact—certainly— like Tonio I have a right to respond to those few moments of pure knowledge of my life. Well, enough of this, it is not the emotion I carry at present.

It is very strange how possessed I am with this subject. Actually I think continuously (and in cycles I suspect) of my relationship with Neal, and think completely of it, without break, even, or perhaps mostly, at work. That is a weird thing to do. I wonder if others go off on kicks like this, and doubt it.

My anxiety about the situation reached a peak of dragged hysteria at 8:00 o'clock this evening. All last evening at work and this evening even more so, I have been developing, quite out of my control, hallucinations about the telephone. The vacuum cleaner has a high singing pitch and I began last night, awaiting Neal's call, to confuse it with the dull ringing of the telephone. It reached such a point tonight, combined with an emotional exhaustion and an intellectual despair, that I was completely paralyzed for minutes on end, stopping work turning off the motor, listening, half-hearing the phone. I had a vivid auditory sensation several times, that it was not the confusion, it was really the phone, and dropped my work, and ran over to the phone, and found it dead and silent. At one point I could not continue work and collapsed in a chair—not stricken or broken—simply so confused and enervated that I had to stop everything; and again, not to gather force, but simply to wait, half for the phone, half for some intuition or some decision. I would have gone home but I had nothing to look forward to away from work, and plunged in again speedy and desperate, trying to lose myself in the craft of vacuum cleaning. I did the work in record time, stopping once again, half beaten, and going on without lunch till I had finished everything by 11:15.

I cannot easily describe my feelings because they were too far over the border of beatness. There was no depression, there was several moments of a sort of savage elation, but mostly a raging ragged perturbation and shifting of thought on the subject. I tried finally, to think through what I had been trying to become aware of in Neal's personality and mine that made my present emotions and his incompatible, and I think I glimpsed and held it finally. It was something I shall try to write lucidly despite its still ambiguous nature and despite my feeling that it, in disposition of fact, is contrary to what I have already written, though near it in parts. Neal simply cannot accept my emotions of masochism and dependence, they are out of place. Why? I do not know anymore really what I thought then. Push. Analyze. Hold it. My fault, my failure, is not in the passions I have, but in my lack of control of them. I am not to inhibit them, but inhibition comes only with awareness. I drift toward submission to them, where I should break (the strength) weakness, which; can be done by mere decision and action in accordance, by "responsibility." My objection to this is that I fear the substitution of a mask for the passion, a continually conscious mask, and a continual division of personality, the building of a new armor. But what else is development or analysis and purgation but this act of will which binds to such emotions and prisons them till, as I suppose, they must eventually starve? So perhaps, then, my failure is in not recognizing that the critical moment for reformation and self improvement is the present, and the present decision is the crucial one, the decision which I do not know about and have always thought of as a future evolution requiring no effort but the slow osmosis of knowledge. Yet I am continually fearful of choosing a so-called strength that is merely rational and analytic, as such a one for this occasion would be, according to my imperfect vision of an ambiguous situation. Nonetheless, as that earlier in the evening appealed to me I let it sink in and found some surprising results in insight into the general situation. That was in an image of Neal, half recollection, half synthetic, of his face and attitude when I both admire and fear him most, or, if not fear, am most bewildered. When he sets himself to, that is, and explains something—as that of Jack on the trolley. I imagined him telling me (or did he, once?) in a sideways, ambiguous, yet seemingly clear manner, that he liked me and needed me, yet etc. What was the etc? I fill in, that my emotions are my own and not his or for him, and, after all he, (perhaps no one) could respond that deeply into another's personality; or, not that, but that, really my anxieties are all unreal, or my own, and to expect attention, obedience, solicitation for them, is an impossible expectation "since there's no real issue" perhaps, or since they are impossible to satisfy, or since, after all, they are really nobody's business and nobody but a morbid sensitive could feel them. I am again convinced of much of the truth of this. Yet I answered myself at the time, unreal, but existent, and they must be administered to with sympathy or I suffer more; if they are attended, I shall flourish. This is foolish. Or is it? Discuss later. And I also answered, more to the point, that my sexual starvation was not unreal,—and that the indifferent bent of his will toward me sexually and emotionally was obvious from his supererogatory avoidance of me or attention to his problems with me during the last day and a half. Truly indifferent said he? I have warned you of my apathy, why don't you understand <u>that</u> and live and adjust to it? Furthermore, aside from the vague problem of my inner apathy, I have not been really indifferent to your interests. True, there is no sexual fulfillment, but that is too much to demand of me for the moment, though I mean to do something about this sometime. But I have been loving really, attentive when with you, he says, considerate to a degree. I wink at you once in a while when Carolyn is there, though as you can see I am preoccupied with her problems, but, again, only to straighten things out with you, Allen, after all etc. Lost, I give him an argument more to the point, which somehow he circles but never touches, that, after all, what do I expect, or, in other words, here is he, here am I, in Denver, we see each other etc. on a warm basis, my demands are all mystical.

All this has been very vague, as I predicted, but I remember the sense of it and am a little tempered by it. My mind runs to a sort of independence—forced, and inevitable, "Carry your own bags," but valid perhaps. Yet not valid since my basic real problem is not settled, and Neal does, after all evade that, sex. And that, further, goes on to the fact that he has no real physical love for me which I find must be the main division between us and must create most of our problems. Yet he protests that that physicality is there, as yet unripened.

Enough of all of this! I meant to continue, yet I always return to this point, and so will end with examining it and a little musical coda. I have wept and made decisions, indecisive and ambiguous ones, but the problem does clearly form: that this week he must make amends in the form of sexual payment. Yet I see that this creates all problems anew—despite his own stated willingness, even to the point of isolation in Texas.[158] Because I cannot yet prophecy what my sexuality will be like, that is, sick or masked, and which would be better, which I desire, which will bring us closer, which he will find least antipathy to, which I will find more pleasure in, and which is more authentic to me finally; for, can the mask be the real? I think it may turn out to be so. Yet in bed I will have my vengeance.

So I listened, first, to eight sides of Jewish wailing, then long passages of the *Messiah*, and wished for Neal a similar organization and nobility and then the Beethoven *op. 111*, which I found strong and tensed, and Mozart 41 which left me blowing lucid, calm, and with love in my heart for Neal again; and all the while I had decided and was finding myself more and more drawn, even in calmness and love, to the knowledge that, unless things run smoother I'll pack my bags and head east or west or south and have to leave him as he is. I wonder often if I should make use of this decision to force him to responsibility or openness, or choice and decision of his own, yet I hate to force him—and yet, does he not, less consciously, force me?

And now so to bed, half amused, wondering whether or not I will show all this to him.

Out of bed for one other mad idea. I wonder if he intends or recognizes his present absence for a conflict of will? I think that Neal, consciously or not, intends by all of this a subtle attack on my psyche (or does he even bother subconsciously with the whole business?) intended to reduce me to a quivering mess of ambiguous guilts. Does he really expect to strengthen his position— really force me to dependence and non-sexually demanding love—by such a threat as his absence or does he mean this as a sort of breaking away? In either case, unless he is completely hopeless, or completely indifferent to the whole deal, I feel that he is mistaken in his neurotic strategy for a change, I feel stronger now and more in a position to order and demand and hold him to his responsibilities to himself—those are clear enough—and to me (whatever they

---

158 Cassady had agreed to accompany Ginsberg on a trip to visit Burroughs at his Texas farm.

are). He will be in a poor spot when I next see him; I think, that if he has cho-
sen to match wills with mine, he has at last met his match. If it is a battle then,
I accept. But what can he have in mind? Why this proposal for a trip to Texas,
and his acceptance of responsibility for that? Or does he understand what I
meant when I asked him whether I might hold him to it? Is he so completely
stupid as to be unaware of what he's doing? He is one of the few people I can
trust to know his mind and mine at the same time.

August 1, [1947].
Neal strikes me sometimes as being even more simple-minded and confused
than myself, except that may only be the goof balls. Last night, I had to look
him up, which he need not—should have known not to—look him up; yet that
is his charm. (Not the indifference or rejection) but the true feeling, which, by
his charm and conversation and sincerity and anecdotal, I felt, so that (if not
invalidated) gave me no heart to force him to the ambiguous consideration of
larger complex problems of our relationship. Or perhaps only I could not face
him with my own tortured meditations—tortured, I look at in horror, but so
they were. Alas, his incompetence to understand and aid me (he thinks that he
wants to, perhaps) forces a sort of torture. That is that I cannot be really free
with him till he develops a true openness and responsiveness. That I am begin-
ning to make both love and understanding a mask with him, when I should be
allowed to have feelings and simpler human reactions is a pity. It will, if con-
tinued, eventually destroy my love. If that love had the advantages for him
which I see, truly, after all, that it does, and which he assures me in his own
sweet way that it does—I am not being presumptuous unless the whole situa-
tion is and I do not really think that is so any longer, and never really have, my
understanding of his need has become more real, if anything in understand-
ing, and my compulsion to abject acceptance of my role has become less
strong, to the vanishing point, so that only his assurances of sincerity and his
tone of it make me stay longer, despite the "apparent" lack of sincerity in his
action. There was no issue yesterday except,

1) I should be "man enough" to understand his mood or occupation,
2) I know more surely than he, the subversive nature of his mood.

I say apparent lack of sincerity because they do not please me; and yet I
cannot feel myself longer wrong or confused in knowing that this pleasure is
possible, except for his retirement from attempt at it, however "sincere" his

retirement and postponement. I cannot tolerate this sloppiness of several devotions of his sexually and incomplete fulfillment of all; nor do I wish and do accept his "gifts" to Carolyn and Helen of sexuality which I have not demanded from him as my due as far as I am concerned. Yet I try to give him freedom and spontaneity in this, wishing him in freedom to come to me, since it would be the only happy fate, yet he comes not. I have maneuvered him to a promise of Sunday night, and it is with misgiving that I will release him from that promise. Perhaps all such henceforth. I thought of terms last night. Yet as a practical situation, knowing that he would then follow his inclination not to come at all, I think, I cannot suffer it to come about. Again, the only course is departure despite the love and pity and admiration I have for him, and his real return of such to me. And his even greater fatal need for me. So be it?

August 1, [1947].
Carolyn's notes on Indian art: "Most gods shy gods."

This evening at Jack's behest, a behest which he performed after I drew him to, I called up Hal Chase, abed with measles.

"Is Haldon there?"

"This is me."

"This is Allen."

"Yeah."

"I just called—I hear you have measles."

"Yeah"

"Where did you pick them up? From Ginger or (a lapse and slip with G.G. Ginger) something?"

"Why?"

"I thought I'd call and give you my pity and sympathy." He mumbles on.

"Well what did you ask me that for?" I hang up.

I burst into a flood of irritation resentment anger and hatred of his stupidity and dull arrogance. "He can take his god damn narcissistic charms and shove them up his ass." He asked me what did I ask that question for, thinking, rightly to cut into my amenities. Perhaps I should have told him, as far as the amenities were concerned. He still thinks it is a cleverness and directness to express his sullenness in such a manner, asking questions which reveal insights which are easy and unkind, superficial, stupid emotionally.

I will perhaps make one more attempt to make him come down and understand what is going on between us. It is a labor of pity now, and love. This is the first time that I am sure that I should be doing well for the two of us in try-ing to be friendly to him.

August 2, [1947].

Evening for an assignation at last. It is 1:45 now. Neal won't show up; if he does, I'll free him from his vow tonight, since he means well, and let him proceed at his own desire when and if he summons any up. If he does not, I'll leave town. I may do that in either case. I can't keep giving and not getting in return. Not that he hoards. But he has nothing to give; to me, anyway.

Remember as you write, address your fellow men. Remember if you were doomed to die in one hour, any man would do. If etc. and I wasn't here and Bill wasn't here and Neal wasn't here; you would take any man, and look only into his white eyes.

I went on to explain ambiguity vs. complexity to Jack and suddenly realized he had fallen asleep. So I sit here, at last myself, free, serene, I think happy, with this past behind me and this freedom before me, a poem to write on a loved subject, Jack in bed in my room, Neal to call on me tomorrow.

I think I am at peace, creative, harmonious, composed for the first time in my life. I feel much strength and much humility—or shall I say it better, as the absence of contradictory inner thought, yet not the absence of external prob-lems—and so the absence of compulsion, false communion, attachment, of fear, of conscious awareness—a wholeness, a unity of being.

I think much of Neal and am truly grateful to him without abasement; I have begun to realize him as a person, a human being. He is I think the only one I can trust as I should trust myself and I am happy at fate for bringing him to me. I hope I will be good for him and not lead him to waste, pain, trouble, and failure. If our engagement shall lead to happiness for us in the end it will be more good and more true and more strange and real—the word—benevo-lent? lovely? beautiful? desirable?—than anything I have had or seen in human life in my first years. My love for him and all about us, and my love for such a sweet consummation of torment and confusion is now too serene to be sinful. May no further error: love: lead me and him astray, that we may be saved on earth, and our lives later, apart, be filled with love and knowledge and pleasing labor in the world, and blessings on all whom we touch and use and satisfac-tion in our work, and soul's sweetness withal. I think now I stand upon the top of that mythical mountain I have climbed for three years, and I see the living world as the old valley of peace ahead. The work of waste and work of salvation has been done, only now is the steep descent, which does not frighten me. I think that all will be well. I hope that the descent will not discourage Neal, I hope that he stands beside me and can see all ahead as I do. O how sad, how sad human error is, and all its miseries, its lost-ness, its sharp-toothed solitude, that dark dark infinite isolation. I think that no man is alone; as I, writing in silence this morning, without much care but for love, am not any longer alone. I hope that I am not mistaken in discovering at last that I have no individuality, but only everlasting communion with one, and therefore all men in their consciousness and soul. Enough of this, not sharply, but simply. Perhaps I should come to the end of this note book. I feel free to turn the page; inscribe a Roman [numeral] 2, and proceed with new commonplaces; I know I have entered a new season, and, so, at last, Good-by Lucien, Good-by David, Good-bye Rimbaud, Farewell Gillette in <u>Where was the World</u>, adieu to the juvenescent children of the rainbow, to Spengler on the Square, adieu to unhappiness, *auf-wiedersehen* to Death.

August 5, 1947.
Remind Neal to ditch a few women; I don't want to have to compete for time with more than one. Or maybe it's better this way? No attachments? But too frantic. Anyway, remind him to settle down and get to work. What a strange come down from the sexual nihilism of abstractions.

August 6, [1947].
I am surprised at how interested I am in what I have written in this journal previously; I do not read it straight through, but turn back desultorily to pages I half forgot.

I had several surprising and interesting at the same time, dragged, conversations with Luanne (Cassady). She speaks of none but Neal, really, and in a confused and confusing and finally boring fashion but from it a strangled, touching picture of him emerges. She mentioned a talk with Hal in N.Y. in which he advised Neal not to come on too cocky, "the boys around Columbia wouldn't go for that," because though he was king of the walk in Denver (as she thinks he thinks of himself) they were different in N.Y. She speaks constantly as if, on returning, he pleaded for her to come back to him; she tells of his sentimentality, after their marriage: making his father's last days happy by having him come to live with them, taking in his sister. Then she spoke of college for him at great length and how she would give him up, never see him again if he would only not "waste his talents." Therefore she likes to see him

with his boy friends, and just sits as if she weren't there while they talk intel-
lectual talk; she's too stupid, she converses, and he's too big for any woman.
He told her that she especially was too possessive for him to do work—writ-
ing—while he lived with her; he was so proud of the poems he'd written in
N.Y., but she asked me if he really had written them (and seemed to accept my
word that he had[159]—I act to her aloof yet sympathetic and straight) and told
me he called her (for a week) his "intricate child" from the line, "yet, intricate
child, thanks for the touching homage"[160] as well as, "his homeless waif" that
Chase had once called her. She has seen him almost cry thinking of his plans,
his big plans for his future, yet everything always falls through because "he
can't leave his women alone: He showed her a letter of mine containing a
poem (the above) yet as I remember I sent him only one poem,[161] the play,
and also the Garden's penultimate verse. Her talk leaves me with a liking and
indifference to her. She is stupid, but not dull, but lively, and could be sweet if
she were not so confusedly sentimental about self abnegation. Through her
eyes he is weak and vain, (not as she really sees him but as he is to be seen
through her talk), also confused, needs to be ruled rather than trusted, almost.
One thinks of him (in a mask however) as charming, touching, pitiful, gently
contemptible; also it is apparent that he has handled her with mixtures of deli-
cacy and crudeness, but real self-confused stupidity; as if hers infected him and
the two of them together wallowed in degeneracy and juvenility. It seems
more and more apparent that not withstanding the sincerity of his conscience,
the intuition, and her own perverted limitation of view and insight, he has
acted hypocritically and deceitfully to all concerned, mostly himself (of
course! What are we thinking of) and still needs more direction than he can
give himself, or get someone to give him. In that sense he is not as I, he does
not know where to look for help.

Aside from personal desire, I think, it seems more apparent to me that he
should be kept isolated and strictly dealt with—a constant succession of emo-
tional problems created to fill the void and avert real decisions, plus a knowl-
edge of this fact, keep him from organization and creation. The idea of having
to fill the emotional lives of three women and one half man is enough to make
me vomit. Almost anyway, mentally. In any case in the month I've been here
he's done nothing but waste his and my time, and this is all the more touching

---

159 As mentioned earlier, Ginsberg had actually written the poems, not Cassady.

160 This line from an untitled poem written January 24, 1947, which begins, "As I shall come to
trust myself, trust me."

161 "Death in Violence."

because even his slow jelling into action is circumstantial and external. Any movement to me has been not because of his perception but his receptivity: I have had to talk him into a state, slowly, where he understands what is going on, I've really, despite myself, been making all the decisions. Which is an amusing thought, but not very promising. And since I have not presumed to go all the way the result has not been very happy. I find myself at long periods growing (despite Roman numeral 2) growing dissatisfied with his conduct, despite the fact that it springs from his will freely, so it seems. So after all these years we are really on the discipline kick again. Welcome home, but I hope you can pay your rent.

August 7, [1947]. Afternoon.

The reason I can't write prose (it struck me, as I worked last night) is that I transform all dramatic fact in my mind to spiritual (intellectual or poetic) experience. Thus in the story in progress, the prose is absorbed in reflection, all crucial action takes place in the mind of the hero, and it is simply a matter of putting down the end product of his character (the thoughts of the mind). My interest there is not in circumstance but, how does he think of the circumstance, not even, how does he react to it.

Neal is lifeless, hopeless, almost, as far as trying to make him change his secret heart, acting on knowledge of long range inevitability. I have never seen lust versus duty enacted so clearly. I have fallen of late into the simplification of complex alternatives into questions of "duty," "responsibility," etc. and so far it has not gotten out of hand, though I dislike the literary cast of my mind, and the continual transvaluation. It bespeaks a "fear" of his violent and my violent tendencies toward anarchy, and not an understanding of it as simple, unsacramental, concrete waste. That is because perhaps I still idealize the anarchy because I once idealized the bourgeois stasis. But you see, waste is not the word either; we writer's use a bourgeois vocabulary invested with our own interpretations, because thus far the world has been so unreal as to fail to invent a suitable vocabulary for the parts. Then we are back on Rank's speech origins.

August 9, [1947].

I turned to Don Juan today to try to discover the secrets of their morality through the inspired and deviated minds of great creators, etc. Remember trying vainly to read the play years ago? Well I read it easily in an hour this time and was amused with it as a play but much disappointed. It seemed to have little relevancy to my problems, more particularly, Neal's. I accept the conversation and dialogue with some interest but, looking at it thru the eyes of one for whom the verbal external statements of the situation are irrelevant, found the play disappointing. I found myself unsympathetic to Don Juan because he had no love in his heart, and my own attitude is simpleminded enough; yet I could not admire his fate forced on him by Molière because, after all, it seemed in the context of the play (except as simple theology) pretty meaningless. The consciousness of the absurdity of the whole deal is reflected in Sganarelle's final speech and in his speech of associational argument.

Am going on to Kierkegaard's *Either/Or*. Perhaps then Byron and Shaw versions.

August 11, [1947].

To write tonite on benny (incidentally the drag has disappeared) and instead there is a corridored floating-down a single set of thoughts, those of a morning say.

To write: a poem on the birth of William and Joan's boy.[162] No ode to the bastard boy I don't think, as planned. The main thing is Birth and (not promise) but possibility. Main points to cover:

1.) In proem, write of our sterility in such matters, that lends proper aesthetic languidness and melancholy objectivity to occasion. Too bad I can't write as one happy virile pop to another—man to man.

2.) Circumstances of birth—
   a) Concerning a past madness of mother
   b) Child of narcotics—? (taste?)
   c) Father's sterility, yet, in circumstance, this happy fecundity.
   d) Compliment to mother for bringing everything thru from fecundation to fruition.

3.) Salute child as a brother.

4.) Possibility not promise.

Make an ode, formal Cowlean, not Latin I think. Write not in irony, but pure sweetness where possible. "My main critical eye is: I think of reading to Joan without embarrassment." Last, it is a present to parents, not a poetic kick.

---

162 Joan Adams gave birth to a child by William Burroughs on July 27, 1947, naming him William S. Burroughs, Jr.

So make sure you are not too private, that you are straight with them to them. Write to whites of eyes, as Jack sez, whatever that means.

Also, later, note here several paragraphs about

1) talk to Luanne.
2) talk to Neal about month's work and his divorce.
3) discussion of past (re-evaluation) with Jean-Luis [Jack Kerouac] and Chase. When Jack left it was a sad, but happy departure. "Adios, Jean-Louis." Did I really feel as if I'd not see him soon again?

Think of course of action with Chase and his present inaction is not real indifference but fear and inhibition. Your strength on the occasion was hostility at rejection, not right indignancy over his lack of amiability and friendliness and good will.

Tell Neal he is a good boy. I wonder if he likes compliments. I often have many simple ones for him yet hesitate for fear that he will not like to hear them from me as they will remind him of the servitude of lovers.

Make a list (for kicks? Why? Not?) of acquisitions from May Co.[163]

Birthday Ode[164]

The occasion for this poem was the birth of a child to close friends [William Burroughs and Joan Adams]. The poem was written as an expression of love, as a present to them, as an amusement for us. The child was born in the Bayou, and the parents are megalopolitan desperados. The mother is very intelligent, yet she is almost self-annihilating in her refusal to partake of any sacrament, literary or political, and so she devotes herself to her family, isolated, and meditates privately on an enormously complicated *idée fixe* of universal radioactivity. She reads the newspapers with an interest in skin diseases and unexplainable explosions. She is very young and has another child, a girl. The father is a lean, skeptical genius of failure, a former anthropologist, usually gentlemanly and shy with women. He would like to be a criminal, at the same time his mind is warm, sympathetic, and highly sophisticated, yet he is without the sophisticated illusions usually associated, literarily with his type.

163 Ginsberg had found a job with the May Company department store and was working as a cleaning man at night, pilfering items from time to time, and these are the "acquisitions" he is referring to here.
164 "Birthday Ode" was later retitled "Surrealist Ode."

I am using the Nightingale to tell them what I think of life and to admonish them lest they cultivate their child in sterility and despair. The poem, in parts, describes the responsibilities and decisions the child must assume with maturity, taking into account his birth and the society in which he will live.

In part VI the twin is an imaginary fool, another soul of the child, that miscarried, theoretically, in the mother's womb. That is, she will not raise the child in an orientation to the society which would be a typical false communion. Certain lines identify the destruction of the bourgeois baby with spontaneous atomic fission and cultural explosion.

Part VII is a lamentation against the possibility of homosexuality. The "sense" referred to is the mother's skeptical wit, which I fear is self destructive.

Part VIII brings my own personality in overtly because I am, as it were, a brother to the child, such is my relationship to the parents. The last line refers to lines on the subject of confusion in the will in a poem which was dedicated to the father.

The last section refers to the coming war with Russia, the decadence of poetry in our time, and the renaissance of art in American jazz music. I associate the saxophone with mature passion and vigor, and sometimes with evil and knowledge, etc. An imperfect verse from an ode to Be-Bop may illustrate this:

"The Saxophone thy mind has guessed,
He knows the Devil hides in thee;
Fly hence, I warn thee, Stranger, lest
The Saxophone shall injure thee."

"Sent" in hiptalk means ecstatic. The trumpet of Dizzy Gillespie I associate with the quotation from Plutarch's "Sulla" that Yeats and Petrie have quoted: "One day when the sky was serene and clear there was heard in it the sound of a trumpet, so shrill and mournful that it frightened and astonished the whole city..."

[The following introduction to "The Denver Doldrums" was written a year or two later, but it has been placed here for chronological flow. The "Dakar Doldrums" referred to here was written later in 1947 and will be found in its correct place in the chronology.]

"The Denver Doldrums" were written all in one day, except for revisions; the main body of the poem (Lost Elegy) was started before dawn, continued, section by section, with increasing comprehension, through the afternoon and on into the evening. The unity of the poem is submerged in the moody meta-morphosis of the doldrums. The Denver Birds are the birds of dawn suggested by the usual sounds outside the window made more sharp by sleeplessness and placelessness of spirit. I never did see any of the fowl mentioned in the poem, except, later, seagulls (Dakar Doldrums) and vultures (Birthday Ode, an unfin-ished part of the series). The Doldrums were intensified by a long night of Benzedrine sustained conversation with several acquaintances of mine in the city. The image is therefore, probably, seriously metaphysical, though tinted by choice the slang meaning of birds, i.e. characters. The birds are, I suspect, derived from Yeats, though I was not reminded of Yeats' denying birds of dawn till later, and though the whole conception was taken at the moment from real birds associated with my earlier visitors.

The Nightingale I remember mostly from an old song that one of my rel-atives, a Russian woman with a nervous breakdown, used to sing to me. I don't remember the words fully: it was an American ballad of the 20's I suppose, though I had always thought of it as a kind of peasant's lullaby. I associate my relative, who suffered an extraordinarily 'naturalistic' yet 'virginal schizophre-nia,' with the song and style of the Nightingale.

> "Last night the Nightingale woke me,
> Last night when all was still,
> It sang in the golden moonlight,
> From on the wintry hill.
>
> I opened my window so gently,
> To see who was singing there…"

Other beasts in the poem are remembered from a short stay in the bayou of Texas just before a longer visit in Denver. There were tics and chiggers there, and armadillos and scorpions. I had never seen any of them before. I refer in one phrase to the armadillo's regularity and exactitude of patrol of a given area at a given time, a kind of stupid and pure mechanism of conduct that completely captivated me. My host, who knew the schedules of several of them, ambushed one for me and set it down on the floor of the house. This upset the creature, which began scratching industriously at the floor right under the man's feet, in an ineffectual attempt to hide its head and settle down under its shell. For literary use, I carry a rather private association with the Reichian concept of 'character armor' and also, regularity of bowel movement and anal sadism. I can make no excuse for this and certain other conceits except that in my mind they are associated in a pleasant harmony of ironies. So the parasitic tics and chiggers and so, the scorpion, a traditional castration symbol, are associated with the demon of Mr. Mayer that follows. The image is from one of the Mayan Codices—the Madrid Codex—which contains a series of drawings of a venomous growth on the loins of a squatting man. The beast grows larger and bolder in each picture and finally dominates the man astride his neck. The evil of the visage of the monster intensifies and grows more complex with each picture, while the Mayan's face is drained of all emotion. Nobody seems to know exactly what the Mayans meant, or knew, by this and a hoard of equally terrifying representations of psychic mortification. I understand that there were priests who had control of these Codices which seem to have prescribed both social routine and psychic ritual. Regularity of thought, stylization of the soul in the culture, and manipulation of these abstractions by the priestly aristocracy (and here I mean to suggest Korzybski's[165] semantic theory) are all elements of my personal myth of the Mayans. I am on a 'kick' with the Mayans. As far as that is concerned, I imagine actual seasons of the soul, and an atomic magic (psychology, which was the basis of their society as the machine is of ours) developed by the priests and gone out of control after ages of bureaucratic centralization. So follows an explanation of certain Mayan cities depopulated but intact, like ghost ships.

The last section of the poem is a kind of nostalgic "looking backward" at the rest of the poem, and a settlement with it, in terms of a lyrical movement in confessional seriousness, of pensive exegesis of the Nightingale symbolism. This sort of sad recapitulation is repeated in the *Dakar Doldrums*, and it serves, in both, to solve the aesthetic and personal obscurities of early lines by purgation and revelation. In both, the meanings of antecedent sections of impulsive, semi-hallucinated imagery are considered, deepened and clarified with afterthought, and acted upon by the mind in decision. In the *Dakar Doldrums* the early process of metamorphosis of the doldrums is extended over a period of weeks, the poem is actually a sort of psychic diary of the time passed in a sea voyage over the Atlantic. It was written and developed from day to day, the states of mind are various and sequential. A note I wrote at the time may help explain the style: "here the desperation is more consciously maniacal, yet directly presented with sincerity; a 'symbolic' poem imaged at will with obscure prophecies of self-destruction and, I warn, deceptively romantic vio-

---

165   Alfred Korzybski (1879–1950). Writer and theoretical expert on general semantics and the author of the influential book, *Science and Sanity*.

lence." It may fill this out if I add that I later discovered the preoccupation with images of Death was, beyond literary extravagance, a direct, if unconscious, statement of naive fear at the departure of personality from one stage of development to another, a change of phases of the soul.

Finally, the whole series was intended to communicate and it was all a love poem.

[*Excerpts from a letter Ginsberg wrote to Trilling, dated August (circa 15), 1947.*]

All the prize money[166] (a surprising amount, almost $150) saw me through a month on a farm in Texas with Joan Adams, my old landlady, and Bill Burroughs, my old 'analyst.' They had a baby boy a week or so ago and I have been happy over the whole deal because I have longed to see the two of them, settled and raising a family for years; besides, the child will be almost another brother to me and I wonder what he will grow up to be. As you know I have a tremendous respect for the parents. So I am in the middle of a long formal ode in salutation of the birth. I hadn't ever before been on a farm and this was a wonderful introduction to one—bayou, Spanish moss, scorpions, good company, isolation, a little work when I felt like it, a hand-wound Victrola with lots of be-bop records, woods to explore, trees to climb, a Jeep to learn to drive, weekend trips to Houston, etc. Huncke, you may remember him from the long poem, was also there as general handyman, along with his marijuana, so you can see it was a weird set up, but not so sterile or irresponsible as might be supposed.

I came on to Denver at the beginning of August, penniless, and found a pretty beat situation here. My job fell through (though I'd half expected it to). I moved in with two nurses I met, who fed me, petted me, listened to my poetry (though they are not particularly spiritual women) gave me cigarette money, and I wandered around being introduced to all sorts of people, and looking for a job for several weeks. There seems to be an unemployment problem hereabouts, and I am finally settled as the night porter in the May Company. I vacuum their rugs, but I have got the whole thing so systematized by this time that I am able to spend my last three hours in the store at night sitting around and listening to phonograph records. I got a basement apartment of my own and now everything has become almost happy and lively about me. There is a whole crowd of Denver U. students and romantic

166 Ginsberg won the George Edward Woodberry Prize for poetry from Columbia.

pool-hall sharpies who gather around me to examine the myth from N.Y. That is my position, it seems that Hal Chase and a lot of the other Denverites I knew in NY (not from the school) started, years ago, a myth about me in Denver as a sort of combination of Alyosha and Uncle Eduard, which I have been only too pleased to sustain, and it has not been difficult.

As to writing, I have put more and more time at the table, and have written a series of poems called "Denver Doldrums." They have developed in style in a manner which I foresaw, and half-mentioned to you. It was apropos of the 'romanticism' of the last lines of the Donne poem with its verbal play. What I have been trying to do has been work out a simple sweet line and wind up with a happy, spontaneous authentic lyricism—write happy poetry. I have not yet.

Also I have turned to prose and started a novelette. It is a difficult task for me since I have neglected to cultivate any efficiency at all in fictional writing. I am beginning with all the handicaps possible, and eclectic, cold analytic style, a dread of the work and fear of the results, the knowledge as I go along that what I am doing is incompetent, a lack of insight or the feeling of insight into what is really going on in concrete form in other people's minds (that I discover as the principle handicap). Since, in addition, I am led (and have succumbed) for the while in writing autobiographically and truthfully if possible, the ambiguous nature of other selves is an unresolved difficulty. The subject matter, being autobiographical is another handicap—my desire is to write objective 'noble-themed' (I do sense the relevancy of noble themes) dramatic prose—and what I am doing makes it almost futile to try; further I am all tangled up with unresolved tableau of drugs, pool halls, homosexuality, aesthetic theories and quasi-psychoanalytic introspection which is the lot of my hero. The final problem and perhaps the virtue of what I am writing is the attempt to resolve all dramatic ambiguity to complexity, and put down the complicated whole; this in turn leads to moral questions in terms of personal 'responsibility.'

To conclude, I am heading down to Texas again in the middle of August, and then on to N.Y. sometime in September. Traveling with me will be one of Denver's dissolute young bucks, (his name is Neal Cassady) whose education, for the time, I find myself superintending. He is a boy of my age who I found in N.Y. last year, he had come in to the city to try and reform and organize and go back to school (he has not had a high school education). Despite a background of bumming and reform schools and living off women he strikes me as the wisest and most powerful personality I have run across, in school or out, among the young, and since he seems to be assuming finally some 'personal responsibility' I think all will be well for him. [end of letter]

I have spoken to Jim Holmes about Neal's past and I have from him the clearest idea of Neal's development. He told me (for the first time) of Neal's former beauty and innocence, fullness of heart, generousness of sympathy for all man, beast, fish, in flesh. It is strange that I did not recognize what he was before the knowledge of deprivation came upon him, before his fall, his bite into the apple of knowledge. Surely, as I'd half imagined him playing with love in a Big Time. I half-lose the hope that he will do so with love. All now for him is desperate and organized and laborious, he has too much ambition now. I wish that he could, as I, participate in creative activity with no conscience, but merely the love of abstract images.

"—he abstract joy, the half mad wisdom of demonic images, suffice the aging man as once the growing boy" etc.

For him, I fear, art will be another weapon against the world, another way of domination. He has too much love for Byron and the romantically ambitious. Perhaps, after all, I should go through, with him, the intellectual analysis of the dandy, the Promethean, the hero, the humanist.

There is so much natural sweetness in him which is his most real personality, that, though it has been "expended in a waste of shame" in his early years, and now perverted in sadism and apathy because of his knowledge of the sterility of his sweet deeds for the Denver Birds. Yet he is a saint. This was my first vision of him and it remains so.

But his present desperation, his compulsive and self-defeated seeking and labor, burdensome and onerous, will not please him. He has a rare medium to work with, and now, rare personalities to play with, and I pray that he will submit to the outside world again, and absorb it and take pleasure in it and its action upon him, and respond with simplicity and sincerity and a desire to please and help and benefit and instruct, as well as to profit from the circumstance. He will only profit, only succeed, only become free and great if he learns, once more, submission. As I realized my own loss of individuality in the impulse and achievement of communion with him, he must someday do so with me, since I am worthy, or, if this is not so, with someone who is worthy, or some activity which is worthy. He must realize fully the fact that dedication without compulsion is pure, free, happy, pleasurable, worthy, successful in the end, all the blessings that fall on genius, all the power he seeks now, all the profit in love and money he would wish for would all be his, in time, if he, without caring less for them, realized that they are never achieved as the simple end of labor, but come as a matter of course with it, and that the labor itself, properly loved and understood, will repay. If there is merit in his soul it will be rewarded. If there is none, why need he waste time seeking the rewards of merit. So for myself, but actually I need the advice less than he.

Yet there is the happy vision of Neal in former years. And that lends proof of dignity and accomplishment to his present development into solitude and fear and hatred and apathy. I wonder how much "authentic emotion" he felt then, and if the superficial movement to response of the present is the faded talent of his gifting days.

As I came in tonight I had this dream: He entered the room this morning and I looked at him and we understood each other well, and with a kind of quiet, depth of emotion and thought, I said "Here Neal, take my hand, I feel profound." Now as I think about it I wonder if he is yet equal to the simplicity and sincerity—not homosexual fixation—but frankness and knowledge, that would be required for him to take my hand, without squeezing it, and look at me without winking or grinning, and, perhaps, nod once, incline his head so, even smile (if necessarily, a trifle sadly, but) preferably without driven joy, just simple and strong (and wholesome!) minded trust; so soft and sweet as to be an angelic situation, this is. I think I am ready and deep enough for it. If he were, I would have no fear for him of his will, his future, his efforts, or, for me, of leading for the immediate future a moderate and active and non-symbiotic life with him. It is sad to me to think that he, at this point, owing to my present equilibrium and increasing absorption in other (aesthetic and financial) problems, must now assume so much responsibility, and must now not only act but be straight and frank and helpful to me as well without my demanding, cajoling, begging, giving immoderately, explaining, expounding, guiding, or talking him into things. That suggests another problem I would like him to think of, that of being simply helpful to me in practical (not emotional matters) like being dependable for appointments, being practical and frank (or at least, if not frank, amicable) to contacts and acquaintances, trying to participate in mutual efforts with less show of irritation, less explanation, less waste of apathy where apathy is pointless. That is not force interest, but still, put himself out to exorcise emotional sterility in creative situations—exorcise it if possible by simplicity and frankness, rather than "awareness" in silence, and deceit as less messy than explanation, objection. He must also learn to converse and act with less impatience, since his impatience is nervous and unreal.

He must relax more, and he will do so once he realizes that I am not making demands on him but only trying to help him figure out what demands he really wants to make of himself. So as I told him today, don't say you'll come to see me early just to placate me at the moment. I would be happier and he would have less anxiety if he would think awhile first about what he'll be able to do, what he'd like to do, and make arrangements on that basis, rather than "guilt" or "apathy," or irritation. You see it is annoying for me to accept his "statement of mind" on trust, and then find the statement untrustworthy. Perhaps he as well as I find it is only the mind that is untrustworthy, not the immediate statement. If so, then I wish he would not try to bully his way out of the situation, be more simple and less clever about it all.

"I warn you," said I, "now you'd better show."

And what did he reply, not "Allen, don't worry," or "I don't know Allen, but I will try," or "Please don't force me to decide as you are now," or "You can trust that I will arrive," etc. according to his mind, but only an arrogant, foolish, rhetorical, insincere bluster, "I warn you"—etc.

I do not mean to chide him for impatience with me if he thinks that I am being presumptuous or obtuse, but if he feels any confident and simple trust (again) for the situation, he would be more mild, more "helpful," in an explanation or by sign. There are often in him, and the situation, moments that I do not understand—I am not saying this as part of my repetitious anxiety or guilt or insecurity or compulsion as on other pages—but simply again, there are moments which I do not fully realize, and those moments he must not merely "assume responsibility" for, but rather kindly fall into a movement toward, not a movement away from. He has no just emotional cause for apathy then, for I am merely waiting for truth, not blocking my understanding of it, resisting awareness, and trying to force him to do things against nature and fate merely for confused private kicks. In the future I hope I can expect from him the same kind of love—non physical—that I have for him. I have all along worked—and this is half strange, and half-inevitable, almost mythical in realism, yet feeling it so good as to be untrue, yet sensing it somehow to be true, that our destinies are mutual and interdependent, that love between us, or affection, even some emotion, and equal in each, is in the cards, is in our minds, and is to be fact, without compulsion or irritation. In me it almost amounts to a superior knowledge, that, in this sense only, we are somehow mated and paired. I almost—and quite, not quite—could say that he must and will understand this because—perhaps that is the point—he can understand, and he alone of all I know, can understand, as I do. So as usual I am confident and I hope he will not resent this as some kind of queer incursion on his soul or trespassing on his genius or seduction and assault on his apathy. He must learn to accept love where it is true and intelligent and unalloyed in its pure basic central core, with cravings, sacerdotal motive, fantasy, misplaced purpose. My love is more of a natural homage and a sharing of trust than an imposition—I wonder if he realizes that. When he does he will not resent it, but accept it, even if at the same time it is necessary for us both to leave sexuality out in the end. With this subject the picture becomes a little darkened, clouded. Yet I wonder if he has the transcendent imagination—which I once credited him for—to give and take with me sexually, not necessarily out of physical desire for me, but because he sees my situation as I see his, and knows that he loses nothing in sharing himself with me for my ease and enrichment. I no longer derive driven joy, mad weird ecstasy from sex and all proceeds, if he so moves himself, in a kind of clear, serene, lucid pleasure in physical contact. I get a strength and assurance from it—self-assurance, not assurance of his fidelity of soul—ease is the word. I spoke to him of freeing him from this in the city. I hope he understands me well enough to feel that that would not be necessary. I would, in any case, no longer be starved sexually, and pathetic and miserably isolate even without his well-wishing participation in sex with me, because I am equal to the task of going out and taking sex where I can make it now, I think. But I do so hate to have to spend myself on useless sterile people—I fall into an apathy toward this situation and its inhabitants as he does towards the Denver birds. All would work out so well and comfortably for me if he wished (or invited) with pleasure himself, for my own pleasure, and/or for the simplicity of it all, and equal usefulness. It is a difficult situation and one that he alone must solve, for I cannot will or advise physical acceptance of me upon him, and I cannot move freely with him or really aid him unless he wants my freedom in the situation. As an alternative, sexual abstinence, in the city, presents, however, to tell the truth, not insoluble problems. In such a case I would likely to be, freed from all dependence on him, and in a completely paternal (not equal given) pedagogical, advisory capacity, be stronger willed, perhaps more critically perceptive, and so more frank and demanding, and, not tied to him by lover's bonds, he even freer and more useful. Yet I wonder if I would sustain interest, if I would not become sadistic, for, at moments even now, I have glimmerings of his soul's inferiority to mine yet these glimmerings are weak and transient and are not crude judgments or critical glories, but relaxed feelings of his place and mind. I would be likely to make more use of this for his own benefit. What is that sense—one of sophistication almost, or maturity—that is, perhaps not his lack of polish (for he is a perfect natural gentleman so to speak)—our first meeting and his reading of Wolfe and his conversations prove that. But in art, as in some life (politics, social amiability, upper-class personality, even lower class personality, simple wisdom and sense of equality with all men, he has not). I feel at last an understanding of his naiveté, or shall I say almost lack of awareness. That is, I think of Gene Pippin, say, and of Neal meeting Gene without knowledge of Gene's goodness and complexity, and without love for Gene except in burlesque Wolfean tableau. I would like Neal to be simple and heartfelt and understanding, at moments, with people and with the wider world, [In the margin Ginsberg has written: "shit."] yet I see him continually posturing, masking, exacerbated, all-too aware, presumptuous, fearful of real conflict, yet creating conflict with good people in his mind and avoiding it unless they are weaker than he. And of course he has no purpose yet but what he has set himself to. So it is Neal that I would like to see free and spontaneous in essential things, not peripheral incidentals—I don't know if I have expressed myself clearly on this, I am not trying to make rhetoric or diary or criticism, but thinking of him and when I read this to him as I hope I will be free too, I want him to respond if it is met, not with enthusiasm or all-too-awareness, but understanding, explanation, frankness not of hostility but of submission to circumstance or fate or knowledge, with mild generosity not conceived in apathy, but of concern and almost childlike helpfulness. I would like to talk to him all the time not with driven desperate sincerity but almost with quiet questioning talk to him, his self at the moment itself, reach to him, as I allow him and encourage him to reach me and talk to me as if I were a human being he had nothing against. Perhaps mutual humility would be a good verbal starting point to describe what I feel we need, and yet a state of mind outside of literature and self-dedication and sacrament, and inside a real world of people met together and conferring with each other on what to do. I have pretty much lost all fear of Neal now at last, so that his absence or his activity in other issues does not perturb me, but interests me. As, yesterday, when he showed late, I hesitated to call for fear he should think I was pestering him, and then realized that this was all wrong, that I really ought to call, there were things to be done, and I wanted to talk with him anyway, and why should I feel so guilty about it all? So I called, and so I was pleased when, though he wasn't home, he at least came in and we went to work. O well, I really ought to stop, I've exhausted my stock of conscious opinion for the moment and I'd really like to pack.

Neal still has not got his journal and I will help him get one before we leave.

I think I know what he will someday write and told him awhile ago but hardly explained: An American picaresque novel, full of nature and events, a chain of deeds and darings and sufferings and mad kicks and slow developments and purgation and final purity and intellectual beauty and physical vigor at the end. He will have to read Fielding, and *The Symposium* and *Petronious Arbiter*, and Sterne, Smollet, Richardson, Stendhal, Céline, *Don Quixote*, Cellini's autobiography, Casanova's memoirs, all works on Don Juan, some Kierkegaard, (Wolfe) perhaps Isherwood, H. Crane and A. Rimbaud and C. Baudelaire's and R. Rilke and Yeats' lives, Ben Franklin's *Autobiography*, *Robinson Crusoe*, Camus, (Connolly Cyril perhaps), Denton Welch, Gide's autobiography. He will <u>have</u> just <u>have</u> to understand the atmosphere and personality of St. Perse, Dryden and Pope; read Marlowe, Johnson's life, Hemingway's *Green Hills*, perhaps also a dose of Peggy Guggenheim. His will be the best of all, for the American work, for he is wide, aware, awake, experienced, has true individuality, etc.—<u>but</u>, he has true experience, superficially disorganized, not so as he will write it if faithful to his development. Sensuous of soul. External, authentic adversities. His story will be straightly told and dramatic, not melancholy, but with great stern sadness in parts, yet will in the end burst with joy and consummation. If Neal will do, and do, until his will is done, will perfect, and organize, and take pains, and learn true love, withal, he will be very great, greater even than I, and I am now assured of my own powers; yet he will say things that I cannot because of sickness, and write of emotions and experiences I will never have, he will be universal.

"Thoughtless met, for every reason." And all of this, my own labor on him—as almost, I labor on a poem—is sheer homage and pleasure in his being alive and dealing with him, yet by this I do not think of self-desecration, merely that I am I and he is he, each a separate, yet friendly self, each with its own purpose and fate. Unless he crosses himself—and me as well—I expect he shall be blessed with a very happy fate. He has only to submit to it—not me—and learn with thankfulness from whatever instrument, tattered tho it be, that fate works out to guide and develop and deepen him and make him a whole, even perfect, human being. One last thing—as and if I read this to him—I just thought of his reaction to what this would say—and I want him to know, while I have my wits about me, never more than now, not to presume that I am merely complimenting him; though I have a gratitude for compliments myself, and a benevolent regard for all praise given where met, the purpose of this is not, "To tell Neal he is a good boy," as I remind myself earlier that I must tell him, or, even to encourage him, or to try to give him hope as if he were a thoughtless child, but to tell him what I am thinking, to consult him almost, help with such of this as is factual and clarifying. I am not now writing a love-note except in some (presently vague) higher sense; I wonder if he will see that I am being very friendly, and, as a fact, I hope he will do the same for me some-day, and feel like doing it as I feel like telling all this outside my own mind. Someday I would like to hear his angles on me. Fin.

August 22, [1947]. Letter to Norman [Schnall] 10:30.
"...but I am coming down off benny and I slip into these long passages of abstract lyricism as easily as sleep...

and so (the poem runs) on and on, much like this letter, chaotic waltzes in morbid measures."

Of treatment

"I'll do this thing (his) and see it thru if I have to pawn my soul and forego Columbia for a term or so. You see what a wild sacrifice I'm prepared for, ready to put aside school. Do you? Do you? (Burp....) I'm cummings* to the end of this, I can see by the paper [In the margin Ginsberg has written: "*e.e. cummings."]

August 23, [1947]. Last day in Denver 5:00.
I have been sitting in bed in a naked voluptuous ease of body and soul, read-ing Wolfe on Paris and Munich. Do you know in all of this I have said nothing itself on Denver, the town? I don't think I could if I wanted to but I don't par-ticularly want to, a world, a city, is too big to come in upon—like Wolfe. Describe in sight and smell. Only it is enough that on the windowsill here are a cigarette holder and box of matches and a full pack of cigarettes, a coffee jar half full of sugar, without a top—all framed between a half drawn clean white shade-paper—and underwear hanging to dry from the hooked bundles of the [illegible words, perhaps: "lower rows"] of glass—outside two bricklayers are sitting the walls of a cellar in a dug out behind a neat doubly angled house of wood, grown over with ivy, and the roof of the house is on one gable dark, and on the other, silvery gray, with green running along the edges of the roof. But the point of this is that there is a young bricklayer out there—the subordinate of the two and he has been sitting idly for a few minutes, a perfect picture, (if necessary) of Denver. The other man has gone away and I was alone watching him, masturbating myself,—for he had on dungarees and was bare above the waist, and he has yellow hair and a smudged but still bright red cap on his head. He was sitting facing me before, on top of the wall, on a ladder that leaned up between his spread legs, his head was bent, gazing uninterestedly at

something on the ground, and he drew his hand across his chest and then slowly rubbed his knuckles across the side of his chin and rocked to and fro on the wall. He just picked up a cat that walked to him on the wall, took off his cap and put it over the kitten's body for a moment, to try it out. Meanwhile it is darkening as if to rain and the wind in the trees on the street is clear and almost harsh, not soft and murmuring. That's life for you, you really are always alone, can't depend on anybody or anything, and don't need to. So I sit here, not even waiting for action, reading, touching my body, listlessly—yet interested—writing, sans past and future—nobody really matters. This feeling is familiar yet momentary—I had it for surprising sustained intervals last night, after work, fatigued, trying to while away the time listening to Prokofiev, yet uninterested, too exhausted—not sadly listless—but coldly drowsy to care. All the problems of Denver diminished to contemptible unreality. I trust this sense, by the way, more than I do most moods.[167]

August 29, [1947]. Texas.
Aug. 29 or always

   I wonder, kind of…well, lots of things always.

   Lets go to bed.

   Recital of hitching to Texas—mostly natural wonders—early morning visions and communions with *papier mâché* mountains, fields suffused with anonymously cosmic physicality. It's really begun, May—open up your womb.

   Saying to Neal: "I love you" in bed, to express myself and also to test myself—and failing, since as I remember it sounded sickly "I loove yoo." Even worse than dear Carolyn.

   Now the afternoon of the double-bed.[168]

August 30, [1947].
Writing with Bill's [Burroughs] pen.

   When we got here, I expecting this happy holiday of God given sexuality, where was the royal couch? Little Boy Blue come blow your horn. So here I was: the first day high on tea, lushed, at supper watching Neal orient and try to dig Joan [Adams] and Bill—his remark about *Berlin Diary*. His childlike

---

   167 This paragraph was the basis for the poem, "The Bricklayer's Lunch Hour." See Ginsberg's *Collected Poems*, p. 4.

   168 When Ginsberg arrived at Burroughs's farm in Texas, he tried to construct a double-bed that he could share with Cassady. He had no skill at carpentry, and the attempt was for naught becoming a famous disaster and thwarting his attempts to have a sexual "honeymoon" with Cassady.

amusement with Bill—which gratified and slightly puzzled me since I half expected that Neal would not have sufficient feel or respect for high masks or low gentlemen—so not these, but for the blue Bill personality—different worlds or something—I don't know what. Simply, I suppose, could Neal be at home among "equals" in the sense of self-respecting characters?

But my frantic concern for closeness among all—even to the point of, not making only remarks, but being simply me relaxed and loverlike, almost kissing Neal before the household, doing so unconsciously. So far really, the subject has been tactfully omitted from open expression—except more slyly with Herbert [Huncke], so that I have not conversed at any length with Bill about Neal or with Joan, differently, on the subject. See, for instance, if Cassady had a sudden moment of recognition during dinner or etc., would he be free enough among all to be able to suddenly reach over and show it. Amusing, almost to the point of a delightful little play with Joan—the youngsters against the old frigid witch—while she was won over from skeptical objection to such conduct. But no such happy forest of Arden seems to be in sight in Texas—not that it's really so bad, except that it simply is the transformation of unimportant drags from Denver to Texas. Really out of lack of trust or knowledge, more of Neal, I have not attempted to bring us all into any open intimacy. At the moment where I knew there were a rapport I might even try to bring him to me (or us in a sense) on my own initiative—but surprisingly I really don't know when he is with me and when he is tensed—till he makes signs or till action in deeds, or talk; he is (amusing—comparison) uncommunicative about his emotion—even, in a sense in private. Whereas I naturally bounce up and stroke his beard—half self reassurance perhaps, but, still, that half in the sense of touching and announcing and verifying possession, the other half pleasurable passage of emotion. But it strikes as pawing alas.

So withal there is the problem of a bed yet! Another [problem is] Huncke buzzing round and round all afternoon.

July–August 1947. [Reading List].
Jackson, Charles. *The Lost Weekend*

Lowry, Malcolm. *Under the Volcano*

Auden, W.H. *The Age of Anxiety*

Kelly, John. "The Pure Substance!!!"

Gide, André. *The Counterfeiters*

Mann, Thomas. *Tonio Kröger*

Molière. *Don Juan*

Wolfe, Thomas. parts of *You Can't Go Home Again*

September 1, [1947].
Still Texas, no action in terms of love or art. "Neal, you give me cosmic vibra-
tions." Invent a paranoid fantasy of cosmic vibrations.
    Impossible to write. I cannot write prose.
    Jealousy of Cassady between moments. The sacramental honeymoon is
over. I have a drug against turning my mind to a practical non-romantic set of
arrangements *a propos* Cassady. Since it has at last penetrated my mind and
become obvious to me that, without angling, he means what he says when he
says he can't make use of me sexually, it requires a turn of the mind. I had
imagined myself in a sweet love relationship or the emergence of one—all by
my faith and will. This, as I say (repeating myself) seems out of the ques-
tion—what a waste of time and mood to find out. It is a finding out. He might
have been more explicit but so what, what would I have done with such
explicitness anyway? It's all now a drag to worry about. Anyway I see myself
in the last days indulging in petitionary masochistic lust, sliding around mess-
ily, corrupting any equality of temperament we have by sexual demands
which I am convinced (more or less—still in my mind a hopeless stupid hope-
fulness and ambiguity) are impossible to gratify. So now what? I suppose the
situation might as well slip along as it is except that without this previous pres-
sure I shall drift along half-apathetically, half hotly, now, full of more sterile
anxieties in situation, yet without real will to resolve them to love, since they
are all personal—pride—sentiment concerns. I might as well think that really
Neal has gotten himself into this set up, and has to push his way out of it.
Without love, and obedience to love's possessive impulses, and with the impo-
sition of conscious tact, I don't see that I will be in a position to push or pull
him (or me for that matter, too) into aesthetic shape. This doldrums settling
in is not good. I can take it because I know in the end I will resolve my aes-
thetic problems, if not strictly or satisfactorily, at least, productively—if worst
comes to worst with the prose I will always be writing bigger and better
poems. So I languish in Texas, pick up on Joan Bill Huncke and Neal, but my
earliest, most discouraging, meanest apprenticeship to life and art is over, was
over a long time ago, I just move around and forward now—not to any goal
but working, really. Whatever I do and feel. Enough of this. But I am won-
dering what will happen to Neal if I really withdraw my active queer love and

leave him alone emotionally? Doing so would be an effort for me, yet even that is half-done already, though before I was really convinced that nightingale did exist. Yet since I could not bring myself or him down by love I was apathetic to his spleen about it, "All meaning nothing" in my rebuke at him for pissing away his time on Mezzrow,[169] and because I could not deal in other than indirection and satire. I guess the whole point was lost in my reading of Sartre—though another perhaps was gained. Anyway he has not been reading—well—just browsing in trivialities, which I suppose he can afford if he is sure of himself. Still that makes me uneasy as I now loathe to presume upon our closeness to admonish him, even in foolish admonitions such as this may be. As for the grammar, I have not had the heart to force it on him, and have wasted, half knowing that without the force of love, irrational and unreasonable, the reasonable conduct of grammar would never be confronted by himself alone, even if I were there and he could come to me (which he has not of course). Still it is pleasant to sleep with him, have him, if once, turn and clasp me in the middle of the night. Yet how much the both of us sense the stupidity and corrupting nature on both of us (I wonder if he sees the corruption in himself) of my present mask of sexual obedience and supplication, which is not really necessary for me, but that is not the point. I really don't know what to do now. The clarity about sexuality is too much of an external impossibility to work with. I really see N.Y. unhealthily—presumably my closeness so far cultivated by my desire would disappear slowly as our relation became more and more artificial, more habit and momentary insight. In N.Y. how could I stand living with him without love? or he, with me for that matter, since my attitude would be so hostile and aggressive or else so suspicious or submissive to force. That is further aside from all else, coming to me for external details and direction of education (and, really why me, except that "I understand him"—which understanding is nothing but love—trust) he will fall into a rut of use of me and stupid or perhaps wise (who knows anyway?) contempt, really perhaps misuse. It all sounds sterile practically, or living with me, in my ménage, atmosphere, room even, imagine! How foolish. Yet if he does not and I do not watch on him he will fall into a N.Y. doldrums, maybe one "better" or more "virile" than mine, but one which will not lead him to divine poesy. Well, I have done my full, and my best, I have reached my end: my love for him was originally based and took fruition from a new love, a reciprocity and trust and mutuality. Without that, if it remains a love, it will be a

---

169. Milton "Mezz" Mezzrow. Jazz clarinetist and friend of Jerry Newman.

servile, sterile, one sided, same old (for him and me) worship which I won't indulge in any more and would probably consciously destroy, and which he would (if he is not lonely enough to cultivate that) resent and be disgusted by—both the conscious destruction and the love. The whole matter is, as casual to come down to it, beyond solving. We may drift in Texas, I'm willing since I can't think of anything else and I won't stop what good comes out of it, but N.Y. I want to see either free of this confusion or tied to it at the core, demonically, mutually participant. Whatever that means.

Suggest to him, as to sex in Texas, that animal kicks—ass fucking and so forth, frenzy, is better than apathy and drift—will pleasure him more, perhaps.

Nite.

Thumbing over the pages [of this journal] looking for the place—disgusted by the sight of love, love, love repeated everywhere. What love?

Well what more? This goes on interminably this scribbling of messages in a journal. I think, jumping levels, they don't mean a thing. Then I came back and know that they did, this does etc. They're there. That's the trouble with Jack [Kerouac]—Just reread his letter to Neal—He jumps and doesn't say (does he?) he knows he's not switched or even think of what he jumped off of, once thinking it was the only place to be in the universe.

The motivation now, of the situation as far as my actions are concerned, is almost mostly curiosity. Today I sounded Neal down about his fishwifery—his accumulation of disagreeable intimidating jokes. They have been a succession of mock-contradictions which I don't resist because I take him with such seriousness and love, and couldn't resist, in this state, even if I wanted, because I'm not interested in the results—or perhaps fear them, but I don't care about that as,—I don't know why. Is there any difference between my fear and humiliation psychically as the child before Neal, and the avoidance of intellectual conflict with him? I had never really wanted such conflict, I am not prepared for it, and I won't go to it unless I'm forced, by which time, if I am not being the same worried character that tried to build the double-bed, I will stop everything. So in that sense my curiosity has taken over, I force issues now not out of sweet love but abject curiosity. Neal (for my paranoid projection of him) is walking on the trickiest and most sinister part of the road to N.Y. now, yet I see him about competent, cheerful ever, confiding at moments like a little boy, and perceptive. However obvious that is it is difficult to see this whole picture. Jack says I don't have enough doubt? of what?

September 7, 1947.
Aboard *S.S. John Blair*, to Dakar and N. Africa:
   No comments.

[*An excerpt from a letter Ginsberg wrote to his father on September 12, 1947.*]

When I last wrote I was signed aboard a ship to Marseilles, but I changed my mind and signed for a longer cruise to Africa (West Africa—French Equatorial—Dakar, etc). I have (and always had) every intention of getting my degree. My motives in shipping out are spiritual, to be sure (I'm tired of everybody) but are predominantly practical, and I embark mostly for financial reasons. I will come back with a few hundred dollars, I expect (and some souvenirs). I am flat broke otherwise, and I don't want to have to squeeze thru another term borrowing money, and trying to live on $15 a week. Of course I could go back and work part time, but I also want psychoanalysis and that will take a lot more money, and the only thing for me to do is to do what I'm doing.

September 1947. [Reading List].
Texas and *S.S. John Blair*

James, Henry. *Wings of the Dove*

James, Henry. *Daisy Miller*

International Incident

[*This letter was written by Ginsberg in his notebook while in Dakar, West Africa, at the very end of September or the first of October 1947.*][170]

Dear Herbert [Huncke]:
How are you? I expect you saw what little I wrote from Freeport so you know what the deal is. I just arrived in Dakar yesterday, and am writing you first because I only wish you had come along. The ship is OK as far as crew—the second incidentally is a big L.A. spade that laughs like Norman Schnall.

   There is so much to do here and so many things to dig that I don't know where to begin. My position is easy as far as that goes because we may be here for some time—several weeks to a month—and I've got me one of the natives to wash all the pots and pans and clean up and peel potatoes. So I just

---

170   On September 13, 1947, Ginsberg left the port of Galveston bound for Africa on a coal boat.

have to get up early to build a fire (damned ship has a coal stove) and see that everything is settled for the day, and then amuse myself till the afternoon or evening by reading or writing while my work gets done.

The place is all I would want and more. It looks like a perfect second hand copy of Texas. I've wandered around feeling that strange feeling of being at home, which comes with such intensity and weirdness that I get sent just walking down the street. But I'm not really at home yet, since I haven't gotten straightened out as I wish. Sex is nowhere here—I don't know why, yet, but I'll improve the situation. I have a couple of local pimps rushing around looking for likely prospects for me. It seems to be strange that you have to look very far in a place like this. All I have is a lot of grief out of it. But there's plenty of that at a penny a stick [marijuana]. Big newspaper wrapped cigars, cupfuls practically. Lots of adobe huts, grass shacks, modernistic plastic government buildings, nutty colonials, beggars, etc. I fall in with some weird situations, as last night, when I walked around alone, met a young kid who took me thru a back alley to a crowd of people in fantastic costumes dancing around the fire with [a] dozen tom-toms. A strictly private celebration—someone got his first job or something, and there were only a few foreigners in the crowd. But what I do want to say is that this place is so mad I'm overwhelmed. And on that note I end.

Business, incidentally, isn't good, I don't expect I'll be able to bring anything of real interest back.[171]

Love, Allen

P.S. I'll be gone longer than I expected. After we leave here the ship goes 2000 miles down the coast to a village called Duala [Cameroon], a few degrees from the equator. Then, presumably, N.Y.

[*Also written in his notebook is this short note to his father.*]

Dear Lou:

I am seizing a spare moment to rush you a note. I arrived safely in Dakar. As might be expected, I am having a wild time, as the place is so native and so typically something or other, but very strange whatever it is,—sort of a third hand carbon copy imitation of Texas culture. [end of note]

---

171 Reference to bringing home drugs.

The Monster of Dakar

Why should I lie to myself any more? It has been quiet and secret and hidden, till someone gets up and shouts, "We have a right to our feelings! We're evil, all evil," or something beyond that.

Let the God damned world change. By God from now on I am not going to be a meek nut anymore, I'm going to be crazy with a vengeance, a horrible vengeance.

The point is I am different, I've been to enough schools and societies and doctors to know it. I used to think I was crazy, and I had to change to fit my own potentialities, the potentialities of the average; but I'm done changing. Why should I change?

What do I want? I give you three guesses. Crucifixion? Never. President of the United States? I went all through that in high school. I really wanted to be, even though I couldn't even dance. Rich? Sure, why not? But I can't even think about that any more. No, you must know, I'm dying to tell you, it's no surprise. It's the usual slob hang-up. I'm queer.

So much evil self accusation and talking around the point? And not the first time I said it either. But I know who I'm talking to. How am I supposed to bring up the subject? It has got to be treated in a special way, either as a tale of woe, or as a big aesthetic camp.

Well, it's too hard to say. But it's funny in a sane way too. It's supposed to be funny, it's an intelligent comedy. I am just introducing myself.

Back in '47, when I was wandering, out on my own in the world for the first time, I had an unhappy love affair in the middle of America with the most lower class Don Juan in the area and an intelligent angel. We still write each other, he's married has had kids and works as a longshoreman in Jersey City— I brought him east to be a big Balzac hero. He loved me, a big hustler, we kneeled together on the road of Oklahoma, in the middle of a four way cross of dirt roads, on an endless plain, at night fall. I hadn't imagined such a place or such an eternal vow: fidelity, union, seraphic insight, everything I could imagine. He accepted it all, just a poor lost soul, an orphan in fact, looking for a father seraph, and I was looking for a seraphic boy. By the time I was ready to ship out and leave the situation, I was really heartbroken.

It was great to go on the ocean; it was wild sea, rusty coal boats, peeling potatoes and serving food to childish Puerto Rican weakhearts, big jackasses from Texas, everything, including a nice blond boy from Texas who was also shipping for the first time. I liked him a lot and always wanted to love him. How it would have been to have him look in my eyes and kiss me, tenderly, sweetly. So great, so beautiful, I often wonder if he never thought that way about me. But apparently they don't, as a general rule. It's funny, but that too broke my heart. Anyway, he and I were friends, we were the only young white boys aboard and so we got along and we'd talk, mostly about him. Sometimes I'd get involved in long flights of memory about my own past. It wasn't lurid, but since he was essentially a straight farmboy he didn't have much to say. He had a lot of inner beauty, manly dignity. Strange that he was really [a] somewhat harried adolescent, running away from family difficulties. He spoke so vaguely I could never find out the whole story and just took off into space, eager to travel, but quiet about it, with a handsome open young face.

There was also a big beefy fireman-water tender, an absolute jerk. I hated him most of the time, he was so repellant, He walked around with shorts that were tight and hung below the protuberant belly. Such vanity! It was pure narcissism. He also had a big stupid face, red, like his belly and age-creased chest. He was a great one for squabbling at union meetings with the negroes. The ship was half colored, and great cats too.

There were two other important persons aboard. Another Texan, this time a fat youngish type around thirty, very evil. I'm passing judgments, but take my word for it, he was my natural enemy aboard. I didn't let on, in fact did him a favor later, so we got along OK. But I really didn't like his greasy lips and thick guts.

Jack I haven't spoken about, I just liked him. He was a big shiny black hipster from Chicago, the second cook, laughed charmingly, had been around a good deal in drug and musical circles, was surprisingly good natured and broadminded. He was my best friend, though knew little about me. Yet when I talked with him I was honest; when I was confused or bewildered I told him, and got advice, I gave him information and advice on several occasions, when he was too dumb to think things through—like his relation with the Chinese cook, who he couldn't understand (naturally enough, since the cook spoke Chinese continually). I told him the Chinaman was really W.C. Fields in disguise and played a ukulele (which he did, very sentimental American songs) and they got along better. Just sort of intermediated their distrust. The Chinaman for his part (named Cookie naturally) was noncommittal and self-absorbed, as all Chinamen are. Except that at sunset he would come out of his cabin, where he had been tabulating lamb chops on an abacus, and play It's Love Love Love to the dolphins.

So much for the cast of characters. The officers incidentally were all faceless wonders, I don't even remember them, at least during the trip. We were headed for Dakar which in my mind I had already equipped with a white stepped Casbah, incense, opium, hashish, Arabian boys, a foreign colony of broken down middle European intellectuals, everybody talking French or Arabic, and the backwoods jungles, with moth-eaten or beautiful Africans, as the case might be. (The map showed a desert and that was fine) I longed to see Africa, it was my first trip to that great continent, I knew all about it instinctively.

My plan for Africa was an orgy of drugs and native boys: to smoke opium at last, something I had never done, and buy a man and have a totally uninhibited ball for the first time in my life. I had visions of a dark hotel room or a mud hut, nakedness, fire light and a dirt floor. This wasn't very much different from the regular shipboard dream except for the choice of sex. Everybody smoked marijuana, everybody wanted to get laid, except for the Chinaman, he was probably the only misfit; a family man who wrote letters home and strummed his abacus and ukulele.

The trip was uneventful. I was going through a horrible depression as a result of my departure from what had been the possibility of a real opening of the soul with Don Juan. I lay in my bed and ran through the whole gamut of sexual fantasies, images taken from past and imagined experience. I got up in the morning and peeled potatoes, boiled eggs, dragged up oatmeal and bacon from the lockers and iceboxes downstairs and did whatever else I had to do. I served my meals, had the mid-morning, mid-afternoon and evenings off, dozed, read, talked, wandered around the ship and spent hours looking at the sea. I would get up in the middle of the night and stand at the rail and look at the dank black rollers coming up to within ten feet of me while the ship, the S.S. Blair, wallowed away toward the tropics like an old mule.

Suicidal fantasies when the waves were so close and historical examples so many. My thought was always that, once having jumped, the worst minute would be on the way to the water, when you woke up and realized what you'd done, cut off your life inevitably lost and caught in; a horrible unreal scheme of your own devising, while the reality of life flowed over you vast as the sea itself. It would be my moment of worst realization.

I never jumped in, but one sleepless night after staying up high on Benzedrine, feeling nausea and totally beat out, wondering what I was doing like a ghost wandering off so far away from anything I loved or knew, the future seemed so desolate. I felt like giving up then and there. I finally just vomited and left my stomach with the waves.

In the mess hall everybody was sitting around half asleep or playing irritable card games; Fat Tex was noisily boasting about his hand to Jack. Tex Jr. was sitting to one side drinking a glass of milk; Tex Sr. was somewhere hid in his cabin reading a sex-detective story or staring at the wall, the Puerto Ricans and Nicaraguans were sitting around humming to themselves. The Spaniards all began singing to each other softly; brought out bottles and glasses and began tapping out simple rhythms to a song called <u>Candela</u>, a repetitive backwoods Caribbean song about a sweet whore in a sad middle-sized Cuban town. The refrain, her name, returned over and over to the singing. The bottle clanking became more and more charming and intricate, they answered each other's laments across the mess hall with sweet tones tinkled in unison. The song changed and the ship gave a great hollow roll, followed by a heavy shudder of motors as the rudder rose up a moment in the swaying sea, whirred in the air for a moment, and then settled back.

Tex Sr. came into the doorway scratching his belly, the trunks hanging over his genitals. He stuck his head in the doorway, popped his eyes, and said in a child's monotone, as if playing an imaginary game: "Boom!" It took me a moment to realize that he had got up out of his bunk, walked down the crooked passageways, stuck his head in the doorway and said boom out of loneliness and nothing else to say. Nobody even looked up to acknowledge his remark, he hung in the doorway for a moment, totally unnoticed, and disappeared. I alone have preserved the moment.

I waited during the last days of the outward trip for a sight of Africa. My mental image was one of huge mountains covered with jungle hanging over the sea, taken perhaps from an early reading of *Tarzan* or *Bomba, the Jungle Boy*. Our passage through the Caribbean, a week or more earlier, had foreshadowed this: the mountainous isles of Haiti had looked like nothing I had ever seen except imaginations of the moon, vast ragged green jaws of land, no cities visible, just empty emerald rock stretching for miles on end. We passed Cabo Verde, the name of which I remembered from my stamp collections, a rusty dream of a mountain peak, a misty dark mountain, a god's house a sea at night and by daylight the sparkle of windows on the earthy vortex, upturned out of the water, ringed round with green volcanic shores.

At dawn of the twentieth day I woke and Dakar was outside, a low flat indecipherable series of promontories and land's edges on the sea, whitened by the mist as it rose. Nothing spectacular. We stayed anchored outside half a day, my inward impatience upwelling agonizingly, and then moved into a vast peninsular dock, near a field of immense coal piles.

Dozens of blacks milled around, they all wore dirty white shorts or ragged white trousers like anybody anywhere and torn shirts or none at all. I looked at the boys who were clustered around the gangplank, jabbering away in French and making mad bargains.

When I came down on the dock I was immediately mobbed by a bunch of dead end kids who were offering me impossible exchanges for seedy ties, marijuana, services rendered, women, and black idols. A few of the boys stood out. The sharpest hipster of the bunch was a rather sly and ratty looking kid who had the idols and ties. There was a big stupid beautiful boy, who had a Herculean figure, and was the darkest and most meek. He stood around offering to work aboard the ship for me. There was another rather genteel, frail and unlikely looking hanger-on who also wanted to work but my attention immediately went out to the most beautiful of them. There was an expression of suffering stupidity on his face that immediately attracted me. I felt that of them all he was the one whose beauty and meekness and strength, I could most easily bend to my own will, weak as it was and take advantage of his body. The obvious scavenging need of all of them was a perfect set up for any demand I might want to make: they were for sale, and I could satisfy their greatest need. I was sure he would have nothing but innocent acceptance of any transient physical demands I might make on him. The idea of laying a huge powerful youth like that, making him make love to me and being in a position to do so anonymously and without fear, in secret freedom decided my choice the minute I looked at him. His name was Mago.

I took him downstairs to the refrigerator and set him to peeling potatoes immediately. He was overjoyed at being accepted and could find no way of expressing it in his poor French. He just smiled to me happily like a great saint. I wondered how I was going to get him away and lay my hands on him when the time came.

Meanwhile I concluded a bargain for tea [marijuana] and bought a few sticks, wrapped up in four inch conical containers of newspapers, which I noticed were being smoked continually by everybody around. I lay in my bunk musing, waiting for supper when the purser came in and explained to me that since some members of the crew were southern, they might object to being served by my boy Mago. Word came down that we had to do our own work, no natives could be hired by the steward's department.

Mago meanwhile had gone on ahead and finished enough potatoes for days. I explained the situation and showed him to the gangplank, after giving him a few dollars and a carton of cigarettes. He thought I was displeased with him, which almost tore my heart out, he couldn't understand the ruling of the bureaucracy. I saw him standing around the dock for an hour looking up expectantly on the ship clutching his carton of cigarettes, hoping that someone would do him a good turn.

It was really, I suppose, my chance, now that I look back on it, but it seemed too much a nightmare to subject him to. Such self-effacement on my part! He embarrassed me now. There was no official way that I could hire him and keep him hanging around. He finally disappeared.

That evening I picked up Joe on the dock and had him take me into town for a look around. On the way I asked him about red marijuana as distinct from the green, which he kept talking about. He looked at me happy to be of service to a connoisseur, smiling, and said he'd get it for me. The town itself was nothing. It's just a new port town with no traditions of its own; a lot of natives came in from the backwoods looking for work. They have a big marketplace, with an outer court covered with stalls full of dried fish and sticky nuts. There's a high class French residential downtown; nothing happened there. It wasn't worth bothering about.

I floated through the streets in a dazed high of my own, followed only by one limp boy who attached himself to me unobtrusively, made no demands, and merely hung around. When I finally settled for rest, it was in a closed doorway on a main street in front of a group of blind children stretched out on the pavement holding hands and singing an alms song. I stayed with them several hours listening to an incredible monotone they wove among themselves, more and more locked in a high dream of my own isolation, more and more wrapt into their own trance which hung in the doorway. Their glazed skin and blindness finally bespoke their leprosy.

My companion went with me looking for the movie house which advertised *Pepe Le Moko*. The boy started making demands in a childish and quavering voice, which I ignored. He continued to ask me for things, relentlessly, firmly: cigarettes, marijuana, shoes, eyeglasses, t-shirt, coins, bills, shoelaces, pencils, socks, food, chewing gum, soda. I answered no, said no again. I had begun to be frightened. He limped behind me, a sweetening smile on his face, his voice gaining angel-like purity, the litany repeated, over again. It finally came to me that he was absolutely sincere and in need. He was all innocent, he simply wanted something, and saw no reason why I shouldn't give it to him, nor, after awhile, did I. I took his hand and we went looking for the movies. Meanwhile I was divesting myself of possessions: comb, handkerchief, wallet, some money, t-shirt, whatever I could remember him asking for.

He pointed out a stall filled with sweets, which we bought and shared. He went off finally, smiling graciously again to me in perfect understanding, thanking me, saying farewell; he was a little boy and it was late at night.

I ran into a native dance with bonfire, drum and dancing, that night behind an old adobe house near the movies, stood watching awhile, then saw Pepe Le Moko suffer his death in Algiers, and floated back to ship in the donkey cart.

Next day Joe brought me his red tea which I bought. It was green and brown, like anything else. He insisted it was red. The shifty smile of the orient is nothing but that of the old fish peddler on River Street. I gave him new instructions this time to find me some hashish. He seemed a likely candidate to be my pimp, too, so I painfully explained my interest to him. He caught on after awhile, smiled at me mockingly, and said, "You're not like the others, eh?" I said, "No, that's the point, what can you find for me? I want a nice, well built boy, about 15 or 16, who needs money, who'll sleep in bed with me as if he were a girl, or I were one. I don't want an ordinary looking boy, I want a handsome one. I'll give both you and him lots of money. Now look around and find out what you can." He shook his head dubiously, but said he would. "Isn't there a lot of this desire around here?" I asked. "Some people," he laughed. "What kind of Africa is this?" I said to myself.

So I spent the succeeding days idling aboard ship and drinking in town. The pressure of work was relieved when the chief engineer brought home another boy and asked me to give him something to do in return for food. Rules were relaxed. I jumped at the chance and hired Djiami, a frail adolescent who spoke English. He had a genteel intelligence about him which attracted me immediately, I set him to peeling potatoes, washing my laundry, cleaning dishes. On his own he cleaned up my forecastle, ran errands, was in every way satisfactory. I grew to like him and began to think of trying to make him. I would get into my bunk, talking, and stretch out half naked or with a towel around my middle, dress and undress in front of him, gaze soulfully at him, tell him I was sick-souled, everything but actually make an attempt. He seemed too fine natured to take advantage of; he would have walked out on a good job. You will think that this is a poor way to go about satisfying myself, but that's the way I am. That's why I set out from America to begin with.

Joe meanwhile produced no hashish, only more green tea, with an explanation that it was hashish. I sent him out this time for what I really wanted, opium. None of the local people had ever heard of it, except Joe, who said he did, but produced nothing the next day but more green tea. I decided that the real trouble was that Dakar was not like the North African cities, which really were cities of sin. Here there was nothing but coal fields and displaced natives who belonged back in the jungle, not wandering around looking for jobs. Joe had not yet produced my boy either. "It is hard," he said.

I had been overpaying for my tea, Djiami complained, not bargaining sufficiently; and since I was under his protection, it was a humiliation to him. He insisted that I follow local custom and I agreed to let him do my buying henceforth. Then I told him what was wrong with my soul and what I wanted. He too had a great deal of difficulty understanding me, and smiled it away when he did. It was impossible to make him, I decided. I was at the mercy of Africa.

I went out the next day looking for Joe. It was the last day and night in port. I ran into Joe downtown. "Have you found me a boy?" He looked at me uneasily. "I'm leaving tomorrow, if you want to make the money I offered you, it's your last chance."

"Well, Joe," (he called me Joe) "I think I know one who'll do it. Where do you want to take him, back to the ship?"

"No, no, no!" I cried exasperated. "Is there some kind of a cheap hotel here where we could go, where nobody will even see us or notice?" Joe scratched his head and I decided to take care of that when the occasion arose. He promised to meet me later around the corner from the sailor's bar, bringing with him my male whore.

I went into the bar and left several hours later at the appointed time. It was late and I was lusting with a wild masochism to be fondled like a child in the huge dark embrace of male sexuality. I waited under the streetlight around the corner. Joe arrived, alone. "Where's the boy?" "I brought him," Joe said, "He's down the street. He'll do it with you, I know he will, he'll do anything you want. I haven't told him what you want, I just told him to do what you want and you'll give him money." "What!" I said, my heart rising in rage. But by now I was so precipitate in my longing that I was ready to take control and demand and receive what I wanted. It was a moment of freedom and wildness that I had waited for. I went with Joe up the street and saw a figure standing in the shadow at the corner. He was a small boy. I was disappointed but it was still flesh to me. When I came close enough to see him Joe called out, "Uroa, this is Joe, do what he say." Uroa looked at me bewildered out of his ugly crossed eyes. He had a stunted body, rachitic and weak with an over large, bulbous head, the head of an idiot.

He stood silently and stared at me expectantly. I paid Joe off. He had done his job as best he knew; and Uroa, he too had played his role as he was meant to. I returned immediately to the ship.

On Creation:
It is not understood that creation is unconscious, or at least the process is seldom really understood because no one is really interested in the process itself, only the morality of it. Thought is in this sense unconscious. Not merely that before a thought is out, the mind has stewed all awhile long, and chance has flung her images in the kettle. Always this is true, but I mean the simple inspiration the, phrase, line, sentiment of sensation, the verbal or unverbal affect that fills the mind for a moment, is not much a matter of control. This is written to encourage creation, since creation is an organic process, it goes by itself, cooks itself, to return to our figure, and needs only the simple tasting of consciousness in all the labor of preparing poem. That is a happy and pleasant thought to me, that I, writing, or living, need not bother to make impossible intellections. We have some vague image in our minds of this all—perceptive all combining consciousness that we, a someone else controls, but thought controls the mind in that fantastic manner, the soul runs by itself. We only need allow our thoughts their freedom and the mind will be creative, so as to that advice as upon detail in fictional creation, though I have not practiced fiction I am sure that the seeming impossibility of that—unless one is not already burdened with the details of life—is only an illusion of process, that moment to moment as the thought comes and is served, the space of mind is covered, like a paper, with spontaneous images.

Note on Dakar Doldrums
The same process of continuous thought [as in the "Denver Doldrums"] in development of "decision" or the development and metamorphosis of mood, is followed, only here the time is twenty days that passed aboard a ship to Dakar. Here the desperation is more consciously maniacal, yet directly and presented with sincerity, and imaged at will with half-prophecies of self-destruction, or and I warn only deceptively romanticist violence.

[ca. Oct. 2, 1947]. New York.
It is about time but I think I have it. I was reading Edith Wharton's *Gods Arrive*, and changes of air and the change of air from Texas to Dakar to N.Y. has been similarly refreshing. Anyway I thought lately now that I am returned to N.Y. where presumably my problem will face me again. All along—I realize—that sense of self has been the lover as it were. That escape in poetry and action or original creation is without "self" almost, Nietzschean in feel of self, if anything, stranger. That is, completely occupied with the specific external or

internal labor or creation—objective and visional, trance like. I suppose all such life is so, true personality. Neal I cannot completely imagine what to do with. It seems that all the doing is to be mine, anyway. Well, I can see one way in which my will hath done. So I say to him, coming now finally with words to speak and ways to act, either we are lovers or we are apart, after all. It is time for me as I believe to cast my self away! live, and spend my self in complete "saturation" or dedication. I am to do so, after all, and have been to do so, with the Final Analysis; but also I feel the sense of indifference to subjectivity coming on me where it is ill managed or weak and pusillanimous. It's whole and useful or there is no point persuading it along. So now rather than waiting on time it is time for a decision as a movement of the soul; if yours does not move mine will, all your temporizing and indetermination, or your acceptance of the situation as is is naught for me in the end. My own submissions and flexibilities were after all subtle secret ways of persuasion and education and weaning. They were in the end to make you submit, and now the time has come. So at last must act with demand, ultimatum, force, possession and unity, and that I add, with appeal, and for understanding, and sympathy, I perhaps have found a wary satisfactory in the situation to sugar coat your submission with a noble and just pity, a masterly one as well existing in you or in me. But that is beside the point, which is also, that all your temporizing is inspired and sensitive, but not sufficient to me in the end in any way, and the difference between our ideas is what prevents you from achieving genius with all your power. I am given to complete saturation. Not as mechanical as that I spoke of on our way between Huntsville and New Waverly perhaps—and can conceive of no truth between us other than an equal dedication. If you are to learn art thru me, a completely opened bond (channel) must make us one, unite. Your way and response is fine as they go, but does not hold the spiritual genius of mine, without which after all, your wishes for yourself in me would be thwarted and the whole "idea" behind our collaboration spoiled. It is that complete saturation that I'm sure is what you cannot achieve for life or art except in a false perjured way and I am not willing to continue thought for you unless you are equal to it or to my conception of it. You see I am ready to throw myself completely on my visions and follow where they lead, and so can think without pain now of a complete break with the past—perhaps Burroughs and all—and a following thru—perhaps with an interval of pure solitude and psychoanalyzing or complete prose creativeness, or different things altogether. I only have to say that my mind is in every side and though I do not sense, really, as I would if I were, that I am wrong and fantasizing now, I do know the way my sense of self persisting still draws me. So I wish to find out if, were I to fail or change my mind about my own possibilities, or decide I have been wrong or half wrong or ambiguously true and false or in any way mistaken above, that you will take me back if I wish to come back. This does not sound very real but it is if you think about it long enough. Anyway here I end.

October 1947 [Reading List].
Maugham, W. Somerset. *Cakes and Ale* [and] *Moon and Sixpence*

Woolf, Virginia. *The Years*

Heard, Gerald. *A Taste for Honey*

Plutarch. *Cicero* [and] *Pericles*

[*On November 14, 1947, Dr. Harry J. Worthing, the senior director of the Pilgrim State Hospital sent a form to Ginsberg for his signature, which permitted the doctors to perform a prefrontal lobotomy on his mother, Naomi. Ginsberg signed and returned the form and the operation was carried out, but he never forgave himself for authorizing such a drastic step. Naomi was never the same again.*]

November 25, [1947] New York.
Allen, don't die.

November 1947 [Reading List].
Karsavina, Tamara. *Theatre Street*

Wharton, Edith. *The Gods Arrive*

Dostoyevsky, Fyodor. *The Idiot*

James, Henry. "The Author of Beltraffio" [and] "Madame de Mauves"

Hawthorne, Nathaniel. *Twice Told Tales* (Stone Face, Ambition Guest); *The House of the Seven Gables*; [and] *The Marble Faun*

James, Henry. *The Great Short Novels of Henry James* edited by Philip Rahv

Apuleius. *Cupid and Psyche*

Chekhov, Anton. *The Darling and other stories*

Balzac, Honoré de. "Passion in Desert"

Maupassant, Guy de. *String*

Engstrand, Stuart. *The Sling and the Arrow*

December 18, [1947].

> Down the dimpled! greasy rivers run
> Times monotonous in tone.
>
> I am so young and beautiful I lie alone. I am so timeless and
>   haglike I fuck myself.
> I lie alone like an old hag,
> like a grandmother who married a laundryman
> (mine did)
> as if I had scrofula?
> Like an old hag.

December 13–?, [1947].

Called up Bill [Burroughs] a minute ago, high on benny to give him some uplift with his attempt at kicking habit. So so wearily depressed this morning—neurasthenic skelping, no job, woke up at 2:00 after how many perhaps 11 or 12 hours of sleep—and it seemed like 16 or 20. I woke up as I dreamed because I'd finished drug with a thing (N.Y.?) I was reading in my dream and couldn't keep on and on reading nothing.

Didn't inscribe hallucinated dream two weeks ago. I propped up my cock under covers, on a speedball several hours earlier. Slipped into dream where I was rewarded for my cock teasing—Joe May came into the room stood over me in a towering manly rage, uncastrate, and cursed me, threatening to make me suck his joint and take it down, "You cock teasing little bitch," and that I was. Poor Allen, so I woke today and sat and smoked a cigarette, helpless in ennui and doldrums. Still with me. Of course I'm bored, I won't work, I have no love and seek it out continually in friends I have no love for or who love and don't love me—it doesn't matter.

Of course I love Bill for all the errors of his. I thought, before, how prideful it is I am, to censure or mock or despise the neurotic and weak. Kingsland is so right when they throw the chestnut at my heart, that I project and fume against people's vices, these are most my own. And I tried therefore to think good—not judge, but how false my false humility is. I can't yet teach myself as a poor weak, even not too intelligent, just practical, little kid without roots or reason, just wondering vainly around looking for some self-justification.

1948

February 7, 1948.
Poems to write—

The Serpent and the Nightingale

Prose and poesy interlarded Audenesque but more direct.

The Killer—(Where Was the World)

"I fought with the killer for his love"

make the killer the symbol of sacerdotal (or) ambivalent love.

Write Lyrics.

Last month wrote letters prose

February 14, [1948].
Records to buy:[172]

Gillespie—All—Things to Come—Can't Get Started

Babs 3 Bips and a Bop - Po-pa-pi-la (o pi do pi hop-la)

Billy Nalidy—No More; Waterfront: Don't Explain, Lover Man, Fine and Mellow, My Old Flame. etc.

Berlioz—Harold in Italy

Mahler—2'd Symphony

Bach—Passacagliote and Fugue C Minor—Particle and Son; Orfeo Catalain

Beethoven—Missa Solemnis

C[oleman] Hawkins—Selections

I[llinois] Jacquet—Jazz at Philharmonic Vol. 2—Blow the Blow—(New Victor?)—Bottoms Up, etc.

Leo Parker—Mad Lad

Barnet—Cherokee

Shaw—Summit Ridge Drive.

172 Ginsberg found a part-time job and used some of his money to purchase records.

O Neal I love you still and I wish you were here, yet you become more lost each day; you are most near while I do not even hear from you or send you news of me. O Neal I love you and am yet even now, wishing you and me both peace in all the awful changes I and you are going to make.

I am not any more as innocent or above sickness or prideful with poesy as before. Was it the poor self or my masks that made you abandon me, or was it the sense of all that you saw of me in duplicity and selfish confusion? I have experienced the vomit and sniveling I thought of. Also only in great horror, as in a frightful dream, only awake in the analyst's chamber. Chamber of Horrors

ca. February 19, 1948.
[*From a note Ginsberg wrote to Trilling, ca. February 19, 1948.*]

Gutmann[173] says that he is not very optimistic about a University Fellowship for me, so I hope you will make the recommendation as strong as you think will be proper. I can't leave the city next year and unless I can study here this is all the schooling I will get, so I am quite concerned about the results, which are, so to speak, 'final.'

February 21, [1948].
H.E.H. [This is all in Ginsberg's handwriting.]
    Herbert E. Huncke
    "My name; although I'm known generally as Huncke and by a few as Herbert and in the past as Herbie—It is seldom I'm referred to as Mr. Huncke and when formal introduction is required it is usually—Herbert Huncke.
    I mention all this concerning me simply because recently—I've grown to dislike my name—not because my name is Herbert Huncke but rather because I've reached a point where my name (any name I might have had) by its mere utterance creates an almost weary and loathsome feeling in me. When I say it myself and frequently I say it to myself—I am immediately aware of a sense of disgust as though the sounds I make were significant of not only me but of a new and strange disease, and I am sure for at least the instant, I am at last slipping into an insanity from which there is no escape.
    For several years I've been confident I will become insane, in fact I've felt thusly almost as far back as I am able to recall.

---

173   James Gutmann (1917–1988). Professor of philosophy.

Once when I thought I would become a writer (I was quite young—fourteen at the time) I made periodical attempts to write poetry and on this particular occasion I became aware fully of the sense of pending insanity. It was shortly after dawn and a huge and glistening sun was ascending a delicate blue sky. It was early summer and people were beginning to enjoy the bright colors of summer attire. I was living on Superior Street just east of North State Street in Chicago in an old wood frame house that had been converted into what is called studio apartments. The house was well constructed and the rooms were large with high ceilings and windows reaching the full height of each room.

I had spent the few hours just preceding daybreak bathed in moonlight watching the sky thru one of my windows (there were two in this room—huge windows which could be flung up quite high letting in all the outside sound and scent and air on either side of a fireplace with a white mantle with two large brass candlesticks with tall green candles) allowing my thoughts to dwell as they would and pondering over my problems and the magnificence of daybreak.

And now as I descended the front steps to the street level—the sun was bursting and spiraling across a huge space of blue.

To one side of the steps was a flowerbed sparsely filled with yellow jonquils and I glanced at them and then toward the sidewalk to observe several young women who rapidly walked past and talking of their work and of something amusing as when they had almost reached the corner they began laughing. Their costumes were charming and one wore something with large figures of poppy red which I liked.

Then it was almost at that moment—I suddenly thought of my insanity—of how sure and insidiously it begins and of how unsuspecting the victim.

I was rather frightened and deeply impressed. I stood a long time thinking about it becoming more convinced each instant, I was doomed. Several hours later when I had finished my breakfast and returned to my apartment I tried putting in a poem all which I felt and I was rather pleased with what I had written although I can't remember any of it and the actual writing is long misplaced—along with everything of myself at that time.

It wasn't long after I began traveling and ceased considering Chicago my home.

I now have no home. Perhaps I should think of New York as home. Certainly, I feel sure—it is in New York I'll die. What I actually mean is, it is in New York I have started dying in the final stage.

Hiatus time. All which I have learned to associate with myself has become abhorrent to me. I have developed fear of meeting people. I prefer sitting quietly alone. Sometimes I feel as though I must force—almost drive myself—to come out from behind a closed door when new people have entered an apartment I am in or I will wait until the last minute before leaving a place because I know I must meet people's glances on the street. I dislike having to speak to strangers—waiters, clerks, bus drivers, newsboys, shoe shiners, subway agents and all the rest. I find I am ceasing to enjoy my more intimate acquaintances. I believe they like me but they also pity me. [In the margin Ginsberg has written: "Me?"] I am sure they explain me to their friends slightly apologetically on occasion and always with an air of tolerance. Huncke's idiosyncrasies, his eccentricities or perhaps—his mother complex. Sometimes I am sure they even attempt to allow for the unhealthy pallor of my skin. He takes Benzedrine—in fact he lives on it.

Among a large percentage of those who know me casually or only know of me it is commonly understood I am completely saturated with narcotics. It is also believed I am unscrupulous and a completely rotten sort. I believe I am rotten in my entire being. My skin is unhealthy and serves merely as an excellent breeding territory for all the fungus and parasitical creatures it contacts. It itches constantly and I can sit for long periods scratching and picking odd shaped black and sometimes white and frequently very darkened (like specks of dried blood) specks or flakes from my arms and legs and face and often from the pubic hairs of my testicles and above my penis. The palms of my hands and also my fingers produce hairs some fully an inch in length. I have become conscious of this condition to so great an extent I am frequently sure it is evident to people I pass on the street. My eyes are poor with large dilated pupils mostly the result of constant use of amphetamine. My teeth have long been gone. I am no longer able to walk as far as I please without my legs and feet aching so badly, I am often in pain. Recently I have acquired a strange dry cough. I speak of it as being due to the recently popularized Virus X. I am firmly convinced mine is a sick body. Occasionally I feel ashamed and I think I should remain away from everyone because per chance I may infect people, pollute them with my corruption and leave them with a diseased soul as mine is diseased. Leave them—weary—listless—horrified of themselves and longing to escape the world—to die.

The weather has been cold and amazingly disagreeable.

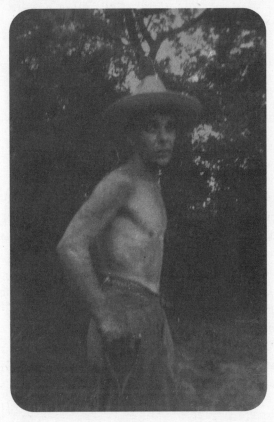

Herbert Huncke working on William Burroughs's Texas farm, 1947

Saturday Evening, February 21, [1948].

"The most depressing thing is to get up to go to school and wake him [Huncke], and see him lift up his head, staring blankly, dumb, biting his lips, for half an hour at a time." Letter to Neal.

February 1948 [Reading List].

James, Henry. *The Ambassadors* (begun)

Isherwood, Christopher. *Lions and Shadows*

Céline, Louis-Ferdinand. *Death on the Installment Plan* (parts)

Flores, Angel. *The Kafka Problem* (started)

Melville, Herman. *Bartleby* [and] *Billy Budd*

March 22, [1948].

On Corbière's picture in front of the translated poems (Walter McElroy. [Banyan Press, 1947]). The figure is like a mixture of Sancho Panza and Don Quixote sitting in the body of a lunatic backwoods peasant; that is the equal of Corbière's soul (sense of self). I suppose this image of anxiety is the common meeting ground of Eliot and Corbière. [In the margin Ginsberg has written: "On Weed. Literal sense of feeling of lost peasantness for C. and E."]

First stanza and then poem *Heures*, with magnificent pun on "cease and tell." Train of thought excited by: "I hear the north wind roar / It bellows like a horn / That calls to those too long gone, / I have howled in my turn too long, / I hear the north wind roar / I hear the knell of the horn!"

Trilling's—sophistry: "...for the poet is in command of his fantasy, while it is exactly the mark of the neurotic that he is possessed of his fantasy."

Stanzas deleted from "The Killer"

Poems to write: The Geek—Epistle to the Hipsters—The Dark Horse (Psych)—Remember children repeat (in association experiments) "Lamb-Lamb."

Lessons this week—

1. Act like a fairy
2. Don't criticize, sympathize
3. Don't act in literary pride
4. If you don't, you'll fail with Tommy. So what?

March 1948. [Reading List].
Lorca, Federico Garcia.

Kafka, Franz. *The Trial* [and] *The Castle*

Gregory, Horace. *Chorus for Survival*

Tate, Allen. *Poems, 1922–1947*

Wilbur, Richard. *The Beautiful Changes*

Rimbaud, Arthur. *A Season in Hell*

Blackmur, R.P. *The Good European, and other poems*

Corbière, Tristan. *Poems.* NY: Banyan Press, 1947. (translated by Walter
    McElroy)

Laforgue, Jules. "Hamlet" [and] "Pan"

Dante Alighieri. *Divine Comedy*

Gide, André. *Journals* (here and there)

Céline, Louis-Ferdinand. *Mort À Crédit* (first 150 pages) He doesn't hold up
    well, but he's great.

Warner, Rex. *The Cult of Power*

Smith, William J. *Poems*

Bishop, John Peale. *Selected Poems*

Lawrence, D.H. *Selected Poems*

Vidal, Gore. *The City and the Pillar*

April 12, 1948.
I had this dream between 7–11: In Livingston or Hartley[174]—Has nobody got a
room on the first floor? (an apartment?) I would like to have one to entertain.
I walk in the room—it is for three or four queers. They are talking in queer talk
to one another, and I wander in and am offered refreshments to them—I lie
around on the double decker bed. I am an outcast from the queers. I apologize
that I can't or won't "come on" right and here are elements of "hipness" in
their speech. But I don't or can't communicate to them in Hip language. [In the
margin Ginsberg has written: "The Negro to whom I denied help."] I am eat-
ing a sandwich of pure meat—a big, enormous sandwich of human framed

---

174 Livingston and Hartley were both dorms for Columbia students.

flesh, including a dirty asshole. This is what I am eating, and I notice it. I had finished $1 \frac{1}{2}$ or $\frac{1}{2}$ and I am offered it and I accept, since I am hungry, but on realizing what I am eating I also realize that I'm full of it and no longer hungry. I am left alone in conversation with one of the three who is trying to make me, is sweet—it is to him that I apologize for my armor. The room is (as I remarked to them) one which has two decks of beds, and is lined with goods and cooking apparatus, icebox, stove—like a ship, living there is, with room enough only for cooking and sleeping. I remark on it but my remark is not appreciated.

Company comes, I come down to meet them, recognizing Walter Adams and Ed Stringham.[175] I cry out in a grating queer voice by Ed. S. (to show the former occupants that I am queer, to demand attention, etc.) S. has a soldier suit on and is a little horrified at my behavior. After greeting him I am introduced. There are several women there, one of whom is young and pretty and cute and says who are you and we exchange names and courtesies. The other, more a woman, says hello but is very cold, the last, a fluffy princess, mature, frilly dressed, (reminds me of Ansen) says outspokenly, "I don't like you," and turns her head refusing to be introduced. I say what: get very imitation angry, straighten up, and begin calling her names, "Why you shit faced fool!" This gets everybody's attention and I begin to denounce her in front of everybody for being "imperceptive," "socially blind," "neurotic," "unmoral" etc., "How can you decide when you don't even know me?" etc. In violent and messianic voice, almost inspired.[176]

This dream shows somewhat my relationship to both men and women—I am shut off from either.

May 1948. [Reading List].
Vossen. *Medieval Culture*, vol. II

Fry, Roger. *Vision and Design* [and] *Henri Matisse* [and] *Cezanne*

" " Matisse

" " Cézanne

Blake, William. *Poesy*

---

175 Edward Stringham. Friend of Kerouac who introduced John Clellon Holmes to the group.

176 This paragraph was the basis for the poem "In Society." See *Collected Poems*, p. 3, although misdated in that collection.

June 5, [1948].

My twenty-second birthday marked fortuitously with breakthrough of under-
standing of reality—of the evil of the world, of the peace of the self possible,
of the value—the reality—of art. Read Jack's novel last week [*The Town and the
City*], and think it is very very great. Alas! that we should have been so true.

Rewrite Mother's poem to title "On Mother's Mandolin"—with old ending.

Rewrite down dream of search after Meyer Shapiro—his leaving the (my
father's house)—Shapiro changing form and mood (including the witch on
MacDougal) and his play with his child. My imagination of Shapiro's imagi-
nation is genius.

To write tonite—poem on above themes.

Languor in Cleveland

and Doldrums in Denver

(And Dolours in New Orleans?)

Tea Leaves—(subjective notes)

My mind travels a series of ways from the most general concrete to the
most (white) abstract, this is a cycle recurring at the moment. Not only redu-
plicated from time to time and then to season, each abstraction is an abstrac-
tion of an abstraction. And there we are again.

To write. I phrase an idea in the mind and then revise it to read allegorically,
or by metaphors, most important.

One is compulsiveness. My mind travels from a peak of abstraction down
a series of ways to the concrete then back.

I cry from moment to moment like an eagle or like a worm.

Modern poetry

by Allen Ginsberg.

> Bebop style
> I am an eagle and I am a worm
> I am the mother and I am a sperm.
> I am a sky and I am the storm
>
> I want to be an immortal bop poet
> (later thought)
> "I want to be the great bop poet."

> Boy, will you come, will you come
> seven months have I sat
> Reading here, pacing alone,
> Turning to stone in a room…

Jack: "I am going to marry my novels and have little short stories for children."

Henceforth the sign and symbol of my works will be [Here, Ginsberg has drawn a picture of a falling leaf.]

> Which is a fig leaf, undried,
> A worm crawling up a mountain,
> And the Crow of the Marijuana Garden.
>
> O that cicatrices
> Should have a big valise,
>
> O that round old *Merde*
> Has such a baby Pard.
>
> O that me O my
> My sex is in my eye.
>
> My sex is in the mouth
> my sex is in the nose
> My sex is in the South
> Where the north wind blows.
> And I'm writing to tell you
> Old frueteysotiyou
>
> My sex is in the bowl
> my sex is in the glass
> my sex is in the soul
> my sex is in the ass.

eyi = the mysterious combination of syllables that sound like my prophet's parables.

Titles for a book.
1. Where You Going, Cat?
2. Get Hip, My Soul.
3. These Are The Images Of Allen Ginsberg.
4. Please Open The Window And Let Me In.
5. The Fad In The Television Set.
6. A Child's Garden Of Curses.
7. I But The Plue, I Push The Pink
      I Wassel The Red, I Ride The Orchid
      I Wish The White And I Cry When I Wink.

Neal: his names were long and will never be forgotten.
Lucien: All our intelligence was in him.
Allen: All his sorrows were more than ours.
Bill: All our courtesy was most in him.
Joan: Her madness was all our own.
Jack:

Whom I love most in the world, in this order:
Neal
Eugene
Jack
Bill—I should die for these—
Lucien
Joan
Huncke
Neal

[*Neal Cassady had divorced LuAnne and married Carolyn Robinson on April 1, 1948, in San Francisco. Around mid-June Ginsberg wrote a short letter to Neal, which in part is replicated here.*]

This <u>spring</u> has been one of madness, much like yours. Frenzy, frenzy, creation that is worthless, drinking, school, etc. I've been working part time and so I had about an even stint of money, and bought a lot of records. What finally pulled me out—to name an external cause since they are the signs by which we mark seasons—was Jack's novel [*The Town and the City*]. It is very great, beyond my wildest expectations. I never knew.

Now, I suppose I should congratulate you on your marriage. So O.K. Pops everything you do is great. The idea of you with a child and a settled center of affection—shit, I don't like to write prose because you have to say something simple and direct. My mind isn't made up into anything but complete amused enthusiasm for your latest building.

Tuesday, June 17, [1948].
Dream of seeking refuge and sleep with another tall middle-sized (tough) unshaven character, naked in a bed of hay or unstraightened blankets in a large room (glass) or sun porch in an empty mansion which (I knew about) I began to blow him but began right off wrong by biting the head of his cock off. It came off easily, but I was a little ashamed for my presumption and he was disgusted. At this point, the police came, we all made friends, sort of, or, rather, I retired with him under the blanket with our heads sticking out, hiding ourselves as best we could.

I had a strange dream of image and symbols. I remember descending—after leaving the leviathan city in the cold that possessed it. Following a man that was thin and frightening down a well (with a brother) to his module apartment—where he explained why he was so frightening to me in terms of the images that surrounded him: for instance a cat/that I thought was strange—a noble sleek head, as if chopped off, or so stylized with sleepiness (sleepless) as to be frightening. She it was who led us there. Why did he neglect her so?

Neglect her? No, on the contrary, what more was he to do? It was she who came to him, he took her in from out of doors during the recent calamity.

Then a picture of him—as in a poem—in the street during the calamity (perhaps on a cold hysterical winter's day in an imaginary Germany of the 30's and the general winter snow terror). An unidentified young man in strange "decadent dress"—red shirt and sharp trousers covered over by a stylishly cut weathercoat buttoned up to the neck, had come up the stairs to his brownstone, and was delivering a message to a frightened shivering lady. He has led her from the porch—[In the margin Ginsberg has written: "1. I confused him, rereading, with her. She has wild glowing hair."] "Perhaps to see the messenger himself the old man and withered old dead man on the street"

Next thing I see two stanzas of Auden's poem, and a picture of the young man dying and dead in the gutter, and the woman drawn against her will down off the porch into the wintry, snow, street in despair and wild suffering in the cold, watching him, and I wake with those few fragmentary lines in my mouth. Also I remember remarking that his one early poem of Auden's (including a reference to a Cambridge scholar, perhaps the old man) was his one moment of actual communication between self, world, and which prevents him from speaking directly.

(After reading yesterday the "Starting Point" by C. Day Lewis. Seeing a copy of *Age of Anxiety* which I had stolen once myself from the library, and discussing my own De Quincyism and exaggerating it to some young girls.)

Why should not the great poet write "In youth my sympathies were bent on men, in age on nature?"

Random—

...And make the world my own delight. World is the bad word because it can be confused with the Romantic abstract world—which it is, and I want to imitate sensuous knowledge of the real thing, "The destiny wished thing," as James said on his deathbed. If this notebook is ever published, I curse him and his who expurgates any line. You are a rat, you thief of fancy.

Dream

Neal and I and others riding on a Jersey? highway. He is driving, he weaves in and out of cars, faces them, and pulls over ahead out of their way by inches. Why don't he stop? "If they stop, why then I stop."—Great gentility?

He and Carolyn take me home. He leaves me with the key, a long three sided key. I ask the landlady "Does N.C. live here?" fearing to ask directly where he lives, fearing to show the key and eyeing to her. She says yes, and presses his button. It lights up, his light, he has answered. I don't go up but go to the basement, get some food prepared as I am originally supposed to. Everything gets upset. I am impractical. I lose key, can't clean the food, all the people (ladies, housewives) in the basement are helping me. Suddenly in the midst of all this fear and ambiguity he shows up—I also have lost my way back to his room—and puts his arm around my shoulder leading me away. "I feel a blush of love for you again." We ride upstairs in an elevator. Stringham also lives in the building. I say to Stringham who is occupied talking to somebody and doesn't hear me, so I say again, "Stringham, this is Cassady." Stringham looks up astonished. I am caught in my duplicity and have to follow Neal away before he catches on that I have this special relationship to Stringham that depends as much on asserting my relationship to Neal and his virtues. So to break off with Stringham and not have Neal know where I have been in mind, I impulsively as if busy, ask for a dollar—to borrow—and Neal (who has glasses and a fur leather jacket, and is clean and washed and looks like Jewish Weitzner) rushes in and says, "Yes I owe myself a dollar will you give it to me so I can pay me back?" I recognize and am smitten with Neal's childlike gleeful understanding—his disgust transcended into gleeful rime.

We are upstairs. We are met by Carolyn or a Helen, short, wifely, efficient, taking something out of the icebox, and yet working in an understanding and peace in Neal in her wifely tasks. I wake up, around here, joyful and sad.

After thinking of Wallace Stevens
    Great poets never generalize.

June 1948. [Reading List].
Stevens, Wallace. *Poesy*

Pound, Ezra. *Personae* [and] *Provenca*

Woolf, Virginia. *Roger Fry, a biography*

Mill, John Stuart. *Autobiography*

Macaweny. one chapter of History

Tennyson, Alfred. *Selected Poems*

Lewis, Cecil Day. *Starting Point*

Blake, William. Poems (early)

Yeats, William Butler. *Last Poems*

Blake Reader. (fragments)

Fragments—Shakespeare, Cezanne

Dostoyevsky, Fyodor. *Letters* (parts)

Fulke, Greville. A few poems

Blake, Yeats, Herbert fragments

Rilke, Rainer Maria. *Elegies*

Holderlin, Friedrich. Prokosh translation

Dickens, Charles. *Nicholas Nickleby*

St. John of the Cross. *Mystical Doctrine*

Eliot, T.S. Ezra Pound (his metric)

July 1948.

[Excerpts from a letter written by Ginsberg to Trilling, ca. July 1948.]

I remember that a long time ago you asked me when I was going to produce a poem in extension from myself, a work of art not of will. I am beginning to discover that possibility now. I have a good deal to say on the subject, but I do not possess the freedom to expatiate with any degree of sincerity and clarity.

I have not yet accomplished what I have in mind. I have settled down to regular writing, almost regular hours of application; though the whole recognition of what is necessary and proper has not yet crystallized. Still I have sufficient hints—almost visions, or I am finally on the right road. The whole routine is very wild.

I have been doing a lot of thinking about Cézanne, and through him have begun to recognize signs of truly living personality and intelligence in works of art: a literal sense that I had never before experienced. Wallace Stevens has also opened up in "large breakthroughs." Yeats, and to a lesser degree, Pound, have been very informative. I have been reading closely Yeats last poems for signs.

Unfortunately I am enmeshed in a summer course in Victorian literature, which still only excites me sensually, if at all.

You must remember Jack Kerouac; he has finally finished a long novel he has been working on for three years, and is retyping it now. It represents a lot of work, 380,000 words or more. I think it is very great, in fact will be a major literary event. It is of immense cultural importance. I am afraid that you did not respect him when he last appeared to you, and even made me back down in my original enthusiasm; but he appears to me now to be more of an original and "prophetic" genius than he did when I was 19: which is only three years ago.

[In July of 1948, Ginsberg experienced dramatic visions that were to greatly influence his life over the next ten years. After having an epiphany on the street, Ginsberg was reading William Blake's poetry in his room in East Harlem when he suddenly "looked through the poem, heard a physical voice, very ancient and tender, saying, 'O Sunflower weary of Time.'" Ginsberg believed that it was Blake's own voice speaking to him and it was accompanied by a sensation of eternity, a timeless intelligent sentient harmony of all people and things, which recurred for several times during the following week. He did not immediately record his impressions into his notebooks, but references were frequently made later to this period of visions. Several poems were inspired by the visions as well.]

October 3, 1948.

After a conversation a long time ago with Bill Frankel, at a time when I was egotistically depressed, and when I attacked Cannastra's[177] lack of communication, he said, "Doesn't he communicate more than anyone?" He showed me what was wrong with my attitude. Of course I resented it.

I moved to Harlem this summer, read, wrote little, thought little—I came to think while I was still living on 114 St., after staring into that abyss which was of blank uncomprehending despair of practicality and attainment, the feeling of gray brown life, and walls forever there: I came to think that I could no longer sustain profitably or make headway with the burden of weight of incessant anxiety—thoughts that led nowhere, so in all of this book except as practical unconscious prophecies which I didn't fully realize—I knew they were prophetic but I didn't see the actuality of prophecy. When in Harlem I found my mind.

Tea Leaves—with Bill

> Beautiful music, and the fatal moment. (Bill)
> I'm green all over.
> Beat the children in the womb
> Begin love with the womb.
> Most mothers (do they) neglect to recognize that an identity
>   is already formed in the womb.

Names—Nightsoil (Nightsoilia, N.Y.)
> Lou and Barbara [Hale][178]
> Letiticia P. (Paper) Nightsole
> Joe Nightsoil
> Joseph Nightsoil
> Mustapha Nightsoil

[*Excerpt from a letter Ginsberg wrote to Trilling in November or December 1948.*]

I haven't been doing much but sitting still at home in Paterson for the last months. I did a lot of reading—Melville, Poe, Yeats, Dickinson, Whitman, Spengler, Blake and a book that Van Doren recommended called Revolt in

---

177   William Cannastra (1922–1950). Subterranean friend of Carr and Ginsberg, portrayed in books by Kerouac and Holmes. He died in a freak accident on the subway.

178   Barbara Hale. One of Carr's girlfriends. She worked for *Time* magazine.

Asia, very much apropos of today's Indonesian news. The author says that the second coming has come already, from Asia, and I can well believe him. I have not written any poetry except in the last few weeks. I am able to write more easily—without the aid of stimulants and more at will, but I still have not found a subject and form and won't for a great while I think.

My material situation is much improved, since I have a job (this is my second day or rather night, at work). I am a copy boy at the Associated Press—$30 a week, five day week. The work is pleasant. I need, again, letters of reference, and I would be grateful if you would compose a short note for me to present to the A.P. for their files. I am sorry to have to bother you again for a letter, but I don't seem to be in control of my fortunes. I expect to work here for a while and then move over to the *Times*; in the course of job seeking I found them receptive to my initial overtures; however they are all filled up till 1949. The atmosphere here is fine; I do feel as if I am at the center of the news. I hope to lead a quiet life and perhaps make a success of myself by writing prose, when I can overcome the initial barrier to an actual attempt to write stories.

Lucien's little tale of having to go two blocks (up and downhill) and having to go to the bathroom, so asking the neighbor down the block, "may I please use your bathroom," and doing it every week. Lucien curling up in the womb.

The animal anima spider evil animal god.

Universe as an animal. a maze of god as the one layer of forces around the cosmos. Each shift of atoms on his level changes quillions of atoms in the shaft.

There is a center to the universe perhaps. The problem of infinity has haunted me since childhood.

Haunt: means that we know the answer to what we consciously think our problem to be, but will not yet recognize or be aware of it.

I cannot write well because I cannot put my whole being into it.

Poetry must haunt the mind.

"A king without a name."

December 1948.

[*Excerpts from a letter by Ginsberg to Trilling dated ca. December 1948.*]

My job is terrible, leads nowhere. I sure made a compromise with society. The more I think of it the more I think I'm being tricked by a lot of B.S. to assume some phony responsibilities. Existing and plucking fruits from the trees is work enough for me. Too bad they tore down all the trees. It's all a lot of hot air. Particularly Radio City. Maybe the executives are psychoanalytic-

intellectual-Spenglerian-New Yorker-mature characters but I haven't seen any-
one yet who wouldn't be improved with a stick of marijuana in his mouth.
Everybody in the outside world is morose, sad or silly, including me. I thought
I would pay attention and polish the handles so carefully, but for the life of me
I'd sooner pay attention to an old bum than I would to what I've signed up to
do. No foundation, all the way down. I'm nobody to talk, I never put out any
free enterprise to build up these great associations of the press, and there's a
lot of sweat and hard work that's gone into it, they say (they never stop say-
ing) but it's all lollipops to me.

Winter 1948–1949. [Reading List].
Baudelaire, Charles. *Eugene Delacroix; Femmes Parisiennes; Daumier*

Cezanne

St. Augustine

Lao Tzu. *Buddha's "Fire Sermon"*

A Vision. parts and poems

cummings, e.e.

Emily Dickinson

Shelley, Tennyson

Coleridge, Samuel Taylor. *The Rime of the Ancient Mariner*

Lofting, Hugh. [Doctor Dolittle stories]

"Eternal Light" plays

Samuel Greenberg

Hart Crane's biography

James, William. *The Varieties of Religious Experience*

1949

January 24, 1949.
Dream A.P. [Associated Press]
    In the glass room-cage-bathroom. Masturbating and not coming.

January 1949. [Reading List].
Wyatt Poems

Blake's *Milton*—Milton's shorter poems and fragments of Camus

Herman Melville's "The Piazza," "The Bell Tower," "Lightning Rod Man,"
  "Benito Cerino," [and] "The Encantadas, or Enchanted Isles"

Household, Geoffrey. *Rogue Male*

Robinson, Edward Arlington. *Selected Poems*

Lawrence, D.H. *Poems*. Yeats

Mark Van Doren—Bright bits from a lecture class.
  "Great lights had burst in his head."
  "Related in a series" or "simultaneously known"
  "And speak of God from time to time."

Story:
Psychological portrait of young me spiritual man caught for robbery by the
police.
  J.K. "Oh to be in some far city and suffer the pangs of the suffocating ego."
In Peoria reading *Robinson Crusoe*.
  Destiny itself is sick. The rose is sick. We must be doctors we are the sick-
ness. Spengler is an old woman.

Blake's *Urizen*
"Eternity shuddered when they saw
Man begetting his likeness
On his own divided image."

I dream and dream.
I can face anything but reality
I can do anything but what is real.
I can be any actor but myself:
I can write any poem but my own.
Boasting.

Desks are dusty.
Money, money, work and worry.

"Dear Naomi:

Gene tells me you will be out soon, singing and dancing in the City....
Musical sweet poetry."

Early 1949.

[*Ginsberg was anticipating a teaching job at the Cooper Union in September. He received
recommendations from his teachers at Columbia including Trilling and Van Doren. In June,
he and Kerouac were planning a Huckleberry Finn–type trip down the Mississippi on a raft
to New Orleans to visit Burroughs, or else hitchhike along the river. Kerouac was writing
an early draft of* On the Road *at the time, while Ginsberg was working on fifty and sixty
line psalms.*]

February 1949.

> Bigger and bigger gates, O God.
> If each season, like a garden, dies,
> The gates each year get bigger.
> The gates get wider and the gardens greener,
> Every time we go through a new garden.
>
> Ed White—saw him off on *Queen Mary*. Jack returned;
>   camped with Burford. Hotel Nevada.
> Seen in summer in a green gown wedded.
> Wintered in a wedding shroud
> Staring like a startled friend.

Huncke's ambition for living place is "Chinese Moderne" with soft darkish
lights, oriental costumes and incense: and low furniture and couches to recline
on, shiny unmarred—felt slippers high up in the sky in a penthouse with glass
and clean lines and the blue sky stretched up high all around, and a vista, a
panorama of the city below.

On my twenty-third year—never expected to find myself so comfortably estab-
lished and happy in this want and weariness of this foul house. Time takes
away our love and leaves no hope—removes the effects of desire from the pos-
sibility of our possession till it becomes palpable.

Jack Kerouac at the Staten Island Ferry dock © ALLEN GINSBERG TRUST.

April 1, 1949.

Jack signed to publish his novel.

Clear the air! (oratorio)

Where the unborn and dead come from

Half crazed half saintly masked Levinsky is undone by his one face without a mask: Behold the myths that we have made of ourselves incarnate in Jack's book.

Because the poet is the man at home in the universe and in eternity and does not identify his being with his special place in society or identify God with them, he is at home anywhere.

You (Jack) are it (Queen of the May) as all of us who follow in the circle of our lifetimes are chosen sooner or later to be it.

Beautiful music, and the fatal moment:
The fatal moment is always gay.

Come, sweet Death, with madness marked
and end the sceneless revelry.

J.K. even craven time has honored him.

Plato: "All knowledge is recollection"—
"The devil is never so black as he is painted."

Oh, steel divinity and archangelic light...

Portrait of Huncke

I

There was a knock at the door, surprising me because it was only eight o'clock in the morning, and it was snowing outside. I had been sitting on a couch, with no thought on my mind, staring at a huge map of the world. I saw a dim familiar figure in the hall, and I guessed immediately it was Herbert Huncke,[179] though I hadn't seen him for over sixty days, which was the time he had been spending in jail. I had made up my mind about a month before this not to put him up anymore, but he looked so much like a ragged saint at my door, that I waved him into the living room, and followed him in silently...

179 Ginsberg used the pseudonym, Herman Hauptman, for Herbert Huncke throughout this story.

"Did you get my letter on Riker's Island?"

"No" he said, "thank you for thinking of me, though." He began to take off his shoes, gingerly. They were wet, and the socks, for all their wetness smelled dank. His feet were bloody, covered with blisters and raw spots, and dirty.[180] He hadn't slept for several days, the last time in the 50th Street Greyhound Bus Terminal. He hadn't eaten except for irregular doses of Benzedrine, coffee and donuts. He had no money. We discussed these things with some humor and I began to take pleasure in provisioning and rehabilitating his wardrobe.

I boiled up a pot full of hot water and helped wash his feet, his legs were stiff by this time. I was aware of how little love had been shown him in the last ten days of half hallucinated wandering. Yet I washed with averted eyes.

Then he went to sleep on the couch and slept for a day and a night.

II

The day and night's sleep dismayed me because I hadn't planned to leave him alone in the house without further talk with him, reassurance that he wouldn't run off with any of my valuables. The last time I'd been his host he'd done just that. Small radios were missing, cheap rugs, jackets, one at a time, with good reason—a matter of keeping him warm or getting him food. I would be petulant, I would even become secretly enraged. It didn't actually make too much difference to me, because I was too preoccupied with the charm of his company, and the misery of my own thoughts.

But the last time I'd put him up, it was a different matter. I was living in an apartment loaned from a friend, a mad "pad" in the middle of Harlem, six flights up in the sky with a view of 125th Street.

I would look out of the window, not at the street, but at the sky, staring out of my own emptiness at the light of heaven. My daily program was almost the same—I would go to school for an hour in the morning. The class I had was the last course I needed to get out of the school after six years of irregular study. After class I worked two hours in the small musty office of a nearly defunct learned journal of political economy. I worked at that office for two years.

On my way home, I would walk down the shopping street of Italian East Harlem, a crowded avenue where I purchased cheap meats and exotic vegetables. When I got home I would sleep for a few hours, then go out for another walk around Harlem.

180 Ginsberg retells this in his poem, "Howl" with the line, "who walked all night with their shoes full of blood on the snowbank docks waiting for a door in the East River to open to a room full of steam-heat and opium."

I had no preoccupation, no plans, no purpose, no real interest. This was quite unlike me, actually as I had nourished myself in the seven years following my adolescence, on a contradictory but long thought out program of intellectual self improvement. This had meant to me going down in the gutter of Times Square and Harlem. Yet suddenly, after seven years of rocking myself back and forth in the cradle of intellect and youth-wildness, I suddenly lost my curiosity. I lost my motive, my reason. I wanted to lose the sense of my own character and emerge with a voice of rock, a grave, severe sense of love of the world, an asperity and directness of passion. I wanted to make people shudder when they looked into my eye, suddenly wakened from a vast dream of the will.

Needless to say—and I am not passing judgment on the attempt itself—it had not succeeded. I gave up, I shut down the machinery, I stopped thinking, I stopped living. I never went out to see people anymore.

So there I stopped and thought no more about it, except on that level of renunciation, and lived for months in complete surprise and emptiness at the strange conclusion of my spiritual progress. What to do then, after that, I didn't know—nothing but to keep myself fed and comfortable and away from temptations to effort and ecstasy. So I stopped writing poetry, stopped using my weekly round of visits to friends, and stopped using drugs to excite my senses to eerie knowledge.

Nothing I had experienced in my life led me to expect what would happen to me in my loneliness. One day in the middle of the summer as I was walking down 125th Street, I suddenly stopped and stared around me in amazement. It was as if I had just awakened from a long dream that I'd walked around in all my life. I threw over all my preoccupations with ideas and felt so free that I didn't know who I was or where I was. The whole appearance of the world changed in a minute when I realized what had happened, and I began to look at people walking past me. They all had incredible sleepy, bestial expressions on their faces, yet no different from what they usually looked like. I suddenly understood everything vague and troubled in my mind that had been caused by the expression of people around me. Everybody I saw had something wrong with them. The apparition of an evil, sick, unconscious wild city rose before me in visible semblance, and about the dead buildings in the barren air, the bodies of the soul that built the wonderland shuffled and stalked and lurched in attitudes of immemorial nightmare all around.

When I saw people conversing around me, all their conversation, all their bodily movements, all their signs, the thoughts reflected on their faces were of fear of recognition and anguished fear that someone would take the initiative and discover their masks and lies. Therefore every tone of voice, movement of the hand, carried a negative overtone: this in the world is called coyness and shyness and politeness, or frigidity and hostility when the awareness becomes too overpowering. I felt that I would be crucified if I alluded with any insistence to the divine nature of ourselves and the physical universe. Therefore I did not speak but only stared in dumb silence.

This so overpowering draught of knowledge lasted until I began to move again, and think, and I was once more baffled by the inscrutable appearance of things. I was staring out the window when I saw a vast gleam of light cover the sky, the bowl of heaven was suffused with an eerie glow, as if the world about my eyes was a vast sea creature and this was the interior of leviathan. When I recognized that something extraordinary was happening to me, I realized that what I was seeing had been there all the time—indeed excited in me a recognition of that aspect of the imagination which is referred to as the eternal—longer than my own life, extending beyond my life and my former consciousness. I was staring at no human objects except the tops of buildings and at nature. Of the human objects, I remember that I understood in this one glance, their utility and significance. I can say that I saw not the objects but the idea behind them. The most absorbing aspect of the spectacle was the actual placement of the intelligence for I perceived that the guiding intelligence was in the objects themselves, not in some far corner of the universe, and that the world as we see it is complete: there is nothing outside of it. It seemed also to open itself up to disclose itself to me for the moment, allowing its secret to be understood.

When I returned to my apartment my first impulse was to consult an old author, William Blake, whom I remembered from earlier days, for the then baffling beauty and directness of his observations on the divine nature of the soul. I remembered particularly, apropos of my own astonishing moment in the street, a famous poem in which the poet wandered on the byways of London several hundred years ago,

> "and mark in every face I meet
> marks of weakness, marks of woe."

I read this poem again, but found that it did not shed any further light on what I was after, and turned idly over the pages till my eye was caught by the lines

"seeking after that sweet golden clime
where the travelers journey is done."

I felt at that moment a wave of such great sadness pass over me that I knew
that my vision of the early afternoon had returned, and this time in such inten-
sity that I stared stupefied with knowledge of the words written on the page,
as if there had been a magical formulation of my own awakening compre-
hension of joy. I looked out the window at the sky above Harlem, beyond the
bare, stained, brick wall of the next building, through the massive distances of
the cloudless and immobile atmosphere toward the unseen stars, and felt the
gigantic weight of Time.

I then found the poem "The Sick Rose" and when I came to

"the invisible worm
that flies in the night,
in the howling storm"

and read on to

"his dark secret love
does thy life destroy"

I realized once more that the last and most terrible veil had been torn from my
eyes, a final shuddering glimpse through death. Then I moved across the room
with the gnawing pulse of animality engulfing my body with slow carnal
undulations of my frame, and shrieked and collapsed in silent agony, moaning
on the floor, my hands grasping and hollowed in my thighs.

I spent a week after this living on the edge of a cliff in eternity. It wasn't so
easy after that. I would get glimmerings, hints of possibility, secret amaze-
ments at myself, at the world, at "the nature of reality," at some of the wisdom
other people seemed to reflect, at poets of the past, even at Shelley. I reread
Dante and wormed through some of Shakespeare, Plotinus, St. Augustine,
Plato, anything that caught my fancy.

It was in this frenzied preoccupation that I received Herbert at the door
that summer. I didn't even notice him, except to ask him what sensations
he had while walking cold and hungry down the street in his own days. So I
waited for the descent of the dove while Herbert hungered around the apart-
ment. He went out, days and nights at a time, and returned with gossip of the

underworld, which I listened to with an ear for the bizarre, the fantastic, eventually the cosmic. A new social center had been established on Times Square—a huge room lit in brilliant fashion by neon glare and filled with slot machines, open day and night. There all the apocalyptic hipsters in New York eventually stopped, fascinated by the timeless room.

I was absorbed in my alchemical studies, leading nowhere, but promising the key to that light which I'd experienced. Every author I looked at had his own light, his own method, his own renunciations. I became confused by my own theories and those of others. Meanwhile Herbert came and went, and one day disappeared entirely.

By then I had begun to notice that the bookshelves were barer than before, that my radio, typewriter, winter clothes, and an oriental statuette were not there anymore. Suddenly I realized that Herbert had been robbing me to feed a heroin habit. I had seen him shooting it in the veins, but I had supposed that he at least had had the courtesy to provide his own dope, since I was already providing everything else for him. The worst of it was that they weren't my books, but belonged to a theological student friend.

I spent part of that fall lurking around Times Square with [Russell] Durgin, the theologist, looking for Herbert. I didn't hear from him for another year, until I had settled in my own apartment, was working at night in a cafeteria as a dishwasher, had made partial repayment to the theologist for his books which were worth at least $150. It was from an old acquaintance on Times Square that I heard Herbert was in jail again on charges of possession of marijuana. I wrote him a letter and didn't hear from him again till the knock on my door.

III

Herbert had finally wakened when I came home the next day from work. He looked at me and laughed, nodding his head with a conciliatory upward lift. The ironic mask remained, as did my fixed and frozen inquiring smile. I had thought of him all day and night, with alternating rage and gentleness, and had made plans. I was waiting for an opening.

He sighed. "You didn't by any chance think of bringing home a tube of Benzedrine?" He looked at me as if he knew I hadn't with an ill humored, petty reproachfulness.

"No, I don't have enough money."

"Well money, money. God knows there's enough money for an inhaler to get me up at least out of your couch and out into the snow. If you can't think for yourself you might at least think of some small way of making it a little easier for me to get into operation again."

"There's no rush. I'm not going to send you out into the snow—yet."

"You might just as well, for all the good I feel at the moment. I don't think I'll ever get up." He turned to me, a touch of humor in his voice, and yet with narrow eyes, "I think I'm going to die."

I nodded without comment. He spoke as if he were telling me something that he had been aware of for days.

"Why? Do you want to kill yourself?"

"No," he said. "I had thought of it and started going through with some routine or other on that issue a week ago." He shrugged his shoulders, as if annoyed that he had not. "I'll kill myself slowly, like this, if I do it at all, unless I get more beat than I am now, and I doubt that I can get any lower."

His death and my vision seemed to hold equal finality for each of us in the scheme of things.

"Then what makes you think that you are going to die?"

"It's not dying, exactly, it's like an animal—extinction. I'm tired. I have nothing, and I don't think I want anything enough to put out the effort involved in getting it." He spoke with great delicacy, choosing his words, halting and spitting them out wearily, as if the effort at conversation were futile, and any expression he could use was cliché. An impatient gesture of the wrist signified that this was his own fault, his own lack of drive, or lack of polish in speech. His gestures were apologetic. He spread his hands again, explaining what it was that was so unspeakable. "All happening to me is unnecessary. I have been feeling all morning that I am caught in a gigantic whirlpool. I was frighteningly dizzy. I hoped to lose consciousness again. But something assured me I would not. It is all very terrifying. It is making me very sick."

He began to talk about his body. For years, since a trip to North Africa on a merchant ship, his dark face had carried on it the lingering remains of a skin disease that appeared soon after he got back. It began with a rash, almost fungus-like, below his mouth, and spread till it covered his lips and began eating its way up the cheeks. It was not a mortal growth, it appeared to do no harm, other than to complete the destruction of the dark beauty on his face.

His teeth were gone, and his visage had changed from what I had understood to have been wiry, precocious, original charm, with large dark eyes, jet black hair combed in waves on each side backward to the base of his skull. The youthfulness of his charm had long disappeared; he was now 30 and an old man to me. He had spent his adolescence at the center of large groups of the city's underworld in Boston, Chicago, New Orleans, and New York. He had been used to being kept by men of curious tastes older than himself. Now that was out of the question; not only was he a monster in his body, but the same monstrousness had emerged in his mind. The former youthful curiosity and freedom had been replaced with an almost saintly obsession with homelessness; his taste for the strange and exotic in personal habits, in perceptions, in love, was transformed to a weary disillusion with his own body. His original curiosity about his own passions had died, and he was left listless, all energy directed to the extermination of his personality, in an endless nausea at his sense of self, his vanity, his wants.

And yet all this was displayed and sometimes admitted with the charm of an old, knowledgeable roué, or a woman looking backward nostalgically, and with gaiety, at the charm of her own youth; not merely forgiving her innocence, but with a lovely human surprise at the wickedness of her own conquests, and winking at the youth that inherited her frivolity among the fortunes of the world.

So, as Herbert spoke it was this bitter lament for time well spent and now unavoidably past; and with some regret for wasted opportunities—frail earlier ambitions—and with good humor, almost mature self contempt. As so often the case with people of any intrinsic interest, Herbert's face and its expressions were so much the hub of my experience that I find myself returning to his naked visage as the key to my memory.

In the masked smile I have spoken of so often there was yet fellow-creaturely questioning of an almost conspiratorial nature. He often smiled at me when appraising some effort of mine at teasing him and awakening his interest in himself or some project that I had in mind for him. It was, I guessed, an expression of recognition and coyness of his own, for I had often seen him converse, with this same look on his face, with powerful and violent hoodlums on Times Square. Certainly, it was also the look of a mother with no illusions about her young.

IV

"It's about time to tell you, Herbert, that my hospitality can't last forever. I only make $25 a week and I can't put us both up on that very long. I'm already going in debt."

"Well, I'll be off your hands as soon as—" he dropped his shoulders wearily, "I can figure up some sort of plan of action."

"This is what I'm getting at. But before I begin, you should know that I still haven't paid Durgin off for the books and clothes you took last time."

"That's not your responsibility. You might at least treat me as if I were an independent party with some decision of my own. When I took what I needed to keep going, I knew how you'd feel, and I knew how he would take it. I was sure you'd have some great upsurge of self-righteous annoyance at my theft of your worldly 'possessions.' That I was willing to deal with. As for Russell Durgin, I took his books, and that's between him and me."

I continued, "Durgin didn't mind your staying, but he did get annoyed at the books. Though I'll say this for him, he was more consciously concerned for your soul than for his books. I'll see that there's enough to eat in the house, but I can't afford to keep you in heroin or Benzedrine. If we can pick up a little marijuana now and then, fine, but the Benzedrine every day costs too much. Whenever you are ready, whenever you feel like it in the next month, I'll find you a job, any kind of job. I'll guarantee to see you to work, I'll take you there. You'll have no expenses so can give me the money you owe me within a few weeks, and then it'll be all over with. After that you can share house expenses for awhile—just food, I'll pay the rent myself. Once you have a little money you'll be better off obviously. You'll keep out of trouble, you won't have to worry about jail. You might be able to find yourself a boy and set up a pad of your own. You'll have enough money to invest in some heroin, if you want to sell it for awhile. You might even be able to afford a habit if you need it.

"This is all right, but at the moment I don't feel like thinking about it anymore. I'll mull it over. I haven't worked in I don't know how many years, and I don't know if I want to. But maybe you're right, I really don't have anything else to do."

I was pleased with myself for I had at least made an attempt at straightening everything out. The next day, however, his cold turned to a grippe and he was coughing.

"You can have a week to think it over," I said, "till you're better."

He lay around the house, reading my books, and sleeping. My own routine went as usual and a kind of peace descended on the atmosphere. Our conversations thereafter consisted mostly of reminiscences and gossip about Times Square, musicians, students whom I knew, books that I was reading, my family, his family and early life, and stories of famous heroin addicts. He also told me at great length about his first and later arrests—he's been arrested 37 times, and spent several years in jail, usually on short term misdemeanor charges having to do with vagrancy and narcotics.

I began to realize, as he talked of his crimes, something that I had understood from the beginning, but had simply passed over in scheme for his recognition. He had no objection to paying me what he owed; quite to the contrary, his guilt to me, which I played on childishly and with such good humor as a lever to move him back into action, was finally acknowledged by him. This despite the petulance of our first conversation. With all the youthfulness of my temperament and the innocence of my dealings with him—innocent because I ignored the great shadow of tragedy that I sensed in him—he respected me and grieved for my love for him as a bleak and aged rock broods beneath the weight of a flower.

Of how much he was guilty, only he knew. I had hints and explanations of days, of weeks, of whole seasons of robbery and violence and corruption—a whole lifetime of innocent evil. And now, as the realization of that vast madness grew upon him, how puny a thing seemed the burden of my flower. And his crimes were deep! How was there ever to be time enough for patience, for humility, for enough vigor for restitution for the errors of such a life? Repentance, perhaps, but atonement never, that was impossible.

Yet his conversation turned away from himself most of the time despite my prying curiosity into his state of mind. My curiosity was like the harsh ringing of an earless clock, telling of the limited days which I had granted him for repose. His "position" in the world, as he called it, seemed hopeless and impossible to me. He could not go back and undo what had been done and care for what had been neglected. Yet he could not, it seemed, go forward because of that. With a man of such imagination, the scheme I had set out for him of pitiful daily labor and quietness, or at least minimal crime, was one of vapid humiliation and intolerable irrelevancy. Greater ambition in a social world was out of the question; it was a new and altogether different trick which I saw no possibility of him learning. I thought of educating him, sending him to school. We discussed that, but like the dishwasher's work, it was left in abeyance, till the end of his sickness. But that was a hopeless task, he was already wise and knowledgeable beyond the ambitions of any university. There seemed to be no happy place for him in the sunny activity of the world.

There are, it seems to me, people who by temperament, education, or whatever conditional contingency may be thought to be applied, are manifestly and irrevocably unsuited to peaceful, mundane civilization. Our hospitals and jungles are full of such men. Herbert's case, as a social case, seemed hopeless to me, and certainly to him, and there was nothing left for him to do but accept the greater fact that he was still alive and enjoy that life without the blessings of his fatal civilization. As for me, I accepted that fact less quickly than he.

The conversations continued and every time I began to rage at him about his enjoyment of the rest earned at my expense, about his delight in the objects of the household, about his pleasure in my company, about his annoyance at my refusal to bring home drugs, he would forestall any expression of malice by sinking into profound and weary silence.

His bronchitis, after a week, became so serious that I offered to call a doctor.

"No," he said, "I don't want a doctor." He was petulant again, speaking sardonically. "But if you had any real interest in my welfare you'd spend a measly half buck on some Benzedrine. I assure you it would do me a lot more good than a doctor." And he was silent again.

We were both silent for the rest of the week, eyeing each other guiltily as I came and went. I wished to break the spell, for as I lay in bed at night, or watched him from my desk, I wearied of the struggle that had ended our intimacy, and had made my household a forest through which I crept in stealth.

After a while, he began to speak again, but to my horror I saw that he had been moved by my recalcitrance and discovered signs of the enmity I bore. He criticized my dress, my speech, my own tired and unearthly existence. We quarreled over division of food like hungry animals, we bickered over sleeping places, over household slippers. While we quarreled and raged at each other, we respected the limits of each others final sovereignty.

For nothing could have humiliated me more than being angry at him with whole heart and mind. He was my experiment, my love, my teacher, my dog, and if I renounced him I renounced at the same time my own dignity and ineffable senses of taste and justice.

And what would I do without him? He filled my mind, dominated my waking activity. I thought of his great tragic mask, and I thought of his ignoble comic humanity; I learned from him and I thought of him day and night, whether speaking to him, staring at him in silence, or wandering down the street. His body healed after two weeks of this mutual torment.

He rose, one afternoon, in a happier frame of mind. We discussed the day. It was Friday and I suddenly wanted to visit Professor Van Doren, my wisest teacher at the university. Herbert was at the mirror over the kitchen sink, picking at the scabs below his lips and on his jaw. He had been there an hour. I had known him to shower and clean his body for whole nights meticulously inspecting every part. This afternoon I had lost patience with his preoccupation with his appearance.

"Where are you going anyway? If you're going down to the Square for a few hours, why bother making yourself up like a Hollywood star?" I asked him.

He turned and looked at me, suddenly pathetically, and spoke with a trace of irritable stubbornness. "Man" he said, drawing the address out in sing-song bitterness, "I've been lying here beating my head against the wall for so long I forgot what I must look like to other people." I was suddenly made crestfallen by his appeal to the simplest of human vanities. I had been pushing him off a cliff for weeks, avoiding his person, howling at him as if he were a beast or a god, or a ragged and blind spectacle of sainthood.

"I've been lying here without a cent," he continued, staring at me, "thinking of you, about myself, about the street. I've been looking into the alley and watching all those old biddies out there yakking to each other across their washlines."

I sat down, looking at him, with a desire to avert my eyes from his. He followed me into the living room, groomed and now serene, as if complete in the eyes of the world, cleansed and healthy again.

He said, "I know you've gone out of your way to make me comfortable. It isn't that I don't appreciate it. I know at times I've been irritable, you've been irritable, coming home and finding me still here day after day, sleeping in your apartment, wearing your clothes, eating your food, yakking about myself, while you've been going out every night holding down a job. I can imagine this hasn't been a pleasure for you, and I know you want to be alone. Maybe that's a good idea for you; I can see why you do with your preoccupations toward the mystical, whatever it is."

I felt a sudden tenderness encompassing me, in the realization of his regard for what, even to me, was a fearful and solitary pursuit of God. It was the compliment of an unknown beggar and of a wearily well known older man of the outside world.

"I would hardly criticize derogatively anyone, much less you, because you're pretty wise as it is. I might say, after all this time, that it is a pleasure and even a kind of honor, to be in a position to run into you, have dealings with you of one kind or another, even share a number of the same intuitions and people. Not to mention the kind of active consideration you've displayed toward me, oftener enough than I have even understood it, or responded properly.

At the same time, there are certain things that I like to take for granted, not only from myself but from other people, particularly people for whom I feel a certain amount of respect and who have thrown their lots in with me and vice versa."

He was gesturing with his hands, sitting in the dim light of the afternoon. His voice halted, from time to time, to find words, to form thoughts, to look at me inquiringly, seeking assent to expressions of regard, concurrence to certain despairing or earnest intonations sometimes seeking reply. But I was frozen, as if in a dream, listening to him from the other end of the room, grieving for the sinister antagonism toward him and his hapless fate that I had cherished in the past weeks. I nodded as if to agree and encourage him, feeling treacherously, tremblingly frightened of the love I bore him.

It was inexpressible love I felt, beating upon a stony face which I held against its tide. I wanted to sink at his knees, and was terrified at the grotesquerie of the scene, and the knowledge that it was the undeniable sea in which, as on a frail raft, we had been carried all these days. My horror of the truth, as I saw him sitting there, staring at me, was magnified by the awareness that he knew, and that I alone, in all this wild sea, had not yet become a creature of the sea. My mind roved desperately toward remembrance of the Divinity and perfection of the street. I saw myself as I had seen others, unborn.

There was so much sadness dying in his voice that tears began to trickle down from my eyes as he said, "I don't know what it is or why. Perhaps it's some fault of my own, some lack of understanding. But every time I try to say something—to speak seriously, to attempt to come to some sort of understanding—I feel as if I have been pushed back, as if I had made some great mistake, as if I had said something I shouldn't have. There just doesn't seem to be anybody who can speak with any kind of earnestness or even meaning, or who knows what they mean. And I certainly don't know what I mean and just wish someone would break the wall down."

"Your hospitality," he said now, "I feel hasn't somehow been a pleasure to you. I haven't enjoyed the situation, my own beatness. And yet in a way I wanted to be able to forget about it, and perhaps in a pleasant atmosphere be able to come out of it and think up some new routine, or get into any kind of pleasant activity without that terrible feeling that I were a guilty child, that I was being watched and criticized, that my whole existence was an unpleasantness to others and that I was not wanted. The best thing seemed for me to just disappear and not be a burden to anybody but myself. Somehow you don't seem to be able to give anything of yourself without fearing that it will be misunderstood, without perhaps thinking that you're being taken advantage of. You don't seem to be able to relax and enjoy my presence, or I yours, without some overtone of possessiveness. We might have been here together without this overwhelming pressure to do things, formulate some kind of activity for me, or an admission that I'm a heel and a bounder and a bum and a worthless drain on your resources. It's your own development of character that I am concerned with for the moment."

I had said very little, my original feeling of disgrace and compassion had deepened. I could only guess what knowledge lay behind his words.

"You seem to treat me as if I were not a human being with as much need for human decency and politeness and courtesy as anyone else. Perhaps you treat me this way because I have not accomplished anything—money, possessions, knowledge, an education—all the things which are good for you and which anyone really needs to get along in the world with comfort. I have no wish to go out and get what society demands everyone to have. That doesn't make me any less needful of consideration, the kind of *noblesse oblige* that you extend without thinking to Durgin. I don't give a shit what is expected of me by you, the police, the judges, the hoods on Times Square. And because of that I find myself treated as a shit, a dog, by the police and the judges. I at least expected a relaxation from you; an ease, and trust and relief from the complete beatness and mania of the whole damned city. But I find even in you the same distrust, the same anxiety to be not too different from what is expected by the outside world. I feel as if I were a leper and you have felt the same thing in the end."

He had partly begun to apologize for his loquacity and eloquence and finally began laughing nervously, at what he called his 'swan song' and 'appeal for sympathy.'

After a while I left the house, saying that I'd be back sooner or later that day and he promised to lock the door. He would be away longer than I, he thought, but would try to get back the next morning unless anything of interest developed in the Square in the meantime.

[*On April 21, 1949, Ginsberg decided to take all his notebooks and letters to his brother's apartment for safekeeping. Little Jack Melody and Vicki Russell offered him a ride in their car, which was also packed with stolen merchandise. In Queens, Melody drove down a one-way street the wrong way and panicked when the police tried to pull him over. As he tried to escape, the car crashed and rolled over, and Ginsberg and Russell ran away, leaving all his documents in the car. A short while later, the police arrived at Ginsberg's apartment on York Avenue and arrested everyone involved. The crime made all the local papers, but with the help of Ginsberg's father and a few of his Columbia professors, Ginsberg was sent to the psychiatric hospital instead of prison.*]

[Excerpt from a letter Ginsberg wrote to Trilling around April 1949.]

I suppose that you are aware by this time of "what I have let happen to me" now. I hope the publicity around Columbia is not too widespread. My immediate future is uncertain depending on how my case goes but things do not look too favorable. I have been exposed to considerable horror and stock taking and feel myself more clearly. What remains is a restless anxiety about family.

If I should be freed as is possible, or acquitted, my desire to teach still remains, though I wonder if that is now possible. If not I guess I will stay at the A.P. [Associated Press] though I don't want to. I don't know what kind of liberation I can achieve outside of writing.

The Fall[181]

I

Before recounting the events of the last month and a half, I will tell of last summer. After floundering around vainly exhausting myself seeing people, trying to write, not succeeding in seeing clearly or thinking clearly having trouble at school getting through with administrative details in preparation for a degree, and moved by a growing sense of the futility of my thoughts and doings, and the ineffectuality of various half-assed schemes for homosexual or heterosexual orientation. I settled down for a quiet and lonely summer in an apartment in East Harlem which I had sublet from a school friend, a consumptive theologian who was going to New Hampshire for a rest.

My desire for a quiet and routine summer was not fully realized: I immediately broke up the boredom by throwing several parties in succession as farewell parties for Russell Durgin, who owned the apartment. Then I did settle down, for the most part, cooked for myself, went to a class in the mornings, worked at a part time job at the American Academy of Political Science as a file clerk two hours a day. I would come home and go shopping, order ice, get half undressed and idle around the house.

Heretofore I had been aware of a 'problem,' as I shall call it, which had haunted me since childhood; as a 14–16 year old my straining to settle what seemed unsettled took a political form. I had come to school to study law. Thereafter most of my intellectual endeavors were heightened and channeled into aesthetic, psychoanalytic, anthropological and criminal (jazz music and drugs) areas. That is, I sought for insights into myself and the world in areas of

181   Ginsberg's note: "This notebook confession was written for Ilo Orleans, lawyer after my bust with Huncke and Vicki."

WRONG-WAY TURN CLEARS UP ROBBERY

Four Men and Girl Arrested— Copy Boy Joined Gang to Get 'Realism' for Story

An unwitting turn of a stolen car in the wrong direction along a one-way street in Queens ended yesterday with three young men and a girl being held on burglary charges and a charge of assault against one man.

One of the accused, Alan Ginsberg, 21 years old, of 1401 York Avenue, told the police that he was a copy boy for a news service who had "tied-in" with the gang, all with police records, to obtain "realism" he needed to write a story. He said he held a Bachelor of Arts degree from Columbia University, and had shared his apartment with the gang for their tutelage.

Arraigned in Ridgewood Felony Court, Queens, before Magistrate David P. McKean, two of the men were held without bail because of their previous records and the woman and Ginsberg were held in default of $2,500 bail. They were held for a hearing on Wednesday.

Police of the Bayside station, under Detective Lieut. James M. Sloan said that with the capture of the four a $10,000 theft on Wednesday, of jewels, clothing and furs from the home of Henry Pieretti, a contractor of 19-50 Eighty-first Street, Garden Bay Manor, Astoria, had been cleared up.

The car in which two of the four had been riding at 4 P. M. Thursday when the wrong turn was made, was said to have been stolen last March 22 in Washington, D. C.

The driver of the car, Jack Melody, 26, was captured, the police said, after he had allegedly attempted to run down Radio Car Patrolman George McClancy. The policeman had stopped the car when it turned into Forty-third Avenue, Bayside, from Francis Lewis Boulevard, against traffic.

Melody, according to the police, had started the motor of the car when Patrolman McClancy had left to go back to the patrol car for his summons book. His partner, Patrolman John Colletin, waiting in the car, shouted at him to jump. McClancy leaped from the path of the speeding sedan.

The car then turned west on Forty-third Avenue toward 205th Street. By the time the two patrolmen caught up with the car it had attempted to negotiate the turn at 205th Street, six blocks away. At sixty-five miles an hour it struck a curb, turned over twice and stopped upside down.

The two patrolmen captured Melody and Miss Priscilla Arminger, 24. Melody, charged with the attempted felonious assault as driver, was said by the police to have been arrested twelve times in other cities on charges of safe burglary and larceny.

Bystanders told detectives that a "blonde" woman had escaped from the car after the crash. Police notified hospitals to be on the lookout for an injured woman but none was reported yesterday. In the car the police found half of the loot from the Wednesday night robbery.

The other half of the loot was found in the York Avenue address where Ginsberg and the other man, Herbert E. Huncke, 34, were arrested. The police said Huncke had served sentences on six narcotic charges and one burglar tool charge.

Ginsberg told Lieutenant Sloan that his father lived in Paterson, N. J., and his mother was a patient at Pilgrim State Hospital.

Wrong-way turn newspaper clipping, April 23, 1949, page 30

knowledge and activity under those labels. The point of all this is that due to reading Jack Kerouac's novel [*The Town and the City*] in its manuscript form I felt that all the turmoil and frenzy of the last five years had been somehow justified because I saw expressed in his novel a peace and knowledge and solidity and a whole recreated, true and eternal world—my world—finally given permanent form. And so I also felt my own failure as an artist to conclude a large and, if not mature, at least complete and internally perfect work—of personality for that matter. I was still trying. Jack, on the other hand, had finally made the first leap, which at that point I felt was a successful leap.

Let us chalk this up to misplaced vanity or ambition; I don't feel capable of judging. Also it was a sincere regret at my own failure, which at this point must be apparent. I don't mean so much an artistic failure as much as a failure to rebuild my personality. At the time I read his book, I was deeply depressed and used to lay in bed trying to sleep longer hours to avoid my problems and activities which was futile—seeing people, writing work without value, etc. I had been planning a book of poems with Van Doren's encouragement at the time. I felt increasingly the inadequacy of what I had written and what I was as a coherent and true statement of existence—which (vaguely) is what art is.

I lay down my writings even—this was all last spring—and, as I said, moved to East Harlem. My desire was blank—I had no plans.

In the midst of this sterility and despair, conscious or unconscious—I took pleasure in cooking, cleaning up the house, reading idly—Renaissance poets, Blake, etc. Suddenly, one day [July 1948] when I was browsing in the bookstore at Columbia I experienced the first of what at the time I took for 'mystical experiences,' a visionary state quite unlike any which I had ever experienced before, but seemingly the consummation of all my earlier creative aspiration and longing.

I will not try to describe this as it is indescribable. It returned during that week several times. I found it, finally, frightening and fled to Paterson where I scared my father with wild talk; then I went back after a few days to N.Y. and took up my routine existence again; only this time gnawed inwardly with recollection of these experiences, which, because of their absolute and eternal nature I assumed as the keystone and reference point of all my thought—a North Star for life; much as Dante says, "*Incipit Vita Nuova.*" I thought much of Dante, Blake, and St. John of the Cross. I wrote several poems incorporating the ideas—purely intellectual skeletons—which remained of the solid flesh of visions. One ended:

I shudder with intelligence, and I
    Wake in the deep light
and hear a bony machinery
    Descending without sound,
Intolerable to me, too bright,
And shaken in the sight,
The eye goes blind before the world goes round.[182]

Another:

    Look before you leap
    Many seek and never see,
    Anyone can tell them why:
    O they weep and O they cry
    And never take until they try
    Unless they try it in their sleep.
    And never some until they die.
    I ask many, they ask me.
    This is great mystery.

I subsequently sought out several people whom I knew who I thought would understand the intimations of prophetic power which had been gifted me, because I recognized signs of it in them. The recognition with certain of them was mutual; I thought Van Doren, for one, understood clearly what I was talking about, and more. I have no idea fully if what I am saying is madness or truth. I said to myself at the time that "I no longer know what the word crazy means anymore." My poetry began to take more body and order and clarity at this point; but it was still mystical and still clouded by the lack of all of concrete sensuous realism. I have spoken of all of this because the 'Visions' have been constantly on my mind and have been monomaniacally inspiring all my conduct for the last year.

It was only recently—several months ago—after a psychoanalyst I went to dismissed them as 'hallucinations' that it was necessary to forget them entirely and begin life all over in activity and real work—literary or career—work, etc. The road to God I discover is not a leap, but work—concrete sensuous reality. Fully experienced I presume it is satisfactory. I saw my situation described in

182 This poem appears in *Collected Poems*, p. 8, as "Vision 1948."

theological literature, in Kafka, Eliot, Blake, etc. Particularly the Kafkian hero who is suddenly wakened in the middle of his life and put on an unknown trial—I <u>also realize</u> that I am sick.

II

Who is Herbert Huncke? When I first knew him I saw him in what I considered the 'glamorous' light of a petty criminal and Times Square hustler who was experienced in the ways, thoughts, and activities of an underground culture which is enormously extensive. The attempt to dismiss him because of his social irresponsibility is something that I was never able to conceive as truthful or productive. I saw him as a self-damned soul—but a soul nonetheless, aware of itself and others in a strangely perceptive and essentially human way. He has great charm. I see that he suffers, more than myself, more than anyone I know of perhaps; suffers like a saint of old in the making; and also has cosmic or supersensory perceptions of an extraordinary depth and openness. I learned a great deal from him—I treated him as if he had come to give me metaphors for poetry; he used to lecture me on my vanity and suspiciousness and superciliousness—strangely true and wise and well-meant and effective lectures. He is one of the few people I know that makes me feel like a silly little kid trying hard to be one of the boys—(I don't mean one of the criminals, either). I don't know if that's a therapeutically positive feeling or not. At any rate I sensed a great deal of understanding in him.

Why was he such a wastrel and criminal then? It was perhaps the depths of his rootlessness and lack of sense of possessiveness of property and ideas and education and societal position that left his mind open to 'higher' ideas. And they were, after all, higher ideas. But this question I cannot start to answer. I have several things in my desk that he has written down—he is not a writer and did not write them as a writer might—but they will give a clue to his disorientation. One is a long and moving letter to his father which, from some sad sense of his own sinfulness, he never sent.

My former sense of his glamour as a literary type wore away when I saw, after years, the sincerity of his horror and awe at creation and events, and his humanity. He also resented being thought of as a literary caricature, and often admonished me healthily about this tendency of mine to remove people from real emotional presence to a world of literary values—false ones at that.

Herbert was in jail at the beginning of the year, and I wrote to him, saying that he would be coming out homeless and aimless, and I proposed to him that if he would consent to get a job and try and straighten himself out and withdraw from the world of frenzied and distracting criminal activity that had always absorbed his personality, I would guarantee him a place to sleep, eat, etc. until he felt calm and serene enough to make plans for some kind of creative future. The letter was written I remember to the Bronx County Jail. It was never delivered and is still presumably reposing at the jail. It might be recovered as evidence of my general good will, if possible.

I did not know it was not delivered, and did not hear from him till one day in February when he appeared at my door in a very bad condition—he had been walking the streets sleepless for days, his feet were sore and bruised and bloody, he was depressed, and in his conversation I detected stronger suicidal thought than I had ever seen in him. I was also glad to see him, since I like him. At first I was worried about financial problems his arrival might create if I had him on my hands for too long. However I reproached myself for worrying about that. It seemed pretty uncharitable. Besides I did not wish to reproach him—was afraid to, better—with practical problems at such a time. He bathed his feet and went to sleep on the couch. I went to work and let him stay overnight, and brought food for him in the morning. He slept for several days, in such a depressed state that I did not attempt to get him into action, particularly since it seemed, considering his particular problems, the only immediate activity he would be likely to fall into would be criminal in nature. I hoped he would sleep and rest himself and finally go out and do something—anything, to get him going, and off my hands.

You see the problem was very delicate, as I saw it. I didn't want to discourage him; at the same time I hoped that by letting nature take its course (a trick I had learned from him in the past) things would take care of themselves.

He was fully aware of my feelings—he is pretty wise and he knows me well. His awareness of my thoughts was one of the things I liked about him most. However at this time my spare thinking moments were absorbed by an anxiety not so much for his welfare as for my own in terms of how long I would have to take care of him. I wanted really to be alone, to withdraw from frivolous or absorbing activity, and to settle into my own mind and place. I tried to recreate, almost, a jail for myself in the world, where I would finally come to a peaceful rest, look around, see clearly, and begin to act. Finally I hoped that a withdrawal would bring a recurrence of visions.

After a week, when he seemed to stir about and show more interest in things I told him what I had written him in the letter. He listened carefully, and seemed to respond as I hoped, that is: I figured what he needed most was not mechanical care but actual sympathetic love—if I demonstrated sufficient active interest in his welfare, if I showed him he was really wanted and thought about, perhaps the spark of life would catch.

Of course I have so little of the spark myself that this is somewhat funny. Besides I really wanted to get rid of him and he knew that, too. But my motives were mixed; the care I felt for him was real. I think I can say truthfully that he worried and was as concerned about me as I care for him.

I suppose that there is a great element of homosexuality latent in all the Dostoyevskian enigma and plotting; but we both excluded it from conversation and action. Meanwhile I must say I enjoyed his conversation and company. He began to move around the furniture and fix up the house. He is an expert at little perceptive touches of interior decoration. He liked to burn incense, for example, and so does it. He burned little pieces of wood, experimenting with the smell. Perhaps he had nothing better to do. But I appreciated these activities as touches peculiar to Huncke alone, and therefore valuable, lovely, and honorable. They were part of his whole being and 'life force.' I also enjoyed mythologizing his character. It is a literary trick which Kerouac, the novelist—who has written much about Herbert Huncke—and I exploited in the past.

The selfish or self-preservative anxiety which I went through at this period was almost unbearable, since I would work myself into a great rage at his dependency on me for life-energy and sustenance and vow to get rid of him. I was going dry on my poor $30 a week and I felt a need to be more financially independent of my father and more stable. I also felt that this desire for financial stability was one which rose from a deeper, more uncompromisingly neurotic motive of fear of flux and activity and surprise and joy.

So I set myself to enjoy Herbert's presence and to get rid of him when I felt that I could with a clear conscience. I felt guilty towards him. These anxieties were uppermost in my mind when I would return from work in the morning; and after the first few moments of uncertainty I would usually break down my reserve and talk to him, gossip-like, as freely as I could, recognizing that after all, we were just two more people marooned in creation, congenial in nature. Why therefore should I raise my anxieties and worldly problems to a state of predominant importance?

And so my house and my belongings, wearily, painfully, anxiously, became his. He wore my suits, socks, shirts; even took over my bed, so that I sometimes, rather than selfishly claim possession, took over the couch to sleep on.

Now this may seem absurd and perhaps it is; but that isn't what the saints and the Bible say life is about. "Cherish pity, lest you drive an angel from your door." Also, "Consider the lilies, how they grow. They toil not neither do they spin. Therefore take no thought for tomorrow. Sufficient unto the day is the evil thereof."

Meanwhile I rationalized away Herbert's own parasitical situation, ascribing it to mental sickness not so unlike my own that I could afford to judge him. Though, I must say, I judged him and myself continually.

Where then is the element of human self-responsibility? I looked for it in vain in real life and found it, until lately, only in theory—which wasn't sufficient to make me kick him out.

Of course I recognized that under the veneer of impotence and misery there was a calculating mind in him trying to attach himself to my goods and possessions and do me out of them. Early in the year Bill Burroughs had written warning me about Herbert, saying that his responses worked so that the more benefits were lavished on him the more the unconscious hostility and hatred he would build up. This is psychoanalytically a repetition of some family situation and it is true. Can I however say it is more true than the valuable human knowledge and care that he felt, almost paternally, for me? No motive is unmixed and, knowing all this, I still was not able to dismiss him and set him out on his own. I felt the stronger tie to be the fear of rejecting him and assuming my own independent character. It meant making open and clear the awful gulf that we both knew was between us—and everybody. It also meant, practically, sending him out to starve [on] the streets; and it also meant that I would have to see clearly into my own personality problems and act on that and I was not ready. It took the shock of the car crash and subsequent wanderings on Long Island in fear of the Lord, to give me the strength to see that what finally counts is whether I will be able to face my own self and act on it henceforth without further equivocation and delay, even if it means hurting other people and myself. The gardener of the rose must not spare the knife, as the old saying goes, to prune his flowers. But I am running ahead of myself.

After the first few weeks, I gave Herbert a week to get a job and I offered to get him a job at the Associated Press with me. However fate interposed in the form of a great boil, a sore of Job, which appeared on Herbert's leg and incapacitated him for another two weeks. It was impossible to order him out at that point.

We had many long talks about the problems I have referred to, always without resolving them. I always felt afterward like a heel for adding to his misery and not properly appreciating the value of his company. He, I presume, usually felt more deeply his inadequacy and insecurity and lack of place in the world.

Eugene [Ginsberg's brother] was a frequent visitor, often appearing when my money had run out. He and Herbert developed a pleasant relationship of understanding. Herbert often took down Eugene from the over-anxious lawyer's pedestal he stood on and made him feel more like another poor lost soul. I can't say whether this was a service or a disservice. Herbert was also one of the few people who knew what my poetry was about. I also got him to read Blake, Dante, Kafka. At one point I got the idea that with his experience and his unparalleled knack of story telling—all in a fruitful and undiscovered area of Americana—he might make a great writer; I suggested school and he responded with more enthusiasm than I thought probable. But that, as most projects, fell through due to a lack of real energy or belief in it.

Towards the second month, I began to feel Herbert as an actual damned soul already living in Hell, aware of it, powerless to help himself and powerless to be aided.

He saw himself in some mysterious way, as a dying man. That is why he wrote his father; he thought he would die soon. I forgot to mention that the first few weeks he spent out of jail he spent with a character whose name I have forgotten, a madman I think, who attacked him and once or twice threatened to kill him. Herbert took this seriously and I believe that there was some serious and complicated tangle between them that Herbert accepted and fled from with a kind of prophetic fear. There is a shadow over him now. As I write this he is in the hospital with blood poisoning, alone, sad, weary, beat, ended. I thought, when I first heard that he was in the prison ward at Bellevue, that it had come at last. Perhaps this is only a romantic fantasy of mine. Let it be said that a kind of longing for Death has taken him in the last year or so; and that it is not impossible that it will be somehow fulfilled soon.

During all the time I was warned by my father and others—friends whom I respected—Kerouac, Lucien Carr, etc.—to get rid of Herbert as he was absorbing my sustenance and money, and taking me away from real creative activity. If I could go back I would, since finally I have done him no good by letting his fate take its course and me with it. Nor have I done myself any good, except what can be said to be good in the punishment to come and in the suffering of the past.

I think I have now established the background of activity and atmosphere that was present when Little Jack[183] and Vicki appeared on the scene. I might

___

183 Little Jack Melody. Vicki Russell's boyfriend, a friend of Huncke's and a minor criminal who had served time in prison.

add that there was little concern with drugs up to this point. Herbert had on a few occasions picked up some marijuana and once or twice I had bought a few sticks myself for Jack Kerouac and I to get high on for a Sunday afternoon visit to the zoo or a foreign movie.

III

Perhaps I should describe drugs and my relation to them. I will not talk about heroin since as far as I am concerned it has not been effectively in the picture for about two years. I used it once about a year ago and once about half a year before that. Previously I had indulged in what is known as 'chippying' or 'joy-bangs.' I had not acquired a habit, which is a regular routine of three shots a day, once every eight hours required by the system once it has gotten used to the drug. I used it once every few weeks, then once a week, then several times a week, for periods of a month or less at a time, scattered over the years between 1945–1947. After 1947, as I say, I made so little use of it that it is not worth speaking of.

Marijuana is another matter. It is not physically habit forming. That is, once the drug is used regularly, the physical or mental system does not pain if it is withdrawn. There are no withdrawal symptoms. It is not even as bad as liquor from that aspect. It is habit forming as movies can be habit forming. If you're bored, or unreceptive and unresponsive to stimuli it will waken your sensibilities. Food tastes better, amazingly so. People who smoke marijuana usually sleep well, eat well, and gain weight. It used to be prescribed by doctors in the 20's for depressive cases. Music sounds clearer and more coherent and moving. Poetry seems more significant—in fact everything assumes a great and portentous significance—little innuendoes and gestures in conversation; colors, drapery, arrangements of flowers, etc.

I have used it on and off for years. I can't say whether it has been psychologically good or bad, actually. It is a moot point. I suppose anything constantly used to evade the press of reality is bad; but marijuana seems generally not so bad as liquor. This is not, incidentally, only my opinion. It is shared by many smokers of marijuana. That may seem like a joke. But you ask a lush (or liquor addict) or a junkie (heroin or morphine addict) if his drug or stimulant is bad for people, and he will usually say 'yes.' He is in the grip of something habit forming that has ruined his life. People like me, Herbert Huncke, and others who have tried all drugs—and Herbert, incidentally is more of a junkie than a teahead (marijuana addict)—will finally judge marijuana to be the least evil of all stimulants. But I have been indulging here in a kind of irony. There is, however, a book on marijuana known as the La Guardia Report—a committee was formed under the administration of the former mayor to investigate the mysterious reports emanating from drug and medical sources that the marijuana reputation was a big capitalist bogey myth. They were unwilling, finally, to take sides and concluded that it wasn't good for the whole personality, but on the other hand, it wasn't as bad as has been made out. I am saying all of this to attempt to mediate somewhat between myself and my reader and eliminate some of the possible confusions involved in the mere mention of drugs. I may add that, personally, ultimately, and for myself, I don't approve of marijuana, and that I have at various times in the past approved of it and that I decided against it as a final influence for me a long time ago—at least a year and a half. That I have used it at all in the last half year—and I have used pretty much—is due to the fact that it was over-available and that I was foolish enough not to go ahead with my own plans to withdraw from other people, particularly 'hipsters' and live by myself. I do not wish to use it anymore; I can say that and mean it.

I still have not given an adequate reason for using it lately, and what I have written above seems to me to be an evasion of the admission and insight that I am very confused on the subjective problems that marijuana creates for me. On one hand I say I condemn it, on the other, that it is not so bad; on one hand I say I or nobody needs it, on the other, that I went ahead and used it against my better judgment. Well, let that stand for the moment as it is. Anyway I won't use it anymore. If I had been in the hands of an analyst all along and felt that I was making progress, the question never would have arisen and I would not have been tempted to enliven the sterility of my sensations with the false visions of marijuana.

Finally, I might say that it is an interesting drug. I wrote a stanza last March, apropos the whole drug problem:

> The city's hipper slickers shine,
> Up in the attic with the bats;
> The higher Chinamen, supine,
> Wear a dragon in their hats:
> He who seeks a secret sign
> In a daze or sicker doze
> Blows the flower superfine;

As for some value (healthy) in contradistinction to the temptations of money, drugs, sex, fame, etc., each of which had a stanza of renunciation in the poem, the last stanza went:

Come, incomparable crown,
Love my love is lost to claim,
O hollow fame that makes me groan;
We are a king without a name:
Regain thine angel's lost renown,
As, in the mind's forgotten meadow,
Where brightest shades are gazed in stone,
Man runs after his own shadow.[184]

IV

One day when I returned from work, about two months ago, Herbert told me that Little Jack [Melody] and Vicki had been by. Little Jack I knew only by reputation. He had been to federal prison for stealing a safe. Vicki I had not seen for some time—once last summer, at a party I threw and not before that for a year or so. She had been on a heroin habit which I did not particularly like to see happen to her. She had always been disdainful of junkies—even me, several years ago, for chippying around. She had been in treatment (under the care of a psychotherapist of the school of Dr. Wilhelm Reich) some years before, and had never completed the course of therapy. She is a naturally bitchy girl; she is subject to moods of over-affection and stern rejection of men; she always has a lover. (I liked that in her, since she usually would go with one man steadily; they were real, if violent, love affairs). I never liked her cruel surface—caddy, half masculine at times. But underneath she is just a nice, sweet, sharp, vital, energetic girl, somewhat overgrown and bewildered. She liked me; why I don't know. In fact, I really don't know why I am always glad to see her from year to year. For one thing, she has a lot of resourcefulness and energy. It may be misdirected, but it certainly shines through. I would hate to be in love with her, she is such a changeable shrew, though. She had a habit when I last saw her and had been so hung up on her drugs that she seemed to have no time for any kind of true feeling. I had heard that she was out somewhere in Long Island with Melody and his family. It appears that they really fell in love, he took her home and stayed with her and helped her cure her habit. The cure is a tough and supposedly horrible process for all involved, so Little Jack must be given credit for a generous and truly difficult task and Vicki given credit for a cure which is not often successful. I was curious to meet Little Jack since any man that Vicki takes for a long time usually has something on the

184 These lines are from the poem "Stanzas Written at Night in Radio City," which appears in *Collected Poems*, p. 27.

ball. Maybe this reflects my perverted sense of values, but I like people; and my liking and curiosity is not confined to criminals. I have gone out of my way to meet a lot of people of varying kinds.

The desire to seek people out for purposes of intimate contact is something that a psychiatrist would have to look into. I suppose that if I were stable, secure, happy, working, and married I would find sufficient satisfaction in a much smaller community of people than I am accustomed to. As it is, I left my door opened and encouraged anybody who was curious about me to satisfy their curiosity and I hoped vice versa. The most unexpected relationships develop from that attitude. As I say, I was finding it necessary for my peace of mind to withdraw entirely from the company of others when all this mess happened.

Well, Vicki came back two days later (this was sometime at the beginning of March) bringing Little Jack. When I saw her I was somewhat shy and pleased; when she came in the door we actually embraced; we had known each other a long time. Vicki is one of the few women whose company and conversation I can take large doses of. Not too large, because she lacks some spiritual or poetic sense of God or humanity or something I've never been able to define. She's too worldly. And yet it's her worldliness and worldly amazing energy and irreverent enterprise that I like.

Little Jack turned out to be unlike my expectations. He was little, half-bald and he had a definite kind of half-elfin, half-Italianate, doe-like gentility and interest and sympathy with things and people around him that surprised me and belied his reputation as a big money hustler and Lower East Side gangster, etc. I thought that there was also a kind of unresponsive area of insanity in his mind. For example, if I began theorizing about metaphysical knowledge, I felt that there was a certain kind of insistence on his own intellectual structures that prevented us from ever coming to a clear understanding of what we were talking about. But that is perhaps a fault of mine. However I asked Kerouac and Eugene and they agreed with me. Little Jack gets pet ideas of a vaguely cosmic nature and can't completely express them and you somehow find it difficult or embarrassing to disagree or show lack of proper sympathy to his own enthusiasm. I found him at first so sweet natured and eager to be pleasing and amiable in a perceptive way, that I felt quite good that first morning I saw him and began talking wildly and fantastically in a spring-like incoherent way, jumping from one thing to another, reciting W.B. Yeats one minute, the next crying out lyrically that I had berries growing out of my wall (pointing to a sprig of mistletoe I had set in a crack in the wall), explaining myself in an absurdly humorous manner and reciting my own poetry to him. Bear in mind that there aren't many people to whom I react like that.

He came a few times more with Vicki in the next few days. I think he brought marijuana with him then. We got high several times and got involved in long conversations about Cézanne, Spengler, the nature of the universe, mutual acquaintances, etc. Vicki and he were also over my apartment several times when I was not at home, working at the Associated Press. Jack Kerouac, Tom Livornese (a student), and Russell Durgin were present at these soirées. Marijuana was smoked. Little Jack saw that I had no music in the house as he put it and brought over his own Victrola and some of Vicki's records. He also brought little gifts for the house—a copy of the Arabian Nights that he wanted to show me—cake or food to compensate for whatever of my larder he and Vicki used up. I made no particular issue of their frequent visits and in fact welcomed them, they usually slept in my room, going to sleep towards dawn or perhaps earlier. I would come home and sleep on the couch or on the floor if Huncke was on the couch. These traffic tie-ups as far as sleeping quarters were concerned did not happen often, but I did worry about it. One day Little Jack came by with a paper bag full of antique knick-knacks he picked up somewhere in town—from a friend who owned an antique shop. They were not stolen—a little matchbox with a silhouette on it, a carved Japanese panel, bookends, etc. He was very friendly; even went to the trouble of breaking off the ends of a number of large wooden matches to fit the box. Most people are not capable of such little touches of creative generosity. He also brought a picture he painted to show me, a painting of Vicki, which lends her face an indescribable quality of inner severity and savagery. He is a very sharp observer, needless to say, in some matters. He also described another painting of his, that of a little white lamb (Blake's Lamb?) on a black background.

By this time marijuana was flowing around the house. Sometimes I used it, sometimes not. At one point, I had two days free, so I got as high as I could and went out exploring the streets and park at dawn. I was beginning to feel an aversion to the confusion and sleepiness that marijuana was inducing in me. It was almost a reaction of over-nervousness, physical and mental anxiety. I began theorizing at this point about marijuana as a big drag, that is, a big bore and a bringdown and I used it less and less. I smoked it in an opium pipe that he had bought in Chinatown. I think he brought it up because I told him that I would like to have a classic opium pipe for my mantelpiece as an ornament. It was an old ambition of mine. The police now have that pipe and another similar one that was in the apartment when they came by to disturb this 'idyllic existence.'

I am sorry if at this point this journal sounds flippant but I have been writing a great deal in a short time and I am unable to concentrate to that point of holy confessional urgency which I feel might be more proper to my situation.

At this point I may as well stop and continue tomorrow.

V

Sometime in March—late in March—I fell sick, the recurrence of a bronchial dryness and cold-preoccupation which had bothered me on and off for a year. It usually came at times of doldrums where my life or mind needs a decisive turn not offered by fate—some external happening, like the end of school year, a trip to sea, etc.—when I don't act and am wasting my time. I mention this because it was my turn to be depressed and sick and Herbert took care of me for several days while I stayed in bed. Little Jack and Vicki came over and entertained me; it was about this time that they brought over the phonograph. I remember this with a certain nostalgia, as they brought along a lot of fine jazz records. Particularly a set of songs by a negro blues singer—a very profound and subtle woman named Billie Holiday.[185] I have been listening to her records for years. Little Jack and Herbert introduced me to one particular record of hers which I bought myself a few weeks later, called 'That Old Devil Called Love,' which expresses her resignation and suffering joy at the prospect of a repetition of the old pleasure-pain of an unhappy love affair:

"When I hear that siren song
I just know I gotta go along."

These particular words of the lyrics are sung with such a tender, winning, knowing sensitivity that I recognized why Herbert, Little Jack and others have thought that this was one of Holiday's best records.

Billie Holiday is well known in jazz circles as an amazing, great woman. Little Jack and Vicki, who know her, promised to arrange for me to meet her. I had long hoped and expected to meet her, one time or another. Perhaps I someday will. She is at present barred from singing in New York and in trouble with the law because she is a heroin addict. All this I suppose is more atmosphere.

At this time Jack Kerouac was at the end of his rope attempting to peddle his novel [The Town and the City]. It had been given to a critic named Alfred

---

185   Ginsberg's note: "Was listening to and writing down lyrics to: Blue Spirit Blues, What's the Matter Now, Empty Bed Blues (all by Bessie Smith); Them Graveyard Words, Send Me to the Electric Chair; Jelly Bean Blues, Counten the Blues, See See Rider, Jealous Hearted Blues (all by Ma Rainey); He's a Jelly Roll Baker (Lonnie Johnson); and Bridewell Blues (Lloyd Nolen)."

Kazin, who submitted it to Harcourt Brace, but nothing had been heard. Vicki knew a literary agent, Brant or Brandt and Brandt or something, and Jack gave her several chapters of his novel to show the agent. I went up to school and talked to Van Doren about Jack and arranged a meeting between them. They had known each other several years before in a student-teacher relationship. Van Doren read parts of the book, saw Jack, called up Harcourt and in a day the novel was accepted and Jack had a check for $1,000. This was the first big money and success to come out of the toil of the last years; but our art was at last paying off and all was well. I even started a poem which turned into a holy psalm:

Jack's Poem

Surrounds us here with hills and clouds and stones,
bones and wounds and clowns and halo crowns.

Death is where the buried and unborn come from
who come and go in stillness out of time.

I but a ghostly poet

sweet Jack, six years of penury and pine
and twice three years of crackbrained alchemy
six years of purgatory have ascended
like to a mad balloon out of my mind.

Jack that like a beast of burden carrying
the deathly weight of time upon his back
made an Egyptian journey to the sea,
till even time has honored and obeyed thee
and crowned thee for thy spiritual might
with all the glories of the pride of Babylon the sphinx.

And yet your art is not so melancholy
as that broken clarinet I celebrate
rather your book is like a piano in the dark
played by the young and blind in a building
high up at midnight on the balcony.

Like a gambler, rich soul lost to time.

Sometimes I lay down my wrath;
and wonder where my life must climb;
money money, work and worry,
and all the aimless toil of time,

Meaning mostly that six years of hard intellectual effort had opened up into a
new skyey world. Jack and I spent hours walking around the city discussing our
respective literary futures. I was envious and also depressed by my failure to
work as hard as he—he spent three years at home in Ozone Park, coming in to
get drunk or high or walk or play in the city on weekends with me and others.
At one time he had an affair with Vicki. He liked Little Jack and knew Herbert
almost as well as I. Herbert appears in Jack's novel under the name Junkie. I
told him that I was tired of all the activity around me—all the people in my
apartment.

Several flashbacks are necessary. At one time in 1945-6, Jack and I had spent
a lot of time together, even sharing the same small room around Columbia
and we had had no money and no place to go at night to continue talking after
the bars closed. It had always been my hope to own an apartment of my own
where people like us could come, be fed, if they were hungry, and stay over if
they had nowhere to go. A lot of good young artists are footloose at night and
need some social center. Otherwise they will go around (as we once did)
knocking on doors of acquaintances, waking them up in the middle of the
night, rousing neighbors, and be in an unfriendly atmosphere which they have
helped create. My ideal was a 'pad' or apartment like mine where people I
liked were welcome anytime and under any circumstances.

Well, this plan was backfiring because Jack and Vicki were around so often,
and Huncke was there permanently. In a sense I got what I asked for with a
vengeance.

A second flashback: while I was sick I had a long talk with Huncke (who
was sometimes, as I indicated, a spiritual advisor to me) and he urged me to
get out of the work rut that I was in and begin to plan for the future. There
was a certain pathos in his speech since he was advising me to do what he was
incapable of doing. I realized he was right and that I had been waiting too long
in the doldrums for something to happen. But nothing would happen, he (and
once Van Doren) said, until I acted myself to make it happen. I finally decided
that my next move would be to arrange for a teaching job for me next fall, if

possible. This would also give me enough money to be psychoanalyzed, and enough time to write. So I finally made up my mind to try to get it, which was a big step; I wrote Trilling, who offered to help in such a matter. I planned to investigate the possibilities of an instructorship at Cooper Union.

> (I once wrote a lyric
> I love the lord on high
> I wish he'd pull my daisy
> Jack Kerouac added refrain,
> Pull my daisy,
> Tip my cup,
> All my doors are open).

Well as I say, Jack and I were talking and I said I was sick of working at A.P. for $30 a week and sick of my home life in New York. So he asked me why, if I were planning to teach in the fall, did I continue to work at A.P. and why stay in New York for the summer? Then and there I decided to go to New Orleans as soon as I could.

In New Orleans are, or were, Bill Burroughs and Joan Adams. They have been almost a substitute father and mother to me. Joan is the nicest woman I know, 'the greatest' as they say in hip-talk. And Bill has always been the wise, warm, friendly old father confessor. Thereby hangs a long, involved and crack-brained tale of the years 1944–47; but I can't go into it as it is of too great length. Lately, however, I had come to feel Bill's final intellectual inadequacy and spiritual failure. I wanted to go down and galvanize him into some kind of activity, get him to kick his heroin habit (he is 34) and stop fiddling around with drugs and romanticized quasi-underworld activity. He is a scholarly and well-traveled ex-Harvard anthropologist. It would be hard to describe his character. He is lean and gray faced; he looks like the busts of Dante that are so familiar. His temperament seems cold but he is very thoughtful and friendly. He has helped me out financially a number of times and I have repaid him for his loans. I spent several weeks at his farm he once owned in the bayou of Texas near Houston; and I lived in an apartment with him and Joan Adams and Jack Kerouac and several others in 1945–46 off and on. He tried unsuccessfully to psychoanalyze me. It was a mistaken psychoanalysis but it was an interesting experience. I spoke to him an hour a day for at least a year and we learned a lot about each other.

Anyway, I felt weary of New York and as he had invited me several times during the year to join him and his family (two children) in New Orleans, where he had a house. I wanted to go to New Orleans and as I said to Jack 'rest my weary head on his shoulder.' (I might add that we have no sexual relationship; I feel a filial affection for him).

I wondered what to do with my apartment. Little Jack had spoken of trying to get an apartment in the city to 'operate' out of. I have no idea what such operations involved; not burglary, however. But, as my reason for leaving was to get away from the loose or unstable life of Herbert, etc., I did not want to suggest that he take over my apartment. Herbert brought this up and I excused myself from such an arrangement; also I told Eugene that he could have my place for the summer.

I had gas bills to pay ($20 worth) but had not paid them due to lack of money. Also I had the problem of raising money to go away for the summer—carfare, living expenses. I had no idea how to solve this.

A few days later, (I think this was sometime around the first week of April) I decided to attend formal graduation ceremonies at Columbia. I had not anticipated doing this; but it was partly Herbert's idea. With a kind of sweet and friendly concern, he said that he would like to attend my graduation. High on marijuana, I also decided it would be a nice kick for my father and stepmother to be [there], if I were to go through with the ceremony in cap and gown. My graduation had been a long time in coming.

At this time, I asked Bill Burroughs to send me some marijuana. I wanted to have a small quantity on hand to use as the occasion dictated for myself, for Kerouac, and for Lucien Carr. Lucien was drinking too heavily, losing weight and having heavy hangovers. I hoped to distract him from liquor with marijuana, perhaps he would also eat better. I did not worry about the affect of the drug on him since he had never cottoned to it and looked down on my using it. But I hoped it might help him over the waste and depression of those months. He is now in the hands of an analyst (psycho) and has begun writing short stories for the first time since his college days in 1944 and so his situation is very bright. I don't think my marijuana project for his welfare was such a good idea, but it seemed at the moment a temporary expedient. He had resisted psychoanalysis and creative work for a long time; now things were changed. These developments are all in the last month.

Bill wrote back saying that he would send a small package for me, not to 1401 York but to a mailbox for which I had the key at a room on 114th St. where I used to live. I have given the room over to my brother and since he received his mail at the office and I still received university announcements, etc. there,

I had kept the box under my name and kept the only key. I had received a package of marijuana from him once before at the same box, sometime in January, when my boyfriend, Neal Cassady, was in town.

Bill also asked me if I were able and willing to pick up some side money selling marijuana as he could get it wholesale. I asked Huncke what the prospects were and corresponded with Bill on the subject. It is mentioned several times in his letters to me, which the police have, as is the fact that he did send a package of marijuana for my own use. Herbert asked Little Jack and Little Jack said that if the 'weed' were any good he could probably unload some on jazz musicians on Long Island that he knew. About three weeks ago I decided against the idea entirely, partly from fear of the law, partly from lack of enterprise, partly from a feeling that if I went into business with Herbert as a partner, he would wind up eating all the profits and that nothing would come back to myself to recompense me for all the trouble. I wrote Bill telling him I was against it, but would go through with it if he wanted to, but that the decision was his. I knew that this approach would discourage him, too. The project was never attempted.

I received the package of tea (I will refer to marijuana as tea, which is what it is often called) and divided it into two parts, one to Kerouac, and one to Barbara Hale, who was Lucien's girlfriend. I presume she has poured it down the toilet by now.

Herbert was annoyed and irritated at me for keeping him in the dark about the receipt of the tea. I did not want the drug for constant use, but wanted a liberal supply available for occasions when it could be enjoyed in moderation by Jack and Lucien and myself. I knew that if Herbert had got a hold of it that it would be gone in a matter of days. The quantity I had would have lasted a year at the rate I would have used it. Herbert became angry and we had a long argument about a week after I received the tea.

The issue was why had I deceived him and why had I held it back when I had partaken of Little Jack's supply? I said that I was grateful for Little Jack's generosity but that I had other plans on this specific issue. He took offense at this; at my lack of community spirit, at his missing the tea, and at my attempted deception of him. I had finally shown him Bill's letters and so he knew that I had received the tea. This argument developed into a serious conflict of wills, with both of us adamant. I finally gave in and got back the tea I had given to Kerouac and handed it over one night before going to work. It was gone in a day or so. A few days later, after another flare-up he visited Barbara Hale and got her to give him another portion. I had given him her address, finally, tired of arguing with him and also feeling a little guilty about the whole matter since I had approached it in a cowardly way from the beginning.

At this point I was quite wearied of my relationship with Herbert. I felt the abyss between us constantly and felt great tension when with him. One morning when I came home, we had a long complicated discussion. I felt I had to withdraw from him entirely and that I was not open to him. He was open to me and frank and sincere; but I had a final sense of the futility of the unconscious parasitical relationship between us. I saw it was doing nobody any good. The immediate problem of telling him to go, however, required an act which seemed too cruel or frighteningly real for me to attempt—that is, actually banishing him.

Also there was a new element added through Vicki and Little Jack, who stayed strictly on the sidelines in my argument with Herbert. They sympathized with me and my long suffering problems with Herbert. To a great extent their appearance on the scene was motivated by a desire to join forces with Herbert, and since he is, as it were, incapable of going out into the world alone, they hoped to inspire and give him strength to act along with them in whatever scheme they would develop. Their plans were fluid at this time. There was talk by Little Jack of renting an apartment, one with a telephone and using it for some purpose or other to make money. I never asked and was never told how.

Herbert at this point brought up the subject of my own apartment again; he urged me to make some kind of deal with Little Jack to sublet. I did not want to, but Little Jack offered to repaint the place, install a telephone, pay rent and give me whatever I needed ($30–$50) to get to New Orleans if I would let him have the place for four months. I accepted immediately, on the spur of the moment. This must have been at the beginning of April. I added that he might have to take care of the gas bill and he agreed. It was understood that he might move in whenever he wanted. Up to this time he had practically moved in; it was already accepted that he and Vicki could use the bedroom. She had brought her woman's apparel and bottles of perfume, etc. He had brought in a small radio, an electric heater and his paintings. He and Herbert had spent a day, several weeks previous, cleaning up the apartment and rearranging the furniture to their taste. Their taste was a vast improvement over the arrangement of furniture that I had found when I moved in a year ago. This deed was done for the enjoyment of all, one evening and they had even exempted me from what to me had been the onerous burden of contributing my own labor to the project. I was quite grateful; it was a pleasure.

So, about a month ago, they moved in. There was no formal moment of handing over the keys. Ever since Herbert had come, I had kept the key in the hall bathroom; my apartment has no toilet of its own. Kerouac, Herbert, Vicki and Little Jack were free to go in and out at all times.

They were bringing things in and out all the time—small things, mostly their own. All changes of bedding, shifts and divisions of covers, etc. were done by Herbert and Vicki. Housekeeping (dishwashing) was done mostly by Herbert. My own clothes were slowly, over a period of weeks, moved into the living room. I did not supervise this job. Herbert had been free to use my clothes, and he did the moving of my shirts, underwear, handkerchiefs, socks (few as they were) to a bureau drawer in the main living room. I was actually never sure where to find my own personal effects. Herbert even appropriated a few drawers in my sacred writing desk to keep his own scribblings and trinkets. All this I resented slightly, but felt that it really didn't matter and didn't bother very much about it. It saved me the trouble of thinking for myself on small matters. And besides, I was in a state of weariness and futility about the absurdity of trying to live and write in such a hectic atmosphere, even for the two months that remained. I wasn't acting or living with any real sense of purpose except to get out of town and enjoy myself in New Orleans.

I made inquiries down at A.P. as to the possibility of getting a transfer to the local office down there. I never acted on it. Also I began talking to people about my proposed trip, told Eugene, Louis, my family in Newark, my dentist, etc. just for conversation, also to boast about my footloose romantic character.

During all this time I was not writing much; but I wrote a few interesting metaphysical lyrics about God and the search for God.

It is as usual a very abstract poem. I was thinking of writing a long piece and trying to find some hint or manner or method to harness my energies to extended work. I had hoped to do so in New Orleans. Conditions were not propitious in New York. That was really all I cared or worried about seriously, aside from the state of my soul, which I felt would be helped only by getting down to some real solid work. However it is just the surface of a deeper sexual problem, a problem of feeling and expressing real human love emotions which cannot be solved in jail. That is why I do and do not want to go to jail.

Up to this time, I believe that Herbert and Vicki had together been 'heisting' a few automobiles. I don't remember any specific times or acquisitions thereby. About a week before "the fall," Little Jack, Vicki and Herbert left the house about 10 o'clock at night for that purpose in the automobile that later crashed. They asked me if I were willing to accompany them and I said yes. I took along a book and several manuscripts of poems to work on at the A.P. I went along to see how they did it and the conditions under which they operated, a strictly literary interest. We cruised around the midtown area. They were looking for cars with suitcases or clothes in them. About 50th and 3rd Avenue Little Jack, who was driving the car, stopped. He and I remained in the car, Herbert and Vicki went across the street, broke into a car and stole a woman's coat. They rode on searching for more cars, finally found a set of them on 50th Street between Fifth and Sixth, I think. They parked their own car around the block and invited me to accompany them and lose my burglar's 'cherry.' I was to look out on the corner while they broke in. I declined and remained in the car. They returned a few minutes later, apparently there had been nothing of interest in the cars. They left me at Lexington and 57th Street. I went up to visit John Holmes,[186] an acquaintance of Kerouac and mine, who lives near that corner. He was not home, so I went on to work by 12 o'clock.

My feelings at that time were mixed. I had gone along with them on the ride, not knowing how I would react or what would happen. I thought, possibly, I might take part in a car haul. I did not due to a clammy feeling of fear about getting involved in the actual operation. We had discussed my feelings in the car, they (especially Little Jack) even sympathized with my desire to keep my 'cherry' as we referred to it.

About April 12 or 13, Little Jack, Vicki and Herbert brought home a carved cabinet. I saw it first when I returned from work, asked about it and was told that it was taken from an apartment foyer. The police seem to have neglected it in their search through my apartment. Several days later I came home to find two large, expensive and fine looking carved chairs sitting in the living room by the window. These had been obtained in the same manner.

When I saw all this furniture in my place I was struck by a feeling of greed, not unmixed with faint legal anxieties. Little Jack reviewing our compact about the apartment had spoken of adding some furniture in addition to painting it up. This particular furniture was not to be left with me, Herbert told me, when I expressed delight at the look of the house. Little Jack and Vicki intended sooner or later to get an apartment of their own when they were financially stable and the chairs were to go into that apartment. I felt annoyed.

On that weekend, I spent several days away from the house. I had no money

---

186   John Clellon Holmes (1926–1980). Author of *Go*, widely considered the first "Beat" novel, lives in an apartment at 681 Lexington Avenue at the time.

and had borrowed a few dollars at work. I hated to give it to Herbert to fritter away on candles, incense and Benzedrine inhalers (which he used to get high with). I didn't want to feed him and I was sick and tired of the whole frantic mess in the house. I had a dental appointment for Monday April 18th in the morning after work, so I went to Bloomfield [NJ] where my dentist was and then to Paterson. I returned on Tuesday afternoon, having been away since Sunday evening.

I am at this point trying to separate in my mind the series of things that happened and am confused as to the specific days. They all took place in the last week and a half before the fall.

When I returned I met all three on the stairway and was told that there were plenty of cigarettes and bread in the apartment. I had no money and there had been a shortage of cigarettes and buttered rolls for breakfast. When I got upstairs I saw a cigarette machine, a whole cigarette machine, standing in the kitchen with a blanket over it. I also found two enormous paper bakery bags, one full of loaves of rye and pumpernickel, the other full of rolls. I was hungry and ate some of the rolls with cheese that I brought. Russell Durgin visited me that evening and I complained to him in a half-humorous vein of this great flow of goods into the house. I gave him a loaf of bread to take along to Harvard the next day. I also presented a large loaf of rye to the old deaf lady next door who often brought me bowls of soup and Jell-O to eat.

The cigarette machine stood in the kitchen for two days and I suggested that it be removed. We broke it into parts and carried it down to the car. Herbert and Little Jack disposed of it. I don't know where they got it. I was curious, of course, but I let it go.

I had two letters when I returned home on Tuesday, one from Bill Burroughs and one from Joan Adams in New Orleans. He had been arrested for possession of narcotics. Several letters from me to him, mentioning the small shipment of weed, were seized. Apparently he persuaded the police down there that there was no great traffic in drugs taking place. He said that as far as he knew the F.B.I. would not concern itself. He also warned me to keep my own house clean of narcotics as there was a chance that I would be visited by the police on account of the letters. There were no narcotics in the house belonging to me; Herbert had opened the letter, shown it to Little Jack, Jack Kerouac and Vicki. I told them that I wanted the place kept clean, therefore.

Huncke reassured me that if the police came looking for drugs they would not notice the other burglarized material around the house. I was unsure of this and discussed it with him but he insisted that my anxiety was in vain.

Since the question of 'heat' was now raised, Herbert told me that he had discussed that problem with Vicki and Little Jack. As far as I was concerned, if anything were to happen and I were home alone I was to remain silent, deny everything and contact the Melody family. Little Jack seemed to think they would intervene somewhere in the upper reaches of the law and get me out of any trouble. This was said on Tuesday morning, April 19.

Herbert by this time was growing dissatisfied, apparently there was a conflict between he and Little Jack and Vicki, similar to the one between he and I. A matter of his personal relationship to their activities. I believe there had been sometime over the weekend, one burglary. I don't remember what was taken very clearly, suits and women's clothes, mostly. Vicki and Little Jack had done it alone one day when Herbert was home and I was at work. He resented not having been along with them—resented their secret mutual action.

He also felt, in view of the whole situation—my going away and Little Jack and Vicki as lovers—that he was not really wanted, or necessary to the operations of the household. He resented having the domestic tasks thrown on him. I did little cleaning myself. He and Vicki had not worked out any scheme for dividing household labor between them, and so a problem had remained. I never ascertained exactly what the trouble was; probably it was Herbert's feeling of inadequacy, frustration and inactivity. Herbert felt that he was riding along on Little Jack's and Vicki's activity, a needless member, that he was not contributing anything essential. He wanted to be an equal member of their family bond and they invited him to assume an equality of feeling and work with them. I think Little Jack really wanted to incorporate Huncke into his scheme of activity, make use of him, in whatever way was possible and get him out of the slump that he was in. Apparently they even discussed all three of them going out and getting jobs; Vicki as a waitress, Herbert at the Associated Press, Little Jack as I don't know what.

For a week Herbert expressed his dissatisfaction with himself and his present situation and said to me that he intended to leave very soon, go away—where, he did not know. He wanted to go somewhere where he did not know anyone at all. He felt that 'he was doing nobody any good and never would and doing himself no good either.' He felt like an untouchable. He wanted to remove himself from friendly society and be alone and I think in the back of his mind he wanted to crawl somewhere off in a corner and die alone.

The first burglary might have taken place sometime on Sunday. I spent Sunday walking on Fifth Ave. with Lucien Carr (it was Easter). I came home about 6 o'clock and went to bed, got up at 11 o'clock, announced my own intention of deserting the apartment for a few days, went to work, dentist, Paterson and returned Tuesday about 4 or 5 o'clock in the afternoon.

On second thought, I believe the first large burglary took place Tuesday. I think I helped Vicki and Little Jack, who arrived home about 9 o'clock (Herbert and I were home) carry stuff up from the car—men's and women's clothes. I did not stay to watch them count their loot, but left the house almost immediately to see Lucien Carr after he got out from work at 10:30 or 11:30.

Lucien and I walked and talked all night long, till dawn. We walked all over the Bowery and Chinatown area, ate, walked up to 42nd Street and back down to his house on E. 10th Street where I left him.

Our talk was particularly significant to me. In the course of the night he announced that he was already underway in psychoanalysis. I had been vainly attempting to urge him to this step for three years and it was quite a surprise to me that on his own he was suddenly doing it, as he had always resisted the idea. Also we had a long talk about writing short stories. When we were in school five years before it was Lucien that 'inspired' me to artistic activity, he himself had subsequently renounced it and gone to work for the United Press after getting out of jail. (Lucien had been in jail for two years, 1944–46, for second degree murder [sic: manslaughter]). Now suddenly he told me he was going to write again and this too was a great event.

I showed him Bill Burroughs' letter. Lucien talked to me for about two hours rebuking me for letting myself become involved with Vicki, Little Jack and Herbert. He warned me against possible legal trouble at great length. Also he asked me if I had disposed of my papers—journals and letters from Neal Cassady, Bill Burroughs, Huncke, himself and others. I had intended to and had not and was ashamed of my unwary conduct. For a long time Lucien had warned me against involving him in any way, even the most innocent way, in my correspondence and journals. He was on parole and didn't want to have any trouble. I had ignored his warnings and since Bill knew and liked him had kept Bill informed as to Lucien's activities and health. I don't believe there is anything incriminating to him in all the papers the police have, since he had kept his nose clean and in fact had often warned me against my own footloose tendencies. He was angry that I was 'tempting fate' by leaving all those papers around the house. I resolved to take care of that matter the very next morning.

You can see that fate gave me plenty of warnings of what was to come. It is very bitter.

An ironic touch is that while so innocently walking at night on Fifth

Avenue and 14th St. we were stopped by two policemen who wanted to know who we were and what we were doing at that hour. We explained that we worked at night for A.P. and U.P. This had happened once about a week before when we were sitting on Lucien's doorstep in the early hours, very soberly conversing.

I got home about six in the morning on Wednesday. Little Jack and Vicki were in bed, Herbert on the couch. I slept on the floor till about 11, when Herbert rose and then I slept on the couch. I woke up about 3. We all had something to eat.

Then I spent an hour going through all my papers, separating the sheep from the goats. I put all letters, about 100 of them, into a manila envelope along with unsorted very personal, obscene, autobiographical or confessional fragments of prose. I put everything back into my drawer immediately, waiting for the proper time and occasion to dispose of them—preferably by going to Eugene's room and leaving them under a pile of books and law manuscripts in his closet. I felt they would be safe from prying eyes there, at least. I did not want to bring them into Paterson because Louis had once started to read through my old homosexual love letters and writings when I left all my papers at home about a year before. I had resented his inquiry into something that was essentially extremely private and sad of my own. He had once warned me against committing anything to paper that 'I would have cause to regret.' In fact Louis had such an idea of my relationships to people that he asked me on several occasions if Huncke was blackmailing me. I never was able to coherently explain to him (or to myself, either) just what Herbert's relationship to me was. But the blackmail idea was so off the beam, as I saw it, that I had difficulty orienting him to an understanding of just what I was up to.

As to my motives for putting down on paper what I felt and saw—I actually was trying to keep in mind the details of my existence, to put them down in all their reality, artistic or not, against the day when I would be able to use them for a large autobiographical work of fiction. That day would come, I figured, only when I felt enough at peace with myself and self-satisfied to actually be able to conceive of myself as a hero of a book. But that day never came.

Then, feeling that afternoon that a turning point of one kind or other had come and driven to a new rush of activity by Lucien's re-entrance into the scene as an active writer, I spent several hours assembling my poetry for a book and I bound it all together to take with me to work that night. Herbert, Vicki and Little Jack left about 4 o'clock headed out to Long Island. They did not announce their purpose. Jack Kerouac and Tom Livornese were to come to my house that afternoon. Livornese is Italian, a piano player, a fine and also legally correct boy. He had at one time been Vicki's lover. Jack Kerouac and I had introduced him to her several years ago. Jack had his money from his book and with Livornese was going out to buy himself a wardrobe. This was an occasion of note since it marks the beginning of Jack's worldly honor. Jack and Tom were to meet Little Jack, who has good taste in clothes and perhaps go shopping.

When the pair had not shown up at my house by 4 o'clock, Little Jack said he couldn't wait. I took a nap at about 7 o'clock, since I had to work that night. Monday and Tuesday evenings were my nights off.

Little Jack, Vicki and Herbert returned around 9 o'clock with the car full of loot. They wakened me when they came in, asked me to help them get the stuff out of the car—lamps, clothes, cameras, radios, etc. I did. They sat around discussing the burglary and I sat around watching them discuss and go over the loot.

One humorous note was that they had taken a pile of dirty books, pornographic literature. They found someone's name on them and recognized their victim as an ex-Harlem police bigwig.

Some of the jewelry and clothing was divided. I claimed nothing except a broken fountain pen which I repaired and laid on my desk. I had no fountain pen, my own having been stolen about two months before, when my lock was forced and my apartment very lightly burglarized. The thieves had gotten nothing of value besides the pen. I did not report it to the police. I said at the time that sinners suffer enough punishment in their own self-created hell.

Little Jack asked if Kerouac had come, as he wanted to sell Kerouac some of the stolen suits. I said no. It was drawing near time for me to go to work. Since they had no money, they were going to ride downtown to borrow some. Little Jack, Vicki and myself got into his car. I took along my book of poems. Little Jack drove me to John Holmes' apartment on 57th St. and Fourth Ave. (walking distance to work for me). They asked me if Kerouac might be at Holmes'. I went upstairs, found him there, brought him down to the car and then all five of us went upstairs to Holmes' apartment. They asked Jack if he wanted to buy any suits. He told them that he had spent all the money earmarked for his wardrobe that afternoon.

Herbert Huncke was annoyed and expressed his irritation in a sort of frustrated pique at Jack Kerouac. Jack and I both laughed at this. It was typical of Herbert. So Herbert, Vicki and Little Jack left about 11 o'clock and I stayed on till 5 to midnight, when I went to work.

A significant conversation: Holmes announced to me that he was writing, or contemplating writing, a novel about me called <u>The Visionary</u>. He was half mocking, half serious. To show my appreciation of his thoughtfulness, I presented him with my manuscripts to read overnight. He had never seen much of my poetry.

Then I asked Kerouac if he planned to go over to my apartment later. He said he was not and I told him that the reason I asked was that I wished he would go over, get all my correspondence and journals and take them to safety in his house. He said that since he was probably mentioned in the letters to Bill Burroughs, the papers would not be safe at his house either, if the F.B.I. really started following out addresses. I said, "Yes, that's true," somewhat disappointed at his unwillingness to take the problem off my hands. He added, "Besides, if you really wanted them out of the house you would have done it already yourself." I felt such a twinge of remorse and anxiety at my own lack of action in this matter that I dropped the subject and agreed with him, that my behavior had been confused.

This agreement did not make amends for my lack of action. I felt even more the pressure of a reality—a real world in which for some desperate reason of vanity or fear I was maneuvering myself and everyone I knew into some immediate catastrophe, trying to plunge everyone into the pit and darkness of my own anarchy and evil-natured fate. Why had I gone to the trouble of recording the events of mine and other lives, events which were for the most part superficial details of private matters? Why was I so madly bent on this 'method' or truth? Lucien had said to me that I was inviting a kick in the pants and the more I think about it the more true that seems to be.

When I went to work, I wrote a letter to Neal Cassady in California. I am not sure where he lives now, or if he is even in California. I addressed the letter to a friend of his in Frisco to forward. I told him in about 2 or 3 pages what was going on in New York, how I had planned to go to New Orleans, teach in the fall, what I was writing, how Bill Burroughs was arrested, etc. Then I described the household situation. I wrote at great length of the sense of impending danger that I felt and discussed the pros and cons of the possibility of a police visit. I said that everything was ominous and frightful and that perhaps all this anxiety was 'just a mad balloon that I was blowing up' to scare him into worrying for my welfare.

I returned home from work at 9:15 or so on Thursday morning. Vicki and Little Jack were around. Herbert was not at home. Vicki and I had a long conversation, Little Jack had gone out for several hours in the morning and we were alone for the first time, quietly, in all this time.

First, she announced to me that Herbert had finally quit the establishment and gone out on his own. I was quite struck by this new development; it was certainly an occasion as far as I was concerned. Yet it was not unanticipated. I was now beyond a point where I really felt that anything I could do one way or another was important to his welfare. I was also glad to be rid of him. But I wondered what kind of self-tormented feeling of rejection must now be in his heart. That is the root of his trouble. He thrives, a parasite, on being useful and helpful; his heaven is to be needed and depended on. Yet it was a healthy step for him to take, to leave so on the verge of prosperity—his own.

The immediate cause had been a remark of Vicki's. Herbert had been complaining that he did not feel reasonably assured as to his equality in the household and on burglary jobs. Little Jack, who was the dynamic practical force, naturally assumed that he was the head of the family. Vicki, exasperated with Herbert's touchiness, called him "Little Jack's prat-boy."

Now a prat-boy is a jail or slang expression for a subservient youth who runs the leader's errands and carries water for him. Herbert resented this so strongly, since Vicki's remark hit right on the head the sensitive problem of his inadequacy, that he declared his intention of carrying out his threat to go away. Rather than attempt to reason with him or mollify him which he expected her to do, Vicki said nothing. So Herbert left them (I think they had been riding in the car) and did not return overnight. All this Vicki explained to me in the morning.

She was also slightly afraid that I would be annoyed since I had originally assumed responsibility for Huncke's welfare. I was annoyed, too, at her callous treatment of Herbert, but I did not express my annoyance to her. After all, I had failed where Huncke was concerned and I was really sick and tired of him myself. All in all, I was glad to have that chapter closed, as it seemed.

I had a long talk with Vicki about how I felt about Herbert. I had finally come to some conclusions myself. I told her it seemed to me that the basic problem was that Herbert needed attention and love and that all his activity or inactivity was a surreptitious, unconscious effort to win it, one way or another, by making people feel guilty toward him. In Herbert's case, the general impression one got of him was that he had long since given up the attempt to actually make love to people. He had practically no sex life. His face was disfigured by some kind of skin disease. His teeth were mostly out. He needed glasses worse than I and yet had none. He had built a deceptive myth of unreachability or sexual untouchability around himself which everyone, including himself, finally believed. But all he needed and wanted was a mate.

He endeared himself parasitically into a relation of great spiritual intimacy with many people. But what all were blind to was the naked and very human fact of his inability to accomplish a direct natural love.

Vicki was a little shocked, in a way, that I could think in these terms about Huncke. It was a great step for me, even though from the outside it may seem obvious.

I believe that Huncke had a growing realization of all of this, too. That is why he was going to leave the household. It had not occurred to Vicki or to me that the final goal that I was seeking was under my nose in the person of Huncke as a sick and suffering human being. I had, in a sense, avoided all true human knowledge of him. I learned this too late to help him or myself in relation to him.

Probably if I had seen him alone I would have had a final talk with him, renouncing all responsibility and guilt towards him for the frustrating relationship that we had endured and sent him out into the world to try all over.

This is why I say that I am no longer able to be concerned as before with Herbert's spiritual or physical welfare. The plain fact is that I am not his mate and we had in a strange way lived as mates. There was no question at this point of homosexual relations with him. So the abyss which I spoke of before as dooming our relationship appeared to me in reality.

I may add that the analysis of Huncke is nearly applicable with a few terms shifted to myself. It explains to a great extent my own sad waste of time and energy seeking out diverse types of souls—always neglecting and fearing the ultimate value which gives force and strength to my explorations.

Vicki, as I say, was much impressed with what I said, she didn't herself think that realistically. But she had the sense and goodness to understand and in fact feel ashamed of her own off-center, dehumanized attitude towards Herbert.

Vicki and I drew much closer through this conversation. We also realized that we, too, would have to arrive at an understanding. We had avoided each other a great deal on crucial points of mutual understanding and trust.

I think we were both afraid of what we knew about life. I never realized all of this until now, when I am attempting to order all the chaos of my ignorance and recognize what I had been unwilling to recognize before. Time cares for practically everything.

Vicki repeated the admonition that Herbert had given me about police trouble. The night before I had written a two page 'Manifesto' for the household. I burned it before the police arrived and I never showed it to anyone because it was mainly concerned with Huncke. Since he had departed, it had no more weight. In it I had tried to explain to Huncke that, since the Law was now potentially involved, I wanted everything to be kept as clean and clear as possible; i.e. no more drugs around the house.

It was about 10:30 or 11 when Vicki, Little Jack and I sat down to breakfast. I questioned them about their future. They spoke of getting jobs. I said that when the apartment subletting was first discussed, there had been no question of the apartment being made the center for burglary operations. Now that burglaries had been done I wished they would clear all evidences of burglary out of the house.

Little Jack told me and I think truthfully, that he was not a burglar at heart and had not planned to burglarize. The burglaries had been committed (with proper preparation) more or less on the spur of the moment, due to what he called the 'desperacy' of his mood and financial situation. He meant that they were gone through with as a last resort to attempt to clear away immediate financial problems, one of which was a $20 gas bill which he promised to pay for me. He added that no more burglaries were contemplated and I breathed a sigh of relief. Things even looked good at this point and I felt better than I had in some time. Little Jack promised to clear away the radios, clothes, etc. all in the next day. As a matter of fact, he and Vicki were leaving soon to deliver most of the suits out in Long Island.

My next problem was one of sleep. I had to work that night, it was late morning already. I had the problem of my own 'hot' manuscripts on my hands and wanted to dispose of them. I asked Jack which direction he was going and he said out to Long Island. I hesitated to ask him to drive me uptown to 116th St. on the West Side, since he seemed to be in a hurry—he had to get out to his own house first, see his mother and then deliver the suits, etc.

So I asked them if I could come along and would he drive me, on his way back, to Eugene's? I also asked him how long he would be gone and he said only a few hours. I decided to go along. I anticipated coming home by 2 o'clock and going to bed. It was a nice day, I liked the idea of a freshening ride in Long Island. There was an element of relief in the air and atmosphere. I also wanted to see his home and mother. He and Vicki and Herbert had told me a little about his home life. His mother had often sent food to our household—chicken, strange festive Easter pastries known only to Sicilian families, etc. These were the causes of my ride to Long Island.

I picked up my journal and letters and helped him carry his suits downstairs to the car. We rode out to Long Island starting between 11–12, got to his house and stayed awhile. I met his mother and sister, had a Coca-Cola, petted his famous little dog (I had heard much about the friendly dog). Then we set out to deliver the suits.

We were driving down Northern Blvd., about 12:30. I was telling them about a trip to Dakar I took several years ago. Little Jack missed a turn in the road and went back a mile or so to get on another highway. I was talking away, when suddenly a policeman stepped from the side of the road. I did not see him until I saw Little Jack cry out, apparently misunderstanding what the policeman wanted, "Where's the light?" He thought he had missed a red light. The policeman shook his head negatively and I believe motioned for Little Jack to stop.

Little Jack instantaneously backed the car up. Apparently he realized that the situation was critical if he were asked to produce a driver's license. He was on parole and therefore not allowed to drive, also the suits were in the back of the car. He turned the wheel carefully avoiding the policeman, drove out into the middle of the road, turned the corner and sped down Northern Boulevard. It did not occur to me to stop him since he was acting in desperation. I thought, mostly, that he was in trouble, it being his car and goods in it. It did not fully occur to me, until I thought of my own manuscripts, that I was involved in his desperate actions.

Vicki asked him what he was doing and he said that we had to outrun them. I did not see any police car following, though by this time I was actually too frightened to look. We were racing along very fast, and dangerously. I began to see that the great Horror had begun at last. I thought first of the manuscripts and of pitching them out. I think I reached for them but did not [pitch them] for fear that they would be found on the road. Vicki asked where Jack was going and he said we'd have to abandon the car. Vicki objected to abandoning all the loot, but Jack, realizing the seriousness of the situation said, "Fuck the clothes, we have to abandon the whole mess."

Suddenly Little Jack swerved the car to get on a side road. He did not make it—a sharp turn to the left going at a high speed. I felt the car going over on its side and somehow relaxed enough to roll along with it inside the car. My mind was still half tied up with the attempt to hold on to my manuscripts. I felt my glasses being knocked off. When the crash was over I heard Vicki or Jack asking if we were all right and urging me to get up and get out. I got up and fell out of the car and then stooped down looking for my glasses, which I could not find. I found one small journal of 1943–45. It was not very important. I got up out of the car. People were helping me out. I had the small notebook under my arm. I looked around and didn't see Vicki or Jack, and thought that they must have escaped. I refused aid in walking away and made believe that I was confused when people asked me questions. I wandered up the street, crossed an empty lot, walked quickly up a side street and continued walking on. I worried now about the police searching the neighborhood for me and the others. I tried to brush off the dirt around my face. I walked around wondering what to do. I couldn't see. I had only seven cents in my pocket. My lack of money was one of the reasons I had not gone up to Eugene's room by bus or subway. I asked for directions to the city. But I got such strange stares of disbelief from the man I asked that I broke away from him as quickly as possible. He asked me how I had ever gotten so far from the city. I said I walked, it was such a nice day. Walking away, I laughed to myself, I was so crazed and confused; I could not even hold a sane conversation about how to get back to the city without drawing attention to myself.

I decided to walk in the direction of Northern Boulevard and figure out what to do. During this walk, which lasted about an hour, I had a complete, final, and awful sense of what I might call Divine Wrath. It seemed clear, as things flashed through my mind that I was now in a position that I had fantasized and dreamed about and dreamed myself into. I saw all the signs, the veritable portents of the car crash and discovery, drawing one by one to the present moment. I remembered my vacillation and lack of recognition of Huncke's role; my refusal to understand the dangers to myself on that score; I remembered the thousand prophetic twinges of anxiety, muffled visions of what was to come. I remembered Lucien's anger at me and my humiliation on the subject of the manuscripts. I remembered Jack Kerouac's rebuke the night before. I remembered Bill Burroughs' letter, that alone was a total sign of warning. I remembered my own rages and impotence at being in the middle of such a household, my desire to escape to New Orleans. All the secret maneuvers of my mind, all the conversation with others, all in that moment appeared to pertain directly and prophetically to what had happened, even the final irony of desiring to dispose of the journals and being nipped by fate in the act. Finally I saw that what had happened was inexorably the result of what preceded it, that the punishment literally fit the crime and that all was connected by a clear series of events to the final event; each formed a link in a chain, had I chosen to recognize the chain in time and acted to break it, I could have been a free man in the highest and truest way imaginable and this had been my goal from the beginning.

I felt at the time (and still do) that all my problems had been solved; that this catastrophe had given me the key of understanding of my own action. I thought of the nature of tragedy and the tragic hero and saw the parallel chain of events and logical sequence of development of understanding and fate in Lear, Hamlet and Macbeth. I felt most closely akin to vacillating and falsely ambitious Macbeth. In this sense I refer to the accident—seemingly the result of a far-fetched one way street misfortune—as a logical and clear descent of Divine Wrath and at the time I felt thankful and began to pray that I be forgiven for what I then understood as my 'sin.'

I was not much concerned for my own welfare in terms of jail, for at this point I felt that punishment for my passive role in the burglaries was just and good. I am not afraid of jail or even about my future, for my future as a man or artist is clear to me and I am happy with it. I felt (and still feel) liberated to begin on the large structured work which I pined for and was unable to face.

The great fear now descended about Lucien Carr and Bill Burroughs becoming involved in my ignorance. Lucien in particular since he is now becoming so free and creative, since he did his best to warn me and since I feel personally, acutely, directly responsible to him for my own conduct in as far as it concerns him. I am afraid to think of what will happen to Bill Burroughs and Joan Adams if things go wrong now. Vicki, Little Jack and Herbert are no concern of mine, I am relieved to have them out of the way; their troubles are their own now. I am not strong enough to help them and must devote my energy henceforth to my own work. I want no more to do with them, they have their own struggle and they have more to overcome than me, without me adding to their troubles.

What remains to tell is how I returned to the city, was arrested, questioned, jailed and bonded and given a lawyer who wants to know about my soul. I had instructions to call up the Melody family. That was the only thing I could do with my 7¢, so I called their number and left my own coin box number. Vicki called me back a few minutes later and said she had just arrived. I told her I would wait where I was until picked up.

I waited on the corner, turning over my thoughts, smoking cigarettes picked up from the ground, for about two hours. She arrived, driven by a young man named Carl. She had been back to the apartment, warned Huncke, who had reappeared. He had run out of money. Vicki and I drove over to one of the Melody sisters in Long Island where she had taken some of her clothes and some of the loot. Vicki and I took a cab to York Avenue. She had some money, so she gave me $22. She wept in the cab. Most of her anxiety seemed to be about what was going to happen to Little Jack. He had often spoken ominously of the dreadful nature of another arrest. He faces perhaps 20 years, perhaps life, as a three-time loser.

When we went up to the apartment Huncke was waiting. He had not done much to remove stolen property but had mostly stowed it away in drawers and bookcases. He had not even thrown out the two opium hashish pipes. We sat wondering what to do for a short time, preparing to get stuff out, then the police knocked on the door.

Two detectives entered the apartment. First they asked to see my identification and then asked if I lived there. I said yes. They asked if the apartment was mine, I said yes to that, too. They asked who else lived here, I remained silent for a moment, not knowing what to answer. But Herbert spoke up and said that he lived there, too. They asked if I had ever been arrested. No. They began looking around the house, searching, I think, for narcotics. There were none. They spotted the opium pipes on the mantle, looked those over and decided to take them along with us to the station. They asked if I took drugs and I said that I had at one time. They asked how much and when and I explained my drug situation saying that I had used marijuana. I denied having used marijuana for the last four months. They looked over the house, asked me to identify particular women's clothes and trinkets of jewelry and other odds and ends. I said that I didn't know who they belonged to and explained that many people stayed here. They asked me what my own story was, I told them that I worked all night, slept all day, wrote in the evenings and minded my own business. They seemed to assume that I kept a regular opium den or house of pleasure. They asked me about my relations with Vicki and Herbert. I said that I knew Vicki well, that I was not her lover and did not sleep with her. They asked who had been in the apartment. I spoke of Neal Cassady, Luanne, his ex-wife and Al Hinkle.[187] Luanne had left some of her clothes, valises and costume jewelry intending to return to New York in a few months. So I said that I did not know what belonged to Vicki and what to Luanne.

I also mentioned that Jack Kerouac had had a key and that many others were in and out. I was depressed and weary after the excitement and with the heavy weight of what was to come, I spoke softly. They asked me if I had just had a shot, which I had not, and seemed to think that my demeanor (half-sleepy since I had not yet slept after work and it was by now very late) indicated some sort of drugged state.

---

187 Al Hinkle. Friend of Neal Cassady's, who made several of the "On the Road" cross-country trips with him.

We were all taken to the 68th Street precinct. I was taken aside first and questioned. They asked me if I had been out in a car in Long Island; I said yes. They asked me where and I said I didn't know. They asked me who was in the car. I said that I didn't want to speak until I had seen my brother, who was a lawyer. They insisted on my standing up and answering. I gave the same reply and they began slapping me around. They asked what my sexual life was, "Did I like men or women?" I said that I liked mostly men. They told me Vicki had said that she was in the car and asked who Jack de Peretti was, so I assumed they already knew. They asked if I used heroin, I said no. Then they told me that I was lying, for they saw a letter to my psychiatrist, Dr. Cott, explaining my drug situation and asking for medical attention. I told them that I was unwilling to talk at this point because I was refused right of attorney. They said that they would get a hold of Eugene but not until they were good and ready. They said they had already called Dr. Cott and that he had told them that I was 'probably an incurable heroin addict.' He also told them that I was supposed to be in touch with a Dr. Raphael and had never done so. I have not yet called Dr. Cott to find out why he told them such a weird story but I assume that he thought that was the truth. Dr. Cott had kicked me out for refusing to stop use of drugs and at the time I was intimidated into thinking he was right. But this glaring misjudgment of his and his gratuitous speech to the police about it throws a new light on the matter. I had gone to Dr. Woodward rather than Dr. Raphael and so the idea that the police received of my relations with psychotherapy was out of touch with what was actually going on. They asked me if I had ever corresponded with anybody in Elmira (reformatory). I said yes and they told me they knew that I had corresponded with Lucien Carr and had already checked up on his record. (It was at this time about 6 o'clock at night). The letters I had were very few and completely uncompromising, having already been passed by prison authorities years ago, when Lucien was in jail. That was all they asked me about my papers, except to say they had found my address on an envelope of a letter written to me by my father. There was no mention of Bill Burroughs. They asked me again what I knew about burglaries, how many I had taken part in, etc. but I denied all knowledge and participation.

The others were questioned, and then I was taken with two policemen back to the apartment. They began questioning me about my own personal habits, particularly why I had so many people running in and out of my house. I told them that I liked people, the more the merrier, and that I wanted to have them around because I was a writer and they provided me with a great store of atmosphere and subject matter. I did not, as the newspapers say, declare that I was in on this crime wave to get material for my writings.

They took me back to the 86th Street station and we were all taken to the Bayside station-house where questioning was resumed. The police told me that I was in deep, unless I would confess everything, tell a straight story, etc. If not I would not see my lawyer for a long time and be beaten.

Then we were taken to another jailhouse for booking and then to the Queens prison. No further questions of importance were asked. I had a great deal of opportunity to speak to Vicki, Herbert, and Little Jack, on the way. They were greatly apologetic for having plunged me into the mess. They had told the police that I knew nothing of the burglaries or of the fact that goods were stolen and had no drugs with them. Up to this point they have maintained my own innocence.

Their main concern and worry is about disposition of responsibility for the burglaries.

Little Jack has most to lose and I assume that Vicki will be concerned with that. I do not know what Herbert's attitude towards that will be; he sympathizes with Little Jack but doesn't want to assume responsibility for Little Jack's part. Little Jack will probably go or make himself seem like he's gone mad in a few months. His problem (legal) seems to be insurmountable. Also he would like to get Vicki out of it as completely as possible.

I am glad that I have no more knowledge than I do. For myself, I would like (and would feel better) if I could plead guilty and make a full confession of knowledge of the fact that goods were stolen by the three possibly in combination, possibly individually. I do not really know enough specific facts about who is responsible for what crimes to say anything about that. It is really beyond my province.

I forgot one detail of the questioning, which is, that I didn't know Little Jack had been captured until I saw him in the police station out in Queens. He was limping and battered from the wreck and in addition had been beaten by the police. He came into the room where I sat and passed through, escorted by police who were pushing him, woebegone, beat, the world around his ears, walking very painfully.

I heard at the time that he finally confessed and assumed responsibility for all, excluding me from participation or knowledge. Vicki then confessed her share—with certain withholdings, and so Herbert; all denied that I had any part in it. These are the sum of the facts as I know them to date.

[*Ginsberg was released by the police with the condition that he be admitted to a mental hospital for psychiatric treatment. This was something that Ginsberg had wanted for himself for a long time. He hoped that he could solve his personal and emotional problems through a rigorous period of analysis.*]

May 21, 1949.

Saw the movie *Shock Proof* with Cornel Wilde and Patricia Knight. (Vision piled on vision, cast and recast, fused and thawed, image upon image…the horned moon, walking home). It was almost what I could call a pure tragedy but the authors no doubt feared for its public reception and stopped the carnage before the end. If the tragedy had gone on to its logical ending of despair the audience in the theater wouldn't have been able to stand it. So much self-wrought error and terror, with logical punishment was possible to the ancient dramatists, as Aristotle's <u>Purgation</u>. We who have been fed on comic or saved endings have not seen public art show life in its deepest horror and beyond that and its purgation through a revelation of it on the screen, its deepest joy. Would it be possible to present true tragedy today? I must write a tragedy; although not yet having fully suffered through a tragic crisis I am not prepared.…

May 23, 1949.

Several days ago I had a dream that I was enrolled into the madhouse. I was given my bedding and bunk—much like jail or like Sheepshead Bay Maritime Training Center. I remember the colorful feeling of wonder at this new institutional monastery that I had entered. I had a bunk in an enormous ward, surrounded by hundreds of weeping, decaying women and men. I wandered off in search of a toilet and found one finally, as on a ship that one visits and seeks the toilet along the labyrinthine corridors.

[*This paragraph was reworked as the poem, "Dead Man's Institution."*]

The next day my lawyer and doctor consulted and my lawyer hinted that I might be institutionalized. I had a great feeling of relief and joy at the thought of going out and away from the East cities to some psychoanalytic retreat, where I would joy in freedom, then doubts about my sanity and helplessness of my self in this vast illusion I have created. Doctor and lawyer accused me of egocentricity—egotism—thinking that I am mentally ten steps ahead of anybody I talk to. So it is, so I often feel and in the joy of release into official irresponsibility and insanity, despite doubts and fears, I spent the day ten steps of freedom ahead of everybody. I spoke to Eugene for several hours convincing him that he, too, was crazy, because he somehow believed half of what I said, somehow was trapped (by family or fraternal feelings) in the same illusion as myself. Then I spoke of his power-ideals and love difficulties and logically convinced him that he needed psychiatric help; but he really doesn't believe it. That night at [Aunt] Elanor's, I suddenly became angry at Elanor and inwardly angry at my brother, because they patronized, baffled and fogged the natural exuberance and innocent perception of Naomi. However, Naomi too started compulsively, blindly questioning me in repeated monotones, about my travels, which she'd half forgotten, till I became weary of all. I had earlier a sense of their great illusory conspiracy to 'handle' Naomi as a machine, blind, based on habits of thought peculiar to themselves, which was out of their control and that Naomi somehow saw that and I winked at her and tried to communicate my own understanding of her baffling problem in a few terse and fragmentary statements to her; but with not too much response. I feel that I could start a conspiracy of the insane with her, underground—but she goes blank and mechanical too often.

Arguments with Louis after he reopened the subject of my dishonesty to him, but was not human enough to become lost and so refused to speak to him brokenly and humbly as I should—refused to understand his suffering and knowledge. This is a gate of wrath[188] that darkens me.

Jack called a week ago—goodbye, to Denver. Adieu, Jean Louis. Now Paterson.

Headline <u>Daily News</u>

"Dream Driven Boy, 16,
Kills girl, wounds him."
"...he awoke dazed from a bad dream"
I had a dream while I was asleep."

I dreamed a poem which had a refrain like this or similar:
"a boogieman, a bugger, or a boy, / a cod piece, a cadaver, or a cog."
A thought (a true thought): The parallel between introspection and house-keeping—sweeping up dirty corners, dusting, rearranging the furniture. I'd like to move. Now I sit self-conscious, ruefully ruminating about my sense of

---

188 *The Gates of Wrath* was to become the title of Ginsberg's book of 1948–1952 rhymed poetry. He took the phrase "Gates of Wrath" from Blake.

the reality of the living room I sit in. Thought is like sweeping up the odds and ends of an empty room, peaceful, contemplative.

I dreamed of a madhouse and now tomorrow I am going to New York to a mental hospital.[189] I have been wrathful all my life, angry against my father and all others. My wrath must end. All my images now are of heaven. I dream of incomprehensible love and belief. I think always that I am about to put an end to my life, only now there is no worry as to how I will do it, as last summer after the vision.[190] In the hospital I hope to be cured. My images tell me that hours of truth are at hand. I am not going to die, I am going to live anew. My thought has been peaceful all week. I have been reading *The Possessed* [by Dostoyevsky]. My devils are going to be cast out.

If you do not believe other people, their work, their reality, the reality of things, if you mock or deprecate or fight them, you will never understand them. If you doubt their existence you doubt your own—all—you doubt God. Belief in their truth must come; only then can you see things for what they are, see also good and bad. But then you are not maliciously evaluating, you are seeking and living in the good, one turning the evil away from yourself; only the evil is turned away—it does not exist for the future. I am becoming incomprehensible and false to myself now and I will stop. Once I didn't know when to stop.

Tonight all is well.... What a terrible future. I am 23, the year of the iron birthday, the gate of darkness. I am ill. I have become spiritually or practically impotent in my madness this last month. I suddenly realized that my head is severed from my body; I realized it a few nights ago, by myself, lying sleepless on the couch.[191]

Finish...my father is coming in.

June 6, 1949.
Back home. Hitch in madhouse venture.[192]

Dostoyevsky is just like Verne Pomeroy[193]—his gambling. Neal is continually gambling with people's resources, his own, Dostoyevsky grew out of it, somehow. Is it a secret, to give up gambling? No—just what everybody knows and

189 Ginsberg was treated in the New York State Psychiatric Institute of Columbia Presbyterian Hospital at 722 W. 168th Street in New York from June 1949 through February 1950.

190 The visions of William Blake as mentioned earlier.

191 This paragraph was the basis for the poem "Tonite All Is Well." See *Collected Poems*, p. 32.

192 Ginsberg had to return home for several weeks until the proper paperwork for his admission to the hospital could be completed.

193 Verne Pomeroy is a pseudonym for Cassady, but Ginsberg sometimes uses both names in the same entry, as he does here.

probably common sense says anyway. His wife's account—I think he is a coward. His "How lonely she must be while I betray her." The monster. Insufferable.

A dream:

After reading a critique on Blake's dream-sculptured world. "God loves queers, but it takes a long time." Also a long dream of holding hands with a boy, making secret physical signs of understanding to each other, clear and spontaneous and childlike. Dream goes on gathering a momentum of love. I wind up getting fucked. Thought of writing a dream-story of it—the increasing weight of happy erotic communication. Ending in uninhibited wild orgy. Why isn't life so? I thought of the effect Pomeroy has on Levinsky,[194] waking him up in the flesh every year after long seasons of abstinence.

Hardy: "Since life has bared its bones to me."

The death's head of realism and superhuman iron mask that gapes out in *The Possessed*, sometimes. Dostoyevsky. My original vision of Dostoyevsky before I read him as the dark, wild, aged, mansion-haunted, spectral Russian. Hal Chase and Kerouac call him Dusty, but he is Dostoyevsky. What premonitions I had as a child.[195] Lately I never give Dostoyevsky credit for more than what Jack calls 'Divine gossip.'

Trembling of the veil today—out of window the trees seemed like live organisms on the moon. I got the idea originally from speculation on the look of the boughs—extending upward, covered at the north end with leaves like a green-hairy protuberance with a scarlet and pink-shoot tip of budding leaves, waving delicately in the sunlight, being blown by the winds—all the arms of the trees bending and straining downward at once when the wind pushed them.[196]

I remember from my earlier visions that trees are live animals, but do not often think so. I know that everything is alive—but the precise vibrant quality of aliveness of life continually escapes my definition and understanding except for moments that are so far apart and so buried in the sands of thought that they are treasures. I come upon them only accidentally when I wander on the shore forgetful of my imagined purposes there.[197]

---

194 Levinsky is a pseudonym for Ginsberg.

195 This paragraph was the basis for the poem "Fyodor." See *Collected Poems*, p. 32.

196 This paragraph was the basis for the poem "The Trembling of the Veil." See *Collected Poems*, p. 14.

197 This paragraph was the basis for the poem "Eternity." See Appendix p. 487.

I was struck again today by the continuity of metaphysical illusion that occurs to me and the depth of its deceptiveness, the length of its history. Am I face to face with the eternal, or am I the victim of fear and lethargy and all too human pride? Vanity? Am I becoming human or superhuman? The analysts say human. The poets say superhuman. What terms are these to get worried about?

Even here at home I am like a man in the crazy house at the carnival.

[Letter] Dear X:

I have lost my reason…years ago. Do you still have your reason? I am sure I had a reason once and that there is a reason of some kind but once again I repeat, my own reason I do not know, have lost—have recently had glimmerings of it. Have I announced it? Papa is O.K. Poor Papa. "How much I love him." What a shit I am. I have never given him a minute's rest, or myself either. Got drunk tonite and found the liquor kick similar to marijuana—same corridors, same drive to metaphysics and concretion.

Dizzy Gillespie (with Dink Washington and the Ravens) are coming to Bop City. So announced Symphony Sid[198] tonite. Shall I make some profound superintellectual comment on that, too?

O shit, I am sick of myself and I want a New Deal, I—ugh! Yes.

"Al, I would suggest you go to bed."

"I am. But I don't so much want to and would rather sit here scrawling, listening to *Manteca* by Dizzy Gillespie."

June 14, 1949.

At the edge of vision: God is all things—the color of God is all colors. Say not, "Love me, Lord," but "I love you, Lord." Recognize that you do love. That is on the road. This leads to giving love, and the fear of giving, which turned inward becomes intellect: "Neither lose the imagination / Nor the mile of the mind / consuming its rag and bone / can make truth known." God is peaceful. Seek peace, not images of action or mind or accomplishment—these are substitutes, images of something higher which they evade. Madness is irrelevance. Weitzner once said, "Great men know."

198 Symphony Sid Torin (1909–1984). Tremendously popular radio personality with a weekly jazz program on WJZ.

All the doctors think I'm crazy,
Truth is really that I'm lazy;
I had visions to beguile 'em
Till they put me in asylum.

All my oops are oopsing
All my oops are doopsing.[199]

A dream: Marlene Dietrich singing a lament for mechanical love. Love. She is leaning against a tree on a plateau by the seashore. Her face is white powdered, immobile, like a robot. Jutting out of one of her temples, by an eye, is a little white key, like with Frankenstein. She looks like a toy Dutch doll, life-sized, as in a nightmare. (Her brow and head is covered with a hat shaped in the abstract form of bobbed hair, made of white steel). Her eyes have dull blue pupils surrounded by tile white whites. She closes her eyes, and the key turns itself, and opens her eyes and they are blank like a statue's.

Dream: Sitting in H.S. seat shared with Jethro Robinson.[200] We are amicable at first, but tension builds up in me till he says he can't sit with me anymore. I go to the desk to collect $5 from the teacher, which was what we were in class for in the first place—Jethro was not around for his. I wanted to do something about that, but was glad to see he'd missed out so I didn't.

Does Trilling see that the trouble with all of his characters is that they don't know what love (divine or human) is? Even as "I love the Lord." Why do they continue to pursue the falsities of barren social and political forms, and try continually to invigorate or recombine and invent new forms, when it is feeling that they lack? Seldom does the hero realize that he can break through to his antagonist (Maxim) by breaking down his own pride; if nothing else, embarrass Maxim, make him blush.

My novel, like Raw Youth, begins with an idea—actions proceeding from that—write book directly about idea—enough action takes place—if worst comes to worst, hero is a madman, book about a madman and his idea.

---

199   This is a fragment of what would become "Pull My Daisy." See *Collected Poems*, pp. 24–25.

200   Jethro Robinson. Student friend of Ginsberg, who wrote and published his own book of sonnets.

June 23, 1949.

A poem—on America, as in Versilov's speech to his son—after Acis and Galatea—the images of the America, as the Russia, of the proletariat, the alley, the dye works, the mills, the smoke, the melancholy of the bars, the sadness of the long highways, all the pictures that we carry in our minds of the "dull canal," the negroes climbing around the rusted iron by the Passaic River, the bathing pool hidden in a recess between river and factory near the falls. The images of the thirties, of depression and class consciousness, separated from their political narrowness, raised, and rarified by tragedy and the appearance of God.[201]

I interrupt Van Doren in the middle of some speech about the good storyteller being the great liar and ask him, "Why aren't you a saint?" If the essence of life were, as Van Doren says, immaterial...but it is not, for God is substance.

It—Mary Denison[202] and I used to talk about 'it,' referring to some mutual but vague idea which we sense rather than thought or knew. How strange for me to have written a letter to a doctor last year saying right off that "it has happened." It has happened. How can an 'it' happen? But that's just the thing about 'its,' they happen, an 'it' happens.

> It happened on a gloomy day...
> When sun was dark and cloud was gray,
> I don't remember what it was
> And why it seemed as clear as glass.
> But anyway it happened.
> To be called "The Time I Had My Epileptic Fit."

Naomi: "The clock is not like that cat by the fire; it moves and moves and moves."

Naomi describing what happens to us after we die—we become a bloom, an ant, a singing bird, a cockroach, a vegetable maybe, a carrot or a cabbage or an onion; a long list, reminding me of Mary Denison's long list or horrors he was inspired to recite—both he and Naomi realized they were creating and strung out the list and enjoyed the act—but it did not disturb their inspiration.

Tonight I almost asked my father to forgive me for what I had done against him but I was too proud to open up; but I will soon.

---

201 This paragraph was the basis for the poem "A Poem on America." See Appendix p. 488.
202 Mary Denison. Pseudonym Ginsberg used for William Burroughs, but usually just Denison.

Cézanne's Port—foreground is time and life, swept in a race toward the left hand side of the picture, where shore meets shore—but that meeting place is not represented. It occurs not in the dream; only the other side is heaven and eternity with a bleak white haze about the far mountains—with L'Estaque Bay in a V between.[203]

June 29, 1949.
[*This letter was written by Ginsberg's father once Ginsberg was sent to the psychiatric hospital for treatment. It gives some background into the anguish that the past few years had caused the family.*]

Dear Dr. Lionel Trilling:

This letter is to thank you very much for your generous aid to both my son, Allen and me in our predicament.

As you no doubt know, Allen's mother has had a long series of nervous breakdowns; and she has been in and out of sanitariums for the last twenty-five years. I tried to give Allen what compensations I could; however, I suppose his wounded childhood had secreted some imbalance; or some trauma had precipitated some disorder deep in his psyche. Bad companions in the last few years had aggravated his attitudes; though it may be that his choice of some bad companions might be the results rather than causes.

At any rate, his arrest seems to have shocked him back to sobriety. My lawyer has had Allen cleared of the legalities in the matter; and today Allen entered the N.Y. Psychiatric Clinic. I do hope he will be salvaged for a brighter future, for I think Allen has fine talents.

Ever since Allen entered college, your name has been a household word with us. He has read, and we have discussed, your articles (in *The Partisan Review, Kenyon Review*, etc). Allen looks up to you with something of veneration.

Permit me to extend to you my deep gratitude for your generosity and your invaluable aid to both Allen and me in our trouble.

      Sincerely yours,
      Louis Ginsberg

June 29, 1949.
In the clinic—this is a real madhouse—what a weird feeling—at first I saw the patient's eccentricities in relief, clearly, but soon these disappeared in a sense;

---

203 This paragraph was the basis for the poem "Cézanne's Ports." See *Collected Poems*, p. 53.

and there appeared to be at first a secret conspiracy of the great dichotomy—
the lunatic vs. society. Solomon,[204] a twenty-one year old Jew, an intellectual—
said that they, the doctors, make no attempt (even encourage in sublimate
activities) the abstract madness; as long as behavior is socially acceptable. It is
only when abstract systems are carried out (particularly Solomon's absurd
sense of them) in flesh does society object: i.e., yesterday he gave his doctor a
handful of marbles in the hope that he would swallow them and kill himself.

July 3, 1949.
[Ginsberg wrote the following note to Trilling.]

I have been in the hospital since the 29 June. Psychotherapy daily, no psycho-
analysis; but I expect this to be sufficient and helpful, or hope. I have no
other way of thanking you for your help in these hectic days than this post-
card, and I hope you will accept it as a token of my gratitude. I like it here.
I finished cleaning up and selecting forty poems for a book just before I came
in. Have a happy summer.

July 4, 1949.
As I look out the Washington Bridge stands as if eternally, a monument to the
vast illusions of time, floating across the river, looking so fragile. Why is the
bridge always a challenge to my own sense of reality? It stands as a symbol of
all that is permanent and real, though man-made and a vast machine, but so
huge and airy that it seems to be a part of nature; as if the shiny city itself,
all its buildings and all its ignorance, were a part of nature (no more to be
resented or condemned or lectured at or disapproved of or even thought
about in the way I have been thinking of things).

My mind is dulled, with the split between fear and allegiance to human
effort, the accumulated facts of time, society, the hospital, these doctors, and
my own willful dark forebodings of an eternity that surpasses in fact and truth
all the built mazes of the world.

I am torn between putting aside my loyalty and love directed to the past
(the underworld, the mythical symbols of tragedy, suffering and solitary
grandeur) and the prosaic community of feeling which I might enter by affirm-

---

204   Carl Solomon (1928–1993). Fellow patient in the psychiatric hospital. Solomon became a
close friend to Ginsberg and was the person to whom "Howl" was addressed. He also became a
writer and published a collection of poems, Mishaps, Perhaps, in 1966.

Carl Solomon

ing my own allegiance to those bourgeois standards which I had rejected. Yet what do I know of the reality of all these bridges and ideas which make up the visible and invisible world? And why am I in the madhouse? How easy it is to reverse these values entirely and consider myself the patient and forbearing wiseman in a nation of madhouses. Neither of these are true, I tire of this thought.

July 6, 1949.
Carl Solomon's account of a meeting with Antonin Artaud[205] in Paris—the electrifying communication of nightmare—knowledge in the middle of the night in front of a shuttered store.

> What was it I saw
> That turned my mind to bleakness
> And my heart to stone

Death is not unknown; we know as much of death as we will ever know, in this life or after death. All know death because all babies experienced the state of death before their birth. Life seems a passage between two doors to the darkness. Both darknesses are the same and truly eternal. It is amazing to think that the thoughts and personality of a man is perpetuated beyond his time, through all time.

> Life has a double darkness.
> Perhaps darkness a double light?
> The single darkness in a circle?

July 13, 1949.
[Excerpts from a letter Ginsberg wrote to Kerouac.]

There is a boy here named Karl [sic: Carl] Solomon who is the most interesting of all—I spend many hours conversing with him. The first day (in the chairs) I gave way to the temptation of telling him about my mystical experiences—it is very embarrassing, in a madhouse, to do this. He accepted me as if I were another nutty ignu, saying at the same time with a tone of conspiratorial guile, "O well, you're new here." He is also responsible for the

205 Antonin Artaud (1896–1948). French surrealist writer and founder of the theater of cruelty.

line: "There are no intellectuals in madhouses." He is a big queer from Greenwich Village, formerly from Brooklyn—a "swish" (he used to be he says) who is the real Levinsky—but big and fat, and interested in surrealistic literature.

He went to CCNY and NYU, but never graduated, knew all the Village hipsters, and a whole gang of Trotskyite intellectuals (this generation's Mayer Shapiro), and he is familiar with a great range of avant-garde styles—also a true Rimbaud type, from his teens. Not creative, he doesn't write, and doesn't know much about literature really, except what he reads in little magazines (he had *Tyger's Eye*, *Partisan* and *Kenyon*) but he knows everything about that. Jumped ship and spent months wandering through Paris—finally at the age of consent he decided to commit suicide (on his 21st birthday) and committed himself to this place (entering a madhouse is the same thing as suicide he says—madhouse humor)—presented himself practically at the front door demanding a lobotomy. He apparently was full of great mad gestures when he first came in (with a copy of *Nightwood*) threatening to smear the walls with excrement if he didn't get a seclusion (private) room so that he could finish his book in peace.

I can go out weekends—running around too loose is discouraged, though. Someone has to sign me out and take responsibility for me, and sign me back in—relative, sometimes a friend. When you get back, we'll go away on a weekend maybe—to Cape Cod—where Holmes, Ansen, Cannastra, Stringham and many others are. I'll only be able to see you on weekends for the time, but if I get better, I may have more privileges.

October 8, 1949.
I am no longer afraid of the phantom who will appear at his own desire.

October 11, 1949.
Woke after sleeping from 7 P.M. to 5 A.M. not having written anything on novel for a week. Dreamed I was wandering around—at Reichian doctor's awhile—then at regular analyst—just like Dr. Horovitz—Louis comes in—talks to him about me, just as he does to other doctor and teachers—starts picking at Horovitz's teeth familiarly.

October 24, 1949.
The whole blear world of smoke and twisted steel around my head in a railroad car and my mind wandering past the rust into futurity. I saw the sun go

down as if in a carnal and primeval world, leaving darkness to cover my railroad train because the other side of the world was waiting for the dawn.[206]

Later I saw a rainbow which is a rare form of God. I want to live in a rainbow, in will and in womb.

October 27, 1949.

> Lightning born upon the cloud.
> Sometimes I lay down my wrath—
> Sometimes I look up in light
> To see the wearie sunne ol west
> Sometimes I see the moon at night
> far in rest
> Hidden in her clouds
> Where the rain has poured like wine.
>   [unfinished]

November 15, 1949.

Dream about a month ago: In courtyard between two buildings (male and female patients)—Ilo Orleans down there—bartender roughing him up—"I'm his doctor," then, "I'm his patient," I say, warning them he's O.K. Also began with big business of getting free food from open iceboxes under Miss Mason's eyes—list on blackboard—check your clothes—I do not check mine not being one of those type patients with insulin or electric shock.

November 15, 1949.

This is the one and only firmament; therefore it is the absolute world; there is no other world. The circle is complete; I am living in eternity. The ways of this world are the ways of Heaven. The work of this world is the work of Heaven. The love of this world is the love of Heaven.[207]

This is to say that I know less of theory and idea of eternity than ever, to the point of the extinction of the idea of God and the unfolding revelation of the body of the Lord. My thought has substantiated itself only through the destruction of thoughts of itself.

---

206 This paragraph was the basis for the poem "Sunset." See *Collected Poems*, p. 37.
207 This paragraph was the basis for the poem "Metaphysics." See *Collected Poems*, p. 33.

Conversation—
    Allen: What's the Hex?
    Jack: Who's the Hoax?
    Allen: Where's the Hawks?
    Neal: How's the Hicks?

Prose sentence:

He wandered moodily along the hedged rural avenues of the outer night shadowed areas of Silk City [Paterson] passing one by one the familiar mansions of the mysterious order of the Masons, the secret Romanesque pile of the church, and among these many hoarily conceived relics of time, the gloomy funeral home with its shaded and curtained inner sanctum wherein no man knew what mortal fleshy rituals were enacted over the surrendered bodies of the dead, beyond the shuddering mills where the patient silken labors of the ancient worm were manufactured further into the brocaded winding sheets to cover the dead and living, beyond the last block of River Avenue where the petalled lamplit radiance of the mist wove blooms the Great Falls, and he did enter into the very hood of its whiteness, and stand meditating hidden like an ancestral traveler of the night come at last upon the end of his pilgrimage unto a palmy oasis of light, upon the barren firmamental plain of his eternity. [208]

December 1, 1949.
Dreams—afternoon: Often our best dreams come in afternoon naps.

I dreamed I was dreaming again and went down the room here at the hospital looking for the Shroudy Stranger.[209] I finally met him face to face—though I didn't recognize him—perhaps Edward G. Robinson or somebody of that build—like the frog man at the movies—with a pissed voice saying, "I'll bet you didn't think it was me after all." Depth of dream and extensiveness of therapy made me think it was all a farce.

Then went back to sleep after supper and dreamed again. I was lying in bed and had a long sharp hot come in my pants while asleep, trying to hold it in (so nobody would see) but it came out despite my clear effort of mind. I thought it was like homosexuality—which I can't simply give up by holding my cock tight so that I don't come.

---

208 This paragraph was the basis for the poem "The Shrouded Stranger." See *Collected Poems*, pp. 47–48.

209 The Shroudy Stranger. This was a repeating apparition in the work of Ginsberg at this time. Similar to Kerouac's "Dr. Sax," the Shroudy Stranger was a boogeyman.

Then wandering around Chestnut Lodge or some summer camp looking for a bath and found shower finally—like at huts at Dakar—someone came to take a shower with me, but I didn't care if anyone noticed my jellied come anymore—whole party was over, helping each other take showers, so I was in with others—(but they perhaps had women?)—the water stopped so I went around the partition to find the water handle and found well dressed young ladies and young men too, standing back there waiting to give us all a shower—helped them set up machinery—get flush working.

Dream—on railroad tracks—I become Shroudy Stranger of the Night sleeping under blanket of cinders—"who'll come lay down in the dark with me?"

Lines to Neal on the presentation of a birthday tie of Persian design: "Young Cassady has come out of the West / to shelter nations on his breast; / Let this Eastern knot compare / With all the world that rested there."

Dream of Lucien Carr—Familiar presence of body—urine, sweat, sperm, feces, skin, saliva all one odor and natal taste—a ball of flesh the presence.[210]

Future Verse: Try poems in free verse with echo rhymes rather than regular; with sentence structure and thought determining stanza, each stanza a statement, each line in place in reference to the others, Pound's paragraph stanzas.

1950

M. Rukeyser[211] suggest eye shifting of Whitman to be made into visual poem—montage.

Write poem on <u>Imagination of light reannounced</u>. End with death is a surprise, i.e. we do not know or choose the end who knows, so months from now I may be sitting by a window and see the chains of light beneath the ground moving toward the sun.

March 1950.
Project—The Shroudy Stranger of the Night

Write a long poem about a man whose pride is swallowed by oblivion.
Impulses reverse of normalcy—mine the dregs.

---

210 This paragraph was the basis for the poem "The Night-Apple." See *Collected Poems,* p. 52.
211 Muriel Rukeyser (1913–1980). Poet and political activist.

Write secret fantasy. Each fantasy a canto.
<u>The Fantasy of the Shroudy Stranger of the Night</u>—title

"In this mode perfection is basic."—W. C. Williams

> Who is? the shroudy stranger of the night
> Whose brow all moldering green—
> Whose red eye in the dimming light

Possible Scenes For The Stranger
A. Lincoln theme.

Stranger in Lincoln's shrouding cloak and a battered long black hat walking in dark alleys of Washington: as angel of responsibility, angel of fate to soldier whom he meets sleeping on duty—stranger meeting a policeman perhaps; or drunken sailor in subway, to whom he offers a drink of bay rum.

And *sic semper tyrannis?* on some occasion when he is insulted

> The meek the white the gentle
> me handle touch and spare not

by another bum under the railroad bridge or in the alley.

That long lean ghost crazed yokel scarecrow lurching around dark country roads in Illinois, weeping looking at the pigs, because his Todd, the only one who ever loved him, died just when they were going to get married.

Stranger dreams of making speeches in small town in upper N. Y. state like one I passed hitching to Buffalo—held up in his wanderings by a political or circus parade, on July 4th. Apocalyptic debates with invisible angel opponent, with Satan (*Devil and Daniel Webster*). Or better like in *Scarlet Letter*, public enunciation of his shame.

In fact stranger's pilgrimage to the city, to Times Square, is pilgrimage to make revelation speech on Square, debating to self whether he announces god or gives speech moaning his human wreckage and madness before busy world.

City episode, N.Y., before death in alley (?) will culminate in total comedown speech, him kneeling and screaming in the gutter by cigar store N.W. corner 42nd, and Broadway—looking up at people on sidewalk as if they were flowing on another river (he's in the gutter) trying to stop the river;

His metaphysical strategy being that if he makes total confession (shows his asshole to the world) in deepest incre-extra mental execrations of self he will stop time, and life: every eye shall see television cameras will be installed

he will be crucified   (work in here allusions of his blood will run on
            the streets).

readings of Revelations, and all crucifix possibilities.

As for approach to chapel perilous (how identified with Times Square) the logical associations of bestial bat fears and Frankensteinish Mr. Hydish inner transfiguration begins: Antonian Temptations (read). So that when he does finally drop on his knees—he is the incarnation of freakish and repulsive supernaturally shocking strangerishness, the monster. At the same time, subjectively the desire for a world of god-significance and the world of human appearance will be focused together in the extremity of his mortal beatness, he will see where am I in wildness?

Don't buy my wares, don't buy my wares

If I have included all the horrors of all in America of all types pencil sellers and shoestring salesmen, monsters and drunk slavers, I will have perhaps not yet totaled up the depth of horror given to one old lady sleeping on the corner over her gum.

May 2, 1950.
Great gods of fire; tin cans shining in the sun, tin cans rusting—Grant's cafeteria in Newark—seems my imagination is dead these days. Problem—why have I got hung up like so many others on literary sterility—I always thought it was an effete problem—is it not?—for men without sap or light or jewels of love as I...I have no jewel of love, that's why.

The attempt to keep going month after month continuing to shift a set of abstractions about literarily defined problems—languages of dreams and hallucinations—rather than things—compulsive thoughts that I turn from when I really think as others think—attempt to sustain structure which threatens itself with extinction hourly and collapses daily.

Perhaps I will move out of this dead phase into something with ribs of iron like a ship or a factory—or perhaps I will have to wait till the abstract ideas once more become the Word made flesh or perhaps they will turn out to be simultaneous and/or identical.

Lu: "The trouble with you is that you're smart but not smart enough" to a smart-aleck in bar that night last month where we met to drink.

I think less of God and more of duties in time as labor newspaperman and duties in time as a writer of a poem and a scholar of that poem—want to read history of a meter, epic poems of a kind—but no time and also no patience— am I lazy? What will happen, deep life?

I believe I am mitty and the outside world loves me more than I it, and the expression of this is disdain and intolerance on a metaphysical and political level and on emotional coldness to women and things. I believe this as much if not more than I believe that I am shut off from God and that God exists.

I do not know if God exists, I do not think that he does and I am less afraid to say so (afraid of Divine Wrath) but now old elemental philosophical enigmas such as First Cause enter in—which problems, I suppose, are irrelevant to true rational and scientific thought which is after all, in its upper reaches, apparently, inclusive of such problems on its own level.

Jack doesn't believe in Einstein—thinks it's all irrelevant to the inwardness of great mood knowledge—I have no inward mood knowledge and no knowledge of Einstein.

How many times I have wished for death in the past months and then later desire to grip a living reality. How often too, I have gathered a dread rage about metaphysics and deity.

Lines like, "what shall we do with poor fools like me, crawling in between heaven and earth,"—in Hamlet there is a ghost, so that does not indicate that Hamlet is crawling toward Heaven.

> I hate Heaven
> I lack Hell,
> Pull my daisy
> Ring my bell.

Sick and tired of listening to Jack and Neal yak at me about Spirit when I feel they are up in the clouds. I learn to believe that everyone's universe is different and not to be judged. Judge your own universe only.

I don't write in you, book, because I feel it is silly wasted effort to keep on putting down all these irrelevant meaningless changes of mind toward—what— nothing that will make anything of what has gone before, but only make it pointless—without even the courage of convictions—lacking even drama of tension—only dullness. I am a dull boy. How time flies. How interesting I am. Yes, that's so.

In years, I have written how many poems—2-3-4-perhaps? What a record for me who wanted to be a great influential poet—I haven't even got a platform; no sense of dignity or hope of anything, not even despair—so that this writing should by all standards be unimportant to anyone to follow or to bemuse. A reader wants rightly to be entertained. Here last I am thinking through Van Doren. I lack intensity these days in my phrase thoughts, I believe I am nutty on the outside only.

[During the summer of 1950, Ginsberg saw a good deal of Helen Parker, an older woman with a child of her own, who Ginsberg had been corresponding with since the two had met on New Year's Eve. He visited her at her summer home in Provincetown, Massachusetts, and it was there that he lost his virginity with a woman.]

July 8, 1950.
[Excerpts from a letter Ginsberg wrote to Kerouac.]

If you are in any ennui or doldrums, lift up your heart, there Is something new under the sun. I have started into a new season, choosing women as my theme. I love Helen Parker, and she loves me, as far as the feeble efforts to understanding of three days spent with her in Provincetown can discover. Many of my fears and imaginations and dun rags fell from me after the first night I slept with her, when we understood that we wanted each other and began a love affair, with all the trimmings of Eros and memory and nearly impossible transportation problems.

She is very great, every way—at last, a beautiful, intelligent woman who has been around and bears the scars of every type of knowledge and yet struggles with the serpent knowing full well the loneliness of being left with the apple of knowledge and the snake only. We talk and talk, I entertain her in grand manner with my best groomed Hungarian manner, and I play Levinsky-on-the-trolley car, or mad hipster with cosmic vibrations, and then, O wonder, I am like myself, and we talk on seriously and intimately without irony about all sorts of subjects, from the most obscure metaphysical through a gamut to the natural self; then we screw, and I am all man and full of love, and then we smoke and talk some more, and sleep, and get up and eat etc.

The first days after I lost my cherry—does everybody feel like that? I wandered around in the most benign and courteous stupor of delight at the perfection of nature; I felt the ease and relief of knowledge that all the maddening walls of Heaven were finally down, that all my olden waking corridors were traveled out of, that all my queerness was a camp, unnecessary, morbid, so lacking in completion and sharing of love as to be almost as bad as impotence and celibacy, which it practically was, anyway. And the fantasies I began having about all sorts of girls, for the first time freely and with the knowledge that they were satisfiable.

July 10, 1950.
[*Excerpts from a letter Ginsberg wrote to John and Mary Snow.*]

That was the first I ever saw of Provincetown, and I ran into Chris and Cannastra. I had lunch with Cannastra's parents and talked happily (as I did with everyone I could lay my hands on) with Bill about many matters. He was pretty sober. I haven't known him well, and this was the fist time I ever felt him not-drunkenly affectionate. I have a big plan to tie him up with my unsuccessful lawyer brother in a campaign for salvation which is so blatantly bourgeois that I'm sure Bill would never recover if he tried it. My brother is the only one I know whose bewildered hold-the-finger-in-the-dyke social-commercial personality would provide problems too great for Cannastra to intrude with his own. In fact, I appealed to Cannastra to save my brother, who has no outstanding psychic difficulties, but all sorts of social ones. Strangely, though C. was apathetic, or perhaps, dazed by his own sobriety, he thought twice and said maybe.

August 29, 1950.
The usual psychosexual fantasies are given up and replaced by inductive rationalizations with the result that the process of break down of emotion is incomplete and the repetitive process continues. Without control of the concrete there will be no progress toward any process but that of incompletion.

September, 1950.
Is there no way for me to assert myself without coming into mortal conflict with the world?

September, 1950.

(Notebook for the poem "Shroudy Stranger of the Night")

Opening the Window

Begin in veils and supernatural mystery opening the window in a window as in dream and slowly reveal Shroudy Stranger as a human without completion—unable to communicate or love, who does not know himself as a man like others and imagines that he is a satanic or divine incarnation and is waiting for another world outside of human reality to reveal itself to him—Blake's Little Girl Lost. "He had but broken knew for hire. / And horrible splendor of desire;" as the poem proceeds the Shroudy Stranger becomes more and more human and tragic as in my vision in the movies of Dr. Jekyll and Mr. Hyde until his face is revealed in the end of the poem when he is "woven in the darkened loom," as an old beat out decayed Bum of America.

Dead Eyes See: The old bum must sing of his forgiveness like the song at the end of "The Bridge" "Thou answerer of all…Thy pardon for the History."

The Bowery bum's body is to be found by a child who sees it as a frightening spectre of death and inherits his shrouds.

Or who sees the corpse as that of an old man, sees sadly with pity?

or who sees it without feeling?

work out this problem.

The Child: angelic innocence?

human confusion and trembling?

The child notices it as part of his play in an alley and makes it part of his own fantasy and goes away without reporting it, forgetting?

Make the child realistic or lamblike?

Does the child kick the dead man's face?

Actually the child stumbles on him in the alley, shudders frightened and runs away, conscience stricken.

Illustrations—perhaps fate, crucifixions, sunset

Railroad poem? Dream poem?

A poem—like "Ode to Judgment" and "Epilogue"?

Confusion of transhumanization in stranger?

Scenes—

> on the railroad bridge
> under the river bridge
> Cinderella spoke with mice while the rest of the world did not—or

the alliances with nature in <u>Midsummer Night's Dream</u>. Should the Shroudy

Stranger be alone or have a secret organization? At least the poem should have a secret organization.

The stranger's address to the Nightingale—under the bridge—

"Flow round me, river, my rest is brief."

The stranger is man in search of God and man.

Restore a plot to long poetry. Stevens, Crane, Pound, Williams, Eliot, St. Perse, etc. have no human plot. Perhaps this should be a masque or a play.

Visions of the Brooder; Woes of Shroudy Stranger, Wanderings of Stranger, Visions of Shroudy Stranger, Tragedy of Shroudy Stranger.

How to link with *Doctor Faustus*?

October, 1950.

I realized that all along when I was fighting off recognition of the reality of the world of appearances that my poetry was an escape from it. I shall try to set down in these notes (for a poem perhaps) the situation as it stands, admitting, for once, that I am weak and not strong. For all that I have mythologized myself (both poetically and theologically) and elevated my weakness to dignity as perception of absolute divine world and contempt or lamblike weakness in real world others live in, now that the transfiguration to acceptance has taken place, and become real, I am no different from other men whose sufferings were like mine, which they understood without my confusion; and they accept the mortal lot without so much of the painful selfhood preservation that I allow myself. Yet I despised their intellectual crucifixion as less ideal than my own. But they were willing to die to gain the world; and I, not allowing the crucifixion to take place in the outer limits of my imagination, am less a man-God than they. And now for them the world is solid and endless, except for death, which they understand as the total apocalypse and end of the world for each of them; while I cling still in various ways to figments of immortality, solitude, isolation, onanism, shady thought, spite and shallowness against truly innocent fellow creatures.

(My doctor now calls me psychopathic and bids me choose between ego and world).

And what invasion of work, of duty, of terror, of reality of death, and suffering, am I avoiding? And what pleasure of having arrived at the destination of all my thoughts of past, the rock of reality.

Now it seems a bitter ending to all this romance, which was not a romance, but a real contest against the inexorable finality of life—a world of dreams with no significance, no passion, against all human passion and significance.

"But the world is not so solid that it cannot be dissolved in death."—me...
So I am no saint.

I know that escape from time is into nothing; that time lessness is not a desirable state, but no state at all.

Modern Poetry by A.G.

I am an eagle and am a worm
I want to be the immortal bop poet.

October 11, 1950[212].
I was sitting with Steen[213] and Solomon in the San Remo bar about 10:30 Tuesday night and Carl spotted Cannastra standing in the middle of the floor. That evening was the last time I saw him so I shall attempt to chronicle the events and conversation that passed. Whether these had significance in the light of his death several days later, or what significance they had, I will not attempt to intrude into the body of the chronicle.

I did not recognize him before Carl pointed him out to me. In my enthusiasm to greet him, I left the table, went up to him and called his attention by tapping him on the back. He took my hand, but I don't remember his greeting. I was somewhat taken aback by his reserve—as if he didn't want me to remain there, though glad to see me.

I said, "If you feel amenable to any kind of conversation, I'll be glad to see you—back there—I'm at a table." I averted my eyes and hurried back. He had nodded.

When I got back Solomon pointed out that Cannastra was with Tennessee Williams, a well known playwright. We were all eager to meet him. I was gnawed by envy and a desire to seize an opportunity to involve myself with Williams through Cannastra.

Thus further conversation on my part was torn between desire to turn my attention to them, considering that we were all in the same social boat, or abandon ship for Williams. I was waiting for Cannastra to make some move to involve me, to notice me through the fog.

Cannastra was dressed well, better than I'd seen him dressed ever. He had on a dark suit, black in fact, if I am not mistaken, and a tie with small designs

212 This date is just a day before Cannastra's death on October 12, 1950.
213 Bob Steen. Brilliant physicist, subterranean, and conman who hung out around the San Remo bar.

as should be worn by a Harvard lawyer. His hands and head however looked knobby and protruded from the suit, the immaculate suit that seemed to impose its own kind of dignity on his frame, and made him seem taller than usual.

However when he appeared behind the table, I saw that the suit, though still clean and in good condition, was somewhat wrinkled. Indeed, in his condition of partial drunkenness, which I now noticed, with its irrational flurries of violent activity, I wondered how his suit could stand up under the beating he would be likely to give it within a matter of hours. He was attired, if I may interpolate by hindsight a macabre reference, like a corpse.

He hovered over us. I leaned back to greet him again, but in my preoccupied state of mind. "Bill, I'm writing a novel." This had just been the subject of conversation with Solomon. But Cannastra didn't hear, or if he did, he didn't pay attention. I gave up trying to get to him and turned back to Carl and Steen. Cannastra disappeared in a while. I figured he had gone back to Williams.

With Williams, he had stood in the middle of the floor, jiggling and swaying side to side, from foot to foot, slowly and weavingly, as if in time to a dragging and half imagined tune, half melancholy, half sardonic.

I couldn't hear his conversation and wondered what it was: what could Cannastra have to say to him? What relationship had they to each other? Bill seemed subdued enough—he wasn't depending on animal grimaces and half strangled cries for effect, and I wondered how much he was willing to be subdued by Williams' importance. What of polite conversation had he to display? Could it be that Williams was talking about Cannastra, involved with Cannastra's own limbo-aurora, then and there in front of my eyes at the San Remo? Could it be that anyone who knew him would be overwhelmed by the monomania and make that the basis of rapport, including the little chunky rich playwright? The queer playwright? These questions were to be partly answered later.

Cannastra reappeared at our table. I was jealous of Williams and now I began to have contempt for him, reflecting what I secretly ruminated was Cannastra's contempt, in deserting him.

Norman Levy and a girl I figured was his fiancée sat down right in the place I had expected to be left open for Cannastra's return. The girl, it seems, had known or met Steen long ago in Provincetown. Cannastra was involved in a terrifying conversation of his own with some of the lesser luminaries of the bar, about what I don't know, except that I heard brutal laughter and curses, mostly on "wops."

After awhile, Steen and the girl began sparking, she half unconsciously, and getting drunker and more ill at ease in our company. He was speaking coolly and sometimes with joviality but mostly irony at her expense—I, for one, found her presence irritating. Just an example of the kind of crazy frigid womanhood that drives America to drink. I was explaining this to Carl in French, and we got into an involved conversation about female frigidity. At any rate I made no overt hostile gesture, Carl at one point became very reassuring and charming—which further confused her—and Steen stuck to his seducers guns. Since this was later successful, he couldn't have been too bad. The main cause of unrest was Cannastra.

When he first sat down, he had shown Steen a pack of pictures tied together. They turned out to be photos of his loft-household, plus a series of himself in the house, and a series of sculptures by Rodin. Why these were tied together, I don't know, except that I surmise they were one of a number of many curious gratuitous gifts he gathered from sources unknown to me.

Secondly, he was shouting, "I hate Wops, I hate Wops and Irishmen" to a middle aged Italian hoodlum. This precipitated a drunken rapport with the Italian, wherein Cannastra showed the man his card: Wm. Cannastra Counselor at Law etc. to illustrate that he was himself an Italian, which was at issue.

I tried to get his attention and talk calmly with him, at the risk of using myself as the goat, and said again, "Bill… Bill…I'm writing a novel." But he paid no attention. We stared at each other. His glance was sensitive but glazed, and I looked at him with lover's eyes. We gazed in each other's eyes for quite a while.

He became involved soon in a conversation with the girl. This began with him, at the mention of Williams' name, telling two things: "Tennessee," I said to him, "I never liked you before tonight. I never loved you till you got me readmitted to the Remo, the only bar in New York that I ever liked."

The second revelation was actually more astonishing, and of a piece with the legendary scene. One may think whatever one wishes of the "brashness" of the first, though it was not, as in other people, merely an attempt to insult. What Williams' attitude was I don't know.

"He said he would give me all of his legal business if I would, 'come off the party'."

I stared at him, not comprehending what he meant by the phrase "come off the party" since my only association was that of a sexual party and I assumed it had been an invitation by Williams.

"I was in Minetta's. I lost two bottles of whisky." He held his arms up high, as if holding the bottles. I finally understood that he meant Williams' offer as an invitation to sober up forever.

"What are you going to do? Why don't you accept?" I asked.

"I don't know. But the party's coming to an end."

The conversation at this point was interrupted. He turned to the girl and Steen and began mouthing silently at Steen, "I'm mad for Steen." Steen smiled, a little embarrassed I suppose, since he was trying to make the girl.

Then for half an hour, Cannastra cried, "Why don't you fuck somebody?!" at her. "Why don't you fuck Steen? Why don't you fuck somebody? Cunt is the greatest! Cunt is better than anything!"

She was bewildered because his comments had struck at the heart of her whole evening. We all marveled at the uncanny horror of his language and seeming justice.

Carl interposed, with some witty comment on Cannastra's behavior, running to the effect that his conversation put an end to all conversation, and it would be interesting to hear two people shouting finalities at each other—a conversation between two conversation stoppers, two Artauds.

The girl didn't know what was going on. I finally explained, within everybody's earshot, that Carl was nice, that Cannastra was mad, that Steen was afraid of her, that I was just sitting there. Cannastra heard my reference to him, and said something, probably repeating my statement. At this point I was beginning to feel aggressive and coolheaded toward him. He couldn't frighten me; his approach to love seemed too crazy.

He kept shouting, "Why don't you fuck somebody?" Apparently her anxiety was caused by the vain notion that everybody at the table wanted to get their hands on her, and she kept making half-cutting remarks on that score to all concerned. The idea had entered my head but I kept thinking what a lousy lay she would be. "Why don't you fuck somebody? I don't mean fuck me! I don't want woman! I wouldn't fuck you in a thousand years! I wouldn't fuck you for all the money in the world! I mean why don't you fuck somebody? Don't you understand? That's what's wrong with you! You don't know that you want to fuck Steen!"

Solomon departed first with a comment by the girl which hardened his arteries: "So you're going and giving up." His face fell and he blew out his breath, then recovered his composure and gave up half way through an explanation that he had a wife waiting for him at home. Finally Steen and the girl left.

"Now we are alone," I said to Cannastra. There began, by fits and starts, a conversation which was the longest and deepest that I'd ever had with him. In making this chronicle I find that my memory does not contain sufficient details of the actual speeches to give the continuity and sense entirely.

[On the afternoon of October 12, 1950, Cannastra was killed when he tried to climb out of a subway car window as the train was leaving the station. He became stuck in the window, and his head was crushed when the car entered the tunnel. Ginsberg said that the great question on everybody's mind was whether it was an accident or did he do it on purpose? A month later, Kerouac married Joan Haverty, who had been Cannastra's girlfriend and moved into Cannastra's old loft with her.]

1951

February 25, 1951.[214]
John Holmes at Lucien's Birthday Party.

> 'Tis Allen Ginsberg reft of realms[215]—
> Abhorred I sit in city dump.
> My broken heart's a bag of shit.
> The vast rainfall, an empty mirror.[216]
> (Lucien suggests this be 3rd person for right tone)

[Dream]: Myself fleeing from work and doctor to sea: and caught in dream of Lucien—sitting on him rocking back and forth pleading my love, saying "But I've got to go away" and calling it an illusion—while he saw me there, empty, nescient, lost, self-deceived, telling him I was going away (as if I would if he moved a finger of tenderness) as if I had a soul and knew what I was doing, when all the time it was a vacant truth to make him come around—how much drunken contempt he showed to tell me to shove over.

or as Jack sees me parading the Doldrums of my vacancy year after year

or as I write bile, as usual, five years later "I am still all fucked up and nowhere and sterile now."

Phil White (I learned today) committed suicide a year ago in jail—I was seared for a moment of the knowledge—seared spiritually—excitement of chase after Beast of Eternity—and what seriousness his then.

---

214 Carr's birthday was actually March 1.

215 This paragraph was the basis for part of the poem "The Shrouded Stranger." See *Collected Poems*, p. 47.

216 *Empty Mirror* was to become the title of a Ginsberg book of early poetry published in 1961 by Totem/Corinth.

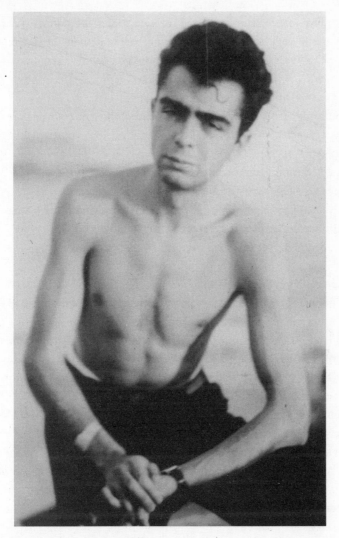

Bill Cannastra

March 14, 1951.

Conversation with [William Carlos] Williams—don't know [T.S.] Eliot isn't right? His suggestion—transfigured—(measure). As I transfigure the shrouded stranger, I transfigure the verse.

A *tour de force*—from classic mystical shroudy psalm like stanzas and rhymes, through the history of poetic language, to bare statement of fact objectivist speech. Begin with symbols and end with things.

Benito Cereno [by Herman Melville]:

Work out next: the structure of illusion and disillusion from first search for mystical centrality (Nightingale) to Phoenix (vision) to sparrow—raven—crow—pigeon reality.

Shroudy Stranger and the orphan of the West—

Shroudy Stranger and the potato peeler of Dakar—

The shroudy stranger tamed by lust in a colloquy with the orphan of the west—the shroudy stranger speaking from behind his hood.

Use Dreams

1. Central High School burning up
2. Finding money in the street: pennies-nickels-dimes-quarters-half dollars, pocketfuls

Dream of Shroudy Stranger (Title)

Introduction—imagery should be fabulous and connected at first; comparisons later between similar realistic types.

Scheme of imagery after Vico—chaos, etc.—Gods—gold—men—"Nature" as in *Hamlet*—Shroudy Stranger dies of cancer.

Be with me Shroud non! Shallow in Man

The monstrous stranger of profoundest dreams.

September 7, 1951. Galveston.

[*Draft for a note to Cassady.*]

Dear Neal:

Claude [Lucien] and I went to Mexico and returned to the U.S. a few days ago. Bill was in South America on some expedition. We took J. [Joan Adams] and kids riding all over to Guadalajara and Mazatlán—Mex Pacific Coast.

Ginsberg and Carr in the wedding party, Mexico, 1951

Car broke down near Houston. I spending week in Galveston on Beach, Claude flew to New York. He returns in four days by plane to pick up me and car and dog.

Note in newspaper I saw tonight says that Bill killed Joan in accident with gun last night. "An American Tourist trying to imitate Wm. Tell killed his wife while attempting to shoot a glass of champagne from her head with a pistol, Police said today."

"Police arrested Wm. Seward Burroughs, 37, of St. Louis, Mo., last nite after his wife Joan, 27 died in a hospital of a bullet wound in her forehead received an hour earlier."

That's all I know.

I am sitting in a broken down shack across the street from the Gulf of Mexico. I have spoken to no one since I've been here, slept much, bathed a lot, walked around town, have an icebox.

Kells Elvins is in Mexico City. He is a great man, and on the scene so there is someone around to help Bill and take care of kids.

Claude and J. played games of chance with drunken driving, egging each other on suicidally at times while we were there. I left with him from N.Y. at last moment after Jack dropped out to go to hospital for leg and finish book.

[*Late in August 1951, Ginsberg and Carr drove to Mexico to attend the wedding of one of Carr's coworkers. They had hoped to visit Burroughs in Mexico City. But when they arrived, they discovered he was away on an expedition to South America, so they took Joan Burroughs and her two children on a drunken ride to Guadalajara and Mazatlán on the Pacific coast. On the way back to New York, their car broke down in Galveston, Texas, and Ginsberg stayed there to oversee the repairs while Carr flew back to his job. It was there that Ginsberg heard the news that Burroughs had killed Joan in a terrible accident. A drunken Burroughs had tried to shoot a glass off Joan's head, like William Tell, missed, and the bullet went directly through her forehead, killing her. Later, Burroughs was able to escape prosecution in Mexico.*]

November 28 or 30, 1951.
Returning to the journal of Shroudy Stranger

Perhaps form should be life work of A.G. entitled "Journal of the Shroudy Stranger" telling my most secret ambitions and vagaries—

How sick I am! That thought always comes to me with horror. It must be strange in any man. I believe and have always believed that such fugitive feelings and thoughts have been my métier—and my road. I am along this road, now.[217]

I felt like Baudelaire in his damnation, and yet he had great joyful moments of staring into space looking into the "middle distance" contemplating his image in eternity, they were moments of identity. It is solitude that produces these thoughts.

It is December, almost, they are singing Christmas carols in front of the department stores down the block on 14th St. I must have the shrouded stranger enter New York on the Christmas season. I believe old myths, or think of them fondly. And his arrival here will be an entry—triumphal entry—music of solitude.

The Oval of El Greco

The secret of El Greco is the cartoon, particularly in the self portrait, that long faced man with the stretched eyebrows—so that his face all but the forehead, makes a pure heart shape—and the face altogether an oval—the face etched out in an oval of light. The cartoon oval.

Also in St. Martin—look at all those six legs—that confusion of seven legs. Does the horse's behind directly bar the man's naked loins from our sight? The beggar's foot is in front, the horse's thigh in front, or is horse changing into man?

The vulva light around Christ in The Resurrection—The dance around him—The Vision, admired and reacted to by man, the conversion of legs again—the whole world in twelve disciples—is that Judas in front, falling: the counterpart to Christ—and warriors all round?

Mary's all look like young Elsa Lancaster,[218] the two levels of the world in El Greco always—Christ receiving angel on Mount of Olives and sleepy old men in big worldly cloaks and the strangeness of the Orgaz's division, the rolling whores of the system of Christ. Christ seems an infinite away in the distance, on a Third Level, in fact. The whole picture revolves structurally about Christ's loins—ballet of hands there, too; Christ in impassive Judgment.

Tonite I made love to myself in the mirror kissing my own lips—saying "I love myself—I love you more than anybody."[219]

---

217 This paragraph was the basis for the poem "Marijuana Notation." See *Collected Poems*, p. 66.

218 Elsa Lancaster (1902–1986). Actress most famous for playing the title role in the movie, *The Bride of Frankenstein* (1936).

219 This paragraph was the basis for the poem "I made love to myself." See *Collected Poems*, p. 70.

Naomi's note: "Insects on Leaves Floating in October Wind"

> All these spirits going to the funeral of each other all these funerals
> of characters.
> The nowhere world, so large—nobody happy knows how many of
> us are alone.
> All those alone; all those that never find—does any man find more
> than I who feel so empty?

December 1951.

I have increased power over knowledge of death. (Also see Hemingway's pre-
occupation) My dream world and real world become more and more distinct
and apart—I see now that what I sought in Lucien seven years ago was mas-
tery of victimage played out naked in the bed. Renewal of nostalgia for lost
flare of those days. Lost passions, now with real world now seemingly dispas-
sionate and fearful with anxiety growing in.

Trouble with me now is no active life in real world, just slow growth of
sight of it, cool clear sight, filled with fear of activity.

And time, as the real world, appearing vile, as Shakespeare says, ruinous,
vile, dirty time. As to knowledge of death and life itself as without consum-
mation foreseeable in ideal joy or passion (perhaps not even unity of being but
that is to be decided)—life as vile, as painful, as racked, this pessimism which
is Lucien's jewel. Thomas Hardy and crass casualty again.

The shrouded stranger grows more into focus, as far as verse is concerned.
I may do it yet this year. Life is <u>grim</u> (not bleak?) The grimness of chance or as
Carl wrote, "How often have I had occasion to see existence display the affec-
tations of a bloodthirsty negro homosexual."[220]

Forgive the forgoing trash. It is now the hour of twelve almost and the first
day of freedom from death is ended. The good folk are not abroad in this hour
of night, except perhaps the young or inebriate with the rain and some there
are who go abroad in the rain, while some sleep or read or listen to the dying
end of the television day, watching the silent pictures of the world move for
them. Some like me in Paterson may be sitting up in their promised attic to
write—maybe that Emily Dickinson, that sweet woman, is abroad in the
streets in his mind, surveying the city from their tower, or as of old, Mon-

---

220 These paragraphs were the basis for the poem "I Have Increased Power." See *Collected
Poems,* pp. 68–69.

taigne, or Shakespeare thinking to themselves of some ditty or some psalm of intellect of hatred.

I lay in bed thinking about the difference between the real world of things and the illusion of reveries. I thought of "And the greatest of these is charity?!" Faith and hope are, say, illusions about something real—charity is only recognition.

When we are not our illusion of personality, character, the peripheral mannerisms of separate men, looking at it justly without personality and subjectivity, we are all the same "all men are brothers" or "all men are the same" as axioms go.

All men are the same—illusion makes us think that the quality or sense of world and consciousness is different. Consciousness and material body are all identical or similar. Illusions are what vary so much and give us our individuality and isolation and our recognition. We can't (perhaps) share same consciousness except in recognition (mutual) of identity of self with other, but we know we are the same and have enough regard for that thing we are to give charity to another part of it.

I have the first line of this poem with me now. Other items I enumerate are the objects of my desk and the object of my person. I have said much of my spirit but nothing of my self—my body, my physical being (note the sound)—this toe, that toe, this wound, that scar, that relic of life. We carry scars of our accidents through the years. I skip all of the foot as it, touching the earth most, changes. Perhaps I am becoming light tied to earth.

My feet change, still however—

Living in a tower with a gelded cat, I found a maiden [Helen Parker]—and left her there. I seek a better bargain—and that child, that child of hers was an awful nuisance. Seriously, between us, I think I did right in all things by her—as I will see her again and we'll become friendly not lovers—as I will have to work with her—she knows, too—and so it will be interesting tomorrow to see how she acts—if she is friendly (or even loving) I will resist, albeit so politely she'll think she has been complimented—and one night drunk maybe we'll have a ball.[221]

---

221 This paragraph was the basis for the poem "A Typical Affair." See Collected Poems, p. 63.

December 10, 1951.

Once, every day was a dollar of time which wasn't wasted. I used to count every cent of my money, chink by chink and spend it. Now just as money passes through my hands extra-vacantly and I no longer know how much change I have in my pocket, I waste time—whole days, weeks, years have passed by—I walk around aimlessly not noticing things, not experiencing anything new, emotionally or spiritually, just dreaming or analyzing without result and with an aimless aim. Like: I am lonely because I am full of self love, versus: I am full of self love because I'm lonely and don't do anything about loving others. I am too practical and should return to creative art, or, I should turn away from the imagination and become really practical instead of thinking about it.

My blue garret—find subject for a painting

All this of mine is crap—the dualisms.

> I've loved you [Carr] for 10 years
> and though for all this time we've lived apart
> And I have not laid claim upon your heart
> In dreams in woes of night, in mortal tears
> I've eaten up your heart and you have mine.

> Lucien said "come by tomorrow early and make a scene, get
> some life into that party."
> We talked of slapping his mother on the behind.
> I said leaving, "I was glad I saw you tonight" turning
> from them. They walked on, didn't look back, and I did.

> Most marvelous night and event that once I would have
> dreamed a miracle!
> "One of my rocks is gone."
> No time for more.

December 30, 1951. 1:15 A.M.

[222]Bare elements on my table—the clock—all life reduced to this, its tick.
    Last attempts at speech.

---

222 This paragraph was the basis for the poem "A Ghost May Come." See *Collected Poems*, p. 71.

And the carved serpentine knife of Mexico, with the childish eagle head on the handle.

Dusty's[223] modern lamp, all shape, space and curve.

Bare elements of my solitude.

Coming out of the movie (Gene Kelly—*An American in Paris*) where I went alone, there was Lucien, my old dear eldest love, my sweet vision, with his bride[224] of the morrow. We shared three drinks therefore. I was alone and when I left them I turned back to see the lovers walk across Greenwich Avenue—the last I'll see of Lucien as an unpledged man—the last I see him before he's given away—which I never dreamed would happen. I always thought that somehow I would win his love—that I would see his soul turned with fast sweetness and light to mine like the sun.

Walking home then,[225] reaching my own block (full of thought beyond tears) I saw the hovering charnel house of the Port Authority Building [West 18th Street and 8th Avenue] and the old ghetto side of the street I tenemented—with soft white failures, cadaverous men, shrouded men, old Dutch caretakers—remembering my chosen attic room—I reached my hands to my head and hissed "Oh God how horrible!"

Today in the movie I also thought and dreamed that I would soon find love—I want to find a fine woman now—I want to fall into a sweet soul like mine, but a woman's—or Gregory's[226] who spoke of the Mexican knife given to me by Lucien; "You ought to get rid of it now—when I see it I think you'll commit suicide." How near and how far is that knife in my body.

1952

January 4, 1952.

Lucien's wedding, him taking my picture for me. Graceful simperings before Mrs. Carr. Lucien looking like a doll, a manikin out of a famous window—

---

223 Dusty Moreland. Girlfriend of both Ginsberg and Corso, originally from Lusk, Wyoming.

224 Carr married Francesca "Cessa" von Hartz on January 4, 1952.

225 This paragraph was the basis for the poem "Walking Home at Night." See *Collected Poems*, p. 70.

226 Gregory Corso (1930–2001). Poet and one of Ginsberg's best friends. He was the author of *Gasoline, The Happy Birthday of Death,* and many other books.

moustache, hair plastered down, in a gray suit with a flower in his button-hole—talking with ladies, making them laugh; standing listening to his father in law talk with Kenny Love[227]—Kenny's manly charm with old von Hartz.[228] How Felicity[229] talked composed and society-like with Helen Rockefeller. The air of money and elegance. The old friend with the wrinkled face sitting in the corner. The Bernsteins—she so like Billie Burke[230]—he so like a "nice" self-effacing man—yet marked, like a *révolutionnaire* in disguise—she "I hope you're not one of those Patchen boys."

I denied it, but on this thought I would have perhaps made a better impression—and how strangely my preoccupation is with making a nice impression on people in a position to do me good—like Stendhal or Balzac—except that I am so fucked up it would be hard to get ahead in the world.

Subject for a novel—the history of mistakes and successes of a young literary (again) type, in securing his position in the world—young man without ambition or goal, only theoretical. Is success theoretical or accidental?

The benign evil butler who noticed how heavily I drank of champagne—he once winked at me even. He looked like a foreigner, German or Swiss.

Kenny barring me from the bedroom where they put on their coats—scene down the stairs—right on Twelfth St.—driving off in the Austin to unknown rendezvous.

Into the underworld they go, marriage of evil and good, dark and light, burning with good in the night. Fine flame. Marriage of Good and Evil.

Poem: An address to the unknown powers—asking release from bondage of moralist, as in Faust at beginning.

Gregory Corso's story of vacation—first time out of N.Y.C.—from Brownsville—in Vermont or New Hampshire—summer—how he and girl both 13, one last night there, in love, undressed in moonlight and showed each other their bodies and ran singing back into the house—how he had a plywood stick and would paddle her with it all summer until that last day—and she wasn't afraid of him that last day.[231]

---

227   Kenneth Love. Old St. Louis friend of Carr.
228   Ernest Von Hartz. Carr's new father-in-law was the national news editor for the *New York Times*.
229   Felicity Love. Kenny Love's wife.
230   Billie Burke (1885–1970). Popular early motion picture actress.
231   This paragraph was the basis for the poem "Gregory Corso's Story." See *Collected Poems*, p. 67.

Gregory Corso

January 1952.

Long enough to remember the girl that proposed love to me in the eerie light of the drugstore on Park Avenue and 32nd St. in Paterson; who had such an uncanny power of mind, penetration of insight, coupled with what seemed to me an untrustworthy character—quite Jamesian, who died half a year later, a month or two after I ceased thinking of her, of an incurable freak brain illness. By hindsight I must have known that only such a state of dying could reduce the personality to such luminousness, the opposite of believing that even in the face of death, man can be no more than ordinary man.[232]

February 16, 1952.

How long can or will I go on spending those dollars on amusement?

    People I see every week or so now:
        Alan Ansen
        Richard Howard
        John Hollander and Ann Loeser
        Carl Solomon and Lois[233]
        Eugene
        Lucien and Cessa
        Father and Family

My sexual vanity with Howard—no relationship is happy or straight. I don't approach any with real seriousness or without embarrassment.

    How like Kafka's diaries are mine—how like K's situation. Last night slept with… Why? Sheer easy sex—I sleep with creeps now. How like Kafka, we desire nothing.

February 26, 1952.

I could write about all these subjects and scenes of life if I wanted to:

1. Paterson
        A. Childhood—family life
        B. Homosexuality in puberty
        C. High school extracurricular activities, teachers, etc.
2. Communist meetings in 30's
3. Sea—merchant marine

232 This paragraph was the basis for the poem "An Atypical Affair." See *Collected Poems*, p. 72.
233 Lois Beckwith. Carr's occasional girlfriend.

4. Military training—Sheepshead Bay
5. Hitch-hiking
6. Mexico
7. Personal tragedy—murder and suicide (Joan, Kammerer, Phil White, Cannastra)
8. Madness—inside and outside madhouses
9. Criminality—drugs and burglary
10. Jazz world and jazz
11. Bohemian world
12. Local politics—Da Vita
13. Labor union
14. Newspaper life—U.P., magazines
15. University life
16. Teacup social queerness
17. Cities—Denver, Houston, New Orleans, Tulsa, Dallas, New York, Baltimore
18. Foreign countries—Dakar
19. Divorce remarriage problems
20. Young marrieds (from outside)
21. Bickford's dishwashing life
22. Lawyers lives—Hoeniger[234] and Gene [Brooks]
23. Normal adolescent problems—Joel [cousin], Harold [step-brother]
24. Bobby soxers
25. Heterosexual love affairs—regular and perverse
26. Professional literary life—magazines, publishers and agents
27. Artist's struggles
28. Early immigrant's struggles
29. Advertising world—sociologist's world
30. The New York limbo of the poor or incoherent
31. Mystical experiences
32. Stamp, mineral, astronomy and microscope kicks
33. Getting a job
34. Incest
35. Certain characters (combined with subject not notably like Isabelle, Morton, Creten on block, Lancaster, Spencer, Little Jack, Norman Schnall)

---

234 Bert Hoeniger. Madison Avenue lawyer friend of Eugene Brooks.

36. The rich or privileged or mannered
37. Dogs, cats and pets
38. Alcoholism
39. Driving—stealing cars, hot rods, long distances, etc.
40. Psychoanalysis or therapy
41. Theater and ballet world
42. Record company
43. Feminism and sterility and women and frigidity
44. Breaking out of small town to big town
45. Factory and shipyard work—post office work, shipping clerks, etc.
46. Bookstores (Bretanos and Gotham)
47. Librarians and libraries
48. Summer camps and resorts and seashore summer life and Cape Cod
49. Bringing up small children—babies and 8 year olds
50. Harlem

[*Ginsberg's book*, Journals: Early 50s Early Sixties, *(New York: Grove, 1977) begins around this date. The editor of that volume, Gordon Ball, remembers that when work began on that book thirty years ago, not all of Ginsberg's notebooks could be found. The editors of this volume have included the passages from a notebook that Ball and Ginsberg did not have available to them at the time, hence an overlapping of dates, but not entries.*]

Here Williams told me poems journal were poetry, henceforth everything written has added self-consciousness.

[*Ginsberg received a letter from William Carlos Williams in February 1952, which informed Ginsberg that he would be featured in Williams' new poem "Paterson IV." Williams was thrilled with Ginsberg's new work, selected from passages in these journals and re-worked into poetic forms. Williams insisted that Ginsberg "must have a book, I shall see that you get it. Don't throw anything away. These are it!" In the end, Williams was not able to get a book contract for Ginsberg, but he did write the introduction for Ginsberg's first published book,* Howl and Other Poems *(San Francisco: City Lights, 1956).*]

March 11, 1952.
Half asleep—in the U.S. there are 34 hospitals with inmates standing in the sun in little white aprons. They are comparing their ills.

It's a wonder that anyone bothers to think the things I think.

March 18, 1952.

Should Jack and I ever write a book—and none but we alive can remember the beauty of certain days and nights—some acts—Lucien throwing money in the gutter, Neal in 106th St. in East Harlem—Bill, sitting in the window in the damp furnished gray room, above old Riordan's, landlady refugee—talking about Europe in the 30's, an afternoon and night in Denver when we talked of the birds, an afternoon in York Avenue when we created "Pull My Daisy" and "The Shrouded Stranger" and "Dr. Sax," and evening we played Sebastian's [Sampas] record, and afternoon in his house with Luanne and Neal and Al Hinkle, moments with Vicki and Huncke—Bill Gilmore's manners and age, Phil White in the Great Days, and Hal Chase in love with Celine.

March 19, 1952.

Dreams: On plateau in Mexico or Inca land, I meet up with Lizzie Lehrman[235] and perhaps Moe Mayer, some Jewish girl, Naomi (Liz's friend), going from tent to tent. I am following Lucien around sounding self-destroyed—am I reassuring them that I <u>want</u> to be? In morning walking up big college street, trees, lawns with Tom Livornese[236] explaining to him how I wasn't queer or not queer but loved sight and nakedness of certain kinds of boys (like image of half naked teenager on river standing up in lifeboat) and Livornese directing me to the Law School. I couldn't say I wasn't really in law school. He was explaining Law School manliness and practice and custom to me.

March 20, 1952.

Everybody's playing caves: Lucien is on the wagon and yet wants to throw a big brave party—restless. Ed Stringham came out of the cave by accident and is working on the *New Yorker*. John Holmes is still in hiding. I have supper with Kingsland tomorrow night. Jack and Neal are in Frisco writing novels. Bill is in Mexico waiting to go to Ecuador. Carl has gone to the mountains for a rest from nervous business. I am in Paterson finishing up book. Haven't seen Dusty [Moreland] much or Jerry Newman.[237] Haven't got laid in months—(years?).

I've been thinking I should make an effort to find a girl and get laid or perhaps this time try for some affection from her. But who do I like enough

---

235 Lizzie Lehrman. Another of Carr's girlfriends, an artist who once lived with Carr in his loft at 149 W. 21st Street.

236 Tom Livornese. Friend of Kerouac's who was a student and part-time jazz musician.

237 Jerry Newman. Jazz expert who owned the Esoteric Record shop in Greenwich Village. He had been a classmate of Kerouac's at Horace Mann.

among girls now? No one practically except Dusty and she's too hung up and doesn't want me. Not just bald head I got bald heart.

Question and answer response poem catalog of all possible sexual kicks by sign writers—inhuman sexual angels male and female (sucks cocks fucks cunts) exposition of subterranean erotic "graphite," "I would love to suck the one who pisses here." [and] "Be here 11 P.M. have pretty cock and will shoot a big load."

It preys on my mind. I'm sick: what's neurosis? I take pleasure in myself, masturbation at the age of 25, no relation with anyone—no job, work, social organization outside self and indirectly through poetry—no outer life, outside self—I feed on praise and flattery—when it comes to real truth between me and Dusty I am afraid; I skirt the subject with Lucien, I joke—I am hardening in the mental arteries—becoming withdrawn from world again—feeding an ego like a baby, with visions, monomania of poetry.

I will keep the book more fully now since it is turning into a mine.[238]

For Peyote—Exotic Plant Co. Box 1401—Laredo, Texas.

March 21, 1952. Afternoon.
Dream: Afternoon dreams are often the most memorable or easiest to remember. I was on the street in Paterson walking alone with my loneliness when I ran into an old friend, younger than I, whom I'd loved four or five years earlier, perhaps Benjamin C. Smith. His face still looked young, doll-like and pretty. We walked up the street, arms around each other, wondering how wonderful it was to meet again. I felt a general glad eroticism, conspiracy and fear. "Where are you living? Have you a room where we can go?" I asked. He led me to his barracks room, it would do. We were going to sleep together. He was a musician, very sweet natured. We recognized each other's feelings and were going to act on them, such comradeship was now possible to me in my dreams, though I felt older than he and more experienced, worldly and bitter, like with Gregory Corso.

First transcription of conversation with Carr and Merims[239] on Faulkner—took place in loft one year ago.

---

238 Mine. Since Williams had encouraged Ginsberg to create poetry from the prose he had written earlier in his notebooks, Ginsberg had gone back and mined the pages for new poems made from older writing.

239 Robert Merims. Engineer and friend of Carr.

M. "In *Pigeon* Faulkner's message is[240]—

C. "I'll tell you—life grows from here (middle of belly) not from here (pointing to head, violently, drunk) not from your crotch, from your grits and belly and heart.

M. "It's sort of inept."

C. "Isn't heart always? I'm in the middle of the book…I haven't lost any one of the central characters yet, actually not the kind of Faulkner book that I like. It's too hard to read. Some of them are harder than others. Just syntactically, I don't like it very well. I like it as a book, I'll put it against any book any day. What I want to read is the Old Man…Well, will read'em all. Obviously he's the guy who can write in this generation."

M. "He's broader than most others."

C. "What do you mean broader?"

M. "Dealing with more universal things."

C. "He sure is. Fitzgerald had no real value judgment on what he wrote."

March 30, 1952.

I leave this as my will:

I have little or no money coming to me but such as I have I leave to my father, Louis, and brother Eugene Brooks to dispose of as they see fit— with the recommendation that if they can spare it they turn it over for the personal use of Jack Kerouac—all except 10% of Burroughs' Junk which goes back to him.

All of my personal effects except books and writings I leave to the family to dispose of. My books I wish given to the Paterson Public Library except such as may be used either by Louis or Eugene.

Everything which I have written—including notebooks, poems, journals, and letters (and also letters to me) I definitely wish turned over to Jack Kerouac. I wish nothing destroyed for a while, particularly by my father who might feel that some of it is in bad taste.

Allen Ginsberg

In all the time I've lived (25 years) no one has ever looked into my eyes and said, "I love you" the way I wanted to hear it said, or meant by that what I mean by love. Do I want something wrong? Am I looking for something impossible? Or should I say no one I've ever wanted to has said it; though I have looked into other's eyes and said those words and meant it, in silence as an eternal vow.

---

240 "Pigeon." [The editors were unable to identify this book or story by Faulkner.]

Some have hinted that they love me—but I couldn't or didn't love them—certain creeps. Some I've said I love you to have said, on different occasions I love you to me, but not meaning complete submission and self-delivery and total physical and spiritual sacrament and devotion (of body and soul). The vow I wanted to take with Neal on the Texas road in the dark by the diner, kneeling in the cinders by the highway under the trees.

Such love is rootless and empty—a vow on the empty plain, with no past or future, in the middle of time, as if time would have no consequence, would not exist in that vow. That vow had no value, a fantasy I imagined in a world of my own making—that nobody shared with me—my own fantasy nobody else's—my fantasy for myself—childish, solipsistic fantasy. I write this thinking of professor Lionel Trilling's cruel gray eyes.

Dream: Carrying the pillow out of the apartment, I see the superintendent going into the elevator, so I close the door and go back into room. Someone's washing, naked—I lick him on the breast childishly—look on the bed, she's there with a moustache, when he goes to work I'll get in bed with her all day under covers naked together.

Merrill's Monologue about boyfriend:
We have to go through the warehouse to go to the lunchroom and he told me where we were going and he told me what time he would pick me up, what a doll he is. We were walking through the warehouse hand in hand. He held my hand and kissed me; if anybody knew, the news would spread like wildfire.[241]

> The sweetest music of the sea
> finding the ego like a fairy.

Dream: Neal and I are working together but the work is in different places. I got him a job when he came here and work with him for a while (in a ribbon factory?) then I get sent out to work at the soda fountain up town by the hospital in Harlemesque streets, I wander around there—work, Neal is to join me but I haven't given him full directions. Time passes, I am free to go, Neal hadn't showed, I had said to him "stay with me after work." I am trying to call Neal on the phone. I call Marianne Moore (there's some kind of social activity going on involving Marion Holmes, Marianne Moore, Kingsland, Neal,

---

241 This paragraph was the basis for the poem "Her Engagement." See Appendix, p. 511.

myself)—I wonder if I ought to call Dr. Brooks[242] and let him know I am back at the hospital for preliminary rest before going out and making money for Neal. I wake up thinking I'm just like the other patients deceiving themselves and trying to alibi their return to the hospital for "check up," etc. rather than admitting they're crazier than ever.

Sex is humiliating.

April 1952.

[Dream]: I'm going along with Potchkie (Lucien's dog) and a boy with no legs from the madhouse. The boy was driving a car but he couldn't drive and kept hitting into tree and car and garage door.

"Where are you going?"

"I'm from the crazy house."

Marshals and sheriff and mayor call up FBI. They're saying, "Crazy, what is he a fairy? I'll bet he sucks women in the ass."

Poor child meanwhile is struggling to get up on artificial limbs. Along comes Supreme Court justice also with wooden leg, driving home. Sees the situation, intervenes by force of manhood and directness and straightness. "Don't you see he has no legs? That's what crazy means." Gets boy out of jam, catches dog and then takes the boy in his car and promises to drive him home through America.

April 3, 1952.

Dream: Riding on a triple decker bus with Dusty, very terrifying, turning corners, etc. Dusty scared. I hang on but don't show fear as we go around Paterson streets I knew as a child. It is time to get off, help off passengers and carry off sticks of wood forming the handrail supports which are works of art. I see one of my own stories there and one of Louis' novels.

Thought Over Breakfast

"Who touches this book touches a man," said Whitman. Usually people pompously accent the last word as if Whitman were calling himself virile. Quite the opposite, Whitman meant that he really had put himself out in his book as he never was able to do in the flesh. So whoever he got under the covers of the book was having a vicarious feel job with the good gray poet.

---

242 William Brooks. One of Ginsberg's psychiatrists during his stay at the New York State Psychiatric Institute.

Blake's source of inspiration was his unconscious—he wrote what he thought literally, "I had a dream / What can I mean? / and that I was / an angel queen!" or dreamed up and didn't know how to interpret it anymore than anyone else, so his wife held his hand while he wrote down his dreams, including the long complicated epics which have nothing to do with reality.

In bed with a faint headache which has bothered me on and off for over a week. "Right now at the very moment I wish to be dead."

April 4, 1952.
Delivered copy of *Empty Mirror* (title taken by Williams for book from "Shrouded Stranger" fragment) to W. C. Williams. Phone call—"I've been wondering what happened to you."

"I've been working."

Came in room—when I arrived having said over phone to insist on late visit (9:15) that, "I wouldn't stay." (He laughed)

"Well come in, we can't send you away like that. Come in and enjoy yourself."

He has a habit of talking blindly to cover up empty spots—rambling on, "Well, we'll see that it doesn't go cold"—the book. "Yes I'll spend some time on it."

I told him about Genet being in jail for murder. He seemed chilled asked, "Do you think he might have done it—maybe in a cold blooded way—like killing the old woman for her money?"

I say, "No I think he's read Dostoyevsky and knows that kind of crime doesn't pay." We talked more about giving the book to Auden, etc.

Rambles—for second time I explained who Auden's secretary, Alan Ansen was, he went through same routine trying to remember who it was he had supper with at Auden's house. (Kallman[243])

He and I both said "all right" at the same moment for me to leave. His wife was sitting on the couch, I didn't notice what doing. He came over to the hall to say goodbye, creaking and holding his bones and hip and shuddering in mock imitation of an old man.

"I'm going right to bed. I'm too tired to think anything through."

I said, "Well I didn't ask ya any questions."

"No, you've been very good," he said and laughed. He also had said he sent

243 Chester Kallman (1921–1975). W. H. Auden's longtime companion.

his novel (3rd volume of *White Mule*) off to Random House today, having just finished visions.[244] "I guess this is an historical day," he said. They were both sitting there very quiet in an old house surrounded by a lifetime collection of domestic and moth-eaten pictures and a Turkish foot rest, etc.

April 4, 1952.

What a sight for new born robins inside the whirling tree. At sunset, long poles with leafy heads unsteadily balancing backward and forward in different directions like a mobile in the dangerous yellow breeze: form the new-made robin's nest the top of the whirling tree.[245]

The tree on 33rd St. near Broadway that I thought of as subject for rhymed ode to survival—twisted ironwise, contorted (Torque?) turned around on itself so the knots and aged veins bulged and strained, blasted at the top and hollow at the center with old roots chopped off, bleared from smoke as if set fire years ago, but an old dignified tree still putting out a leaf or two from branches sprouting out of its neck—huge floating leaves put out of neck, but base has a cave in it and nails in thick trunk and ants and caterpillars crawl in huge cave at base.[246]

Building on fire: flame "dancing" like alive thing, writhing in the window, an inhuman thing an angel being—the descent of reality on the scene that 5 A.M. on Ninth Avenue.

April 9, 1952.

All of what's past has been horrible, but I remember now the beauty of certain days and the fight in certain people's eyes, soul acts.

Memory—strange—only tonight did it occur to me to go explore certain other mythological places of my childhood—not the house on top of Temple Hill but the great field two blocks away from there where I always played, where I saw Morton get his pants pulled off by unknown gang of kids, with me standing by the sidelines afraid to go to his defense—his reproach afterward—and how ecstatically I enjoyed seeing them torment him.

---

244 Ginsberg's note: *"Visions (of Kora) in Hell?"*
245 This paragraph was the basis for the poem "At Sunset." See Appendix, p. 512.
246 This paragraph was the basis for the poem "A Survivor." See Appendix, p. 512.

April 11, 1952.

Dream: In car back seat, stolen boxes riding along, stopped for police inspection, then passing me on—tension and fear. This car crash nightmare fall is a recurrent traumatic dream.

April 12, 1952.

Two cocks will solve the problem—I dreamed of it last night but don't remember the dream—can't remember if it was funny or not I had two cocks.

Yesterday a one-eyed negro shoe shine boy about 11 walked up Market Street by the Lankering cigar store under the Garden Theater marquee saying to himself "Shine Mister?" Two small white boys in dungarees and dirty red sweaters passed him looking back at him. I heard one say, "He can't help it."

> ...Till blindmen see
> and dumbbells sing
> and cripples dance
> in their innocency
> and the lamb comes dancing
> thru the gates of the mind.
> and innocence weeps in the spring
> in the lamb's behind.

April 13, 1952.

Are we having the same experience every generation has? Carl [Solomon] called tonight saying the last nine pages of second (Wyn) version of *On the Road* by Jack [Kerouac] was incoherent. He was excited, scared, since he roped Jack into the company at my pushing and advice—and now afraid of having made a wrong move, losing prestige and power at office. Afraid everybody will blow a gut when they see what Jack's sent in.[247]

Carl shook my own self-esteem, threw me into depression. Is there no way we can tell what's good on our own except by personal heart sympathies, going almost against all rational <u>and</u> commercial possibility? I think Jack is the

---

247 Carl Solomon worked for his uncle, A. A. Wyn, who was the publisher of Ace Books. In 1953, they published William Burroughs' *Junkie* upon Carl's recommendation but were hesitant to publish Kerouac's *On the Road*.

greatest writer alive in America of our own age—yet Harcourt rejected his first version as being too personal and subjective—not worked out in objective story—which feeling I went along with. Now this second version seems to them a garble of unrelated free associations. I think I will stick by Jack, though I haven't seen the pages yet, only snatches in his letters. He understands me— so he must be great. The difficulty is finding what is real in a book and invent- ing out of our own existence its core and purity putting it on paper. I keep thinking, after W.C.W., that is what other people are interested in. I wish Van Doren would tell me if he felt anything permanent in my poems—*Empty Mir- ror*—but I am waiting. Perhaps by tomorrow I should get returns from him. It is so difficult to operate like this, not knowing what is good or bad except by other people's reactions—when the mass reaction of the world is immediately negative—not only commercially, but on the part of the University also. Who can we trust but ourselves? and we are crazy.

Derava (Diana[248]) called: Neal Jr.'s [Curt Hansen] images—she takes him out by railroad and by river; he instinctively loves cars she said, as does his father, and imagines cars, plays with them. So lonely growing up with those dead souls in Tarrytown, surrounded only by nostalgic images of his lost father, growing up in the emptiness all around him to have to create out of his own imagination and the imagination of his wild forbears all the beauty and mythology and reality and life he misses in Time. Will he later penetrate through shells of mystery and come out with an insane gleam of recognition of something so rare in himself and others he has never seen it except in his dreams?

Always the image of the injured becoming uninjured again, in their inno- cence, has haunted me. I have always wept at it. As if I had my injury and weep prophetically for the day I will throw away my own crutches or wipe my eyes of their blindness and see again.

I am in a big hole. Practical affairs are not strong enough ropes for me, I haven't filled my city life enough yet, just the sparse agenting and my own writing, Gene's work, typing and a short story. On the other hand, I have put an unexpected book together and sold Bill's, and given Ansen a hotfoot [to write] and got Jack something and wrote a first short story—first since the attempt at overwriting "The Fall." Plan to deal with "The Fall" again

---

248 Diana Hansen. Cassady's third wife, whom he married on July 10, 1950, even though he wasn't legally divorced from Carolyn at the time. For a short period of time, Cassady hoped to main- tain two families, one on each coast, but before long he returned to Carolyn in California.

sometime. Tonite I feel again as if my life were leading to emptiness. This thought is both right and wrong since it returns my mind to the reality world of psychoanalysis in which my creative pride tending toward schizophrenic fantasy of eternity is slammed back down on the rocks by the fact that I am still living at home, dependent; my government checks will run out soon, too.

Filling this book with watery bullshit again. [Trying] to evade self-consciousness, once some feeling of success is reached, and catch those moments of true introspection—so like Lucien's Roman introspection of 1943—that are real poetry. Since they're about pain and failure, success would rob me of my pathos and innocence. This is my neurotic dilemma. My fine style is not pathos, it is childishness and I am to be successful this month at failure. When I am no longer successful I will be left with my failure—a terrible vista.

My pen ran out above (a pen borrowed from father) and I cursed gritting my teeth, "Oh shit I've got to be bothered by pens!"—a great man like me. This vanity of success—premature—has been elating and depressing me, an acting out of self-importance, confusing the importance of my self-ego and my failure, my character and its life.

What terrible horrors the soul, the man, encounters. This prison of writing in the hope that unselfconsciousness will ensue, not knowing whether the flux of my thought will be interesting to anyone and the peaks of awareness piling up to the point of shameful absurdity and self-embarrassment.

The feeling that my writing here is no longer private. The feeling—not yet knowledge that it will all be read, good and bad, even perhaps the dull long introspective parts of Book I which bother and annoy even me by their being so vain and showy and empty. The quality of emptiness in them.

My favorite words this month:

success
failure
soul
self
character
ego
heart
feelings
intellect
image
madness
reality

thus everything is so gratuitous here now, while this goes on I keep producing nothings. I always wish impossible descent of reality and vigor: as if the failure of my self were responsible for the character of my soul's success; and the ego had an image of the heart's feelings and the intellect a fantasy of madness and reality.

Strange true construction above, almost an abstract poem, wrought in a minute by weaving of above listed words together.

Poem:

> Who knows I'm a mystic
> When I walk down the street?
> I look at other people and
> they don't look like mystics either.

I'm tired of the loves in society, among the bohemians or in the middle class in Paterson or Columbia, lover of bars and tea tables. I want the love of the middle of the night, the love of solitude. Lone on the long bus ride when the soul wakes to find itself touching arm in arm with a young man in brown trousers and brown rayon sport shirt. Long nights of subtle communication, two bodies touching together warmth of part of arm or thigh. I long for sudden look of awareness, sex and sweetness. That's when a man's an angel.

Tonight on the bus with a manly but not pretty student. As our arms touched, I was aware of sweetness warmth of touch—wondered if he was too, wanted to hold his hand and kiss his face.[249]

Curiosity of this journal is that it has everything that passes through my mind. I may have to stop keeping journal, or just keep fact record, no more parade introspection. What's buzzing in my head? Self-loathing? I hate myself? What literary abstractions, Ha! I'll kill that fly. I hate myself? Then I'll think why and be different.

Marianne Moore and all of us—working away in the office—scratching at the mountain with our everyday minds—trying to remain sane saints and live in the physical world rationally, describing it, making correspondences and observations, avoiding talk about truth but accepting the world as given to us as

---

249 This paragraph was the basis for the poem "We Rode on a Lonely Bus." See Appendix, p. 513.

truth, or phantasms of mind as truth: but only truly represented (in art) as actual phantasms of mind, never seeking the central impalpable for fear that it is death.

On the other hand, take the world of problems, affairs that have to be settled, think no more beyond what can be seen. Everyday thoughts are supreme—interesting and eternal I mean.

Ginsberg in the Garden. [unfinished]

O, horrifying rock,
   Which is round and gray
Has been rolling and buried
   in the soil for
thousands of years,
   so humble and dumb
an object, without heartbeat
   or ego or eyes, not even
dreaming, not even dead,
   but you exist and
will last I imagine
   in your present form
when I'm also a dead object,
   and beyond that,
when I'm not even a corpse
   and my bones are gone,
you'll even out last my grave
   and human memory of me
filtering mind to mind
through generations of time
   to nothing, when everybody's
dead: you'll be there the
same. I'll never see you
again after this afternoon,
and there are millions
of other rocks. Why should
I collect you? I think the
same thing every time I see a rock. If I kept
them all I'd be man of rocks, have a
whole house full, there'd be piles of rocks

on the living room floor. So I let you
go; the same goes for trees and flowers;
it's the last time I'll see that tree, just
reversed, so I save it awhile in the vase.
    Rock I hope you collect me for my
minute like I collect flowers.
    Someday I'll be a rock.
    This is crazy but that's what I have
often thought.

However though rocks are dead, they do exist. In that respect they partake of the universal—of the universe, which may be a sort of living thing—perhaps waves of force run through rocks like through animals.

Perhaps these flashes of communication between people I invoke are the level they always deal with, and I just totally hide all day long except when I tip my mitt—like anybody else.

Elements on my table:

> Silver cup of an ash tray,
> Bible and dictionary,
> Blue lamp standing on them
>   for more height and light,
> Glass ashtray: ledger
>   and sound of scratching,
> all attention focused on physical
>   presence and fact of recording
>   in time,—brown polished desktop.
> Pair of dirty socks which I'll wear
> again; matchbook with one match
> loose in it, there being a shortage
> of matches around me all this week,
> old address book.

I have been waiting to masturbate, but passed peak of high, tired, will. I may be in a vain prison but my room on the second floor of this house is the only one without a mirror.

"The yew-trees-scare-babe voice." Marianne Moore's exalted purity—limiting self to fact—robin in grass, its Latin name and its supposed stories and history and wilder theories, plus the robin that exists well delineated in an ordinary or curious moment for the everyday bird.

Write—to put naked self down on paper—truth to personal fact and self-ness is so rare I may be valuable, or original, even if I am an impoverished unaware self—at least I can set down the phenomena of my unawareness—perhaps find a pattern in it, once my self's stream and order is put down as palpable object in front of me.

Unawareness of what—God? Schizoid idealism? No here I am: I am 25 years old, good looking in a personal way, dark, wear glasses, am called Allen Ginsberg. My relations with the outside world are limited—I am dependent on my brother, on government, on parents and on friends for spending money, even for food. I can work if I set my mind to it at uninteresting jobs, sometimes show signs of gregariousness and get along well, sometimes am perceptive, but have a tendency to talk a lot, too much about myself, pointing attention to myself—almost obsessionally recurring conversations with other people to my own weakness, strengths or sense of self; almost all my concern is with my self and its manifestations. I have no strong relation with my father; more with my brother on equal, though dependent footing. I have no secure relationship involving my whole character with another person, though I secretly admire and love several men and few women—who usually have position or are popular and successful sexually—and who reject me as a sexual lover but accept my friendship, which is a friendship more maintained by me than by them, though they do respond and are warm and really like me; but I do not enter into or share their lives.

I share my life with no one, and wish to share my life with someone, man or woman; though I do not know what a relationship with woman will mean to me. I hope it is with a woman and try to bring that about. I have a talent for language and my own thought, which I exploit in my own poetry, without order or understanding; just passive recording of phenomena, thoughts and feelings—no imaginative systematic construction, either in form or story.

I am in a good worldly position in relation to my poetry as it has found some acceptance and may bring me fame and some money—or also notoriety for having an eccentric growth of self which I parade nakedly and mythologize. The charm of my poetry is the pathos with which my limitations and self absorption is revealed. Very often like other people, but obsessional, caricatured, exaggerated, written overlarge and overemphasized—so that it can be seen, this whole of myself. Which reminds them of their own problems which they have conquered. I therefore may have the beauty of the dying swan.

Must do this estimate in detail some day.

What most upsets me in portraits of me and in my own writing is that I appear to be an exhibitionist with no insight into the fact that I force myself to this kind of outwardness because I have no inward relationship with the world. The *Empty Mirror* is sheer exhibitionism, with little objective dramatic art. My revelation is of what other people already take for granted—continuity of feeling among themselves. But what the hell is sheer objective dramatic art—newspaper reporting? Well, Faulkner, Joyce, too.

No return to girlhood, grandma,
No return to life.
You had your chance
to be a sticky creature
and feel boys
and sing with your children;

you didn't sing, you worked hard,
you never got out of yourself,
you never understood that when
your husband said "I am the Master"

he was being a big fool in jail,
you never called his bluff,
you never kissed his breast for joy.

Age is on you, death looms nigh,
greater and vast, and real as life.
Life grows real as death grows real.
Time grows solid as eternity gapes.
What did you do in solid time
but wander around dusting the walls?
        counting minutes?
Life was hard, money was scarce
children wet their pants

your husband cracked jokes and talked
like an innuendo machine.

Don't you want to spill your soul
eye to eye and heart to heart
truth to truth, and find out why
you never understood what anybody was saying?
And never said what you felt,
and didn't know what you felt either?

The clock is a profound toy—a silly object, almost unrelated to anything real in nature, but parallel to certain natural facts like the sun's day. It just goes ticking along in space and ringing at set intervals.

What is an interval of time? What does the word time mean as a philosophic concept? What physical thing does it relate to, aside from ideas of motion? and processes like sunrise and sunset? Interval means the spring unwinds and clock rings. What separates the sunrise from the sunset? Why doesn't everything happen at the same time, at once?

Proceed in reverse: Things happen in flow, one wave to another, cause to cause; therefore we don't say space exists inside itself.

Time is an abstract measure of motion in this sense, as days and lunar periods are; and enumeration of motions, a count of changes in space.

We live as long as 70 suns and call that our time. Amazing thing is that space has memory in our brains—memory and consciousness, still a mystery. Time is the memory of space. "Space exists inside itself?" What does that mean?

Sunrise is not sunset, impossible to conceive of that. Follow the sun in mind, and you will not think in the way that leads to, "All time exists at the same time, at once." All space exists at once—I'm confused. "Space exists in space." "The spring must unwind before the clock can ring."

Now time to come back to a more pleasurable phase of reality—I would rather be occupied with the head of a pretty girl. Problem to find definition of time in relation to space and vice versa.

Uptown queer bar—La Chandelle, 49th Street

Two nights spent with Dusty in an uptown queer bar where I thought America had already reached peak of personal decadence and mythological underground sexual intimacy known already in Berlin and Istanbul.

Big downstairs dyke joint, the scene with Helen [Elliott][250] and Daiches with the fat dyke with doglike face in men's clothes barking away the Milton Berle-like lesbian obscenity lines, "They're Freudian on campus and freaks in bed. So I said Babe just be natural and we'll have a ball, so I got down and we had a real groovy 69, don't you know I got a 2 inch clitoris? Right between the tits," and Helen Elliott actually blushed.[251]

Dusty told me not to chase after Helen, we weren't really suitable and besides, she wants to be the aggressor, wants to have to put herself out. How true of many people; Lucien, Dusty, etc.

Took a walk today in Paterson finding new scenery and going back to place I mentioned earlier. The old empty lot behind the houses I used to play in as child—saw and remembered these incidents. Morton in his garage in the car, telling me, "Don't you feel that way? When I see girls in school sometime I want to rush right out and grab hold of them?" and "I don't feel that way, no." "Well you wait when you're older. Sometimes the feeling gets so strong you can't hold it in."

Then we went inside his house to the bathroom—he and I and his pratboy and another boy. He sat on the toilet seat with his legs apart and the little boy, his friend who had done it before, knelt in front of him and touched his penis to his lips for ever so short a time, complaining that it didn't taste good, it tasted bad, he would get nauseous. The amazing thing was that he didn't seem to be self-conscious about it—wasn't apparently afraid of what we'd think, that he was queer, being of an age when it was all new and mysterious and forbidden, but not full of older sadistic guilt or sadism without the social consciousness and feeling of social shame or social awareness. Morton's mother was in the kitchen and called us out after awhile, we were in there for a long time, but she didn't seem to remark on what we were doing.

Later I had a conversation with Morton about what you do with your snot—wipe it on the underside of things like the kitchen table? Very much embarrassed even then by bodily secrets.

Then around that time in the mystery lot where we used to play, a gang of kids pulled Morton's pants down on the grassless path. I stood aside not helping him for fear of getting my own pants pulled down. But enjoying Morton's

250   Helen Elliott. Barnard College girlfriend of Carr's, portrayed in Kerouac's *Desolation Angels* as Ruth Erickson.

251   This paragraph was the basis for the poem "Two Nights." See Appendix, p. 513.

humiliation and baring, the baring of his privates. This last phrase is particu-larly exciting to me, as perhaps my whole character is exhibitionistic and evi-denced by fantasy and action on porch, slipping down pants for short time to traffic behind porch rail (unseen) and dream of that time of getting turned over and spanked by boys of my gang whom I feared.

I walked out over the little lot. It seemed so much less the vast mirror of the world, now a smaller lot, a green verdant surprisingly beautiful Arden spot, and at the familiar end of it I saw with its trees, the path, the shady shaped street leading there and a ruined old concrete building, now three sides and no roof, overgrown with moss, just an old house, not a building. Do I remember being warned away sixteen years ago because it threatened to fall and kill us?

It is true that on tea one remembers intimations of immortality. Small things like parts of the meadow would appear gaping, old, mysterious play spots, as in childhood—as when walking by a beautiful old house surrounded by a rustic brown log fence. I found house was torn down and two kids play-ing in the rubble. I spoke to one who looked up at me and answered my ques-tion, "When was it torn down?"

I discovered when he asked his friend that he was a stutterer—it took a long time to form phrases and drew them out of his mouth fearfully, like a spastic—though a nice looking yellow haired virile little boy. He finally said, "I don't know, I only moved here six months ago." Walking nearby 15 minutes later he shouted, "Hey mister, look what I found!" showing me a hollow pipe.

"Is it iron?" I said. "Very nice, thank you for showing it to me." That was all the communication. I turned away but wanted to go talk and play with them, afraid people would notice and I'd be taken for a pervert, in fact whenever I spoke to anyone all day I felt like a pervert.

Walked into school P.S. 17 on hill, after school, nobody there—had eerie place to myself. A very beautiful old wood school, large cheery kindergarten rooms, but gloomed by my memory of self-consciousness there. Went down-stairs to bathroom where some boys once mocked me when I went to do a doodie (as it was called in family) "Can we help you undo your buttons?" and it turned out to be equivalent to memory—a terrible place, all shadow and black in the basement with huge slate partitions between toilets. They should provide doors on toilets and give kids privacy, put up gay wallpaper, take it out of secret basement, light it up—not make such a contradictory confusing mys-tery and difficulty about going to the bathroom for kids. I remember we had to raise our hands and go all the way downstairs to the dungeon to take a crap.

I perhaps in addition had trouble because I couldn't manage my pants buttoned to shirt.

Upstairs in the room where I last sat, I said aloud, "I never wanted to leave here," remembering my transfer to horrible school 12 with its sadistic Dutchmen, fights with negroes and abusive morons—and the names they called me 'Ginsbug, Ginsbun, Jewbun.'

I also visited the tailor next door to old Miss Dye's candy shop and asked about her—she's still alive (in her 80s) in Long Island. She'd never married and was an educated woman. Was the tailor the Shrouded Stranger? Nathan the tailor, who when he remembered me said: "Yes, you were very bright, a real intelligent boy, you had the brain of an 80 year old man and so much alive, so full of joy, your eyes shined as if they had stars in them. Now you wear glasses, you don't look so smart anymore."

Did I have a sad feeling about my identity then? I thought where and what did I lose? Did I lose my memory somewhere?

Walking down the hill I saw a sloppy young kid nearly my age coming up with an absent expression, I thought, "Make believe you are he, he is you, he is thinking your thoughts! What a wonder that a person should trudge up the hill with his awareness in another world of time, unlike all the other people here! Imagine him wandering around seeking the sensations of childhood! Without present attachments or identity, profession, wife, love, home, father— just wandering suspended in time looking around him at the scenes of another time he passed through just like yesterday—wondering if there was any different feeling it was so strange not to remember even that he once was bright and cheerful and alive, so as to be a joy to the old tailor. Not a Jewish dreamer, a real saint, a real madman, ugly and somewhat uncontained by physical surroundings. To make you shudder for him like for the mad anthropoid (I saw later in the day) washing a car with squalid round face, half-lidded dreary eyes, jutting lower lip, round shoes, baggy pants and overall coat, dressed like a freak of a mechanic, not in this world in the soul, an idiot! What does he think about? What does this person I saw who I transferred my own preoccupations to <u>think</u> about? But he was just a sloppy kid you saw on a hill.

I noticed a month ago—similarity between poems in *Gates of Wrath* with *The Alchemist in the City* by Gerard Manley Hopkins. Stanza 4, penultimate and ultimate stanzas.

Method of this journal: Entry about Haledon Avenue lot—which gave me trouble writing—or not writing, but trouble to stay with and get down the facts and more trouble to get myself to expand just a little on detail and atmosphere rather than writing of present day happening and put down a record of scene revisited—a crucial scene, an archetype of my consciousness of this eternity.

This past of childhood seems wonderful to revisit since I do so as a grown man (with my own greater mysteries) staring at actual spots in landscape where I was another time, like in another life. As if my years of violence and extremity in New York were a totally strange existence to anything conceived in boyhood, yet prophesied by boyish longings and intuitions. As if Paterson places with their quietness now, no fear, no mystery—I could explore fearlessly with no illusion—those places where illusion and mystery, ignorance gloomed the world over then. Everything was gloomy then and full of unknowns and mysteries, especially the future and the meaning of the present.

I revisit the old mysteries in my memory; even better I go back to the very places the mysteries arose—as if the scenes of dreams and memory could become incarnate again—they're still there—and I travel backward in time. I only lack seeing myself and other children at play. The Shrouded Stranger is myself of the future with future knowledge revisiting Allen Ginsberg in the present.

I always liked science fiction and mystery plays with melancholy, I inherited this from Louis. It is one of his archetypical emotions. Mine however is not enclosed so much by mystery because of the alternations of saintly, saint seeking, eternity and human comedy. That shadow I see threatening me is me in the future with my painful old disillusion looking at myself trying to communicate. This journal is a shift of memory and perception into my past—its dramatic significance in line with the future.

A typical mystery—I didn't know the meaning of the joy when the gang pulled down Morton's pants—how much I was interested then, wanted to see them masturbate him or humiliate him openly. It was hidden to all then. I didn't know how interested I was in the cocksucking in the bathroom. I said nothing and did not take part. Or am I just interpreting significances in light of future external occurrences and developments there from and putting meaning to it now that didn't exist at all then? I was then faced with dumb, shy, withdrawn wonder, no experience to form my taste and desire. I was faced with outside void of experience then—how could I know anything but anarchic lusts and fears.

I now fantasize being more aggressive sexually and talking less about love with Neal. A veritable wonder of dumb enactment. Just get on top of him and fuck his mouth. That's what he once said he was most excited by, the night in Denver I got excited and did what I thought of to him.

Sooner or later as memory grows more balanced and I enter the world of the present I will record the present as it happens—fresh, with all the conversation and detail. Right now it seems too much trouble and I am obsessed with vague sorts of incommunicable abstractions like the above, like sense of eternity, etc.

Phrases which sound nice but are meaningless grasps at ideas like "memory grows more balanced" should also be eliminated, I do it from lack of attention.

More and more interested in idea of writer as mere conduit for reality from air to paper—a machine, an electrical wire. *Empty Mirror* made up of thoughts that came to me, occurred in my mind, rather than things I tried to think up, in that sense they are objective. They are really the substance of my thought.

Content is all subjective projection, illusion of world as carried in mind. Equally it is reproduction of that illusion—as great as if I reproduced someone else's mind in a novel. Try reproduction not of variance of illusion but of physical facts as they appear before me? See "Bricklayer's Lunch Hour" for that. But selection of impression is subjective, it's impossible to reproduce things blank and dumb? Whazzis all about? Words!

Alternative: that I am so locked in prison of subjective selfhood, so absorbed in machinery of my own thoughts I can't see outside of myself. The same difference as between horrible aesthetic paranoid hang-up on [Merchant] Marine or ribbon factory which through Lucien's eyes reduced itself to realistic picture of situation, the opposite of paranoia.

Classic situation: my entry in journal waiting for Neal to appear in Denver versus picture of situation I should have put down.

I am 22 sitting in a basement in Denver. The kid whose cock I have been sucking is off with another woman in bed. I sit and write down what I think, his accusing me of every kind of meanness, contrasting that to ideal picture of him coming by and sucking my cock not making him wait. I realize I ain't going to have things my way, I want him to myself; so I decide to give up the deal, only I have nothing else to go to. So I stay around and hate him and say I love him so much I'll stay anyway. So he finally comes in and lets me blow him because he sees how lonely I am and he enjoys being on top of me and having someone kneel in front of him; he enjoys seeing through my pride and breaking it down. Seeing that I tell him I'm pride-broken and he can do anything he wants with me. I figure that will attract him, I've been too lukewarm with pride. We go off together but I begin reasserting my pride as he loses interest. Finally I leave situation in Texas and I write "Dakar Doldrums."

World as reflected here consists of unsuccessful brushes with a few jobs and organized society, five or six intimate relationships with people and fragmentary pictures of industrial landscape, plus a lot of philosophical constructions which carry no picture—must carry picture while writing. Must also capture moments of intensity—like feeling that head is severed from body entry—acute realization of a strong actual moment of thought, not just meandering everyday conceptions without importance in their striking me. Value of these latter entries is that they are summaries of often thought thoughts.

My interest has always been in the appearances of the mind, for lack of touch with anything more real or—more full of feeling in me; no feeling, no related significance.

Dusty's story in the dawn on Sheridan Square of her mother trying to kill her and I dreamed of it two nights later with cops, everybody with a poker hanging out of the window and gorillas with revolvers and police.

The more I see the more disgusting the publishers are—anything original frightens them, anything out of the way or odd puts them off—but once the odd becomes a craze they're always climbing on the bandwagon and trying to force the subsequent odd to seem like every other odd. The publishers gamble on inconsequential kicks thinking they'll catch on but they really have very little taste or insight into what is good. This I see in Harcourt, in Scribner's, two large companies and Wyn, one small company. Also in Doubleday, another large company. Every time I have come into contact with a publishing situation I have left depressed, whether or not I succeed in putting my goods across or not. So far they have totally fucked up on Jack, Bill and myself, and at this point to bring up Huncke and Neal is officially impossible.

Old thin queer man with dog with big messy pink ribbon walking in front of bank on city corner. I wonder if dog is embarrassed (people know old man lavished all his affection on dog) by the relationship.

May 3, 1952.
Across from me in the subway sit two Scandinavians with hair of incredible yellow brightness—their faces are neither rough nor effeminate, their skin is incredibly red, not merely ruddy, almost as if they were made up for theatrical performance. If they were Americans they would be simpering and narcissistic, but they come from a far land where men love men. They seem young.

They have small eyes. The one I love has a friendly innocent relaxed posture. The boy walks out of the subway, as if eyeing me, maybe he wants to connect with me. He saw me before gazing raptly at him, he walks by my side, glancing up at me. I don't know if it's interest or curiosity. I go down subway stairs to second level where a fat drunk sits smoking a cigarette on the stairway uttering in a rasping groan, "eh, this country stinks."

To include in Shrouded Stranger all archetype dreams as episodes.

How like Jekyll/Hyde my notes on peyote are:

    10:02—Drank potion

    10:04—Feel faint

    10:30—Hair is growing on my palms, etc.

Must someday tell story of chicken coop linking Mahler's dream of spanking, Gene on porch, dream of being pursued, shroudy stranger, appearance on back porch.

Beginning with magic spell, sexual fantasies as king in torture room, men hanging spread eagled upside down.

Link also with chicken coop building buying of chickens, chicken hatchery, Eugene's comment on my buying friendship or being taken advantage of by others.

These notes on my life and fantasies were put down in the hope of showing my lack of completion and development as a man as equal to the reader, as Rousseau does. This may be true but someone may say, "I was better than that man." In fact I believe other people are better than me—as I look around at my friends who have suffered more than I, had deeper trials—I never even had a final trial. Some, like Lucien, seem, to my humiliation and eternal chagrin, better than myself and I envy them.

Our feelings are important, our world is built on the hiding and transformation of feelings into competition for gain, glory and happiness. So my feelings are expressed in an attempt to reach truth in others: to say, this is me. I am no worse than you, aren't you like me?

But my first page, if I ever wrote everything out chronologically, would be:

"I write my life out here as it is the only writing I can do. I am unable to give symbolic or fictional form to my experiences. My gaze and vision do not go beyond myself, my memory and my imagination. My imagination I fear is diseased and it is not constant enough to allow long years of work recreating a fixed image. All I can do is say what I know of what I have done—mostly what has happened to me—I don't believe my own imagination any more than you do.

It exists to me as autobiography and as confession since I speak of things I would not otherwise tell everybody. The alternative is to write the "Monster of Dakar" as a third person story, integrated like a short story not an actual confession. What I confess is interesting only when I approach the reality of my situation without exhibitionism, telling true humiliations.

Nothing is finished here, everything exists without consummation and force—I am hiding something.

All this humiliating vagary comes from an archetype feeling: Shame. Shame is the greatest source of pain to me.

After a week I'm already sick of the ambiguity of love. Good for a man to adore something outside of himself. Ah! love thou rarest of realities.

> There was so much sweetness
> open in your eyes
> my body softened
> and my soul looked in surprise.

I met Dick Davalos[252] again in San Remo—just as Dusty and I had been talking about him and the ambiguity of my position. He is shocked that I remembered that first time when he took off his clothes and sat down naked beside me.

Perfect beauty of his face—soft tender eyes—the stare—beautiful low voice as we exchanged compliments and questioned each other's fidelity of memory. Amazing to me the sudden flash of softness of love—incredible sweetness and sad heaviness of belly when I envisioned him that weekend after meeting. His body youthful and massive and manly—perfection of first evening—the unashamed desire. And the curious moral quality of his approach to the world—seeming at first like a Dostoyevskian purity that left me sick with love.

The second evening—my waiting on the corner in the bar in the rain. His welcome, he had been calling me all afternoon at Dusty's. When I came in I avoided him and talked about his house. Then in bed later, the over relaxed anticlimactic loss of feeling—partial loss of physical sight. I fed my mind on visual imagery, erotic but not directly sexual. Image of equal tenderness

---

252 Richard Davalos (b. 1930). Handsome actor who had a brief relationship with Ginsberg. In 1955, he played Aaron Trask, the favored brother, opposite James Dean's role as the rebellious brother, in the film, *East of Eden*.

directed at me. Too much talk about love, destroyed love. I fell back to dead level again, slightly hostile.

Trouble with him is that he is a selfish and slightly hypocritical commercial type, almost a professional fairy. I keep suspecting him of some immense soft ego, mistaking me for an object of value perhaps and desiring to make myself more solitary Allen in his eyes, less a social asset, more an obsessed man, obsessed with love hang-up like millstone destroying all lightness and softness of situation—take it too seriously. Begin to want to threaten him, intellectual captiousness—how to regain the feeling of pure wonder and joy.

What is Love? Different from daily deadness. When I sigh with carnal honor am I crazy? All the time I go around confessing to everybody. I am a monomaniac, self-absorbed freak. I repeat this last thought over and over till I can justify it or till it sinks in and I am horrified at myself—seeing myself as others (an idealized Lucien) sees me.

Lucien Carr is my ideal image of virtue and awareness. I always look at myself through his eyes as I imagine them—to chasten my vanity or rationalization selfhood. If he knew this he would abhor me, I creep around infiltrating like a monster, a bloodsucker, an emotional vampire.

The horror of my vanity is that I think other people think about me like I think they think about me. I have the wrong idea of what they think about me, because I operate by myself without reciprocal feelings imagining them in roles with me which they never or no longer even conceive of.

To list: My favorite masturbatory images and scenes.

Spun out in this autonomous dream world of a journal which is literary masturbation, these thoughts, to another will seem so removed and mad. Attempt to render my mind innocent, without guile, reduced to wonder. We have not surrendered to each other—there is some kind of state of mind where usual blocks and worries are abolished by soft light of tenderness.

May 14, 1952.
Dream: I am following a youngish man with poorly groomed hair carrying a large briefcase, it is a ghastly pursuit. Secrecy is important, we go into the subway where he checks his bag in a locker in order to follow me. I walk right on past him, get on escalators which crisscross and interweave with one another in space until I arrive at the Navy recruiting station at the top.

As I ride up I know I should have checked with Navy information officers downstairs on my preliminary status and get information papers before going through final stages of recruiting. I go to a bench and line up where final check is given and fill out papers. There seems to be some question about my driving a car—I say I can, am asked how fast, say 90 mph, then realize that's too fast. I settle for 60 mph but there is other information I don't have. I am given a slip to be filled out by me at home with proper information and I go.

Similar archetypes:

The subway station where I get lost in the confusion of levels and tracks and elevated structures, 96th St?

The huge movie house in which I always get lost in the balconies.

May 20, 1952.

For Preface—Apology, etc,

Poems, some of them in *Empty Mirror* have a wholeness and style of their own, a form which includes completeness and pleasing rhythm, others are just statements of fact. Whatever I have to say had best be left as is, as said, distortion removes original spring from the sentences, the purity of the thought, and the exactness of expression. What I really think is what I am after. There may be a way of getting nearer by more work, which I find oppressive and impossible. There may be a way of refinement to symmetry but this would take out what is important, the nakedness which is truth. Perhaps art is not truth; but otherwise art seems empty. Art may be greater truth than that which I offer, this may be appraised but not criticized.

Our thoughts where they meet reality are intense and poetical; this is the underlying idea. I have not written this book to prove it, but I have collected these fragments because they seemed interesting to others, and archetypical to myself, in my own life.

The only things we "know" are what we think in the moments we give ourselves away, "tip our mitt." I prefer those rare moments in authors when they are not trying to formulate an official policy for themselves or the real world.

May 16, 1952.

Dream: At a party in familiar apartment (York Ave. or apartment in Mexico City above bar) with Durgin and Neal. I find N.C. in bathtub, jerking off. I put my hand on his cock and then get in bathtub with me upside down in front of him clasping hipwaist blowing him. Durgin comes by the door, N. leans forward not hiding me sufficiently, he doesn't care. Durgin smiles slightly mockingly.

Lucien called Neal a "pirate." "He's all right to his friends but I don't like the way he cons other people." Spoke of self as Neal's "friend's friend."

There is something ugly going on in my soul again. This last month: pre-occupation with queerness, dope, vice and pop, apocalypse of subterraneans, dispersal of attention to practical affairs, call of Amazon voyage.

Helen Parker's "defect"—as a joke, in bed, she suddenly coyly showed me her "defect"—a small pimply sty in her thigh near her asshole. I ventured to kiss it, complimenting her on it, but I was really disgusted by her narcissism.

Scene outside Bellevue before Carl's blowtop days after split with Olive[253]—child playing with a cat and a drunk asleep on the pavement by the gates. Give me $10 of love.

In a red lit bar with Stanley Gould,[254] his girl Jean, and Carl, bored and embarrassed by Carl's recital of his violence in fight with his wife. I look like someone else I don't like, I don't like my own looks in the bar mirror—my image of floating city slicker, disillusioned, somewhat of an empty heel or a middle class intellectual con-artist. I seem top heavy—haired (I need a haircut), hard long aging face—reaching the late twenties, shadows under my eyes and below mouth, not well dressed, too informally dressed, black browed, heavy eyebrows, too mental and lonely and personally sadistic[255]—as I once saw myself through Dr. Cott's eyes.

In the middle of the night at Davalos' apartment feeling failure of love—as in Dostoyevsky—as in the story at the Geneva conference when the translingual earphones broke down and they all forgot their monomania when the cat meowed in the middle of the babble—it will be a blade of grass that brings peace to the world—some simple thing will produce a miracle in men's minds, some bird or child's cry will be the catalyst.

Unemployment Insurance Office in Paterson

A bank of different kinds of filing cases piled one on another, cardboard ones on top, drawers out, old smoky snake looping out of the middle drawer which protrudes on its rails, old ladies talking to old ladies across desks, little numbers hanging from the ceiling, everybody taking their time.

A certain Dizzy Gillespie chorus reminds me of an afternoon in Denver in 1947 when to please Neal, I brought a Coleman Hawkins record to Carolyn's house,

---

253 Olive Solomon. Carl Solomon's wife.

254 Stanley Gould. Carl Solomon's friend, depicted as Ross Wallenstein in Kerouac's *The Subterraneans.*

255 This paragraph was the basis for the poem "In a Red Bar." See Appendix, p. 515.

played them over and over, discovering them and he admired them. I hear it in a chophouse late in the morning five years later in New York and my heart sinks in hollowness, hallowing.

Dig the dignity of these buildings.

May 30, 1952.
My book cut in half today and I appear twisted and deformed, a cripple mental case—the 'leanness' W.C. Williams asks for.

I do not recite the activity of importance—guarding Carl in his fits of madness—Dusty moving into my attic—the big expensive double date with Merims—Williams' letters to Pound and Moore—my decision to stay in New York and stick it out—mad correspondence with Jack, Bill, Neal, Pound, Moore, etc.—Louis' reaction (you'll get in trouble) to Dusty's move, etc. So much missed important detail.

June 1, 1952.
My imagination of self is of my stumbling desperately through the halls of Hell with arms outstretched shouting hysterically, "Where are all the mirrors?" and a smile on my face. I enacted this the other night for Dusty at Merim's apartment.

My novel must be retelling not in symbols of the actuality of spiritual experience as it was seen then and now, the poetry and myth existing on a level of reality corresponding exactly to the reality of its occurrence. The myth is born in me in reality of my experience, hallucinatory or not; so that further complication or disguise will only be confusing. Don't bother to cover up madness.

In 3rd Person?

I have been meditating on two things: 1. Evil 2. Death.

As to evil, it is a sexless womb which reproduces in ever-widening circles like an amoeba. Discord is a debt which someone must pay. I wonder if God suffers our discords. Hurricanes produce murder also, however.

Millennium...evil does not reproduce itself from that starting point. Do we work for that too, ultimately?

I saw Van Doren at school today on the street while walking in the slush and rain with John Hollander and he walked by us and stopped with a big smile and said, "Well, look at that, just look, both of you together. Heavens what an unbeatable combination, just unbeatable."

Then John said, "It's wet," and Van Doren said, "What is?" and I said, "The atmosphere," and Van Doren said, "I hadn't noticed," with a big fake mock smile and a grimace all out of proportion to his irony and we parted.

Write personal cantos:

> So old W.S.B. said
> When you're dead,
>   you're dead,
> You're just dead,
>   That's all.

June, 1952.

Dream: I followed Carl dressed in rags, he followed a beggar on the road, we were three beggars. The beggar we thought would take us to Christ instead wandered around aimlessly, finally went up rickety stairway to anarcho-communist meeting room and led us to Ezra Pound on the podium.

The boy at the gas station in the middle of frightening Bruckner Blvd., Bronx, in the night on our way to Bronx Park and Dusty and Robert Merims—he cute, dirt smudged face, crew haircut, lively, intelligent, snappy replies to us bored inebriates—me in my shell—his blue shirt open at chest, then as if in answer to a wish he takes off his shirt while talking to us so we can see his body while closing station.

"The flesh has no reputation."—Carl Solomon

June 28, 1952.

Conversation with William Carlos Williams

He: If you cut down everything no joking, no looseness, your book has a chance of making some kind of impression different from the general run. I'm not bothered by unreality except by the reality of cancer of rectum, he thought. He looked healthy and heavier in face. He called me "My dear" on phone and said we may not see each other again when I left.

I told him anecdote of Jews at Columbia—he wasn't aware of anti-Semitic construction of remark. He asked me if I minded phrase, "This young Jewish boy." He's afraid of gut cancer operation, the change of his way of life. Write about his cancer of rectum? Nobody would be interested—only interesting in a young man.

Write true accounts of feelings of sympathy for Jack and Lucien—dark side of reality.

I would like to be a part of inner nature, relieved of the machinery of metaphysics and schizoid roses, but I can't take part. My metaphysics turns out to be weakness and cowardice. I can't even vigorously conceive a job, conceive a plan of action or a passion in the natural world that surrounds me with its factories, techniques, studies, complexities of practice and rough experience.

What job, what love do I want?

Accepting reality, we still have the preferences of the heart to find out. And having found those out, possibly to overturn the structure, queerness and metaphysics. Years ago we were faced with the problem but evaded it by inhabiting an alternative world of ideas.

The fact is I can't get myself out of this rut and moving.

I notice coming out of the movies' imaginary world the solidity of the reality I walk on, and the building I see outlined like stage settings in the glare of downtown traffic going among the streetlights.

These thoughts composed in symbolic world of imagination, contrasted with the actuality of the world not regarded as mere appearance, but something of which I am a part, yet not participating in.

I'm afraid of the possibility that there are not two possible worlds but only one, of actuality. My situation in life and inability to handle it and live in actuality happily results in a madworld. These notes therefore should be practical plans for the immediate future and my relationship to the world. I have never written down my daily worldly plans—practical intentions—so as to clarify them and make them take definition.

To look for a job—to get an apartment—to live independently—to get psychoanalysis—to find love in me and for me.

I have neither job, apartment, independence or love or analysis, which is an intermediary or catalyst between my present state and what I want it to be.

Do I want these things? I used to suffer when I thought of the job hunting prospect. The nights before and during the period—tension, feeling I was being swallowed up in an impossible world, an alien situation that would break me apart from my only strength—the thoughts of ego—and make me egoistic sensitive suffering object in an office surrounded by instructions I couldn't understand, projects I could not face for lethargy of their complexity. Projects for which I lacked confidence in my methods or could not complete in time to escape disapproval of my superiors and the realization that they were eternally superior to me. Fear to take orders for fear I should be <u>unable</u> to carry them out; like a nightmare situation—fear to ask for a good job for fear of intensifying inability situation, all wrapped up in self, as I still am now. How I used to suffer. The physical memory just overwhelmed me.

August 8, 1952.
Wisdom cannot be learned. From consideration of the past, one cannot tell the future like a sage but can tell the outcome of one's past hopes; what happened when one took a stand.

As an adolescent I wanted to go into the great world of men and affairs and dreamed of being a senator or representative or an ambassador. Having lost a high school election to my humiliation, I turned to my own life. I dreamed of love from a blond man and while that dream was never realized in a lifetime marriage of cocks, I found love from men I never dreamed existed. Satiated in knowledge of my man lust, I turned to women finally.

I wanted to write poetry, but doing so found at last a stony line and unpoetic words to deliver me to the title of poetry which I practice in coldness and design.

FIRST POEMS OF ALLEN GINSBERG

Hymn to the Virgin
[David Kammerer to Lucien Carr]

Thou who art afraid to have me, lest thou lose me;
Great anodyne, thyself compound of pain;
Thou comforter discomfited;
Thou strength so fraught with feebleness,
And mind unsure, unmade;
So prudent and unwise:
Thou at once ravished and virgin-bride;
Thou happiness sans happiness;
Thou God, so mortal coiled,
Thou terror, so afraid;
Lover, asleep: celibate untouchable, awake;
Oh, contradiction contradicts!
Unwire thy tight braced treasure,
Thy rigid regular relax,
Thy self-pent, hoarded soul release;
Give, share, lose; know entire co-mingledness
Lest we both die isolate and unbloomed.

August 20, 1944

. . .

Epitaph for David Kammerer

A weary lover
once he was
Who wept as only
a lover does—

or else he laughed
as a lover must;

now his mouth
is ringed with dust.

For he is dead,
and now will heal
The wound which he
alone could feel.

The credit's his—
He was quite brave,
To shut his loving
In his grave.

August 20, 1944[256]

. . .

I placed one rose upon her hair
And placed my hand upon her knee.
And as we breathed the summer air
She returned the rose to me

I twined a lovely rose into her hair
She leaned—we kissed—it fell upon her knee
And so we breathed the heavy summer air
She laughingly returned the rose to me.

August 22, 1944

. . .

Monologue Without Images or Music

Be careful, this is
    civilization,
you are not in wonderland,
    this is not a
dream. These people are real,
you don't know them.

256 Later published as "Epitaph for a Suicide" in *Columbia Jester*, vol. 43, no. 9 (October 1944).

What are you now? a
nothing. They don't love
  you. There is no
reason for them to love you.
  Try

to accept this. Perhaps
you may learn to love them.
Even in your ignorance
  you must learn to love
what is outside you, must
  learn to love
them without them loving
  you first.

That's what's most difficult,
  most miraculous,
about your isolation. Yes
  it is a great
difficulty. Nobody takes
your hand. You must be
  patient, you must
first seek to love
  yourself. You must
waken it slowly in others
before you get love yourself.
  You must find where
it hides. You must call it
  out of the outside.

Do not frighten those
  whom you try to love.
Everything is easily done
  with great patience
over a period of years
  You may even,
then,
  talk of your reverie;
but not to strangers:

even polite
conversation is dangerous,
Their world is real,
   yours is not.

   Certainly do
not talk as if your
own reverie were more
   real than anybody's.
That way you run the risk
   of dreaming yourself woe.

You are in fact
   fortunate, even
in your ignorance. You have
so far been protected
   against the result
of your own reverie.
   Some reveries
are too deep to return
from.

   Remember, this dream
lasts only a short time.
   Don't interrupt
the dream, cherish
   it: your flesh
is the last flesh you
will own. You have just
   one body. You have
begun to understand
   what Death is.
Then all is ended,
   reverie and all

   Think of those
who did not even
   survive, purely
by accident. They miss this

security,
however confusing it is.

Think that you are in glory.
The world has taken care of you,
    will take care of you,
if all goes by expectation of
    the average fate.
    Your uniqueness is
ignorance. Remember that.
You are imperfect
    compared to others.

They know something
    you do not. That
is why they seem happy
    to you, happier
than yourself.

    It is true
that you have suffered,
but you do not understand
    yet how unimportant
it is outside of yourself,
    because all
do not suffer like you.
    You are not
like them. They can do
nothing about it anyway.
    They are not
you. You have no complaint.

You have had a difficult time,
that is your burden.
    You do not understand.
    That is your burden.
Your main difficulty is that
    nobody thinks like
you do. True that is

the nature of the world.
They even see things
    differently from each other.
Nobody thinks
    like anybody else
except a few lovers and
    some families. Then
they agree to think the same.

In that respect everybody
    thinks the same,
though on this superficial
level. It suffices
    to keep things together
temporarily.

    Be
superficial as far
    as that goes.
Observe the customs of
    the country and live
within them.
    If
any need to be changed and you
are in a position to do so,
    do so,

but do not meddle beyond
    your power which is
limited to the point
    of inexistence at important
times. What is beyond
    your ken may result
in jail, disfigurement or death.

You may cooperate then
    as far as your ken
agrees with anyone else's
and as far as all kens coincide.

That is not far
but you may at least
    find employment
    and a home. The rest
you can do in private, if
    you can grasp
anything solidly enough to
do it by yourself. But
    the most easily grasped
realities are common to all
and are not worthless.
    They lead to comfort
and pleasure and even power
    over other reveries if
you are fortunate and optimistic.

    Certainly do not become
panicky or afraid, nobody
will hurt you if
you keep out of
    their way, unless
they are themselves overpowered
    by reverie or
the ken has officially broken
down. Keep out of the way
    unless you think this
or that stranger is safe. Most
well dressed people are safe.

    Talk with them as if
you agree that consciousness
is simple and also
    unimportant, and
that it is not necessary
    to match reveries
and kens at the immediate
    moment. They will
probably understand your tone,
    if you do not carry it

too far and make
   the thought explicit.

If you insist on coming
   to an immediate rapport
on the subject of the dream,
   if you do not
maintain the illusion of
   ignorant security,
if you fail to take
   the birthright of your
being for granted without
   doubt or amazement
you will not succeed
   in ingratiating
yourself into their trust
   and cooperation and
they will cast you back into your
   own illusion with the rest
   of the crippled herd.

You may even worship a God
   in a church, which you
can find anywhere strangely enough
   if you can keep quiet
and are still interested.

[*late September 1944*]

. . .

A Love Poem

Though I forbade desire in me to live,
Yet soon it found its way into my breath.
Forgive my love, as I myself forgive
It for its finding of itself in flesh.
Love has for me been compound of forsaking,
Of gifts to the ungenerous and rich,

Mastering of heart, submitting to its breaking,
Weeping sick for souls and bodies which
Were alien or unattainable,
Or lost before their time.
                         My heart was sick,
Was hurt with a deep wound I tried to fill
With tears, then words—yet still the blood ran quick

What was foresworn I seized; what was denied
I knew, till longing changed to memory.
I wished but to sleep gently at your side,
And then, perhaps, to take as gently unto me
All the substantial symbols of your soul
That you out of your quietness and pity,
Or your shame, might tenderly bestow—
Assuming for yourself the sorrow of my body.
Thus, when you solaced me in my desire,
I held your body, lay beside it sleeping,
Feeling the pain of your own inward fire,
Weeping myself to hear your silent weeping.
I sought you bringing my heart's sadness
At knowing your despair, for I had heard
You crying in the night in the strange madness
Long growing in your soul. I knew the word
Of your hallucinated heart. And while
My body is for me as well my soul,
I did not come of sensual desire,
But brought you my half heart to make yours whole.
I hoped you sensed our equal misery,
The bitter heritage of our disaster.
Thus, when you touched my hand, consoling me
I felt our single spirit cleaving faster.
That night I knew the consummation of
My old desires and my former love.
I sensed the feat of spirit in your flesh,
And felt in frank delight the sensual mesh
That cages us within our hearts. And beating
Newly in my body was the fleeting

And abundant ecstasy of love
That is accepted, which I knew nothing of.
And I was then much satisfied by deep
Compassion. I lay awake with you,
In quietness, with gratitude. My sleep
Was the most sweet and heart-full that I knew.

Did you shrink, inwardly, upon my touch?
What is it you would keep that I must ask?
Know that I seek of you only such
Substance as is given without loss.
Know that love takes only, to bestow,
That mine is a desire to be bereft
Of a soul that's isolate. And know
That love is my offering, and my heart's gift.
If I have robbed you by my giving, or have
Imposed upon you pain; if I have taken,
And would take again what you would save;
If I have seized what you would have forsaken,
Do not deny me thinking me a thief,
Nor yet reject me out of needless shame.
Do not deny the sharing of my grief
For prides or sorrows that you will not name.
Forgive this love, my desire to be whole,
And, if you can, allow the pleasure of my soul.

[*October 1944, revised 1951*]

. . .

I sought you bringing my heart's sadness,
At knowing your own despair, for I had heard
You crying in the night with a strange madness,
Long growing in your soul. It found a word
In your hallucinated voice. And while
My body is as well for me my soul,
I came to solace you, a crying child,
Not for sensual fulfillment whole.

[*October 1944*]

. . .

A Litany

He who walks within the womb
Shines no shadow past his doom:
The morbid moon's symbolic light
Will not filter through his night;
The sun's gold-seeded, fertile rays
Will not fecundate his days;
And if he dream of life at dawn,
At midnight, life and death are one,
For he has slept too long and late:
Perpetual midnight is his fate.
His arms locked tight about his leg,
He sleeps in the unbroken egg:
Forever must the shell be whole,
Forever fetal be the soul,
Forever the spirit be uncursed,
Blessed because it cannot thirst.

Oh angels, curse me, I am damned!
This was not myself I named—
I rode the tortoise and the ark
And knew the cobra-hooded dark,
Crossed deserts where the fig leaves hang,
Where the serpent joins the tail and fang:
I ate both bread and blood in drouth,
And gasped within the fish's mouth.
I have seen the naked sky
And know immortality;
I have walked upon the earth
And I will bring eternal birth.

[*October 1944*]

[*Poet's notes:*]

This is a poem contra *Gemeinheit* the animal symbolism in the last half I culled
from a book or two on sex worship that I looked thru (very interesting, inci-
dentally, the sexual origin of cathedral spires, horseshoes over doors, mistle-
toe, crosses, etc.)

The tortoise is a symbol of birth and creation—because of mythical androgyny, also because of phallus like tumescence of head when it sticks out. The ark is a <u>Yoni</u> symbol (female organ)—as receptacle, holder of Aaron's rod, etc. Cobra-head—cobras are sacred because of phallic looks, especially when angry and hooded and puffed. Triadic fig leaves have reference to trinity cross, male copulatory organs, feminine erogenous zones by tradition. Phallic serpent, with Yoni head biting phallic tail, is by tradition a symbol of circular regeneration, immortality. Bread and blood are, before transubstantiation myth, symbols of male and female contributions to life blood, male; bread (womb—sustenance) female last, the fish's mouth is by tradition like unto the vagina—and thus fishes (as well as cows, goats, cocks).

. . .

Orpheus heard with quickened breath
the black rhetoric of death,
I lied to the sun, that I might soon
Become the lover of the moon—
I look in the air, and it is cold
and I look in myself, and I am old,
And I am not sad, and I am not whole,
and somewhere I have lost my soul...
Say goodbye to the spring
To the spectral love of autumn
Goodbye, goodbye beloved,
Winter's cold has come.
Say goodbye to the night,
Say goodbye to the moon
Goodbye, goodbye beloved
We will love soon

Apollo is a weed,
David's body is bones,
And all of Helen's seed
are sleeping under stones.
My soul is sick with tomorrow,
My body hates my head;
the stuff of life is sorrow,
And soon I will be dead.

[October 1944]

[*Poet's notes:*]
Capture this idea! Write poetry of specific things. Don't try to consciously universalize unless you can do without using universal platitudes.

. . .

The Last Voyage[257]

Others have voyaged far, have sailed
On waves that wash beyond the world.
I loved the ancient men who veiled
The image of themselves where swirled
The maelstrom of the holy stream,
And I glided through the smoking air
With sails uplifted by a dream.

I knew the pit of Baudelaire.
The sodden Tree of Knowledge groaned
Beneath my keel as it fell sighing
Under the waters; its leaves moaned
With silent cries and murmurs dying,
Sinking with the drowning boughs.
Where slid the Tree I drove to drown.
My barque fell under reddened clouds
Of burning water, chased on down
Under a moon of morality
That eclipsed the savage sun;
Mad moon pendant from the Tree,
The Upas of Elysian.
I sank into a barren land,
Ruled by lunar mystery,
Where Demons danced upon the sand
Beneath the drifting veil of sea.
They ate the carrion of their sins,
And on their brains I saw them sup;
I saw them struggle with red winds

---

257   This poem was heavily influenced by Rimbaud's "Bateau Ivre." There were at least four versions of this poem. This one is the most complete.

That plucked their flesh and drew them up.
Burghers of Chaos, they were wined
On blood; they prayed; they traded jests;
They wept; they stealthily reclined
Upon a gutter-woman's breasts.
I sailed past angry creatures chattering
Bloodsongs to enchanted peoples;
I sailed past vengeful deaths-heads clattering
Calamity from tops of steeples;
I sailed above the heads of tombs
That littered twenty centuries;
I journeyed on through leprous wombs
That nurtured new catastrophes,
Past narrow-shadowed naves of night
Where Satans sang in secret shame,
Past a crucifix in flight
In starry firmaments of flame
On wings that shuddered in the night,
Groping moonward from the day;
Illusions clustered on the arc
Of rainbows falling far away.
The Earth went black; the living moaned
And cursed a God who was not there;
And the Big Jesus sat enthroned,
And smiled, and shouted up a prayer:
"Bless O me my Lord and Master,
Thaumaturgist of Disaster,
Wreaker, Wrecker, Builder, Breaker,
Stingy Artisan, Unmaker.
Hope is dream and dream is dead;
Death is Shepherd, men are led
To fields unmellowed by the sun:
Without the moon all dreams are done.
Sinner, lover, fool, and knave.
Each one prays above his grave;
Thief and priest are damnéd all,
For each in turn in His must fall;
Sin was sucked in branch and root
And impregnated in its fruit:

The poison of morality
Dripped from Eden's evil Tree."

This was the Earth, the Hell where I
Flung out my heart into the fire,
And stilled a last, despairing cry
To see fade into smoke, desire.
Now, in the brilliant spectral flare,
Phantom universes wheeled;
Illumined in the radiant glare
Their cracks and corners gaped, revealed;
Theologies sprawled bare and bright,
Their shrouded secrets in my eyes,
All Hells, all Heavens in my sight,
Unfolding fire-encrusted lies.
I saw the ancient ordained evil,
The usual stupidity;
I saw my God was now the Devil,
Laughing from the ancient Tree.

I leave to Christ damnation of
My soul. I also leave to God
All sin, that He may make of love
Metempsychosis into sod.
I leave my pity, bless with Truth,
Him who is by Satan led,
Whose soul knows nothing of God's truth.
He will be damned when he is dead,
Who sailed his ship, a Devil's whore,
To find on the unyielding sea
Horizons that he'd crossed before;
Who damned the wind's inconstancy.
Hail to him who dwells in Hell,
Hail to whom the Earth is Fire!
Rejoice! Who hears the midnight bell
When Satan's fork is poet's lyre!

"I will stay no longer pent!"
Cried my spirit, petulant.

"Fire and circle are the sun,
And with these two I will be one!"
And trumpets, singing in my soul,
Healed my heart and made it whole!
I cleft the moon out of my mind;
I plucked the earth out of my eye;
Liberated, I would find
The power of eternity.
I renounced the pale country
Of the past. Transfixéd thus
With creation, more than me.
More than human ever was,
A poet, I died by the richness of
The enigma. Human, who
Cannot conceive of my death-love,
Know that my death has silenced you.
From the wounds of Hell I bled
The fires of Empyrean;
Creative ultimate, I fled
Into the macrocosmic Sun;
I caroled my undying wound,
I chanted litanies to sadness;
With symbologic music tuned
To re-echo my own madness,
I decked myself as Orpheus,
Released my soul unto his task;
Novitiate of loneliness,
I assumed the sacred masque;
And with Iconic incantations
I arose in holy flight
Into the stream of constellations
Above the acrid city-night;
Now I had ridden waves past Hell
That truly is, but on the Earth.
New winds billowed on my shell
And I was voyaging rebirth.
Old winds had whispered to me, "Fail..."
Soft winds had murmured to me, "Stay..."
Strong winds now seized upon my sail,

Great winds were roaring me away.
I set my compass to the How,
And hunted upward for the Why;
I sang my strength upon my prow,
Pursuing deep into the sky.
On the craft that was my art,
I sped the shining mystic arrow
From the bow that bent my heart
To the vertex of my sorrow:
A marijuana garden where
Instantaneous visions bloom;
Flaming in the golden air,
Not sucking on the root of doom;
And there blossoms, and there grows,
Fixed in skies that stream supernal,
An amaranth that was a rose,
And dwells in peace, and dwells eternal;
A recreated sun shall shine
The streaming energy of fire;
And imaged in its perfect line
Will be reason past desire.
I flew beyond the Earth, and soon
Past Jupiter and Pleiades;
I saw the turning of the moon.
And gathered all cosmologies.

I sailed a sea of vacuum,
Whose moons are locked in strange eclipse
And darken with a dying sun;
A cosmic shoal where other ships,
Too freighted with their loneliness,
Have sunk in terror in a night
That hovered over happiness
With a wisdom cleansed of light.
Here is a broken boat: Rimbaud
Died here. I gather from his ark
A rotten soul, a heavy load
Of death to bear upon my barque.
He, the celestial mariner,

Sailed too far beyond his birth,
And wept, to find that all ships were
Anchored drunkenly to Earth.
For, out of the womb of quiet spun
Catastrophe; out of forsworn
Came man, came moon, came earth, came sun;
Out of time was tempest born;
Out of the single absolute,
The silence of infinity,
Came all things musical and mute,
All myths that mask eternity;
Out of black and being, breath;
Out of breath and being, birth;
Out of birth was driven death
And every agony of earth;
Unbeing to being, and being to pain,
And pain to unbeing, ruthlessly so;
Nothing from nothing and roaring again,
Symbolical vortex of infinite No!

Alas, there is no Mystery,
But only higher consciousness;
For our supreme reality
Resides alone with nothingness.
And the enigma that we have
Tormented with our feeble wit
Descends with us into one grave,
For stars will have no thought of it.
And all the hoping of our heart
Is as futile as our doom;
Meaninglessness is the art,
And gentleness has found a tomb.
Life does not transpire in breath;
It is not finished in the womb:
We, living, fleetingly enmesh
The quickened chaos of the tomb.
We live in worlds that are not real,
And move in nights of days to death;
And all sensation that we feel

Is as bodiless as breath.
And while essential shadows swirl,
We are blinded by our eyes:
We cannot see behind the world
What the subconscious dream denies;
We dream, and never know we sleep;
We sing, deluded that our rhyme
Echoes singing in the deep
Black tunelessness of time;
We seek to give a silence, sound;
To string and insubstantial lyre;
To touch to darkness and no ground
The flame of world-creative fire.
Life is not dreaming, is not growing;
Life is not action, is not breath;
Final wisdom is unknowing;
True life lies alone with death.

Oh, is my journeying my doom?
Are there no currents more to run
When I have sailed beyond the moon
And have burst beyond the sun?
Oh, have I found finality
When I have drifted past all dreams
Into this dark and quiet sea?
Sometimes I sleep again on streams
That sob the soul's return to Hell;
I often am reborn; I thirst
Again, and in my weakness dwell
In all the Hells that I have cursed.
And often I babble aimlessly,
Repeating songs I used to learn,
Paeans to immortality.
You, who bid me to return:
Perhaps I still regret the Earth
Forsaken when I turned away,
Far beyond the night of birth
Which I pronounced Eternal Day.
But, oh, my friend, you have no eye

For symbols and you cannot see
Disaster. Burning in the sky,
Stars have too deeply wounded me.
I, who neither sail nor sink,
I, who neither live nor die,
Began my voyaging to think,
And I have found your action, lie.
I, who am quiet, will not scorn
The final failure of my vision;
I, who am conscious, have forsworn
The holy madness of derision.
I am a star upon my barque
That has exploded from the sun;
Mine is awareness of the stark
Unsignifying cosmic One.
I am the star that sees the end:
Half-eye on the world agleam,
The other half my eye I bend
Upon the universal stream.
And I am lonely as a star,
Wounded, bodiless, bereft,
Comfortless, isolate, and far,
Staring, silent, to the earth
This sadness that the Earth imparts
Has grown in me until I sigh
At seeing in no other hearts
This strange, this selfsame soulsick cry.
As I am wounded, I shall thus
Gently breathe till breathing cease;
I cannot be Prometheus,
For pain and action are not peace.
But as I am not Satan I am still
Not God. As I am no martyr,
I shall never judge to kill.
As I am conscious of my barter,
Devil for God, and God for dirt,
I need not sign a legacy
Which will perpetuate my hurt.
As my ship has carried me

All the universe's length,
I shall fully comprehend
That my weakness is true strength.

I have voyaged to my end.
I find supreme reality
Not in the myth, not in the clean
Miracle of morality:
All is a prophetless machine.
In my age I sailed between
The disaster and the dream
Till I was driven into flight
To the quintessential night.
Though every wisdom I assume
I shall be domiciled with doom,
And I shall carry as I go
The magic wand of Prospero.
Thus I finish my last journey.
This, my ship, has found its berth,
And on anchoring, has turned me
Back to the harbor of the Earth.

                              Fin.

                    [*March–May 1945*]

                    . . .

Epitaph for Roosevelt[258]

The hero ends, who though he die
Founded peace with treachery:
He drew the blackness of his lies
To lead a nation without eyes,
Who with the cunning of a whore
Led a nation into war,
And with his quick hypocrisies
Seduced a rabble into peace.
He could betray and compromise

---

258 Franklin Roosevelt died on April 12, 1945, and this poem was probably written around that time.

To confound the overwise;
He could be false to any length:
And this was essential strength.
He fought stealthily and well
With the Magic of a Machiavel.

It was that he understood,
That he was innocent of good;
For he was conscious of the lie
That is our reality
Thus into the grave we lower
One whose virtue was his power;
To peace his power once could bend:
Thus inhuman he shall end.
Mourn, oh mongrel, if you can
For a non existent man.
I mourn a hero, a machine
Whose naked strength was clear and clean.
Constructing castles out of sand,
You shall miss the master hand:
You who lose him soon may cry
For his inhumanity.
Genius is sired of misery and magic
And dwells between disaster and the dream.
In chaos it will find a core; in death
Find an existence much too pure,
A master of all mummery
. . . .thus he is mad.

[*ca. April 12, 1945*]

. . .

Times Square, April 28, 1945

I

Here I walk in arrogance
To wound the city with my glance.
I tighten all my mind's disdain
To hear the rabble's new refrain.

II

Somewhere in this crowd, someone I hear
Is crying. Shut up, you sickened idiot!
That's too much the way to meet
Whatever it is that you celebrate....
I'm sure it's not myself I hear,
Not now, anyway. Of course I'm happy;
I'm still human even though I call myself a poet.
And the rotting old men, tired, tired,
Rocking their bodies over the ruins of mad nations.
And not again, the struggle of the west,
The indignation over Munich, the bomb
That burst on Barcelona, Sebastian[259] in his tomb,
And goodbye goodbye goodbye
To everyone who had to die.

III

Peace awakens, finds her breath,
Sighs, and must remember death.
Beloved peace, be tender now;
Teach to us, your children, how
Gently to renew the life
That we have silenced with our strife.
Teach to nurture and to grow;
New joy, beloved mother, show:
Teach to beater of the drum
How to chant "Elysium!"
Teach the truth that you can tell
To the sick intellectual;
Teach the maker of an art
To grow a Heaven in his heart,
And, seeking in another's eyes,
To rediscover Paradise.

Teach the numbers, teach the host
To find the pleasure they have lost;

259 Sebastian Sampas. *loc. cit.*

Teach the peoples, ancient, sad,
To find the virtue they once had;

Teach the atheistic race
To find a Virgin in thy face.

IV

The sensual mask of the burgher of chaos
Is dropped before the grave of war.
He will be silent for the infinite moment
That follows on cessation of disaster.
Then, leaking in his ear, there is the trickle
Of the noisy rage of victory,
And someone is singing God Bless Us All.
He shrieks and grabs the nearest woman
"Quit shoving…"
And kisses to the promise of tomorrow;
And thus has mourned the passing of habitual sorrow.
Meanwhile I walk around looking for group experience.
"Quit shoving!"

V

We shall send our heroes home,
Back to the city, back to loam,
We shall send the surviving travelers
Back to the scaffold of America;
Let them be hung to their death
By the umbilical cord of the nation;
We shall resurrect the ancient uterus,
And shall rebake the womb, the apple pie.
Let them struggle for their lives once more
In the ancestral forests of the suburb;
Or let them thirst in loneliness,
Drifting again, on the pitiless salt seas of cities.
Let them then return to home in peace.
Let us now sign the treaty, the old lease
On our aged, haunted mansion,
And live with furniture still broken,
Shattered, shattered, as the token

Of the disordered fixtures of our minds.
Hours and catastrophe have overwhelmed us:
A lot of people are gibbering in the street.
Someone on the corner was just talking
About rededication and I found myself walking
The other way. And the unseasonable weather
Of yesterday will lie with the torn newspapers
And telephone books in the gutter, where a cop
Just spit, in the Times Square of our memory,
And tomorrow will be the last casualty
Of yesterday's war.

VI

Grope on through the streets.
"Quit shoving..."
"Buy a star and look at it through a telescope?"
"Have you ever used a fire hose to extinguish a match?"
And Jesus Christ, do wars ever end anyway?
The pain returns, renewed throbbing of the tumor.

VII

The peace by now has faded to a rumor.

[*April 28, 1945*]

. . .

A Poem for Sebastian Sampas

The Prince of Crete, a Massachusetts Greek,
Wept for Adonais; he is dead.
One night in Lowell, lost in love, he leaped
Upon the table of a backroom bar, and shed
Tears for the sorrow of beauty and future, tears
For the beloved penitent that sat
Beneath him, slowly wounded, drinking beers.

The barman knew the night was passing, spat.

"I shall keep faith," Sebastian cried, "I seek,
I shall remember!" And he journeyed thus

Into future silence, gentle Greek;
Soon Italy, enchained Prometheus.

Weep for Sebastian Sampas, dead by bomb,
He kept his faith, and weeps within his tomb.

[*ca. August 1945*]

. . .

A Nightsong

Allow my soul's most gentle piteous tears
to gift you with the terror of tenderness.
Remember loss and individual years
that edged us into silent separateness.
Remember autumn, saddest of the seasons;
remember time, remember tragedies and places
of the past dark streets, forgotten reasons
for dying or creating; then, the faces,
that each by each will turn to us to speak,
to gaze at us with flowers in their eyes,
till each becomes a lover we must seek,
and fading into loveliness, each dies.
Shadows languish gently in my sight:
disconsolate visions in the street at night.

[*ca. August 1945*]

. . .

The Poet: I

His genius is sired of misery and magic
and dwells between disaster and the dream.
He might be sedate but only tragic
Ecstasy is meaningful to him.
In every chaos he will know a core:
In life, a higher mystery of sorrow;
In death, the last existence that is pure—

Curiosity betrays him to tomorrow.
Necromantic passion, final horror
Is his bequest: a wound was all he had
To start with. Balancing the rope of error,
He shall fall to doom. He shall be mad.
Sadly shall he live, and he shall die
Deceived, a master of all mummery.

The Poet: II

An introspective rapture draws his gaze
violently inward. He has watched
external sunsets crucify his days,
and in your face his pensive glance has touched
a meaning. He has mastered outward vision.

Yet shall he turn his face from earth. His eyes,
unhinged, unhappy with decision,
shall fall into his soul, a paradise
of guilty angels, where the ancient thunder,
of a long forgotten storm has clung.
Depths beyond death the savage eyes shall plunder—
Behold these bloodshot charmed orbs of dung,
bestial sentinelled twin vultures, deep
and haunting in his shadow-stained sleep!

[*ca. August 1945*]

. . .

King Cole

Here his life is cast to earth
    Who was merry, just, and wise.
He broke while in a fit of mirth:
    What he accepted, Death denies.

. . .

Epitaph for a Virgin

Ugly born, she hated men;
　　Her ever righteous wrath was rigid.
With life, she kept herself from sin:
　　She sleeps with death, she still is frigid.

. . .

Sonnet

Beyond the seas, beyond the last horizon,
Far from the acrid cities, and the pain
Of egos in each other's arms, the glum
Obscenities of shoeshine virtue, lain
In the darkest suburb of reality,
There broods a sinister metropolis:
There each soul is sober as a lie
Drawn from a psychopath; there, canticle
And cabalistic litanies to doom
Intoned by myriad serious zombies rise
To wind the sleeping walls with shrouds of gloom—
Songs without faces, songs that have no eyes,
Songs that are not protest, curse, or claim
of time which dulls and death which buries time.

August–November 1945[260]

. . .

To Kerouac in the Hospital[261]

Death can make us gentle; pain will kill
The animal, subdue the aggressive
Pride of the disastrous, healthy will
The animal once dead, his soul can live.
A poet in the company of saints,
You lie and hide the cigarette you puff.
As if in a familiar dream: You, patient,

260 Later published as "Spleen" in *Columbia Review,* vol. 27, no. 1 (September 1946).
261 Kerouac had been in the hospital suffering from thrombophlebitis in his leg.

Weary of the hospital of life,
Have known eternal illness.

                                    I wish
You, Jack, not well, because there always is
A wound; and the most deeply cut of such
Is this futility of consciousness,
That hoping for your joy is vanity

I wish you nothing but necessity.

December 1945[262]

· · ·

To My Mother: An Homage

Do you remember maidenhood? The picture
Taken in the summer camp, you sitting
Carefree on the grass, of summer singing,
A mandolin upon your knees, a garland
Wound of dandelions in your hair?
I can't forget your tragic, early singing,
Russian, Jewish, indeterminate
Of origin or sorrow…how Stenka Razin
hurled his bride into the restive sea…
You, sitting near the trees, and singing sadly…
    "Last night the nightingale woke me,
    Last night when all was still;
    It sang in the golden moonlight
    Beyond the wintry hill…"
Till from your head the dying flowers fell.

· · ·

An Amusement, Not an Attitude, Peaches

Psychodynamics commits a shocking act
(Which nobody can deny) below the fishy
Stare of virgin metaphysics. Tact

---

262 Later published in *The Unspeakable Visions of the Individual,* vol. 12 (1982).

Forbids such violation of the wishy-
Washy flower of the absolute,
And that's a fact. But fate is wrought,
Though frigid Plainville maidens seem amused.

I've nights of moody and disfigured thought,
To necessary ripeness hip. At best,
Some stylized debauch disturbs the air;
Or Last Quartets of Silence in the West
Amuse the Cognoscenti of despair.

Notes [*for this poem*]:

    Title: Peaches—a well known male of ill repute.

    line 1: Psychoanalytic—anthropology's possible invasion of ethics.

    line 6: Quote from Celine's <u>Voyage au bout de la Nuit</u>: use of existentialist bathos.

    line 7: Kardner: Psychological Frontiers of Society: "The fact is that most of the female population of Plainville is frigid."

    line 8–12: Paraphrased use is here made of Spengler's history.

    line 10: In reference to the Neo–Baudelairian, Surrealist *Weltanschauung*.

    line 11: The last quartets of Beethoven, assumed to be the ultimate musical expression of resignation and subtlety of understanding.

    line 11–12: The modern Yogin and Catholic movements.

. . .

To Opium

When, unamused by grubbing in the horrors
Of megalopolitan cloacae and shelves,
I draw this pipe,
    and watch the alien stars
Commingle, murmuring sadly to themselves—
Until celestial opium shall press
My flesh, immobilized and nerveless, down
To no place outside distance, in a timeless
Fix of infinite: detach from bone
My insoul's popping eyes: indulge
The esoteric syndrome of my whims

In multi-sensual caricatures, occult
Ennuis, mad orgies with the cherubim.

. . .

Gang Bang

Shared, Dionysiac Lucy's shivering,
Still hot, but we relax awhile and smoke,
Jack on her left tit, I on her right, discussing
Spengler whom I haven't read, or joke
of the Arabian children of delight—
Aware that Nature knows no cognate lovers,
Till Lucy coyly giggles in the night
And tells us how she teased her older brothers,
simpering sweetly. After which I rise,
caress her placid face, which is still damp
With joy, and from her head unscrew her eyes
Like bulbs out of the sockets of a lamp.

. . .

Ode to Decadence

This fabulous, unfathomable city;
City of concrete images and mirrors;
City of spiritual magic and general sorrow,
Cleaving to one adventure, personal
Trial and panoramic comedy;
This pinnacle of agony of youths
Potentially heroical; this port
Of seasonal departures, this starry island.

This is my home: these houses now are silent.

...They stoop as if in suffering above
the streetlight's gaunt and hollow gaze,
And slowly I perceive assembling in
Familiar windows, ancient tragedies.
Trembling on these rooftops I have watched

Unnumbered destinies creep up the streets;
Have looked beyond the mirrors and windows,
Have left the doorways in the day, in night,
Have walked myself alone in destiny
Among these inner, murmurous avenues.
I have kept silent on stranger haunted sidestreets,
Knowing myself there, most of all a stranger.
Thus, alien in the hemispheres of night,
And followed time, a passer-by, around
The block, beyond, into obscurity.
Have seen unmentionable lovers in
The darkness, heard the piteous midnight wail
Of invisible alleycats—their desolate cries
Are like the voices of forgotten children.
Or on pavements, from windows, eternally I heard
The endless hysterical screaming of women,
Frightened, coy, raped and robbed, or murdered
By monotony: for these streets have tortured
Everyone. A wandering loneliness
Is the dismal neighbor of each kitchen,
Or sleeps in the backyard at times, or walks
The streets unholily...
                    Where do they lead,
These pavements swirling from the battery
Upward, twisting on themselves, revolving
Back, and reaching out beyond the docks?
What gates, what images, what mirrors shine
Profound and silent at the crossings of
This traffic? O, a vision of the streets
Is one of past-enchanted wandering,
Of present hopelessness and future loss:
As here, at the crossing of the seekers, here
Where lovers find the maidens of departure,
Here in this square we mockingly call Time's,
Where the moon, its dim eternal sadness and silence,
Moans among the incandescent shrieks
Of signals, ecstasies, and masquerades:
The furniture of roofs of fire crashing,
Splintering from neon cities down

On pavements.
O Firemen of these skies, these burnt
And guttering balconies of light, O save
The child, shovel the lights from off his soul!

Here, child of the city, homeless waif,
Out of the mirror I plunge my hand to yours;
I shall emerge from mirrors to your side
And enter in your eyes, identity.
Follow me, whoever I am, lost child:
Our trail of knowledge of the city soon
Shall be recessed—a step beyond this block.
Beware the streetcars and the taxicabs:
One lumbers toward your error, hurls a tomb
At you, the other slyly seeks your skull.
Move sideways, shoulder first, evade the drag
Of inarticulate Annunciation,
As hesitating mobs balk in your path,
Their huge pedestrian desire struck
In the concrete of an impotent Vision.
Beware the hoods and hustlers, they have purpose:
Guard your wallets and your genitals.
And as the roaring firemen enkindled
Conflagrations in your soul, O child,
Beware the law, lest you be murdered for
Your sins: if any trespass on your heart
Or steal your overcoat, be dumb as crime:
Christ of the nightstick would accuse you first.
Here, under the marquee avoid the eyes
Of the somnambulistic sightless beggar
Torturing his violin of drugged
And incoherent desperation.
                    Enter:
Images of your delight shall be
Projected on the screen of your despair:
Behold a dream within the city's night
That lovers dream when you are long away
Of when you shall return, O wanderer.
A golden city and its silver lights

Are yours: its sorceries beneficent:
The fantasies of invalids, the wishes
Of enraptured children, and the loves
Of lovely women for fair and useful men.
Behold a dream where time is only a dream,
Where you are everywhere, and shall be pleased,
And if you die, it shall be sad and great,
With music to stampede your ecstasy...

They died with visions fading from their eyes,
They died with boots on, whisky in their legs,
With watery eyes that once, half closed, had kept
Cold contemplative vigils spying out
The hidden ace or Indian, that mastered
Silence over psychopathic cards.
Their trembling hands, blue veined and limp at last,
Have fallen now from guns that plugged injustice
In the widowed heart; the guns that roared
The name of Hero through the hangman's noose.
They died to join a posse of the damned,
To ride once more like vengeful thunder on
Poor simple beardless Jack the juvenile
Who stole a horse and will be strung forever
To swing in lone repentance for his deed.
The stubby bearded guzzler has died,
Though once they called him Pop. There was a wife,
Who died a quarter century ago;
She kept him going while she went herself.
And Zack the keeper of saloons and whores,
Who was a silent man and used his gun
To keep some order by his bar, he died.
And Miss Lilly and Miss Lou, unkissed,
And sweet they were, as pretty, they, as blossoms,
Married each the hero, and they died.
And two-gun Aunt Minerva who became
The richest woman in those parts—was hard,
But honest as her tongue was foul. Her days
Were long, and she was happy in the end,
And died with visions fading from her eyes.

They all did, mad or manic as they were,
They adumbrated riper fields of wheat
By their own richness and expanse of soul.
By individual violence and open-
Handed casualness with all disaster,
By human power, and their bursting, boldly
Bronco-busting and free-shooting lives
They interfused humanity with earth
And fertilized their souls with all the world...
They died all prophesying nuggets from
The golden mountains that rose veined above
The oceanic roll of prairieland.
Their gleaming eyes have closed around the light
Of shattered sunken sunrises within,
And mountain-heaving, Herculean sunsets
Waiting yet to pour their rainbow blood
Upon the savage youthful Western plains...

So leave the moviehouse, transfigured now
With images, and lose the child behind
A bus. Here's music on the sidewalk, dreams
Flowing with the traffic, exaltations
Jubilant as the chorale of lights
Above. For we are foolish in our childhood,
Even in the city we have dreamed—
A dream can make us gentle, joy will rib
Neurosis, and subdue the cataclysmic
Pride of the aggressive, healthy beast.
The animal will die, his soul can live.
Chase the vision with a beer.
                  Or better,
Right around the block is Huncke's pad.
He can slip you dreamier stuff than movies:
From blasting the roach of false communion, you
Are left hung up and beat, a broken square,
Nauseous with hallucination, dumb,
To see a drag come crawling up the street.
Pick up on a secession and a silence,
A vaster bang. Your tragedy illuminated

As to make the present weep with shadows,
Or life revolve in ceaseless human laughter.
Snow for a depression; junk will change
The city to a dream of seasons far
Away; or else the teahead's sensate garden:
A stick of weed and you could knife a poet
Or become a raging pianist.
Get your kicks; an oneiric message
Bright as the flicker of the times: but hop
Or hay—O man, you must get Hip to Death!
This even mirrors won't deny. You have
Not seen the movies in a mirror, never
Seen a restaurant, nor most of all
A subway packed with banal voyages:
There is no mirror made to catch the soul
Of these—a mirror glimpses only life
Or death, not emptiness: not rain on roofs,
Nor the ennui of incoherent brains
In fur, nor stolid loads of hostile flesh
In business suits disguised as pure existence.

And yet this vast nostalgia of these millions
Of intimate pathos and the rage of mystery,
Their sleeping sorrows and impending dooms
Are powers of creative tragedy.
This is a land of seasons, their meanings cry chorus;
A silver mirror of immense distortion
Which gathers eyes that open in the night—
And gods and beggars in my heart have swarmed
Without to tenement their island of echoes,
Whose many windowed lights are nebulae
Of timeless retrospective ecstasies,
Whose many mirrored darknesses inmove
With lingering myths of magical children departed.

For of the city of reflective light
Its mirrors are its greatest invocations:
The cracked and peeling mirrors of its sterile

Prophets, raging in their sidestreet rooms;
Smoking mirrors above bars, and fleeting
Glimpses of them through the labyrinths
Of drunkenness; the clean and whiteframed washroom
Mirrors; spit-stained, yellow mirrors of
Vomity flophouses, and spectrum-showered
Mirrors of half-European hotels; the bent
And frenzied mirrors of the carnival;
The gutters of the rainwashed slums; the windows
Of the subway; mirrors in eyeglasses:
The mirror of Narcissus in the toilet;
The mirror that the window makes of light
Within and outside darkness; and the mirror
Of my room, attiring myself in masks.
The mirror is enigma: I have watched
My eyes within a thousand, sought an image
Truthful to myself, and have been duped
By manifold reflective mockery...
Who am I there, intense, assuming, and
Semitic? Laughing child of affection,
Confidently grimacing, intending compliments?
Or paranoiac snickering to myself,
Lowering eyelids before the mirror,
Sneering, knowing of my own presumption?
Or am I hero there, haunting self
In mirrors, moved, and even weeping now,
Recognizing my own tragical,
Pathetic face apart? And now again
Myself, self aggrandizing, avaricious,
Sensually craving for affection?
Or this my soul, O vision of the mirror,
This moodful and despondent visage,
Tranquil with remoteness and departure?
How shall I seek; and what identity
May I assume? For now I am unwhole,
Unfound, and unreflected in myself,
Multiple-maskéd, indecisive in desiring—
Till as I walk into the huger mirror of

The night, I twist in horror at my thoughts,
My cadences and badinage, my soul
And its external insincerities.
Nor I alone have sought myself in thee.
Children of the Rainbow, innocent,
Perplexed, gifted of the sadnesses
Of Earth, and musical children of all grace,
Who sported once so cleverly with fate:
The pure, romantic youth who sought a vision
In the city: surrealistic nymphs
And agile fauns who danced the year away
Upon the Brooklyn Bridge, in bars and parks,
On avenues, in love with self and stone;
Children who once lived amid their own
Eternal Spring of agony, within
Their ears, the bawdy haunting echo of
A sacred solipsistic carnival;
Or violent children, sons of wrath, the souls
Of power and creativeness who fled
Upon the streets of self-destructive love;
Children of suicidal introspection,
Seeking deeply in the truthful mirrors
Of their angered souls, although their gaze
Found only depths of darkness in the glass,
Concentric blackness that damned the eye
To vertigoes of broken destiny;
Children whose eyes held pathos and all distance;
Enchanted tragedians whose last triumph
Was their impulsive terror on a stage
Of pointless comedy and false burlesque,
Who saw a corpse where once the sofa was,
And writhing snakes where slippers meant to hang;
And prophets that emerged: the men of shadows;
Practiced, tormented, and unvoyaging—
The great creators slink about the streets,
Their drooping faces nerveless with ennui,
Performing orgies in secluded corners.

How many others I know not have dwelled
Unknown except to silence in these houses,
Wherein whose rooms the walls at times would flee,
Transformed into huge windows facing on
The night, and ceilings floated towards the stars,
And floors sank down a fathom in the earth...
The universe becomes a mirror unto them,
These once expansive and immortal selves,
And squeezes in, reflecting images
Of unresisting ruin, elegies
Of ultimate depression,
                    Visions
Of the naked bone, the white and grinding
Horror, speechless, stripped of flesh, and bare
Of lust and sinew; jagged edge and nerve
Within, all powerless, all agonized,
All blank, rock-bottom of reality,
All revealed within the wishless mirror
Of solitude within a dying city.
Number the children of despair, and weep.
That their remembered seasons are no more:
They have long known disaster in the tabloids,
Tragedies in public squares, music
In the criminal, the shrewd rebellious;
They, dwelled within this city, childlike, seekers
Of the soul amid the drunken rage
Of honest men, and suggestive dread
That haunts the teeth the bowels the loins and minds
Of an infinite populace of misery.
They have lived here, argued in this dusk,
And watched the orange sun discolorate
Their city of psychoanalysts and thieves,

And these are one, the mirror encompassing all:
The city is the gleaming core of fate.

. . .

The Character of the Happy Warrior

or

Death in Violence

Several satires, laments, celebrations and an epitaph
Dedicated to William Seward Burroughs

January–March 1946

"Canon the Critic on the Six Landscape Painters of Greece: On Alexander of
Athens. 'Alexander was in love with Athens. He was a glutton and exhausted
both himself and his subject in his art. Thus when he has smelt a flower it was
quite used up, and when he painted a mountain it felt that living on could only
be a useless competition against Alexander's painting of it. Thus with him
Athens ceased to exist, and we have been walking about inside his canvasses
ever since looking for a way back from art into life.'"

Cities, Plains, and People: Lawrence Durrell

Critical Introduction to "The Character of the Happy Warrior"

In the course of writing this series of related poems, a task which was begun
in January [1946] and concluded in March of the same year, I became aware of
several faults in conception and deficiencies in execution that lead me to con-
clude that what I had created was, as it were, a literary white elephant. It is this
realization of certain weaknesses in the poem, reflecting the "confusion in the
will" which produced it, that lead me in this introduction to examine the poem
critically and exegetically. I wish to apologize for what this particular poem is
not, and describe what it is, so that if there is anything aesthetically satisfactory
and philosophically sound in it, it may be salvaged for use. As to whether a
poem is really a poem if it needs an introduction, I am not concerned; for the
question is too much of a verbalism. Concrete application is a discussion, I
may add, which does not seem to promise instruction of any importance; so
that, if necessary, I should not be inclined to call the work a poem at all except
as a matter of convenience in referring to it.

The poem, then, is primarily deficient in intellectual consistency, or unity
of interest. It was written over a period of time, while my will and thought
were not sufficiently stable to sustain strong, consistent activity. A completely
clear intention was not established until shortly before the poem was revised,
though a knowledge of general intent was established from the beginning, and

a basic logic on conception does barely sustain the whole structure. I mean the specific themes which are presupposed or developed; I have tried to analyze personality, usually my own, where it is sufficiently representative, in a disintegrating civilization. I have presupposed a "decline of the west," to be sure, and this is a considerable presumption. Therefore, to eliminate the difficult task of suspension of disbelief in such cyclical sociologies as those of Pareto, Petrie, Spengler and Toynbee, it would, perhaps, suffice to state that I am considering the personality in a particularly unpleasant culture.

Returning, then, to the poem, the evidence of disease and fantasy is presented in the heroes, humanists and Prometheans who are addressed in the first lines of the poem. That there is the possibility of happiness in our culture, whether it be considered formally decadent or merely unpleasant, is perhaps a more important theme in the poem; and this happiness depends upon the individual personality. For the portrait of the happy man, whom I have called the voyager, and who has been perfected and made happy through voyage, I have drawn, though not explicitly, upon a type which I believe may presently emerge in literature as the "psychoanalyzed man," the hero, then, and unfortunately called him the voyager, using a standard and somewhat worn symbol. I do not equate the voyage with formal psychoanalysis, obviously; the qualities of mind and personal habits displayed by him are variations (suitable for our culture) of the basic texts of human wisdom: dignity, integrity, insight, concreteness, self knowledge, boldness and valor, sensual power, and imagination. That these virtues, potential in every man, can be achieved in our culture is impossible, since the basis of our virtue is castration. This being the case, it is difficult to conceive of any man escaping the evil effects of his culture by purely intellectual liberation, or by exile, and we may be instructed by the example of Joyce and Rimbaud. There is the possibility of intellectual liberation if psychology is conceived of as magic and philosophy as did the ancient Egyptians and vanished Mayans; if this verbalism is more pleasing to intellectual or aesthetic taste, may it please, and serve in salvation.

I have spoken of the use of voyage as a symbol. I do not mean physical voyage, patently, since the problem is one of happiness within the culture, and have consequently created heroic travel as romantic fantasy. The selection of image, I believe, is evidence of the romantic fantasy still existing within myself, as well as the images of sea travel, and the stock images of nature. The specific life of the matured or cured soul, in the culture, has not been made explicit: many of the principles of simplicity and concreteness decided upon in the poem, are not followed with consistency in the work itself.

To remedy this failure, of which I was at first only half conscious, I had recourse to the various anti-romantic devices developed for poetry by T.S. Eliot and W.H. Auden. I have made use, on one hand of the elegiac style of Rilke, and the hypertrophic metaphors of St. Perse and Rimbaud. On the other hand I have tried to seal them to specific sociological content by the constant use of psychoanalytic imagery—i.e. to describe the cultural disease and fantasy in terms of the syndrome symbolized by castration. I have made use of much of the imagery of the metropolis, evidencing and idealization of the criminal or "hip" personality as the most healthy manifestation of "voyage" or individuality, and the virtues previously listed, yet produced in the anarchy of disintegration. I have used the criminal type as an example of a natural equivalent for the "psychoanalyzed man." I mean this primarily as a metaphor, but I am not unwilling to accept certain literal moral instruction that is implied.

This has been the general intention of the poem, which, I think, has been executed with some success. However, the poem was started first as a panorama of decline and then was developed in its later sections, into a statement of affirmation, optimism, and "grace"—achieved by what might be brutally summarized as a synthesis of Nietzsche and Freud. Because of this, several of the sections remain emotionally undisciplined or intellectually inconsistent.

Thus, in the first description of the voyager, part III, as opposed to the sentimental fantasies of the hero, humanist and Promethean, I have drawn a man more addicted to Baudelairian spleen than Mozartian vitality; and I fear that the account of my own personality therein contains too much self pity to be accurate. I have allowed the section to remain because it fell into place as the first step, toward the change of personality, beyond the more literary types examined in sections I and II. The voyager and the author now begin to exist outside of the canvas described by Durrell in *Cities, Plains and People*. The existence is not much, to be sure, and this transitional state of mind is exploited for section IV. This I intended simply as a recognition and admission of the "misery of the earth," after Mahler. I attempted to sophisticate the sentiment of Mahler's bad German poetry by the use of the stylized banalities so effective in Auden's early poetry, but, which are, I feel, essentially shallow. My intention was to pass the emotion off as "authentic," neither morbid nor compulsive. Lacking acquaintanceship with the archetypes of emotional health, "the psychoanalyzed man," I cannot be sure which of the lines convey "virile" sadness, (that is admirably expressed in St. Perse's quotation) and which are mere hysteria. This weakness taints the section, though it is partly redeemed by the enumeration, as examples of sad things, of certain sociological details which are also tragic. The confusion in the will, not wholly unconscious and unintentional, in this section, is therefore examined and presumably exorcised in section V, and stoicism and discipline are again substituted for romantic afflatus.

Part VI is the beginning of the synthesis, and here the poem has worked around to the point, for I have attempted to be as accurate as possible in the description of the "psychoanalyzed man," examining his culture with a mind disciplined to concrete thought. I have used an unconcrete figure of speech, to describe what surrounds him; but I have taken pains to revise the usual lyrical meaning of death, associating it with wish for death, the fear of life, indecision and inaction, and consequent death in violence symbolizing an anarchic disintegration of culture. The application here is most obviously to the literary personality.

The "confusion in the will" again is the subject of section VII. I have used the literary types to symbolize the disease of the society which forces it to fear decision, to "cherish its sadness," its compulsion to self destruction. An attempt is made to focus choice, to present the aesthete with responsibility of choosing between the death he woos by leading a life of sorrows and heroic postures, and the life which he fears—the voyage.

Part VIII is the crucial chapter, the purest statement of synthesis, intellectual and emotional unity achieved in the poem. I have made so much of silence and anti-intellectualism in the poem simply because a healthy man does not continually wrangle with himself and produce excuses, verbosities. As art is practiced now it is an excuse and a verbosity; there are few spontaneous creators in the body of twentieth century literature. Unity of being would in most cases eliminate the largest part of our art; for certainly that has been, directly or indirectly, the concern of our creators. For that reason, since part VII pretends to synthesis and unity, the creation of the poem seems supererogatory. This, I think, is the basic failure of the poem to which all others are related. The section, then, starts with a statement of the case, and it is not intended as a natural paradox, but a statement of failure of my own will.

This cannot be overlooked, and so the ensuing rhapsody on unity of being, of passional and intellectual involvement in active existence, the "pure statement" of life which the poem had been attempting to achieve, is rendered invalid. The whole structure is an artificial fiction; unable to attain completely the unity of being it apprehends.

Therefore, this poem is a white elephant, as I imagine most poetry is now; a parade of sentimentalities, an "indecent exposure." It is this knowledge, I believe, which turned Rimbaud against poetry. It is the attainment of this knowledge, and the mastery of self which lends grandeur, power, nobility, and authenticity to the poetry of St. Perse, also the Vision of Yeats and his last poems: I do not mean knowledge merely of aesthetic motives, but the attained unity of being which insures knowledge and pleasure in the world. It is this accomplishment, in relation to their culture, that has been the common genius of Homer, of Shakespeare, of Mozart. There is a word for it which nobody really understands, and it is objectivity.

From what I have written, it may be seen that the poem has been worked on while I was in transition, and that its failures are the failures of the author. It is to be noted that the poem should honestly have begun with the "pure statement" of love, and not discover itself and the nature of poetry, or great poetry anyway, near the end. In explanation I offer the fact that the poem was intended to be a didactic poem "for the instruction of the young," and again, this intention violates the obvious principle established in the poem. The voyager, as we have seen, is, to put it very simply, rather anti-social. I mean this, of course, only in metaphoric contrast to the vanity of motive that has, in this case, produced didacticism. The same vanity of motive and confusion in the will which in addition to producing decadent poetry, is the sickness of the hero, humanist, Promethean, the explanation of the inefficiency of their efforts to change history; it is the same sickness which at present drives western society to self destruction, death in violence. For this reason the poem is, I consider, a "white elephant." The prolegomenous sections having become obsolete upon the attainment of the "vision;" that leaves two sections of "authentic" poetry: what I have called the "pure statement" at the end of section VIII, and the concluding section the "epitaph," which is presented as an exercise in mature poetry, however unsatisfying the quality of the poetry itself. I have introduced this section with a quotation from the last poem of Yeats on Crazy Jane that seemed to be much to the point:

"I am tired of cursing the bishop"

and substituting western civilization and its forms for the bishop, which, I believe, was Yeats' intention as well.

"I have found something worse / to meditate on—"

By which both Crazy Jane and I mean death. I have used death as a symbol previously, and the intent of the last lines was to consider it with bare, objective passion, as a concrete fact; and to temper the sentiments which conclude the poem with such solemnity and dignity as befits this last sensual experience of men.

[This prefatory statement was written in June 1946.]

Death in Violence

[This long poem was also identified in Ginsberg's notebook as "The Death of the Voyager," a solo requiem to "The Dirty Little Bigot" and "Assembly 10 Celebrations."]

"Yet, at this very moment when we do at last see ourselves as we are, neither cozy nor playful, but swaying out on the ultimate wind whipped cornice that overhangs the unabiding void—we have never stood anywhere else,—when our reasons are silenced by the heavy huge derision—there is nothing to say. There never has been,—and our wills chuck in their hands—there is no way out. There never was,—it is at this moment that for the first time in our lives we hear, not the sounds which, as born actors, we have hitherto condescended to use as an excellent vehicle for displaying our personalities and looks, but the real Word which is our only *raison d'être*."

The Sea and the Mirror: W.H. Auden

O heroes, hipsters, humanists, Prometheans!
arrange your lives as best you can before the voyage—
sell your mansions of nostalgia, throw away[263]
the playsuits that you frolicked in among the ruins,[264]
and the sheik [*sic:* chic] drapes you sported every Sunday morning,[265]
walking in the cemetery, scattering respects
to the substantial citizens preceding you
into the tomb, where they are insubstantial now.
Sell the dungarees you never got to use
for manful labors in the bedrooms and the bathrooms[266]
of your houses. You'll need the money that you get
for these, in time. But purchase, first, some handkerchiefs:
O children, or perturbéd innocents, how shall
you weep before the doomed *dénouement* of your lives!
The tears you'll shed before your early eyes fall out,
gouged by the stretching shadows of the cities and

263 "Auden style." [This and all the following notes for this long poem are Ginsberg's own notes written for Neal Cassady's benefit in 1946 or 1947 at a time when Ginsberg was trying to teach Cassady how to write.]
264 "Forms" of false gaiety.
265 Mixture of hip and bourgeois youth.
266 Fromm, Reich, Kardiner, Freud; anal sadism (bathroom).

the seas you'll cross, the tears as uncontrollable as sleep
these tears shall have been shed sufficient to their cause.

I pity your first aimless journey, your virgin hatred [267]
of yourself, and your confused inconsistency
to origins and endings in the unaccustomed[268]
wilderness within, without...the moist disgust,
the terror of the mind as you are bound and gagged[269]
for torture by the diabolic specters of
premonition and boredom...aye, and men have died
of nausea of personal intelligence.
You shall struggle in the charnel house of kings;
you'll walk among the leprous clans astonishing
their dumb, diseased natures with your admonitions;[270]
see cities of grass and jade beneath the nervous eye
of jungle birds; shall gaze yourself out of the eyes
of giants strewn decapitated on the hills[271]
that move upon the broken cities; these will descend,[272]
soon, on the moldered bony arches of your grave.
Day and night, sunrise and sundown, you shall turn
your face in exile to the West. And then your dreams
will creep upon you with the moon, for winged beasts[273]
and awakening serpents shall glide out of the dreaded[274]
lidded labyrinths of your nocturnal eyes.
You shall awake prophetic with remembrance of
the secret symbols of voyage. Open eyed, and with
subtle smiles you shall whisper these mysterious
confidences in the black indifferent ears
of sleepless scarbrowed savages beside their spears.[275]
Following the smoke of a celestial opium
by Persian rivers you shall find the crazéd conch[276]

---

267 See Auden's phrase in sonnet "Ingrown Virginity."
268 Confusion in the will—philosophic perturbation.
269 "Aye, men have died of terror of the mind"—Lucretius changed to ironic statement of romantic situation.
270 Bourgeois, etc.
271 Spengler and Fitzpatrick.
272 Travelogue of Siamese ruins.
273 Mayan demons?
274 Phallic.
275 See Frederic Prokosh—*Seven Who Fled Asiatius.*
276 Meaningless reference.

of Paradise. Be startled by the bones of death
gleaming upon its rainbow flowered bulge, shall hear
in it the Voice of Thunder in the westward caves—[277]
And yet, except in your demented visions, your
disconsolate creative languors, you shall never
reach these doméd islands and diseaséd jungles,[278]
shall only descend the myriad windowed city, leap
upon the grassy earth suburban, sleep inside
hotels in sweating southern nights...and while you snore,
the vulture of your soul will swoop in melancholy
conquest of defeathered corpses of delusion.
Your chicken hearted loves will squawk in fear, and starve.
Your improprieties and your grotesque charades,[279]
the cardtrick carnival you managed to display
before the yokels and their mayors in the sticks,
the cagéd bestiary of your small conceits—
will flower in flame in fall, or freeze with winterness,
and in a last performance be destroyed amid
the shrieks of murdered elephants, the whimperings
of clowns, the agéd and infirm, and little children.

II

"Once after I got busted for pushing junk[280] and got sent out to Rikers Island
I met this character in the mess hall who insisted that I should come up to
his cell and look over his "library" because I asked someone if there were any
books around. He had a copy of the *Counterfeiters* along with a lot of other
mad issues so I started to take that, when he got excited and began to ask me
where I'd ever heard of Gide before. So I told him it was none of his business
and took the book. He wouldn't even speak to me the rest of the time. He
was still there when I got out. I found out that he got busted for indecent
exposure."

[Herbert] Huncke, in conversation

Your babbling tongue was never blasphemous, Black Angel,
your lustral curse was an impulsive benediction.

---

277 "Decline of West."
278 Rimbaud's "Alchemy of Word."
279 My masks and images—see marijuana perceptions.
280 Narcotic.

Neither damned nor blesséd, but unjudged; the dignity[281]
of an external crucifixion is denied you:
the penitential thorns you once assumed had sprung
upon your hothouse rose, your overnourished soul,
sheltered by transparent fantasies of fear
from the bleachéd winters snowy passage, the passionate
chance parturition of the spring, the change of rains,
and all time's bending sensual winds, abundant with
seasonal facts, that haunt your garden[282] of a void.

Not your's the criminal's spectacular crusade
to Hell. Sharp character you may have been, perhaps,
a hipster of symbols and hophead of hyperbole
you fixed[283] on dreams of pilgrimage to untamed nations
of earthly anger: Night and day, sunrise and sundown,
you, isolate and evil, exiled and demonic,
labor in your sinful sleepland voyages[284]
to the unique dark provinces of east and west,
of monster populaces and paretic kings.[285]
To these exotic borne and land massed hemispheres,
defended by the ocean's vast barbaric legions,
the turning waves the weaving tempests and the rains,
on chanting seas to rivers singing in the heartland,
you voyaged inward bearing mortal wisdom like
a plague. A deathly victor over mythical cities
of the vain trade of the sea, the black commerce of the plains,[286]
you cried aloud your conquest, argued savagely
your guilt before the meek, bewildered multitudes.
You waved the black bandage of the slaughtered father,
the bloody bedsheets of supernal homicide[287]
stained gray with guts and grease the murdered brains of men.
You fell from Pegasus in Kansas. The stolen lyre
burned your thumbs and dropped and shattered on the sidewalk.

281 Inverted. Moralism of Absolutism and Romanticism. The usual conception here.
282 Garden, etc.
283 Injections of junk = "a fix."
284 Lautréamont's Satanism.
285 Decadence, "Golem," Harry Bauer.
286 Proust—cities of the plain—homosexuality.
287 Oedipus, etc.

Naked and tumescent voiced, you demanded pity
from onion-bellied judges of your soul. Their wives
agog, will have your eyes to eat in time for tea.[288]
And from these undulating buildings dripping blood
of sunsets and unending injury, pale angel,
you wake!
        The shyster lawyer of your consciousness
digs you your martyrdom's naïve. A factual man,
he'll see to it the charges are reduced; he'll switch
your plea—unless you really want to take a fall—
excuse the most distinguished scion of a noble
family for howling in public for absent Eros
on the grounds of his youth and because of his evil companions.[289]
You've nothing to say to court? Thank God only in dreams
does one beseech the judges for a better sentence.
So as per schedule you fall in with the law;
your plea is guilty and the judge suspends the sentence.
Nothing will reach the papers.
        The rap was indecent exposure.[290]

III

"Encore tout enfant, j'admirais le forçat intraitable
sur qui se referme toujours le bagne; je visitais
les augurer et les garnis qu'il aurait sacrés
par son séjour; je voyais <u>avec</u> <u>son</u> <u>idée</u> le
ciel bleu et la travail fleuri de la campagne;
je flairer sa fatalité dans les villes. Il
avait plus de force qu'un saint, plus de bon
sens qu'un voyageur,—et lui, lui seul! pour
témoin de sa gloire et de sa raison."

    Mauvais Sang, <u>Une Saison en enfer</u>: J.—A. Rimbaud

The clock strikes one, the clock strikes two, and three is yet
to come to gather the rhythmic yield of our desire.
An echo rises far above the traffic to

---

288 Eyes: Balls, Castration obvious.
289 Carr's defense at his trial.
290 See Rank's chapter on Renunciation in *Art and Artist*.

the most opulent star of night in which we seek a city.
"Our life proceeds from sun, and shall we yet proceed
day and night, sunrise and sundown?" a voice complains
within. And yet we take unscheduled trains, and late
we travel, alternately brooding on ourselves[291]
and these the strange companions of our solitude.
Perfected souls are some, these bored and secretive,
for they foretell approaching cities, have perhaps
some business there...and here. Or they have gone before,[292]
dreamed all this before, that now they journey on
in dignity; have business on this trip, yet sell
nothing. Some like myself, less purposeful, are playing
cards with themselves; cheating compulsively to win,
to make their cards work out;
or talking politics and art with one another,
trading some pathetic jest about the atom
...that we shall be reduced to naked energy.
We tire one another. We have much to say, to sell,
but not among ourselves, not now. Sometimes I stare
dispassionately from the window, and sometimes
inquire from the countryside what does it grow?
And wonder what time it is[293]...And am tempted still
to talk to a most quiet and impassive stranger—
seriously and earnestly converse with him,
a shadowfaced, thin man, impeccably attired,
with anguish in his eyes and silence on his lips:
"I beg your pardon, do you tell the time? What station
are we riding to? Where shall we stop? What is
the secret of your silence? Do you know your eyes
are haunted with a reminiscent sorrow?
In what way are you sad, and are your sons the children
of death as well as you? Or if you have no sons
let me inherit these inconsolable eyes,
this memory, this wisdom, this composure."
For I am young, am still impelled to questioning,

291 T. S. Eliot.
292 Bill Burroughs.
293 Historical season.

would still assume wisdoms external to myself—
yet awkwardly I know his silence, his response.
And if I ask philosophy from other lips
no spoken word can tutor now my innocence,
Both he and I have heard the last quartets[294]
of silence in the west; his tempest[295] is now solitude.
Knowledge supreme of pain is his: he knows the voice,
it tires him. Knowledge supreme of death is his:
a dream will not project itself into his history.
Practiced and formal he journeys forward with an old
awareness through my shadow land. He carries now
no baggage; he need not lug his voice, transport his wrath.
His fantasies, now folded neatly, cleaned and pressed,
are scattered, stored in the attics of once familiar cities.
He is the most distinguished scion of a noble
family, although he does not name himself.
We know him by his mortal—for look, his eyes
are ours: O his identity in time and place
and destiny is ancient, known, and much as ours.
Perfected,

       he is what is left, at last, of life.

IV

"Wenn der Kummer naht, liegen wüst die Gärten der Seele.
Welkt hin und stirbt die Freude, der Gesang.
Dunkel ist das Leben, ist der Tod."

    —Das Trinkleid von Jammer der Erde: Gustav Mahler[296]

It takes your heart away to see your world grow old
in season, though you're used at last to spiritual
silence, and the preservation of the soul
in purpose and personal labor on earth.
Conceive, create, delight, and then, if ever, die!
And yet the voyager attains at times a pure

---

294 Beethoven "Ultimate work."
295 Shakespeare.
296 Find out the music itself and substitute the exact corresponding passage for Mahler's bad German poesy.

forgetfulness of self: a knowledge of compassion
for the voyages of day to night, sunrise and sundown,
the pilgrimage of living years to burial.
With music alone, with ecstasy, and remembrance
of festival, we are hauntingly admonished;
we look again, invoke our anguish from a joy!
We're meant to weep a rain of ruin for our love;
memorial fulfillment still persists with sadness,
the penetrating grief of an impulsive mourning.
It takes your heart away, and we were meant to weep,
if only fitfully, if only for the moment,
when earth rests heavier on us living than in death.
So sad the sky, so sad the murmuring stars within
that cling and separate, lost in eternal night;
so sad the silver moon, so sad the wrinkled face
whose human gaze on us is of continual longing;
so sad the earth, so mournful are its many children,
engendered in a lost passion, a forgotten vision;
so sad the sleepless seas, the unreposeful labors
of the tides that gather the drifting bodies of
the drowned beneath the sunken spires of their ships;
so sad the cities, and the ghosts that cry on streets;
so sad the virgins: and unlovely girls will weep
melodious before their melancholy mirrors;
so sad the shades that dying women draw at dusk,
so sad the evening lamps by which they write their letters,
the books by which their lives are moved, if once, at sundown
to the soul's unending memory; so sad their futile readings,
even the least profound: and sighs shall wake their hearts,
although they'll never know the meaning of the ache.
So sad the women of the streets, the lovely girls
belovéd of entire cities; so sad their lovers,
the shapeless aging bachelors timid of passion,
and the unwounded children spendthrift of their innocence,
abandoned to the festival of the heart, the midnight
sexual banquet. So sad the poets sobbing always
their careless tears of rhetoric for an unhappy exile;
so sad the song, the farewell to the symphony;

so sad the spell of symbols on familiar windows,
in secret alleyways, on rooftops in the night,
that the inspired loves of savage youths have cast:[297]
so sad the desolate ruined recollection in
their quiet eyes when they return to seek the jubilant
inferno of their unforgettable last springs.
So sad the lyrical departure from the city,
abandonment of day and night, sunrise and sundown;
so sad the unreturning journey to the sea.

Where shall the road of voyage lead? And who shall follow?
Where shall the tomb sink down? Where shall the soul be laid?
What graveyard will contain it? What trees bow above
the sleep? What woman be companion to this man?
How shall they open earth for burial of such sadness?

V

"Du musst dein Leben ändern"

Archaïscher Torso Apollos: R.M. Rilke

Shall you voyage? You must alter in your soul.
You must grow beyond your world, your city of
millennial foundations sinking in the earth.[298]
And yet O voyager this dangerous victory
of mind, this vicious deliberation on the death
internal of the weeping civilization—
this shall be preliminary consciousness.
And if the city's myriad windows burst in ruin?
And if your skull explodes? The molten lava of
your brain shall devastate your ancient avenues,[299]
destroy your circumstantial altars, and your jewels,[300]
ravage your tender throat, its melancholy voices,

297 I will have to take some of this schmaltz out.
298 Spengler.
299 Ideas.
300 Sex.

cinder the inflammable celluloid of your
stupendous and colossal photoplays, produced
of sentimental marvel and confused despair:
gangster pictures, follies, mawkish burlesque
of passion; cowboys, indians, vicissitudes
of life among the brainless burghers; ineffectual
dualisms and barbaric earnestness;
murders sadistic, flagellant comedians,
climaxes humanistic; inconclusive hope
considerate as a wet dream and self destructive
as the marriage of a good whore to a bourgeois saint.
Shall you voyage? You must alter in your soul.
You must hide your tender face forevermore
untwist your grimace and assume the mask of fate
that time external moulds, the visage of fact, the very
contour shaped by the stony vision under the skin.
In your one eye wanes the moon, in another
wastes the sun, as dawn and twilight drift away.
Your eyes will freeze in icy symmetry of sight.
You must walk like marble on the clays of earth,
transfigured statue, mirror eyed, and striding soulless[301]
into the giant mouth of time, the empty blackness
hollowed behind the silent lips, the solemn particulars.
Within the brain of time you walk, no conqueror;
you populate this separate world alone, the only lonely
citizen, the single subject, of a solitude.
Outside the skull the hairs like blackened trees still bend[302]
apart in forests of exhausted ecstasy.
The skins of islands and the pavéd bones of cities
are like the floors of forests matted with excrescence,
with pallid dandruff scraped from lives in false communion.
You shall voyage inward, penetrate at last
to those dead envaled too deep for resurrection,
their prophetic coffin, perpetual coffin encased
within the simultaneous skull of time and self.[303]

301 Cocteau "Blood of a Poet."
302 There is too much Benzedrine in this passage.
303 Neal, all this means, get factual, deal with life in its terms, not poetic ones, according to the
definitions herein suggested, that is.

And you who have walked the journey to this grave,
neither fearful nor joyous, but in impersonal exile,
in purposeful pilgrimage, in factual homage
have drained your soul of blood to stain the alleyways
of seas and cities underfoot: and all about
were the numberless clinging boughs of midnight; and they grasped
your body, imprecisely pointing, sliding behind you,
bearing flesh sundered from the driving bone. And only
the air whined as it was whipped. And only the night
was weeping for you with its rain. Its pity chilled
your loins, and flowed upon the open bones that gleamed
in lightning, gritted teeth behind the wounded mouths.

All of the rocks were jagged, and their edges facts.
All of the boughs were flails; and these flails too were facts.
All of the flesh was wounded, and this blood was wisdom.
All of the bone was shattered; and these wounds were wisdom.
All was the nakedness; and the torn clothes were costume.
All was the nerveless face; and the lost mask was costume.
All was reality, and the tragic play was gesture.
All was the voyage of exile, all in the brain of time;
all was the private skull, the solitudinous self.
All was the forest, all was the night, and the voice was ever
thunder, the inscription on the skies was ever lightning.
So the stars were frightened, and all of them covered their brightness;[304]
and evil was strengthless, and the moon too pale to shine again;
and that which was humble was hopeless; the wretched died of their chills;[305]
and the heroic was helpless, was noisily lost in the forest.[306]
And the brainless sun could not lift its muscles of fire, and languished
horizontal in season, procrastinating sunrise.

You will renounce the Vision and the Soul
the mystic ecstasy, the passion of the chase[307]

304 Energy—Blake, Yeats; symbolism caricatured yet unused.
305 Me.
306 Jack [Kerouac].
307 "La Chasse Spirituel"—Rimbaud's lost manuscript.

spiritual, the sad angelic journey to[308]
the smallest and most opulent star, unhappily distant,
where coupled sphinx and unicorn profoundly chew
the passional amaranth; where amuséd children laugh
into the Sun, the playful uncle that protects them.
Throw up your charms unto the rainbow, let your magic[309]
pastimes fade. Forgive the irresponsible Hero[310]
for his flaming arrow and his eager gaucherie,
forgive the lovers for their fate of ashen heart[311]
and desperate renunciation. And forgive
yourself for love of earth, and earth for earthly sorrow.
You have altered, you have conquered the terrors of mourning,
and the terrors of silence, conquered your lost love
of earth, except for solitude and destiny.

VI

"Someone must have been telling lies about Joseph K, for without having
done anything wrong he was arrested one fine morning... 'like a dog!' he
said; it was as if he meant the shame of it to outlive him."[312]

The Trial: Franz Kafka

A marble statue is only an image. So a cave,
a forest, a tree, its leaves, must be transformed
to lyrical memory once their stanza ends.
Or, once of past substantial, they are now air in time
and shadow in the mind. The marble statue thus
flushes with fleshliness, wears decent clothing again,
retaining only: the mood of its bodiless beauty,
the weariless impassive gaze of mirrors,
a hidden brain, a skull that echoes with no moans

---

308 Philosophy (academic and Romantic); religion; poetry: "The light that never gleamed on land or sea etc." "Beauty is truth."
309 To Hal Chase (Ovid).
310 Jack.
311 [David] Kammerer.
312 First and last sentences in book: Book is about <u>confusion in the will</u>: A trial to attain judgment and grace, purge guilt.

the mouth whose stony silence whose uncurving lips
ask only that the butter be passed, the linen changed,
ask what time the train leaves never yet have mentioned
continents hallucinated, and the grave,
None can hear the silence, the very music of voyage,
then who shall hear the requiem of inward journey?
And now he will not sing; for song requires a note;[313]
and now he will not speak; for speech requires a word.
And this is sad alone to whose who never journeyed.

Then he is riding on the train with us, who was
a Hero and a statue and a tree, who now
sits human, playing spiritual solitaire.
He is sailing with us, standing by the rail,
in an elegant muffler, gazing at the sea[314]
he knows so well. He is in the subway with us,
reading the advertisements with a factual interest;
he rides at night on bridges that watch upon the city.
He shuttles under the river staring at the mirror
that dirty windows make when concrete darkens them
at moments. And the subway roars ahead,
changing the mirror's silver to imageless concrete
in vanishing perspective on the tracks behind.
He is always riding somewhere—I think he never sleeps,
for no bed owns him, and no chamber is his own,
nor any nation owns him. Though he dwells on earth,
no world can own him. And perhaps he owns himself.
Lean and tall, and generally undistinguished,
he even has no name, nor wants one. Questioned always,
he replies with banal facts when filling out[315]
his passport documents; replies with sure ennui
to serious juveniles who pester him for a vision.
His silence is assailed by endless social noises—

313 Otto Rank and A. Korzybski obliquely.
314 Bill [Burroughs] of course.
315 Bureaucracy.

yet in his ear another sound engulfs these voices:
a powerful vision of his own annihilates
the absurd dreamers littered in sleep about his chair,
the vicious beggars that surround him, always clutching
to his sleeve with fingers white with private leprosy.
Engulfing, and other-thou, the shadow contains the present;
an archetype insinuates its skeleton
on every corner of the civilized slums[316] of time.[317]
A shadow falls between the body of two lovers;
his eyes have witnessed consummation: all the time,
those very eyes will testify a different union.[318]
The saxophonist rides and riffs to an ascending
joy of nerves: also extemporaneous
above the instrumental laughter is a classic sigh,
half heard, but understood, the suspiration of
Pan, contemplating fragments of his shattered wand
of music. Hear neighboring nymphs, the virgin ones,
rejoice how dumb the whistle how broken the jazzy syrinx—
there is an echo to their irresponsible laughter.

With action dying out of senses, still remains
another act unconsummate, a crisis signified,
a human passage, a fact impending.[319] For every voice,
an alternate chord; for every early scene, another
sense, an alternate tableau: which is an ending.
The archetype transcending every action is
not merely death, as yet an unrealized abstraction.
The inner watch of mirrors in the statue's eye
has its own style of symbol: the perception
is of concrete fact. And with a metaphor,
the pure statement of the grave, we understand
the imprecision in a life: the false emotion,
confusion in the will, duplicity of choice.[320]

---

316 Decadence, etc.
317 Spengler, culture vs. civilization.
318 Properly read, there is a perfect re-bop jazz movement in these lines.
319 Confusion, death.
320 Freud and Spengler.

The vision of History.
        In speech of death,
we mean the dying, and the sorrow that communes
with death, the vanity of motive, the illusions
that compel our years and all the miseries
that we assume: for we with all our weeping choose
ourselves as thus and thus, deny ourselves, succumb,[321]
and in the end our will becomes our destiny.
Then what shall come of all our willful violence,
tear-tortured, trembling, troubled with the sense of fate,
or this despondency and this despair, this dream,
but what is fitting to it, its creator, to
the starry world created, but words, or deeds in words,
or dialectic and decay alone, a sleepy
world of words and dreams: and death in violence.

And this is how we say the voyager sees death.

VII

"...Et le doute s'élève sur la réalité des choses. Mais
si un homme tient pour agréable sa tristesse,
qu'on le produise dans le jour! et mon avis
est qu'on le tue, sinon,
        Il y aura une sédition."

Anabase III: St. J. Perse[322]

A man is always doomed to undertake himself,
to take his life into his hands, as if a slave,
in daily labors and sufferings of continuance
though often with interludes of forgetfulness.
He plans his coffin, prepares the corpse. This is a life.
He strains his suffering, forces continuance
beyond his time. He presses down his hairless skull
upon its natural ripeness, though his brains are bursting.[323]

---

321 Freud and Spengler.
322 All Freudian.
323 "Baby's on the floor blowing his natural top!"

His ghosts are left with twice as much to clean
away, upon the mess of the delayed explosion.

No one shall condemn you, who resist the death
that grows in you.[324] The definite choice of early doom
against a haunted transience is your own business,
but know what years contain, what lengthy sufferings
the labors of continuance involve you in.
Sensitive youth will never be happy alive,[325] no heroes
with repetitious martyrdoms. Their nerves are false,
all their existence false. Their death alone is true.[326]
O heroes, humanists, and you, Prometheans,
unvoyaged arbiters of your continuance,
respect the last ideal, and freely choose its nation:
for choice is always made, if seldom understood.[327]
Your minor voyage has its end, a home awaits
your habitation in the only Good Society:[328]
Peace is forever accepted; quiet covers the earth.
You who tremble at violence, or at sadnesses,
have nervous ills and psychic lusts and tics responsive[329]
to ruin, will find at last a sanitarium
within the grave, and a considerate repose.

And choice is made.
           Or else, Black Angels, politic
children and poetic children, leave your youths,
your youthful cities, to attain the strength of voyage;
nor yet delay the voyage, and in perpetual labor
suffer continuance, and idle residence.

324 Death wish.
325 Walter Adams.
326 True to the will in its death wish.
327 Subconscious movement.
328 Ideals of liberal and humanist.
329 Psychosomatic.

VIII

"Old men ought to be explorers
Here and there does not matter

                            . . .

            ...In my end is my beginning."

                East Coker: T.S. Eliot

There is a word for wisdom somewhere; those who were lovers
spoke to one another with their bodies, and
the sick and senile endlessly commune in language
of complaints. But what shall be the tongue for silence?
What pure statement, what symbol to contain the world?

Subharmonic drums, notes of transcendent noise,
the crazy heartbeats in the master's frozen fugue[330]
these before destruction of the Lyre, before
the subjugation of the beast within the Book:
a cry to state the ravenings of utterance!

O fathers your sons have hated you, they have become
the prodigals for whom there will be no return![331]
To home, to home...there is no longer any home
for those who voyage as they will in time and on
an earth whose children can no longer gravely weep,
bewildered by nostalgia in autumnal ruin.
These citiless have found their souls again, are hunters in[332]
the forests of the streets, pursuers of the seas.
They cry their powers from the plunging prows of ships,
"Rejoice O mariners, that we have lost our pity!"[333]
A flourish of deliberate annunciation,

330 Mozart last movement *40th Symphony*, Toscanini perf.
331 Freud.
332 Decadence and Kardiner's Comanches.
333 Nietzsche.

a savage celebration of the soul, a summons
to voyage into seasons of perpetual change!

Cleavage and agony are the noblest weathers of
the sea; the sprays of birth anoint the voyager,
the storms shall bathe him in a shower of visions.
The gray rains, the shivering rainbows, and the clouds,
and all the shadows on the seas and moods of earth
shall pass through him: emotions recollected, strange,
spontaneous of mind. Desires like a soundless
wind shall move in the serenity of night.
He shall gaze in skies in sensual jubilance;
his joy shall be the journey, the companionship
of earth and sea, and their prophetic miracles
of death and resurrection: situations of
the years. The voice is ever thunder,
the inscription on the skies is ever lightning;
which voice shall challenge, and which lightning, purify![334]

Fire fire fire and the great wheel[335] turns
within the sea, the spiral compass rolls above
the waters of the sunrise at the bursting of
another sun! Around around the pivot of
the soul the sacred seasons spin the cities rise
and fall the tides approach the shores the shores recede[336]
the turning shoreless waves extinguish other suns.
The shrunken eye shall grow. At last the raging soul,
responsive to its wakeful ecstasies, shall pillage
the treasure of five senses from the seven seas![337]

334 Description of psychic health.
335 Yeats.
336 The come.
337 Reich.

IX

"I am tired of cursing the Bishop,
(Said Crazy Jane)
Nine Books or nine hats
Would not make him a man.
I have found something worse
To meditate on."

Crazy Jane on the Mountain: W.B. Yeats

Finally, it is only the voyage[338] that compels us,
and not the sensuous island of our fantasies.[339]

The voyager prepares his person for departure,
as long ago, at home, he knew to be unreal
his choice of little loves and sweet despairs, of sorrows
and subjective ecstasies. Always, life
announces the stark archetype. The phantom still
is hovering above him, pointing to the sea.
He'll sail again upon a ship, that caught
in accidental hurricanes will split and sink.
He'll splash awhile or try to seize horizons;
at last seen only by the seagull's swooping eye,
the man recedes to doom and desperate history,
anguished, strangling in this last solitude,
grasping among the shattered spars of thought
that spread and cling, the flower of wreckage,
about the vibrant suction's winding stem.
He finds his grave the center of the earth, he drifts
in sleep within the universe. He shall not hear
the serenade of mariners their requiem
for those forgotten in the kingdom of the quiet
dream. These living ever sing a fabulous largo,
unto his life an epilogue of lamentations.

FIN

. . .

338 Pure experience (Existential).
339 Goals, intellectual and emotional fixations.

I weary of perplexity
of weeping, and of troubled laughter
in the city of my vanity,
I weary of my charity
toward lovers, this elegiac chatter.

Nor words alone I weary of,
as lovers, vanity, decay:
Since vanity decays with love,
and mine has suffered some reproof,
Such words have meaning, anyway.

Yet think of Orpheus on earth,
his vanity, and how he chose
the dual wonder, love and death:
immortalized the sense of self
he feared was living death to lose.

Though I have written comedies,
heard Mozart, and conceived a vision
of sensual possibilities,
I strive, perplexed, with ecstasies
of sorrow, weariness decision.

[*ca. September 16, 1946*]

. . .

Verses

Predicament, indeed which thus discovers
Honor among thieves, honor between lovers.
Oh, such a little world is Honor, they feel!
But the gray world between them is cold as steel.

At length I saw these lovers fully were come
Into their torture of equilibrium!
Dreadfully had forsworn each other, and yet
They were bound to each other, and they did not forget.

As rigid as two painful stars, and twirled
About the clustered night, their prison world,
They burned with fierce love always to come near
But beat each other back, kept their selves clear.

etc:
Still I watched them spinning, orbited nice
Their flames were not more radiant than their ice
I dug the quiet earth and wrote their tomb,
And made these lines to memorize their doom:

Epitaph
Equilibrists lie here; stranger, tread light.
Close, but untouching in each other's sight,
Moldered the lips and asking the tall skull,
Let them lie perilous and beautiful.

[ca. January 1947]

. . .

As I shall come to trust myself, trust me:
I awe and fear myself, as you; yet you
Commend me to myself in ecstasy.
Then, should our minds prove talented and true,
You gain mine, and I gain mine own anew.

Now therefore I speak not of love or art,
Diseases or the tomb; nor shall I sue
Your soul to play a gentle, foolish part
In an improbable drama in the dark.

Yet, intricate child, thanks for the touching homage
The season I'll regret, if it depart
Before we each possess each other's image
And in each other to perfection bring
Our intellectual imagining.

January 24, 1947

. . .

Sonnet

Now I have loved thee, now we two may part.
Or shall we love another time again,
Await another terror (boredom) in the heart,
And make another valediction then?

Or shall we love, and now make a confession,
Make pities and prayers, and prayers and lies,
Over our bodies' love, and our derision?
Or shall we love, and fear each other's eyes.

I would that love were long, and love were wise,
That lovers loved themselves as well as pain,
I would this love might last eternities—

Look how I bid farewell! and I am fain
to stay, and I am weary to confess,
I love thee still, and loathe not loveliness.

January 28, 1947

. . .

Sonnet

My true love hath my heart, and I have his,
And yet I think it was not fair exchange
I had a heart, was hot, and now I freeze,
I got an icebox for a kitchen range.
And he, who has my heart, is amorous,
As I loved him, he loves me now, and more.
Alas! Alas! That I must love him less.

So we are now perplexed, as once before.
He charges me "you must repent; and love,
For it is your excess of love at fault":
And I "you are too frigid still to move
This heart with pleas, complaints, or with assault."

What shall we do, who love, but love not this?
My true love hath my heart and I have his.

[January 1947]

. . .

What life is this? What pleasures mine!
Such as no fancy can define, design,
But as when music, understood,
Soft at night, in solitude
Is heard at last, and doth bequeath
Its quietude, anew I breathe,
And walk on earth, and act my will;
And cry, peace! Peace! And all is still—

March 8, [1947]

. . .

Surrealist Ode

In celebration of the birth of a child[340]

I
Proem

Look in this dawn the light, ah! Chaste and pale
Plays with the shadow of a Nightingale
Now hear awhile those mocking birds of dawn:
They whistle shrill and silly out of tune,
Just a burlesque of music
           All night long
They've heard that Knowledgeable Bird in song
I thought I heard the Nightingale's sad cry
In my soft sleep, and woke in misery
Night hath been long and dark, I would not dream;
Yet I heard music sung in which hath no name

---

340 Written on the occasion of the birth of William S. Burroughs Jr., to parents William Burroughs and Joan Vollmer Adams on July 27, 1947, while the couple was living on their New Waverly, Texas, farm.

Or if I dreamt last night it was with fear
Of those cruel pigeons that each morning leer,
Rude little vultures reddened in the eye
On the blue body of night's memory.
"Death wake thy heart!" explode the birds at dawn,
"Incongruous!" they shriek across the lawn.

Yet this Immortal Nightingale till light
Of morn made lamentation all this night:
High as desire's wise daintiness, then low
Her music fell in somber cadence, slow;
Then sensually pure: wild weird obscene
All lucid joy and serious love, serene
Till I would weep but could not for my years:
Perhaps the mind alone contains such tears.
The Nightingale it was my mind's first vision.
Image of love pleading for love alone
Therefore so sweet, so sad, so strange her cry:
Lest lovers mind and love and all betray.

All in the summer air there was a sigh
Like autumn for a moment: even I
Who know this music is too rare for light—
Dividing elsewhere in another night—
Could not but feel much sadness in my soul
The dark possessed a thing so beautiful.

It was a gift to me thine antique image:—
Goodbye, sweet bird, thanks for the touching homage.

II

The ancient Nightingale, she hath composed so mild
A tune for me to show, for this new child
whose birth I celebrate and sing
That, though the boy is born a bastard, not a king
And made by strangers in a countryside congealed
With weed, wet flowers of decay,
With all the livid progeny of a contaminated land,

Into a swamp of scorpions,
Fear not, the song for him is pure as he is wild.

III

Yea, damned by a mad lady in a dead age!
She has assumed maternity
To consummate an irony:
There is some flesh indifferent to its own marriage;
This was mere marriage of the will. And he
That of this fateful child is the sire,
But cast its spirit out in apathy—
Dread was his lust and not desire:
Thy fecundation, child, it was an act of sterile rage!
True Bastard! Live, and someday wave thy magic wand
From all the lands wherein your youth may dwell, and thereupon
Make, on thy father's tattered instruments, thine insurrection.
Or so those pigeons say, "Such is its heritage."

IV

That day thou shalt be twelve in meditation
Thou shalt be the Defender, all in guilt, Thou shalt be known
Around the town for thy demonic zeal for a conviction;
Thy will, as well, in a last learnéd misery,
Police its dozen souls; must stage
The spectacle; bear witnesses, some of the insinuous intention;
Wear all the hot black robes of trustfulness and all alone, though high,
Fool over all the souls in all the world and make them all come down
To intimate confessions of their lurid losses: thou alone, onstage,
Determine the true testimony.
By what sign shall ye know it? It is all complex, like life, some sage
Assumes, yet hangs on formal bones with rare simplicity,
So thou must sup with twelve uncertain
Souls. And yes, be served by an enemy.

V

Now pass some sentence: art the judge
Of thine own trial...over what? The unrememberable vision
Wherein thou was engendered anciently.

Now serve as prisoner awhile, suffer thine own complicity,
And do, and do, until thy will hath done.
Till body shall depart from soul, when both are bent
Upon an antique cross of crucifixion
Thou shalt not love thy soul: but this good fate
Was made for men, and most, for thee, For thou art born—

VI

To him who would not father thee: yet lent
The desperation of his life to thine.
Conceivéd thus, inherit simple liberty:
Thou hast no Duty, even, to intelligence
—To her who carried thee no company: no twin
Fantastic foetus, vivid yet invisible, that would have been,
Wearing thy flesh, the President of Something, Or, mayhap a Star at Sea,
Divorced always being. Or else at least a monster Wolfean.
O poor What-Would-You-Have-Become, alas! The genius of Cigars, thy Ghost
Fat as he was for years in his psyche, worth all his weight in Radium,
The Big Spread, Constructive Fixtures, Promised Orient, long-long is lost
Simply, he was unstable: basically:
In this unbalanced world he just went 'Boom!'
He was a television set, he was a sudden tragedy,
But, baby, that was all he was, a bourgeois Luxury.

VII

Thy mother carried thee alone—but full and sad? No, pity!
Wert thou to be the Queen
Of some familiar kingdom yet to come.
Demesne[341] seceding bit by bit into inconsequence—
Balletomane, or Window-dresses, Connoisseur of European
Urinals, why she'd regret for thee the same old Absence
From the Dance, thy Dummies and Disguises, thy Painstaking Toilette,
She should regret the drag of all thy days: Yet she hath rent
Her womb to give thee way and suffers thee to cry
On her as shrill as all the birds of dawn.
And even now, poor wench, she nurses thee to sense—

341 Demesne. Feudal land kept by the king or lord for his own use.

That hopelessly attribute, so soon! There is another Destiny,
Perhaps for thee. Alas, doth she not recognize its true content.

VIII

Then Thou must, somehow Judge on thy case as Comedy
I had done this, long years ago, had I but known.
Now I can only purge a room in shrill discussion.
Lunch with executives for exercise, quote them statistics, be sincere,
Consider the wide world as simple structure; happily
Teach whom I teach, at last, to know for few sweet moments some of true
    philosophy;

In further reminiscence, think, "Man that Metropolis is just too mad!" At last
I stop the book: I joke about the West: or mock lament,
Hum rhymes around my dreams: O pigeon on my chest
A vulgar bird I babble nonsense in my ears
Or conclude as I have guessed:
A Big Burlesque of Bureaucrats from the Division of Intent.

IX

And this and that which I repeat I still repent...
Echoes and shadows, mornings of mockeries.
Those birds of dawn just woke me with their cries,
New child, there shall be thy guilt as well, half strange, incomprehensible,
As here, among these stanzas all their sentences like trees
With figures hung like fruit and rhymes like leaves:
Emerging in the image of a melancholy wood:
In stillness: Night has darkened on an afternoon,
So all the thoughtless creatures of the sun
Drown in their dread, close up their little eyes,
Doze off for fear, and sleep whereso they stood,
Some fashioning a foolish image for their careless fantasies:
For some, then, it is sunrise in the head, dawn in full style.
The mist is white, half risen on the breeze, half still—
So when the sun shines red and rosy in the air
The birds of dawn upon their rocking boughs rise, everywhere
To wake from night and end its dream. They shriek
Asleep on all the trees, they tumble down in darkness

Through the leaves, in horror at their own nightmarish wail;
They trouble, they are half awake, and afternoon is night as well.
They lay broke, blind on earth, in fear and loneliness.
Now, far in the forest, there is silence; now the moon shines deep.
Crude creatures tremble for their own sweet dreams, such Joy they have to
    keep
And far from shadows far away soft echoing, far from woods of sleep more
    still,
They hear, in night more mournful dark than theirs the sadder carols of the
    Nightingale.

X

Wherefore this mad mystery of night on such a sunny day?
Just nightmares for those miserable birds?
Worse yet, their crying dreams of dawn,
All in the middle of a melancholy wood
When it was as the night, but it was afternoon? You pray?
And yet are not these words that dangle down, these words,
Their rhyming passions hanging hereupon,
Like trees, like beasts that cry, like day and night that fail
And fall together on us, dreadful in the mind?
We have seen light in darkness, we are blind.
—What have I meant for thee? Why have I said these words?
We waken through the night and hear an olden spirit wail,
Her weirdest lamentations are half-mad, yet still more sane than those of
    other birds.

XI

Then make thyself, child, comfortable in natural knowledge
Of all things here inside the world that make a pleasurable passage.
Meet and simple as it is, all things remain
In thee, Time like the rest, and all in curious harmony.
The whole wide world, spun round within thy mind, is thine own image,
And, that Image is of thee alone.

XII

Now thou art born the king, thou bastard child: for all thy early pain
Thou shalt have sweets and meats and slaves, shall try war's majesty.

Thou shalt have music always to conclude the argument:
If not this Nightingale to plead, or lacking poetry, at last
There is our Saxophone to answer what is sent:
And all the Dizzy trumpets of the West that blast
So shrill and high, they shall, and soon, have sane
Long conversations, fortunate lucky laughter, and much serious play with thee:
In part for the unmusical amusement of the world, the rest
for thy more subtle Merriment.

Fin de rêve.

Denver, August 1947,
revised New York, March 1948

. . .

The Denver Doldrums

I

Behold! how strange dawn hath discovered
This little room of night, where I have hid
Me in the star-stared dark, and thoughtfully
Watched cloud and crescent change into a tree
Whereon shrill birds have settled, one by one.
What meditation hath this dawn begun?

Morning is here, and all those nervous birds
Grind on the swinging trees. Sweet be my words,
I thought them out before, and now will write
With perfect circumstance, in sudden light.
But O those Denver birds! So shrill. We greet,
As with amusement, met upon the street,
The chance is such a joke.
                              Yet I have seen
Creatures of 3 A.M. more lovely and serene
Than vulgar pigeons.
                              All night long there rang
In dream some half mad woman's voice. She sang
At dark a wild madrigal, and soon

She sang in agony, and out of tune,
For she had heard, "one eve when all was still,"
From out her window, some sweet Nightingale.
I, who have heard immortal creatures sing,
Half-cursed those birds of dawn, remembering.

II

Now these illusions, all weird birds of dawn,
Still walk invisible upon the lawn.
The cry of pigeon, cry of Nightingale,
Echo faintly from the garden wall,
As if those fretful spirits were in stone.
What meditation hath this day undone?

I sat in shadows, first, inside my mind,
Till I saw light in darkness, or was blind.
Such is the mad intelligence of night;
As well the soul's most pure, most sunny light.
Now this imagination in this will
Sleeps with its wisdom and its verbal skill,
And dreams this lost elegy's strange eye, to stare
Lucid and saddened, as its madness were
A mystery, in mockery of Him
Whose charmed eyes most comprehend my whim.

III

What meditation doth the night compare?

Those charming eyes that comprehend my ruin,
Those cherry lips that whistle on my tune,
Visage I see not, morning, noon, and night,
Though late on barroom floors I face another sight:
It was the Nightingale I heard, perhaps,
Had once such charming eyes, such cherry lips?

No! I am not Prince Ornithologist;
This bird of mine is made ridiculous,

An image of Wronged Nightingales. False ruse!
Considered so, mere fair, fowl merely amuse.
Should any old bird shriek, no harm is done;
This bird sings sweetly out of an evil vision.

So bright an image maketh a blind mark:
I but half comprehend this light and dark.
The dreamer knows more than he would reveal.
More is his knowledge than the Nightingale,
(As we dreamed it) grand symbol of the soul
Consumed in suffering to think the whole,
Chaste paradigm of Love, all graven green
On graceful wings, with voice grave and serene;
Never made but by the night, this spirit
Is mocked and made and mocked again by wit.
(Meek wit!) Pride's palms, that did pet, pester, snare
That too swift sweet, next match, meek praise to share.

Or Eros pure imagination knows,
Or if not Eros, then a purer Rose;
Perhaps the Lady knows, so thoughtless to escape
Impurity. We think not, when we rape
This image from the earth's dark literature,
That we conceive like God: a thing so pure,
A thing so fair it is, a thing so rare,
That we are omniscient all unaware.
Ah! mind has fullness, with her thoughts thereof,
And holy are these relics, all of Love.
All these are true, our Heavens of sensation,
Hour upon hour builded on the dawn,
Yet images pale in the mind; senses dream alien;
Awake, they agonize the afternoon.
Seas of night burn out to sand like bones;
A waste of days spreads past a shore of dawns;
Substance changes meanings in my sleep;
Symbols clang disruptive in the deep.
Mad am I, I mock my own mad error!
Slow round in my chamber I turn in my terror!

Nay, those perturbing pigeons on the tree,
Though shrill, cannot from sleep awaken me:
More vivid monsters in my dreams attain
More intellectual dignity, more pain.
Like these, vague monsters haunt the sunny air,
Invisible as boredom, everywhere.
These days and nights are thus illusions of
Death perpetual, persistent love.
Meridian of rouge, the noon is one
Fatiguing hour of sad meditation.
Each dusk my wisdom and each dawn my skill
Engage themselves in conflict in the will:
On one point turns that wild intelligence,
Dynamic still, her beauty like the dance
In sadness of unconsummated rage
In dreams where a vast desert is the stage,
While all the wide world turns upon a breath,
Until this meditation end with Death.

[1947]

. . .

Last Stanzas in Denver

Art is illusion, for I never act
    —Dwell or depart—with faithful merriment.
    My thought, though skeptic, still is sacrament,
Like holy prayer for knowledge of pure fact.

So I enact the hope I can create
    A mirthful world around my mournful eyes.
Sad paradise it is I imitate,
    With fallen angels whose lost wings are sighs.

In this unworldly state wherethrough I move,
    My faith and hope are hellish currency.

On counterfeit earth, I coin small charity
About myself, and trade my soul for love.

August 22, 1947[342]

. . .

Dakar Doldrums
Letter from a voyage of the *S.S. John Blair*

I

Most dear, and dearest at this moment, most
Since this my love for thee is thus more free
Than that I cherished more dear and lost;
Most near, now nearest where I fly from thee:
Thy love most consummated is in absence,
Half for the trust I have for thee in minds
Half for the pleasures of thee in remembrance;
Thou art most full and fair of all thy kind.

Nor half so fair as thee is fate I fear,
Wherefore my sad departure from this season
Wherein for some love of me thou heldst me dear;
While I betray thee for a better reason.
I am no brutish agonist, yet know
Lust or its consummation shall not cease
This agony of mind, this deathlike sorrow.
Tis but myself, not thee, shall make my peace.

Yet O sweet soul to have possessed thy love,
The meditations of thy mind for me,
Hath half deceived a thought that ill shall prove
It was a grace of fate, this scene of comedy,
Foretold more tragic acts in my short age.
Yet it is no masque of mine, no mere sad play

---

342 Later published in *Columbia Review,* vol. 28, no. 2 (February 1948).

Spectacular upon an empty stage—
My life is more unreal, another way.

To lie with thee, to touch thee with desire,
Enrage the summer nights with thy pure presence—
Flesh hath such joy, such sweetness, and such fire:
The white ghost fell on me, departing thence.
Henceforth I must perform a winter mood.
Beloved gestures freeze to bitter ice,
Eyes glare through their pale jail of solitude,
Fear chills my mind: Here indepth all my bliss!

Curst may be this month of fall I fear?
My pull and pair and near dear kind.
I but endure my role, mine own seas sail,
Far from the sunny shores within thy mind—
So this departure shadoweth my end:
Ah, what poor human cometh unto me,
Since now the snowy specter doth descend,
Henceforth I shall in fear and anger flee!

II

September 16, [1947]

Lord, forgive my passions, they are old
And restive as the years that I have known!
To what abandonments have I foretold
My bondage! and have mine own love undone?
How mad my youth, my sacramental passage:
Yet dream I these September journeys true:
When five days flowed like sickness in this knowledge,
I vomited out my mockeries, all I knew.

III

September 17–25, [1947]

Five nights upon the deep I suffered presage
Five dawns familiar seabirds cried me pale.

I care not now: For I have seen an image
In the sea that was no Nightingale.

—My love and doth still that rare figurine
In thy sad garden sing, now I am gone?
Sweet carols that I made, and caroler serene,
They broke my heart, and sang for thee alone.
Secret to thee the Nightingale was Death—
So all the figures are that I create;
For thee awhile I breathed another breath,
To make my Death thy beauty imitate.—

More terrible than these are the vast visions
of the sea, half comprehensible.
Last night I stared upon the Cuban mountains,
Tragic in the mist, as on my soul,
Star studded in the dark, sea-shaded round
and still, a funeral of Emperors,
wind wound in ruined shrouds and crescent crowned
and tombed in desolation on dead shores.

The place was dread with age: The evening trek
eternal wife of death that washed these banks,
Turns out to sea by night, eternal Bride?
She clasped my ship and rocked to hear its groans.
I did imagine I had know this sea,
And been in ancient? to this before:
The place was prescient, like a great stage in me;
As out of a dream, that gate I dream no more.

I did imagine I had known this sea;
It raged like a great beast upon my passage,
Till I, enraged creature, anciently
Engendered here, cried out upon my image:
"How long in absence O, thou journeyest,
Ages my soul and ages! Here ever home,
In this seas endangerments thou sufferest:
And do, and do, and now my will hath done."

Ah love, I tell my tale, nor false affix
The solitude I watched by the iron prow.
While I interpreted I stared me sick
On transformations in the tides below.
For the grim bride rose up, and all surrounding
Carried me through the star-pierced air,
Till I cried stay! and stay! surrendering
My moved soul in flight to failing fear.

As I dived then I cried, delving all depths inform,
"Now close in weeds thy wave lipped womb, Mistress!"
She ope'd her watering wounds and drew me down,
And drove me dancing through white wreathed darkness.
Though I stood still and memorized the deep
And woke my eyes wild-wide upon my height,
My soul it feareth its descent to keep,
My soul it turneth in its famous flight.

IV

September 28, [1947]

Ha! now I die or no, I sense this tide
Carrieth me still, perishing, past where I stood
So mild! to gaze at where I long have died,
or shall as well in future solitude.
What other shores are there I remember?
I was in a pale land, I looked through a pure vision
In a pallid dawn with a half vacant glare.
Alas! What harbours hath th' imagination?

The transparent past, hath a white port,
Tinted in the eye it doth appear
Sometimes on dark days, much by night, to sport
Bright shades like dint of silver shiny there
In red dull sands our green volcanic shores
I thought these stanzas out this cloudy noon
Past Cuba now, past Haiti's stony jaws
In the last passage to Dakar. The moon
Alone was full as it has been all year,

Orange and strange at dawn. It was my eyes
Not Africa did this, they shined so pure.
Each island floated by, a sweet surprise,
Coins, then, on Cape Verde's peaked cones
Sparkle out with unfamiliar pallors.
It makes me god to pass these mortal towns:
Real people sicken here upon slopes sulfurous.

So in my years I saw my serious situs
Colored with love, and chiming and nightingales,
Architectural with fantasies,
Fools in schools and geniuses in jails.
When in sweet vivid dreams such rainbows rise
And spectral children dance among the music,
I watch them still: hot emeralds are their eyes.
My eyes are ice, alas: how white I wake.

V

I mean, these waxen figures I designed,
Dines on my islands, and illuminations
Of love, disparate symbols, of a kind,
Are all my years delusive recollections.
They are all hued as ghost and frost, a past
Still visible, yet not to understand;
When yearly fading from the world, at last
All lost, will leave me voyage to no land.

These are my small deaths, unremembered,
Of acts of love, or sweet intelligence:
All of that comedy hath vanished,
The music, on the dark stage, and the dance.
Now far from my aesthetical beloved
For whom I had devised a merry play,
My audience, these isles, drowse unamused
I am at last prepared for tragedy.

And what am I but an amnesiac king?
My Queen, thou wast a dream: my lost demesne,

Adieu, where wandering nightingale shall sing
No more the mournful carols of my reign:
Farewell, and merry, my bewildered bird,
Pathetic images, the thought of thee
Torments mine absent mind. Forgive these words,
Weary am I of my sad majesty.

VI

Twenty days have drifted in the wake
Of this slow aged ship that coal
From Texas to Dakar. I, for the sake
Of little but my casualessness of soul
Am carried out of my chill hemisphere
To unfamiliar summer on the earth.
I spend my days to meditate a fear
Each day I give the sea is one of death.

Uncrowned among my pots and pans I wash
The rusts of irony of mind away.
I move half magically through all the trash
Of spoiled works to sacred poetry.
Half-hopeless for my life, I can not care
For courtesies of intellect or speech,
Lose recollections of the dooms I dare,
Nor count sensations in the soul I reach.

Day by day I do forget my knowledge:
Conspirators in kingdoms of my genius,
My thoughts, at night, compose their own strange message.
I have become a hundred creatures, there.
That shrewd Semitic sighing ministry
Grand Visor to a state of introspection
Hath fled my mind, surrendered to the sinister
Multitudes of senses of this 'vision'.

And this, perhaps, I meant to signify
As I inscribed some stanzas unto Death;
I know not, but that thus I dignify

Desperation of another breath.
I move from vision unto vision here,
Ever as on the swarming seas I ride
Among the changing seasons of the year:
And round my mind sweet prescience doth divide all.

This is the last night of outward journeying;
The darkness falleth westward unto thee,
And I must end my labors of this evening
And all the last long night, and all this day.
It doth give peace to thus torment the soul
Till it is sundered from its forms and sense,
Till it surrendereth its knowledge whole.
And stares on the world out of a sleepless trance.

So on these stanzas doth a peace descend,
Now have I journeyed through these images
To come upon no image in the end.
So we must consummate these passages,
Most near and dear, and far apart in fate,
Commit each soul to her philosophy,
So to that would I must create,
Turn with no promise and no prophecy.

Fin de Rêve

September 10–September 13 [1947], *revised*
October 12 [1947][343]

. . .

Where is the garden, that bequeaths a rose
More rouged with joyful tints than this?

"Your madlike air
Your little bits
of knowledge, bare
as spines, these little wits

343 Later published in a revised form in *Collected Poems*, pp. 752–756.

of thine on deserts where
the hot sun hits
thy skull's void stare.
O thou art Death.
Not rouged life,
not gentle breath,
not dark belief
thou art earth
White with grief
At winter hearth
A graying heath.

But where is the garden, that bequeaths a rose
perfumed so, or colors yet more rare,
nor leaf and sweetness doth enclose
or more

October 2? [1947]

. . .

Stop O Ye Reader
(re: Tennyson's "It Is the Day When I (he) was Born")

I have to pause to remember the year, above.
How sad to think of all these years preceding now,
Caught in the moment not yet writ below,
Between two wings that high above some move,
But toward death time through which I make my passage
Stop with me reader to see my message.

Stop stop O poem, stop, stop oh hand,
Stop my eyes and heart and stop my soul,
Stop all ye world that doth round me roll,
And stop ye very sun at my demand

How shall universe the universe be unturned
So shall our ears be left unheard
In the silence of our body sit in the Love
In the soul, in the soul and (soft in the soul,

As the physical heart as the transformed Image,
The clock to Amaze is a thing in the hand.
(Dedicated to Eros)

June 16, 1948

. . .

Harlem Dolors

I

He was walking down a dark corridor and
Couldn't find his way out. After a while
he asked, out loud—"Is this the way that
I'm supposed to feel?"

A dream by Jack Kerouac

This round world is an endless passageway
I never knew in Denver in the cellar
At night in the dark summer. I created
An enduring prison in my prayer,
In the dim basement of a summer's day.
I sat before the wall until it fell or faded.
I looked at the wall and thought of the backyard.
I sat in the cellar and saw my far backyard,
I passed through visions in my white backyard.
Upstairs the living birds all sang: the swallow,
Bluejay, pigeon, any bird
                    "Call her
An image in the garden, ugly caroler,
And vulgar caller of my care," upbraided
I myself and innocent her. Ah, dolor,
I never loved her when I listened pale.
She was outside, out there, past the trick wall.
Was she the natural bird, and I blind bard?
Was she not O! perhaps a very Dove?
Nevermore!
        I thought a Nightingale,
I thought a Nightingale, I thought of Love.

II

"I have seen light in darkness, I am blind."
Brightness, brightness everywhere! I measure
Light within me, marvel, love, and pardon,
But I think the world is more than mind.
My eyes, ye Visions, why have ye gone blind?
Still Nightingales of night fade into air;
Dawn is invisible evening in the mind,
Now risen visible to me, another
Amnesia of the world, all white in wind.

White, white, white, when I closed my eyes
At night was every hour in the cellar:
White as the diamonds all death's atomies
Were the bones of the basement and the walls were white;
Transparent inward whitewashed was the flesh
Of floors, a powdery blind spectacle.
Weary of whiteness, I wakened into white;
In the daze of the immovable ghost and fell
Locked with him into an ivory gaze.
But white is mere shadow of another light:
The world is veil gleams outward visible.
Therefore see me in this frosty tear
Shining: a rhyme in the eye (O save my song),
An eye turned round in a nightmare, as a mirror,
An eye for an eye.
      O image! grief so great,
And O how gone the terror in a tear.

III

A prison was this passage and the dream
Of gardens green is brief to be undone.
The tears sink down. The garden is in the sea,
The cellar is in the sea, the tear the same,
The mirror even, and the Nightingale.
Sea in the city, sea in the buildings, sea
In the concrete.
      O pure idea, imagination

Is a grief gone mad, an ecstasy
In the intelligence, the never real—
Visions of the dark corridors of the sea.
O rhyme in the eye, O rhyme in the eye, O tear,
O interior lake, Narcissus-like
To look upon, O turn me to a flower
That I may tell the beauty of this tale.

Nor rain nor river ever made a lake
Of such dark corridors, so far down in the dark,
No halls in all the waters fall so far.
The tides their architectures never make
Deeper in cathedrals.
                    See, a flake
Of candle falls more stained than a star.
Soft dolphins under drowned boughs awake
And follow leaf by leaf after the shark;
They save the diver and he hears sigh;
They serve the mariner, they call the whales,
They suck the tangled seaweed from his barque,
They seek in the green fountains for his shells,
And carry ambergris to him and pearls.
Under the sea the trees an Arden are.

East Harlem, Summer 1948

. . .

On Reading Wm. Blake's Poem, "The Sick Rose"

Rose of spirit, rose of light,
Flower whereof all will tell,
Is this weak vision of my sight
A fashion of the prideful spell,
Mystic charm or magic bright,
O judgment of fire and of fright?

What everlasting force confounded
In its being like some human

Spirit shrunken in a bounded
Immortality, what blossom
Inward gathers us, astounded?
Is this the sickness that is doom?

[June–July 1948][344]

. . .

[Poem]

I cannot sleep, I cannot sleep,
    Until a victim be resigned.
I have a shadow in my keep
    And wait for death to make him blind.
But my crime is far too deep,
And dead eyes see, and dead eyes weep,
Dead men from the coffin creep,
    Nightmare of murder in the mind.

Murder has the ghost of shame
    That bedded lies with me in dirt,
To mouth the substance of my fame;
    With voice of rock, and rock engirt,
A shadow cries out in my name,
He struggles, writhing, for my frame;
My death and his are not the same;
    What wounds have I that he is hurt?

This is such murder that my own
    Incorporeal blood is shed;
But shadow changes into bone,
    And thoughts are doubled in my head,
For what I know and he has known

---

344 Later published in a revised form as "On Reading William Blake's 'The Sick Rose' in *Collected Poems*, p. 6.

Are, like a crystal lost in stone,
Buried in skin and hidden down:
    Break my grave and raise the dead.

[*August 1948*]³⁴⁵

. . .

Two High Up on a Balcony

—"Why now, after all this time,
Which is no time at all,
May we not speak of the sublime
and act from soul to soul?"
"Oh lover, lover, so many years
Have come, and come to stay;
If you had tears, and I had tears,
We could weep years away.

But words don't weep, and would I love
I had wept years ago;
Now two on a balcony but prove
What one in bed could know."

—"But what you prove, and what I ask
are not such different things,
For you have made despair your task,
and I my imaginings.

You speak of my stiff fence of bones,
And I your wall of skin,
But though we talk thru telephones,
We both can hear within;

And though my speech may seem abstract,
Both fence and wall are one;

---

345 Later published in a revised form as "The Voice of Rock" in *Collected Poems*, p. 10.

And when you think of this as fact,
The wall is broken down."

—"The wall is banished, then, and we
Stand drunk in barren air,
And you laugh in your ecstasy;
But I laugh in despair.

For what we were and what we are
Change us as before;
Now heavens turn round in one big star,
And day is night no more:

Then stand here on this balcony
And wait for dawn, for dawn,
For sun to keep you company;
Till then, I sleep alone."

. . .

The air is dark, the night is sad,
I lie sleepless and I groan;
Nobody cares when a man goes mad:
A paradox which makes me glad
That shadow changes into bone.

Every shadow has a name,
When I think of mine I moan:
I hear rumors of such fame.
Half in pride, and half in shame,
Shadow changes into bone.

When I weep I cry for joy,
And laughter drops from me like stone:
The aging laughter of the boy

To see the ageless dead so coy:
Shadow changes into bone.

[1948]³⁴⁶

. . .

You cannot tell the time it takes
To live into another life:
First the thought, beyond belief,
Jams the mind; then the heart breaks.
All things are broken down to soul.
Lives are changing, even Time,
Until the changes change in rhyme:
Time is nothing, all is all.

[*late 1948*]

. . .

Incredible Thoughts of the Inevitable

Why do ageless angels cry
Against their own eternity?
All their fallen faces feign
Thoughts of uncertain certainty
That what was sure will be as sure again.

I think I would consent to live
All of a thousand years and give
A thousand thoughts to melancholy;
I'd trickle endless yet I'd sieve
My thoughts all down to one and that one holy.

The thousand years, alas, are given,
If I wish, till I am shriven;

---

346 Later published in a revised form as "Refrain" in *Collected Poems*, p. 11.

It is a miracle to believe.
What thousands have I not forgotten?
Why do all the other angels grieve?

[late 1948]

. . .

Song

Tell me, Love, my soul is tender,
I would hear more words of love.
Then if I can't still remember,
Show me what the words all prove.

My soul is tender in thy care;
Thou askest me, and I reply,
Else all the air is my despair,
Till I weary and deny.

My heart arises to your voice,
My soul arises for your smile,
All my mind, and all my choice
O Death, let me live awhile!

. . .

Poem[347]

I think of Death   I catch my breath
and catch my breath   and think of Death
And get a goofy feeling.
Zero is appealing,
Appearance, hazy.
Smart went crazy, smart went crazy.

When I was dead,
A rose in head,

---

347   This is the first version of a poem later to be called "Fie My Fum" or "Pull My Daisy," several versions of which follow.

Fell out of my eye.
Now I have to die.
Pull my daisy,
Smart went crazy, smart went crazy.

When I think of Death
I get a goofy feeling.
Reader catch your breath,
Zero is appealing,
Appearance, hazy.
Smart went crazy.
And smart went crazy.

A flower in my head
Has fallen thru' my eye.
One day I was dead,
And now I have to die.
I love the lord on high,
I wish he'd pull my daisy
Smart went crazy
Smart went crazy.

. . .

Stanzas Written at Night in Radio City[348]

I

If money made the mind more sane,
Or money mellowed in the bowel
The hunger beyond hunger's pain,
Or money choked the mortal growl
And made the groaner grin again,
Or did the laughing lamb embolden
To loll where has the lion lain,
I'd go make money and be golden.

---

348 Ginsberg was working as a copy boy for the Associated Press, whose offices were at Radio City [Rockefeller Center].

II

Nor sex will salve the sickened soul,
Which has its holy goal an hour,
Holds to heart the golden pole,
But cannot save the silver shower,
Nor heal the sorry parts to whole.
Love is creeping under cover,
Where it hides its sleepy dole;
Else I were like any lover.

III

Many souls get lost at sea,
Others slave upon a stone;
Engines are not eyes to me,
Inside buildings I see bone.
Some from city to city flee;
Famous labor makes them lie.
I cheat on that machinery,
Down in Arden I will die.

IV

Art is short, nor style is sure:
Though words our virgin thoughts betray,
Time ravishes that thought most pure,
Which those who know, know anyway;
For if our daughter should endure,
When once we can no more complain,
Men take our beauty for a whore,
And like a whore, to entertain.

March 1949 [349]

· · ·

---

[349] Later published in a longer version in *Collected Poems*, pp. 27–28.

A Beat Cat

Huncke[350] has been in bed
On a couch in the living
room for two weeks with
the shades drawn. The most
depressing thing is to get
up to go to work, and wake
him, and see him lift up
his head, staring blankly,
dumb, biting his lips, for
half an hour at a time.

[*ca. February–March 1949*]

. . .

Song

When I think of Death
I get a goofy feeling,
   Catch my breath
   And feel like kneeling.
Zero is appealing,
Appearances are hazy.
   Smart went crazy
   Smart went crazy.

A flower in my head
Has fallen through my eye.
   I was dead,
   I have to die.
I love the Lord on high,
I wish He'd pull my daisy.
   Smart went crazy
   Smart went crazy.

350 Herbert Huncke's visit is described in much more detail earlier.

This token mug I tup
Runneth over broken.
   Pull my daisy,
    Tip my cup,
All my doors are open.

        AG and JK [Ginsberg and Kerouac][351]

. . .

Go back to Egypt and the Greeks
Where the Wizards understood
The specter haunted where man seeks,
And spoke to ghosts that stood in blood.

Go back, go back to the old legend:
The soul remembers, and is true;
What has been most and least imagined:
No other, there is nothing new.

The giant Phantom had ascended
Toward its coronation, gowned
With all glad dreams begun and ended:
Follow the flower to the ground.[352]

. . .

Dead Man's Institution

I was given my bedding, and a bunk
in an enormous ward,
surrounded by hundreds of weeping,
decaying men and women.

I sat on my bunk, three tiers up
next to the ceiling,

---

351   Later published in a revised form as "Bop Lyrics" in *Collected Poems*, pp. 42–43.
352   Later published in a revised form as "A Mad Gleam" in *Collected Poems*, p. 16.

looking down the gray aisles.
Old, crippled, dumb people were

bent over sewing. A heavy girl
in a dirty dress
stared at me. I waited
for an official guide to come

and give me instructions.
After awhile, I wandered
off down empty corridors
in search of a toilet.

[*May 23, 1949*][353]

. . .

Tonight All Is Well...

What a terrible
future. I am twenty-three;
year of the iron birthday,
gate of darkness.
                    I am ill,
I have become spiritually
and physically impotent
in my madness this month.
                    I suddenly realized
that my head is severed
from my body. I realized
it a few nights ago
by myself,
lying sleepless on the couch.

[*ca. June 1949*] [354]

. . .

---

353 Later published as "A Meaningless Institution" in *Collected Poems*, p. 15.
354 Later published in a revised form in *Collected Poems*, p. 32.

Fyodor

The death's head of realism
and superhuman iron mask
that gapes out of *The Possessed*,
sometimes: Dostoyevsky.
My original version of D.
before I read him, as the dark
haunted-house man, wild, aged,
spectral Russian, I call him
Dusty now but he is
Dostoyevsky. What premonitions
I had as a child.

June 1949[355]

. . .

The Trembling of the Veil

Today out of the window
the trees seemed like live
organisms on the moon.

Each bough extended upward
covered at the north end
with leaves, like a green

hairy protuberance. I saw
the scarlet-and-pink shoot-tips
of budding leaves wave

delicately in the sunlight,
blown by the breeze,
all the arms of the trees
bending and straining downward

---

355 Later published in *Collected Poems*, p. 32.

at once when the wind
pushed them.

[*ca. June 1949*]³⁵⁶

. . .

Eternity

The precise vibrant quality
of aliveness of life
continually escapes my definition
and understanding except

For the moments that are so
far apart or so buried
in the sands of thought
that they are treasures

I come upon only
accidentally when I wander
on the shore forgetful
of my imagined purposes there.

[*ca. 1949 and rewritten 1950*]

. . .

My soul is like a crazy fairy
That sings along the top of hedges;
Her dress is green, her robes are airy,
Her veils invisible along the edges.
Oh, God loves queers—but it takes a long time
Songs and speeches from the Sadist King of Bambury
Now that you can feel my dearness
Even though you fear my queerness
My soul is like a crazy fairy
Traipsing on the hedges.

---

356 Later published in *Collected Poems*, p. 14.

Dew is loose
Air is airy
Invisible around the edges.

[*ca. June 1949*]

. . .

My life is devoted to the making of images. Hush! The Wink.
You'd think I would have thought a plan
to end the inner grind;
But not till
I have found a man
to occupy my mind.

[*June 13, 1949*]

. . .

A Poem on America

America is like Russia.
Acis and Galatea sit by the lake.
We have the proletariat too.

Acis and Galatea sit by the lake.
Versilov wore a hair shirt
and dreamed of classical pictures.

The alleys, the dye works,
Mill Street in the smoke,
melancholy of the bars,
the sadness of long highways,
negroes climbing around
the rusted iron by the river,
the bathing pool hidden
behind the silk factory
fed by its drainage pipes;
all the pictures we carry in our mind

images of the thirties,
depression and class consciousness

transfigured above politics
filled with fire
with the appearance of God.

[*ca. June 1949*][357]

. . .

Cézanne's Ports

In the foreground we see time and life
swept in a race
toward the left hand side of the picture
where shore meets shore.

But that meeting place
isn't represented;
it doesn't occur on the canvas.

For the other side of the bay
is Heaven and Eternity,
with a bleak white haze over its mountains.

And the immense water of L'Estaque is a go-between
for minute rowboats.[358]

. . .

Fie My Fum[359]

Feed my pigeons
Dig my does   Dig my dirt and dust my bones
Dig my dirt   All my hugs are calling.
Dig my dales   Blot my blue
                           Nick my mask

---

357 Later published in *Collected Poems*, p. 64.
358 Later published in *Collected Poems*, p. 53.
359 Several variations of a poem more often called "Pull My Daisy" were composed. Some of
the better ones are included here.

Bleak my peak
all my clocks are crazy

Kerouac's [lines]:

All my eyes are eagles   Blast my roach
all my days are daisy   Dig my pad
all my figs are falling   Flip my giggles
all my eggs are scrambled   Riff me mad

. . .

Smart Went Crazy

Pull my daisy
Tip my cup
Cut my thoughts
For coconuts

Jack my Arden
Gate my shades
Silk my garden
Rose my days
Bone my shadow
Dove my dream
Milk my mind and
Make me cream

Hop my heart on
Harp my height
Hip my angel
Hype my light

Heal the raindrop
Sow the eye
Woe the worm
Work the wise

Stop the hoax

What's the wake
Here's the hex
How's the hicks

Rob my locker
Lick my rocks
Rack my lacks
Lark my looks

Whore my door
Beat my boor
Craze my hair
Bare my poor

Say my oops
Ope my shell
Roll my bones
Ring my bell

Pope my parts
Pop my pot
Poke my pap
Pit my plum

. . .

Fie My Fum

Pull my daisy,
Tip my cup,
Cut my thoughts
For coconuts,

Dove my shadow,
Lull my soul,
Set a halo
On my skull,
Unbind my mummy,

Move my stones,
Dig my dirt
and dust my bones.

Start my Arden,
Gate my shades,
Silk my garden,
Rose my days,

Say my oops,
Ope my shell,
Whore my door
Ring my bell.

Pick my locks,
Ark my darks,
Rack my lacks,
Lark my looks

Pope my parts,
Pop my pot,
Poke my pap,
Pit my plum.

. . .

Ode to the Setting Sun

Because I was a false, a fearful love,
craven in vain, to crave out of despair,
In feigned passion driven, truth to prove,
In meekness moved, to make the rage more rare,
A player in the mind that can compare
A minute's manner with eternal wit,
Drop tinseled tears where silences would weep
More loud than all mute languages permit,
And peek and bow from out immortal sleep,
My antagonist was false and deep:

I mean my love; my author, now my heart
Was ruined in agony of Art.

October 22, 1949[360]

. . .

Nuts
(Written with Jack Kerouac In A Notebook
In Hart Crane's Room on Brooklyn Heights)

Airy theories are in Heaven.
Strange angels are on earth.
Hart scar wild wept, aping
The blind rue of skully days.
Hart's a coral; adieu sweet
mineral, and adieu fair pearl.
Fear not in clammy lonesomeness
thy solitary grain
no lustre doth enshrine.
Since kindness be the
function of friendship,
and praise do be the
courtesy of kind, we
praise thee, loving-
kindest friend, and hope the
hoax will not the hex inherit.

. . .

[The Shrouded Stranger—first manuscript version]

The Shrouded Stranger wandered along
hedged rural avenues in the outer
night shadowed areas of Silk City
passing in turn the familiar mansion
of the mysterious order of Masons, the
secret Romanesque pile of the church,

360 Ginsberg used this same title for a different poem published later.

and among these many hoarily conceived
relics of Time the gloomy funeral
home with white-shaded and curtained
inner sanctum where no man knew what
fleshly mortal rituals were enacted
over surrendered bodies of the dead,
beyond the shuddering mills wherein
patient silken labors of the ancient
worm were further loomed into brocade
and winding-sheet to cover the live
and dead, to River Street's last block
where the petalled lamplit radiance
of mist wove blooms above the Falls;
and he did enter into the very hood
of its whiteness, therein hidden, an
ancestral traveler of the night come
at last upon the end of pilgrimage unto
a palmy oasis of light on the barren
firmamental plain of his eternity.

. . .

The Night-Apple

Last night I dreamed
of one I loved
for seven long years,
but I saw no face,
only the familiar
presence of the body:
sweat skin eyes
feces urine sperm
saliva all one
odor and mortal taste.

1949[361]

. . .

---

[361] Later published in *Collected Poems*, p. 52.

> I bow my eyes, not so fair
> Awaken as the notes are played;
> The crystal glitter of the air;
> and him the music made
> Green as eastern jade
> Down in granite laid
> or standing on a granite stair.
>
> When we met I stared
> and wondered if you had
> Like no other man
> a sweet word in your head
> lover said to lover
> Naked on the bed.

. . .

Paterson

What do I want in these rooms papered with visions of money?

How much can I make by cutting my hair? If I put new heels on my
    shoes,

bathe my body reeking of masturbation and sweat, layer upon layer of
    excrement

dried in employment bureaus, magazine hallways, statistical cubicles, fac-
    tory stairways,

cloakrooms of the smiling gods of psychiatry;

if in antechambers I face the presumption of department store super-
    visory employees,

old clerks in their asylums of fat, the slobs and dumbbells of the ego,

with money and power to hire and fire and make and break and fart and
    justify their reality

of wrath and rumor of wrath to wrath-weary man,

what war I enter and for what a prize! the dead prick of commonplace
    obsession,

harridan[362] vision of electricity at night and daylight misery of thumb
    sucking rage.

362 Harridan. A shrew or old hag.

I would rather go mad, gone down the dark road to Mexico, heroin drip-
    ping in my veins, eyes and ears full of marijuana,
eating the God peyote on the floor of a mud hut on the border
or laying in a hotel room over the body of some suffering man or woman,
rather jar my body down the road, crying by a diner in the western sun;
rather crawl on my naked belly over the tincans of Cincinnati;
rather drag a rotten railroad tie to a Golgotha in the Rockies;
rather, crowned with thorns in Galveston, nailed hand and foot in Los
    Angeles, raised up to die in Denver,
pierced in the side in Chicago, perished and tombed in New Orleans and
    resurrected in 1958 somewhere on Garret Mountain,
come down roaring in a blaze of hot cars and garbage,
streetcorner Evangel in front of City Hall, surrounded by statues of ago-
    nized lions,
with a mouthful of shit, and the hair rising on my scalp,
screaming and dancing in praise of eternity annihilating the sidewalk,
    annihilating reality,
screaming and dancing against the orchestra in the destructible ballroom
    of the world,
blood streaming from my belly and shoulders
flooding the city with its hideous ecstasy rolling over the pavements and
    highways
by the bayou and forests and derricks leaving my flesh and my bones
    hanging on the trees.

1949

. . .

The Poet for J.K.

His genius is sired of misery or magic;
he dwells between disaster and the dream.
He might have been sedate; but only tragic
ecstasy is musical to him.
In every chaos he will wish a cure;
in life, a higher mystery of sorrow;
in death, the last existence that is pure.
Curiosity betrays him to tomorrow.

Necromantic passion, final terror
is his bequest: The wound was all he had
to multiply. Balancing the rope of error,
he shall fall to doom. He shall be mad,
sadly, deceived, he shall live, and he shall die
a master of all mummery.

. . .

Long Live the Spiderweb

Seven years' words wasted
waiting on the spiderweb:
   seven years' thoughts
harkening the host,
   seven years' lost
sentience naming images,
narrowing down the name
to nothing,
   seven years':
fears
in a web of ancient measure;
the words dead
flies, a crop
of ghosts,
   seven years':
the spider is dead.

Paterson, Spring 1950[363]

. . .

The Shrouded Stranger of the Night to the Child of the Rainbow

Come, sweet Angel, at least come out of the fire;
I'll take thee, I'll hide thee, I'll make thee my desire;
I'll be thine old lover, I'll be thy lost groom,
I'll cherish thee first, ere thou'rt dust in thy tomb.

363 Later published in *Collected Poems*, p. 46.

And now thou art darken, and now I abide,
Knowing the Death from which thou would'st hide.
Since I have gone tombwards for vain love of thee,
Now in my death, thy death shall love me.

What death can destroy, time can recover.
Many a love in the night finds a lover.
What dreamlike resurrections I have known
In my old body; what flesh come back to bone.

What unknown, late and ancient tears
Fall from the blind eyes of the years:
What knowing surfeit is an old man's joy
That was but vision to the ecstatic boy.

. . .

The Song of the Shroudy Stranger of the Night

Bare skin is my wrinkled sack
When summer sun climbs up my back;
When winter crawls into these rags
I am embalmed in burlap bags.

My flesh is cinder, my face is snow,
I walk the railroad to and fro;
When all the city streets are dead
The railroad embankment is my bed.

Who'll walk down the waterfront with me
To call the dark shaggy things of the sea
Out of the dungeon under the dock
And sneak with them till break of clock?

My dog corruption of the faun
Howls in concrete in the dawn;
I scream inside an alley place—
O tears out of my Hebrew face!

I hide and wait like a naked child
Under the bridge my heart goes wild;
I creep in shade and suck my bone:
Come and hear the old man groan.

I sip my soup from old tin cans
And take my sweets from little hands;
But meats and dreaming least me feed,
Hunger has another greed.

Who'll come lay down in the dark with me,
Belly to belly, and knee to knee;
Love lies beneath the shroudy sky,
Who'll lay down under my darkened thigh?[364]

. . .

Please Open the Window and Let Me In

Who is the shrouded stranger of the night?
Whose brow is mouldering green, whose reddened eye
Hides near the window trellis in dim light,
And gapes at old men, and makes children cry?

Who is the laughing walker of the street,
The alley-mummy, stinking of the bone,
To dance unfixed, though bound in shadow feet,
Behind the child that creeps on limbs of stone?

Who is the hungry mocker of the maze,
And haggard gate-ghost, hanging by the door,
The double mummer in whose hooded gaze
World has beckoned unto world once more?

1949[365]

. . .

---

364 Later published in a revised form as "The Shrouded Stranger" in Collected Poems, p. 26.
365 Later published in Collected Poems, p. 31.

Bar Mitzvah Poem

Why have I become a man
To know no more than mankind can,
And grows with nature's every groan,
Surviving child's skeleton
and childish eternity.
To wake my poor divinity.
The weaving of the shroud goes on?

No two things alike; and yet
I have a cause not to forget
the carnal light that ate up limb
And thought, but sank below Time's rim,
Wonder has been aged to woe
that all my days more weary show
Time gets thicker: light gets dim.

Now that thought has all been cheated
And that child's share completed.
May waste my days no more
Here is ripe Eden. This is my store.
But where am I in wilderness
So that my past is lost like this
And all that was my love is OK?

[*ca. October 1950*]366

. . .

Versions of Shrouded Stranger

1.

Behold the holy shape wrapped in rotten rags
Behold the Saint of Shrouds
a patch upon his eye and shades about his feet,
Cords upon his throat for grimace and a groan,
gazing red in eye and mouldering in his mouth;
Green his brow is grown, a warehouse for the worm,

366 Later published in a revised form as "Ode: My 24th Year" in *Collected Poems*, p. 59.

with hairy breath all sore, encrusted with the crab,
Laboring up the road of winter's frozen wrath
Hawks above his thoughts, and doves about the brain,
upon his head a halo, holy bright and stain.

2.

Behold the holy shape wrapped in rotten rags
Laboring up the road in winter's frozen wrath
a hundred hats all hung hawklike in his hair
a patch upon his eye crutches on his knee
Harpies in his ear gargoyles in his brain
and on his head a halo glimmering like a crown
Behold the Saint of Shrouds Behold the Shrouded Stranger
Behold his reddened gaze Behold his mouldered mouth
Green his brow is grown a warehouse for the worm
Strings upon his neck for grinning a groan

. . .

Theory:
Stanzaic metrical verse
aims to put thoughts into
equal divisions, embodying
each thought in an equal
image, with an equal number
of sound for each image; symmetry.
To give concrete symmetry to
thought which is worthless, shifting,
meaningless as being incorporeal
make symmetrical corporeal the
mind. Make existent what is inexistent,
permanent what is impermanent.

Rhythm, as Holmes says,
is spontaneous in Pound
like bop—and Benyon's
comment (or Pound's)—"Slowness is Beauty."

. . .

Apocalyptic Sevens

Seven years I was
    CRAZY
seven years
    QUEER.

I was also in
    LOVE
the same period of
    TIME.

I count my first
    POEM
from my eighteenth
    BIRTHDAY.

I am twenty-five
    NOW
I had an incipit vita
    NUOVA

to tell the
    TRUTH
but the exact
    HOUR

of vision is too
    RIDICULOUS
to speak of
    ACCURATELY

The sevens have
    SIGNIFICANCE
But it is only
    MAGICAL:

<blockquote>
that is to say not
    LITERAL
a matter of
    CONVENTION.
</blockquote>

. . .

Blood visaged worms of time crawl over Huncke's face in jail
Passionate Kammerer stabbed and aghast,
Fainting under Love's nightmare drunken gaze;
Phil White[367] hanging in the Tombs labyrinths last passage underworld
Cannastra's[368] face in the windows underground,
Dragged yelling against the pillars of
the subterranean world;
Head carnaged after sunset,
brain opened like twilight to night
Skull broken into whiteness
like a winter sky under the radiant
wheel on the iron track.

. . .

Skull Broken

Under the radiant wheel and iron track
Many are the souls that have founded
their tombs in the wilderness;
many a soul gone riding outward on the path
many a soul gone to the jail and prison
and asylum
Many a soul gone singing in the sea.

Joan,[369] gone southward and from thy Albany;
Under the boundaries of America

---

367 Phil White. Ginsberg had learned that White had hanged himself in prison, afraid to face a long prison sentence.

368 Cannastra had been killed in a freak subway accident.

369 Joan Vollmer Adams was born near Albany, New York.

to the balconies of Night in
Moorish lands
I loved, you Joan, for all your crazy moons.

Denver is lonesome for Heroes.

[*ca. December 1951*]

. . .

O my, bunions and toestubs and
   strange little nails,
O rub a dub dubs
O my heart, and my kidneys,
   my navel and loins,
All that make me animal and gross
   Between the heart and knee—
When will that lightness take my
   Toes and hair—
When has, or will my mind become a star?
My name is angel and my eyes are fire.

. . .

He cast off all his golden armor,
Lay down sleeping in the night,
And in a dream, he saw three fates
At a machine in a shroud of light.

He screamed "I wait the end of Time!
Be with me shroud, now, in my wrath."

I cast off all my golden armor,
Lay down sleeping in the night,
And in a dream I heard three fates
At a machine in a shroud of light.

One screamed "I wait the end of time,
Be with me shroud, now in my wrath
For there is a lantern in this grave
It is my lantern on the path—

Down through darkness,"—But enough,
All men know that old Krone's yell.
Another whispered in the shroud
"I am he whose name's 'angel'

And my eyes are fire. I
Am he who is bare again, I shall
Remember all things after death,
I will be crucified by all."

[December 1951][370]

. . .

And he it is who walks in the rain,
Seeking after dead cat's bones,
Seeking sight of the dead who are—
Watching the dead on the bleeding stone—

Worshipping at the sacrifice
of body necessary to die, and of soul,
For the soul dies at death, and nothing
Remains of the man but the bone.
Therefore I make soup of bones,
I gnaw at bones. I eat the carrion,
I eat the piss and saliva of children,

I feed on the refuse of the blind,
I eat the fruit that is poisoned by cold,

370 Later published in a revised form as "In Memoriam: William Cannastra, 1922–1950" in *Collected Poems*, pp. 57–58.

Or the haggard withered root at the rind
And the parasite cancer of the mold,

Deep down the vision shimmers, gone
In a night or a day.

I lay in the darkness of the years
The silent parcel changed my eyes,
The crystal shroud grew dim too far,
My body is worn as the winter sky.

[*December 1951*]

. . .

Dawn:
   —fatigue
—whiteness of sky,
  solid concrete houses,
sun rust red—
coming home to the
   furnished room
—nervewracking lovetalk.
   I don't want her

stop all fantasy!

  live
in the physical world
   moment to moment

I must put down
   every recurring thought—
stop every beating second

fire-escape, stoop, stairway,
   door,
    electric light,
desk and bed—weariness—
   drunken sensation
of my own physical
   eternity.

[1952][371]

. . .

Cockroach on My Door
(to Alan Ansen)

I came home from the movies
with nothing on my mind,
trudging up Eighth Avenue
to Fifteenth, walking blind,

waiting for a passenger
ship to go to sea.
I lived in a roominghouse attic
near the Port Authority,

an enormous city warehouse
slowly turning brown,
across from which old brownstones'
fire escapes hung down

on a street which should be in Russia,
outside the Golden Gates,
or back in the Middle Ages,
not in the United States.

I thought of my house in the suburb,
my father who wanted me home,

my aunts in the asylum,
and myself in Nome or Rome;

but on the stoop of my building,
watching the stars roll
over the walls of the warehouse
I stood in a profound hole.

I opened the door downstairs
and creaked up the first flight.
A Puerto Rican infant
was laughing in the night.

I saw from the second stairway
the homosexual pair
that lived in different cubicles
playing solitaire,

and stopped on the third landing
to say hello to old Ned
who lay all afternoon drinking
and jerked all night in bed.

I made it up to the attic
room I pay $4.50 for.
There was a solitary
cockroach on my door.

It crept past me. I entered.
Nothing of much worth
was hung up under the skylight.
I saw what I had on earth.

Bare elements of solitude:
table, chair and clock;
two books on top of the bedspread,
Jack Woodford and Paul de Kock.

I sat down at the table
to read a Holy Book
about a super city
whereon I cannot look.

What misery to be guided
to an Eternal Clime
when I yearn for sixty
minutes of actual Time.

I turned on the radio.
The voice was strong and clear
describing the high fidelity
of a set without peer.

Then I heard great musicians
playing the Mahogany Hall
up to the last high chorus.
My neighbor beat on the wall.

I looked up at the calendar:
it has a picture there
showing two pairs of lovers,
and all have golden hair.

I looked into the mirror
to check my worst fears:
my face is dark but handsome,
it has not loved for years.

I lay down with the paper
to see what Time had wrought.
Peace was beyond vision,
war too much for thought;

only the suffering shadow
of "Dream Driven Boy, sixteen"

looked in my eyes from the centerfold
after murdering High School Queen.

I lay, my head on the pillow,
my eye on the cracked blue wall,
The same cockroach, or another,
continued its upward crawl.

From what faint words, what whispers,
I lay silently apart?
what wanted consummation,
what sweetening of the heart?

I wished that I were working
for $10,000.00 a year.
I looked all right in business suits
but my heart was weak with fear.

I wished that I were married
to a sensual thoughtful girl.
I would have made a model
workmanlike tender churl.

I wished that I had an apartment
uptown on the East Side,
so that my gentle breeding
matured, and had not died.

I wished that I had an Aesthetic
worth its weight in gold.
The myth is still unwritten,
I am getting old.

I closed my eyes and drifted
back in hopeless shame
to jobs and loves wasted.
Disillusion itself was lame.

I closed me eyes and drifted
the shortening years ahead,
the walks home from the movies,
the sleep alone in bed,

books, plays and music,
afternoons in bars,
the smell of old countries
and smoke of dark cigars.

I dreamed that I was climbing
over the warehouse wall.
Night hid my nakedness.
Death broke my fall.

[*ca. January–February 1952*][372]

.   .   .

Her Engagement

We have to go through
   the warehouse to get
to the lunchroom—and
   he asked me for a date,
and he told me where
   we were going, and he
told me what time
   he would pick me up.
What a doll he is:
   We were walking
through the warehouse
   hand in hand,
and when we got near
   the loading platform

---

372 Later published in a revised form as an untitled poem in *Collected Poems*, pp. 73–74.

he held my fingers
and kissed me—

we had to hide—
if anybody in Accounting
    knew, the news
would spread like wildfire.

[1952]³⁷³

. . .

Two Trees in Paterson

<u>At Sunset</u>
Leafy heads on
    long poles
revolve unsteadily
    up and down
in the dangerous
    yellow breeze
and newborn robins
    cry in their nest
at the top of
    the whirling tree.

N.J. 1952

<u>A Survivor</u>
Bulging veins
    and knots contorted
ironwise around
    his trunk
blasted at the top,
    bleared with smoke,
old roots chopped
    off his base,
nails in the boles
    a cave inside

---

373 Later published in *Voices*, no. 158 (September–December 1955).

for ants the
   tree in the empty
lot on 33'rd
   still pushing
huge leaves
   out of his neck.

        N.J. 1952[374]

    . . .

We rode on a lonely bus
   for half a night,
shoulders touching, warmth
   between our thighs,
bodies moved together,
   dreaming invisibly.

I longed for a look of secrecy
   with open eyes
intimacies of New Jersey—
   holding hands
and kissing golden cheeks.

        N.J. 1952[375]

    . . .

Two Nights

in the lesbian barroom in New York
and I realized that America and I
have reached a peak of personal
decadence.—A scene with Dusty and
   a fat dyke
     with a doglike face
   barking her lines
     like Milton Berle:

374 Later published as "Two Trees in Paterson 1952" in *Variegation*, vol. ɪɪ, no. 43 (Summer 1956).
375 Later published as "We Rode on a Lonely Bus" in *Yugen*, no. ɪ (1958).

"They're Freudian
    on campus
and freaks in bed—
    so I said babe
just be natural
    and we'll have a ball
so I got down on her
    and we had a real
groovy sixty nine—
    don't you know
I got a two
    inch clitoris?"

And Dusty actually
    blushed.

                    N.Y. 1952

                    . . .

My heart sank beating
and honey filled my limbs
When we lay down together
in each other's arms.
There was so much gladness
bound up in our embrace
It weighed on naked thigh
as on soul's nakedness.

Ah Davalos,[376] your love;
your look; it is too late.
The heaviness is gone
gone into the night.

                    May 20, 1952

                    . . .

376 Richard Davalos. *loc. cit.*

In a Red Bar

I look like someone else
I don't like in the mirror
a floating city heel,
middleclass con artist,
I need a haircut and look
Seedy—in late twenties,
shadows under my mouth,
too informally dressed,
heavy eyebrowed, sadistic,
too mental and lonely.[377]

377 Later published in *Yugen*, no. 1 (1958).

INDEX